Italian For Dummies®

Cheat Sheet

Greetings

Buongiorno! *(boo-ohn-johr-noh)* (Hello! *and* Good morning!)

Arrivederci! *(ahr-ree-veh-dehr-chee)* (Goodbye!) (Formal)

Ciao! *(chah-oh)* (Hello! *and* Good-bye!) (Informal)

Salve! *(sahl-veh)* (Hello! *and* Good-bye!) (Neutral)

Buonasera! *(boo-oh-nah-seh-rah)* (Good afternoon!; Good evening!) (Formal)

Buonanotte! *(boo-oh-nah-noht-teh)* (Goodnight!) (Informal)

Mi chiamo. . . *(mee kee-ah-moh)* (My name is. . .)

Come sta? *(koh-meh stah)* (How are you?) (Formal)

Come stai? *(koh-meh stah-ee)* (How are you?) (Informal)

Bene, grazie. *(beh-neh grah-tsee-eh)* (Fine, thank you.)

Being Polite

Per favore? *(pehr fah-voh-reh)* (Please.)

Grazie. *(grah-tsee-eh)* (Thank you.)

Non c'è di che. *(nohn cheh dee keh)* (You're welcome.)

Mi dispiace. *(mee dees-pee-ah-cheh)* (I'm sorry.)

Mi scusi. *(mee skoo-zee)* (Excuse me.)

Sì. *(see)* (Yes.)

No. *(noh)* (No.)

Days of the Week

Domenica	*doh-meh-nee-kah*	Sunday
Lunedì	*loo-neh-dee*	Monday
Martedì	*mahr-teh-dee*	Tuesday
Mercoledì	*mehr-koh-leh-dee*	Wednesday
Giovedì	*joh-veh-dee*	Thursday
Venerdì	*veh-nehr-dee*	Friday
Sabato	*sah-bah-toh*	Saturday

Practical Questions

Parla inglese? *(pahr-lah een-gleh-zeh)* (Do you speak English?)

Chi? *(kee)* (Who?)

Cosa? *(koh-sah)* (What?)

Quando? *(koo-ahn-doh)* (When?)

Dove? *(doh-veh)* (Where?)

Perché? *(pehr-keh)* (Why?)

Come? *(koh-meh)* (How?)

Quanto? *(koo-anh-toh)* (How much?)

Permesso? *(pehr-mehs-soh)* (May I?)

For more information about Wiley Publishing, call 1-800-762-2974.

For Dummies: Bestselling Book Series for Beginners

Italian For Dummies®

Cheat Sheet

What to Say in an Emergency

Aiuto! *(ah-yoo-toh)* (Help!)

Emergenza! *(eh-mehr-jehn-tsah)* (Emergency!)

Chiamate la polizia! *(chee-ah-mah-teh lah poh-lee-tsee-ah)* (Call the police!)

Chiamate un'ambulanza! *(kee-ah-mah-teh oo-nahm-boo-lahn-tsah)* (Call an ambulance!)

Ho bisogno di un medico. *(oh bee-zoh-nyoh dee oon meh-dee-koh)* (I need a doctor.)

Dov' è l'ospedale? *(doh-veh lohs-peh-dah-leh)* (Where is the hospital?)

Not Too Many Numbers

zero	*dzeh-roh*	0	diciannove	*dee-chahn-noh-veh*	19
uno	*oo-noh*	1	venti	*vehn-tee*	20
due	*doo-eh*	2	ventuno	*vehn-too-noh*	21
tre	*treh*	3	ventidue	*vehn-tee-doo-eh*	22
quattro	*koo-aht-troh*	4	trenta	*trehn-tah*	30
cinque	*cheen-koo-eh*	5	quaranta	*koo-ah-rah-tah*	40
sei	*say*	6	cinquanta	*cheen-koo-ahn-tah*	50
sette	*seht-teh*	7	sessanta	*sehs-sahn-tah*	60
otto	*oht-toh*	8	settanta	*seht-than-tah*	70
nove	*noh-veh*	9	ottanta	*oht-than-tah*	80
dieci	*dee-eh-chee*	10	novanta	*noh-vahn-tah*	90
undici	*oon-dee-chee*	11	cento	*chehn-toh*	100
dodici	*doh-dee-chee*	12	cinquecento	*cheen-koo-eh-chehn-toh*	500
tredici	*treh-dee-chee*	13			
quattordici	*koo-aht-tohr-dee-chee*	14	mille	*meel-leh*	1,000
			duemila	*doo-eh-mee-lah*	2,000
quindici	*koo-een-dee-chee*	15	un milione	*oon mee-lee-oh-neh*	1,000,000
sedici	*say-dee-chee*	16	due milioni	*doo-eh mee-lee-oh-nee*	2,000,000
diciassette	*dee-chahs-seht-teh*	17			
diciotto	*dee-choht-toh*	18	un miliardo	*oon mee-lee-ahr-doh*	1,000,000,000

 TM

References for the Rest of Us!®

BESTSELLING BOOK SERIES

Do you find that traditional reference books are overloaded with technical details and advice you'll never use? Do you postpone important life decisions because you just don't want to deal with them? Then our *For Dummies®* business and general reference book series is for you.

For Dummies business and general reference books are written for those frustrated and hard-working souls who know they aren't dumb, but find that the myriad of personal and business issues and the accompanying horror stories make them feel helpless. *For Dummies* books use a lighthearted approach, a down-to-earth style, and even cartoons and humorous icons to dispel fears and build confidence. Lighthearted but not lightweight, these books are perfect survival guides to solve your everyday personal and business problems.

"More than a publishing phenomenon, 'Dummies' is a sign of the times."

— The New York Times

"A world of detailed and authoritative information is packed into them..."

— U.S. News and World Report

"...you won't go wrong buying them."

— Walter Mossberg, Wall Street Journal, on For Dummies books

Already, millions of satisfied readers agree. They have made For Dummies the #1 introductory level computer book series and a best-selling business book series. They have written asking for more. So, if you're looking for the best and easiest way to learn about business and other general reference topics, look to For Dummies to give you a helping hand.

Wiley Publishing, Inc.

5/09

Italian

FOR

DUMMIES®

Italian FOR DUMMIES®

by Francesca Romana Onofri
and Karen Möller

Berlitz® Series Editor: Juergen Lorenz

Wiley Publishing, Inc.

Italian For Dummies®

Published by
Wiley Publishing, Inc.
111 River Street
Hoboken, NJ 07030
www.wiley.com

Copyright © 2000 by Wiley Publishing, Inc., Indianapolis, Indiana

Published simultaneously in Canada

For general information on our other products and services or to obtain technical support, please contact our Customer Care Department within the U.S. at 800-762-2974, outside the U.S. at 317-572-3993, or fax 317-572-4002.

Wiley also publishes its books in a variety of electronic formats. Some content that appears in print may not be available in electronic books.

Library of Congress Cataloging-in-Publication Data:

Library of Congress Catalog Card No.: 99-69716

ISBN: 0-7645-5196-5

Manufactured in the United States of America

12 11 10

1B/SS/RR/QS/IN

About the Authors

After her university studies in linguistics and Spanish and English language and literature, **Francesca Romana Onofri** lived several years abroad, to better her understanding of the cultures and languages of different countries. In Spain and Ireland she worked as an Italian and Spanish teacher, as well as a translator and interpreter at cultural events. In Germany she was responsible for communication and special events in a museum of modern art, but even then she never gave up her passion for languages: She was an Italian coach and teacher at the Opera Studio of the Cologne Opera House, and did translations — especially in the art field. Back in Italy, Francesca has edited several Berlitz Italian books and is working as a translator of art books, as well as a cultural events organizer and educator.

Karen Möller is currently studying Italian and English linguistics, literature, and culture. Before entering academia, Karen worked in the field of public relations and wrote articles for all kinds of fashion magazines and newspapers. Recently she has had occasion to work with Berlitz Publishing on German-Italian projects, including verb, vocabulary, and grammar handbooks, and Italian exercise books.

Berlitz has meant excellence in language services for more than 120 years. At more than 400 locations and in 50 countries worldwide, Berlitz offers a full range of language and language-related services, including instruction, cross-cultural training, document translation, software localization, and interpretation services. Berlitz also offers a wide array of publishing products, such as self-study language courses, phrase books, travel guides, and dictionaries.

The world-famous Berlitz Method is the core of all Berlitz language instruction. From the time of its introduction in 1878, millions have used this method to learn new languages. For more information about Berlitz classes and products, please consult your local telephone directory for the Language Center nearest you, or visit the Berlitz Web site at www.berlitz.com, where you can enroll in classes or shop directly for products online.

Dedication

Francesca Romana Onofri: I would like to dedicate this book to all the people who supported me: my family, for believing in me all the time, and my friends who haven't forgotten me in spite of the distance. Special thanks go to my nephew Simone, without whose help I'd have never won my battles against my computer, and to Violetta, for her very special support. But my deepest thanks are for Karen: I can't imagine a better partner for a "four hands work," from both human and professional points of view.

Karen Möller: This book is lovingly dedicated to all those people who bore patiently my working on it, including: my brother Frank, who always gave me a hand whenever I had — not seldom — questions or problems with my computer, and for his and his wife's patience at hearing me type night and day for some months; my grandparents, who encouraged me with their loving pride; all my friends who had to accept shortened phone calls; Francesca Onofri, who was an excellent and amicable co-author; and, saving the best for last, my boyfriend, Paolo, for being there and supporting me on sunny and rainy days.

Authors' Acknowledgments

Francesca Romana Onofri and **Karen Möller** want to express appreciation and gratitude to the people at Wiley, including Mark and Holly, and the editors at Berlitz — Sheryl Olinsky Borg, and especially Juergen Lorenz — for their encouragement and support.

Berlitz would like to thank the following:

Karen Möller and Francesca Onofri, an outstanding pair of writers, for their tireless dedication to creating this book.

Our New York audio producer, Paul Ruben, for bringing the written Italian language to life, and the audio post production team at Big Media Productions in New York City — John Sheary, Philip Clark, and Tim Franklin — for endless hours of listening, cutting, and pasting.

Our editors, Juergen Lorenz and Sheryl Olinsky Borg, for their professionalism and commitment to putting together this challenging and exciting project.

Duccio Faggella, a great voice and an outstanding editor, for giving this book the final "Italian touch."

And our deep appreciation goes to the staff at Wiley, especially Holly McGuire, Pam Mourouzis, Mark Rohe, Kathleen Dobie, and Tracy Barr, who guided *Italian For Dummies* from start to finish!

Publisher's Acknowledgments

We're proud of this book; please send us your comments through our Dummies online registration form located at www.dummies.com/register/.

Some of the people who helped bring this book to market include the following:

Acquisitions, Editorial, and Media Development

Editors: Mark Edwin Rohe, Kathleen A. Dobie, Tracy Barr

Senior Acquisitions Editor: Holly McGuire

Copy Editor: Corey Dalton

Acquisitions Coordinator: Karen S. Young

Technical Editors: Dolores Pigoni-Miller, Alberto Mari

Editorial Manager: Pamela Mourouzis

Media Development Manager: Heather Heath Dismore

Editorial Assistant: Carol Strickland

Reprint Editor: Bethany Andre

Composition

Project Coordinator: E. Shawn Aylsworth

Layout and Graphics: Beth Brooks, Barry Offringa, Tracy K. Oliver, Brent Savage, Janet Seib, Brian Torwelle, Dan Whetstine, Erin Zeltner

Proofreaders: Corey Bowen, Rita Milandri, Marianne Santy, Charles Spencer

Indexer: Mary Mortensen

Special Help
Tina Sims, Donna Frederick, Seta K. Franz, Sherry Gomall

Publishing and Editorial for Consumer Dummies

Diane Graves Steele, Vice President and Publisher, Consumer Dummies

Joyce Pepple, Acquisitions Director, Consumer Dummies

Kristin A. Cocks, Product Development Director, Consumer Dummies

Michael Spring, Vice President and Publisher, Travel

Brice Gosnell, Associate Publisher, Travel

Suzanne Jannetta, Editorial Director, Travel

Publishing for Technology Dummies

Andy Cummings, Vice President and Publisher, Dummies Technology/General User

Composition Services

Gerry Fahey, Vice President of Production Services

Debbie Stailey, Director of Composition Services

Contents at a Glance

Cartoons at a Glance

By Rich Tennant

"Don't feel bad-even though asking the gondolier to 'revolve us around a zebra' was a mistake, he did compliment you on how well you rolled your R's."

page 217

I know how to ask for directions to a McDonalds in Italian, I'm just afraid to.

page 41

"So far you've called a rickshaw, a unicyclist and a Zamboni. I really wish you'd learn the Italian word for taxicab."

page 7

"I'm not sure if I'm stressing the right syllable in the wrong word, or stressing the wrong syllable in the right word, but it's starting to stress me out."

page 311

Magnifico!

Molto bello!

"I insisted they learn some Italian. I couldn't stand the idea of standing in front of the Trevi Fountain and hearing, 'gosh,' 'wow,' and 'far out.'"

page 333

Fax: 978-546-7747
E-mail: richtennant@the5thwave.com
World Wide Web: www.the5thwave.com

Table of Contents

Introduction

A s society becomes more and more international in nature, knowing how to say at least a few words in other languages becomes more and more useful. Inexpensive airfares make travel abroad a more realistic option. Global business environments necessitate overseas travel. Or you may just have friends and neighbors who speak other languages, or you may want to get in touch with your heritage by learning a little bit of the language that your ancestors spoke.

Whatever your reason for wanting to learn some Italian, *Italian For Dummies* can help. Two experts at helping readers develop knowledge — Berlitz, experts in teaching foreign languages; and Wiley Publishing, Inc., publishers of the best-selling *For Dummies* series — have teamed up to produce a book that gives you the skills you need for basic communication in Italian. We're not promising fluency here, but if you need to greet someone, purchase a ticket, or order off a menu in Italian, you need look no further than *Italian For Dummies*.

About This Book

This is not a class that you have to drag yourself to twice a week for a specified period of time. You can use *Italian For Dummies* however you want to, whether your goal is to learn some words and phrases to help you get around when you visit Italy, or you just want to be able to say "Hello, how are you?" to your Italian-speaking neighbor. Go through this book at your own pace, reading as much or as little at a time as you like. You don't have to trudge through the chapters in order, either; just read the sections that interest you.

Note: If you've never taken Italian before, you may want to read the chapters in Part I before you tackle the later chapters. Part I gives you some of the basics that you need to know about the language, such as how to pronounce the various sounds.

Conventions Used in This Book

To make this book easy for you to navigate, we've set up a few conventions:

- ✔ Italian terms are set in **boldface** to make them stand out.

- ✔ Pronunciations set in *italics* follow the Italian terms.

- ✔ Verb conjugations (lists that show you the forms of a verb) are given in tables in this order: the "I" form, the "you" (singular) form, the "he/she/it" form, the "we" form, the "you" (plural/formal) form, and the "they" form. Pronunciations follow in the second column. Following is an example using **divertirsi** *(dee-vehr-teer-see)* (to enjoy oneself):

Conjugation	*Pronunciation*
mi diverto	mee dee-vehr-toh
ti diverti	tee dee-vehr-tee
si diverte	see dee-vehr-teh
ci divertiamo	chee dee-vehr-tee-ah-moh
vi divertite	vee dee-vehr-tee-teh
si divertono	see dee-vehr-toh-noh

Language learning is a peculiar beast, so this book includes a few elements that other *For Dummies* books do not. Following are the new elements you'll find:

- ✔ **Talkin' the Talk dialogues:** The best way to learn a language is to see and hear how it's used in conversation, so we include dialogues throughout the book. The dialogues come under the heading "Talkin' the Talk" and show you the Italian words, their pronunciations, and the English translations.

- ✔ **Words to Know blackboards:** Memorizing key words and phrases is also important in language learning, so we collect the important words in a chapter (or section within a chapter) in a chalkboard, with the heading "Words to Know." Italian nouns have genders, and the gender of a noun determines which article it takes, how you form the plural, and so on. So, in the Words to Know blackboards, we indicate the gender with either [f], for feminine nouns, or [m] for masculine nouns.

- ✔ **Fun & Games activities:** If you don't have actual Italian speakers to practice your new language skills on, you can use the Fun & Games activities to reinforce what you learn. These word games are fun ways to gauge your progress.

Also note that, because each language has its own ways of expressing ideas, the English translations that we provide for the Italian terms may not be exactly literal. We want you to know the gist of what's being said, not just the words that are being said. For example, the phrase **Mi dica** *(mee <u>dee</u>-kah)* can be translated literally as "Tell me," but the phrase really means "Can I help you?" This book gives the "Can I help you" translation.

Foolish Assumptions

To write this book, we had to make some assumptions about who you are and what you want from a book called *Italian For Dummies.* These are the assumptions we made:

- You know no Italian — or if you took Italian back in school, you don't remember a word of it.
- You're not looking for a book that will make you fluent in Italian; you just want to know some words, phrases, and sentence constructions so that you can communicate basic information in Italian.
- You don't want to have to memorize long lists of vocabulary words or a bunch of boring grammar rules.
- You want to have fun and learn a little bit of Italian at the same time.

If these statements apply to you, you've found the right book!

How This Book Is Organized

This book is divided by topic into parts, and then into chapters. The following sections tell you what types of information you can find in each part.

Part I: Getting Started

This part lets you get your feet wet by giving you some Italian basics: how to pronounce words, what the accents mean, and so on. We even boost your confidence by reintroducing you to some Italian words that you probably already know. Finally, we outline the basics of Italian grammar that you may need to know when you work through later chapters in the book.

Part II: Italian in Action

In this part, you begin learning and using Italian. Instead of focusing on grammar points as many language textbooks do, this part focuses on everyday situations, such as shopping, dining, and making small talk.

Part III: Italian on the Go

This part gives you the tools you need to take your Italian on the road, whether it's to a local Italian restaurant or to a museum in Italy.

Part IV: The Part of Tens

If you're looking for small, easily digestible pieces of information about Italian, this part is for you. Here, you can find ten ways to learn Italian quickly, ten useful Italian expressions to know, ten things never to say in Italian, and more.

Part V: Appendixes

This part of the book includes important information that you can use for reference. We include verb tables, which show you how to conjugate a regular verb and also how to conjugate those verbs that stubbornly don't fit the pattern. We also provide a listing of the tracks that appear on the audio CD that comes with this book so that you can find out where in the book those dialogues are and follow along. Finally, we give you a mini-dictionary in both Italian-to-English and English-to-Italian formats. If you encounter an Italian word that you don't understand, or you need to say something in Italian, you can look it up here.

Icons Used in This Book

You may be looking for particular information while reading this book. To make certain types of information easier for you to find, we've placed the following icons in the left-hand margins throughout the book:

This icon highlights tips that can make learning Italian easier.

To insure that you don't forget important information, this icon serves as a reminder, like a string tied around your finger.

Languages are full of quirks that may trip you up if you're not prepared for them. This icon points to discussions of these weird grammar rules.

If you're looking for information and advice about culture and travel, look for these icons. They draw your attention to interesting tidbits about the countries in which Italian is spoken.

The audio CD that comes with this book gives you the opportunity to listen to real Italian speakers so that you can get a better understanding of what Italian sounds like. This icon marks the Talkin' the Talk dialogues that you can find on the CD.

Where to Go from Here

Learning a language is all about jumping in and giving it a try (no matter how bad your pronunciation is at first). So make the leap! Start at the beginning, pick a chapter that interests you, or pop the CD into your stereo or computer and listen to a few dialogues. Before long, you'll be able to respond, "Sì!" when people ask, "Parla italiano?"

Part I
Getting Started

The 5th Wave   By Rich Tennant

"So far you've called a rickshaw, a unicyclist and a Zamboni. I really wish you'd learn the Italian word for taxicab."

In this part . . .

Ciao! See, you already understand some Italian, although you may think we're saying good-bye before we even say hello. The truth is that **ciao** means both "hello" and "good-bye."

These first two chapters introduce you to the basics of Italian: Chapter 1 reminds you that you already know how to say a number of Italian words and gives you guidelines so that you can pronounce all the other Italian you'll encounter. Chapter 2 gets into the basics of grammar — how to construct a sentence and so on — and, because numbers are so basic to understanding a language, we introduce you to digits, also. **Andiamo!** *(ahn-dee-ah-moh)* (Let's go!)

Chapter 1

You Already Know a Little Italian

You probably know that Italian is a Romance language, which means that Italian, just like Spanish, French, Portuguese, and some other languages, is a "child" of Latin. There was a time when Latin was the official language in a large part of Europe because the Romans ruled so much of the area. Of course, before the Romans came, people spoke their own languages, and the mixture of these original tongues with Latin produced many of the languages and dialects still in use today.

If you know one of these Romance languages — French, Italian, Portuguese, or Spanish — you can often understand bits of another one of them. But just as members of the same family can look very similar but have totally different characters, so it is with these languages. You find the same contradictions in the dialects in Italy (and in the other countries, also). People in different areas speak in very different ways due to historical or social reasons, and in spite of Italian being the official, common language, Italy has a large number of different dialects. Believe us: Some dialects are so far from Italian that people from different regions cannot understand each other.

If you visit Italy, you'll hear various accents and dialects as you travel through the country, but despite the number of different dialects, you may be surprised to discover that everybody understands your Italian and you understand theirs. (Normally, Italians don't speak in their dialect with foreigners!) But be careful lest this book helps you become *too* good in Italian — you may be mistaken for a local! In that case, please, give us a call!

We don't want to go into detail about these regional differences here. Language is a means of communicating with people, and to speak to people from other countries, you have to find a way to understand them and make your meaning clear. Because using gestures to make yourself understood can be very hard after a while, we present some helpful expressions to make life easier, at least as far as Italian is concerned. We also give you some cultural wisdom to convey a picture of the Italian people. This can also be very helpful, because you know the old saying "other countries, other habits."

You Already Know Some Italian!

Maybe you already know that Italians love to talk. Not only do they enjoy communication, but they also love their language. Italian is very melodious. Not for nothing is Italian opera music so famous.

Although Italians are very proud of their language, they have allowed some English words to enter it. They talk, for example, about **gadgets, jogging,** and **shock;** they often use the word **okay;** and since computers marked their lives, they say **"cliccare sul mouse"** *(kleek-kah-reh sool mouse)* (to click the mouse). Finally, there's **lo zapping** *(loh zapping):* It's sort of a fashion to spend hours in front of the TV switching channels. These are only a few of the flood of English words that have entered the Italian language.

Vice versa, many Italian words are known in English-speaking countries. Can you think of some?

How about . . .

- **pizza** *(peets-tsah)*
- **pasta** *(pahs-tah)*
- **spaghetti** *(spah-geht-tee)*
- **tortellini** *(tohr-tehl-lee-nee)*
- **mozzarella** *(moht-tsah-rehl-lah)*
- **espresso** *(ehs-prehs-soh)*
- **cappuccino** *(kahp-poo-chee-noh)*
- **tiramisù** *(tee-rah-mee-soo)*

Incidentally, did you know that *tiramisù* literally means "pull me up"? This refers to the fact that this sweet is made with strong Italian espresso.

You may have heard words from areas other than the kitchen, such as the following:

- **amore** *(ah-moh-reh):* This is the word "love" that so many Italian songs tell about.

- **avanti** *(ah-vahn-tee):* You use this word as "come in!" and also "come on!" or "get a move on!"

- **bambino** *(bahm-bee-noh):* This is a male child. The female equivalent is **bambina** *(bahm-bee-nah).*

- **bravo!** *(brah-voh):* You can properly say this word only to one man. To a woman, you must say **"brava!"** *(brah-vah),* and to a group of people, you say **"bravi!"** *(brah-vee)* unless the group is comprised only of women, in which case you say **"brave!"** *(brah-veh).*

- **ciao!** *(chah-oh):* **Ciao** means "hello" and "goodbye."

- **scusi** *(skoo-zee):* This word stands for "excuse me" and "sorry" and is addressed to persons you don't know or to whom you speak formally. You say **"scusa"** *(scoo-zah)* to people you know and to children.

You've heard at least some of these words and phrases, haven't you? This is just a little taste of all the various words and expressions you'll get to know in this book.

For the moment, we say, **"Chi si accontenta gode"** *(kee see ahk-kohn-tehn-tah goh-deh)* (Contentment is happiness, or Enough is as good as a feast).

Cognates

In addition to the words that have crept into the language directly, Italian and English have many cognates. A *cognate* is a word in one language that has the same origin as a word in another one and may sound similar. You can get an immediate picture of what cognates are from the following examples:

- **aeroporto** *(ah-eh-roh-pohr-toh)* (airport)

- **attenzione** *(aht-tehn-tsee-oh-neh)* (attention)

- **comunicazione** *(koh-moo-nee-kah-tsee-oh-neh)* (communication)

- **importante** *(eem-pohr-than-teh)* (important)

- **incredibile** *(een-kreh-dee-bee-leh)* (incredible)

You understand much more Italian than you think you do. Italian and English are full of cognates. To demonstrate, read this little story with some Italian words in it. They're so similar to the English words that you can easily understand them.

It seems **impossibile** *(eem-pohs-see-bee-leh)* to him that he is now at the **aeroporto** *(ah-eh-roh-pohr-toh)* in Rome. He always wanted to come to this **città** *(cheet-tah)*. When he goes out on the street, he first calls a **taxi** *(ta-ksee)*. He opens his bag to see if he has the **medicina** *(meh-dee-chee-nah)* that the **dottore** *(doht-toh-reh)* gave him. Going through this **terribile traffico** *(tehr-ree-bee-leh trahf-fee-koh)*, he passes a **cattedrale** *(kaht-teh-drah-leh)*, some **sculture** *(skool-too-reh)*, and many **palazzi** *(pah-laht-tsee)*. All this is very **impressionante** *(eem-prehs-see-oh-nahn-teh)*. He knows that this is going to be a **fantastico** *(fahn-tahs-tee-koh)* journey.

Popular expressions

Every language has expressions that you use so often that they almost become routine. For example, when you give something to somebody and he or she says, "Thank you," you automatically reply, "You're welcome!" This type of popular expression is an inseparable part of every language. When you know these expressions and how to use them, you're on the way to becoming a fluent speaker.

The following are some of the most common popular expressions in Italian:

- ✔ **Accidenti!** *(ahch-chee-dehn-tee)* (Wow!)
- ✔ **Andiamo!** *(ahn-dee-ah-moh)* (Let's go!)
- ✔ **Che bello!** *(keh behl-loh)* (How nice!)
- ✔ **Che c'è?** *(keh cheh)* (What's up?)
- ✔ **D'accordo? D'accordo!** *(dahk-kohr-doh)* (Agreed? Agreed!)
- ✔ **Dai!** *(dah-ee)* (Come on!; Go on!)
- ✔ **E chi se ne importa?** *(eh kee seh neh eem-pohr-tah)* (Who cares?)
- ✔ **È lo stesso.** *(eh loh stehs-soh)* (It's all the same; It doesn't matter.)
- ✔ **Fantastico!** *(fahn-tahs-tee-koh)* (Fantastic!)
- ✔ **Non fa niente.** *(nohn fah nee-ehn-teh)* (It doesn't matter.) You use "Non fa niente" when someone apologizes to you for something.
- ✔ **Non c'è di che.** *(nohn cheh dee keh)* (You're welcome.)

✔ **Permesso?** *(pehr-_mehs_-soh)* (May I pass; come in?)

Italians use this expression every time they cross a threshold entering a house or when passing through a crowd. A more familiar equivalent for "May I?" is **posso** *(_pohs_-soh)* (Can I?), but you wouldn't use it in the situations described here.

✔ **Stupendo!** *(stoo-_pehn_-doh)* (Wonderful!; Fabulous!)

✔ **Va bene!** *(vah _beh_-neh)* (Okay!)

Mouthing Off: Basic Pronunciation

Italian provides many opportunities for your tongue to do acrobatics. This is really fun, because the language offers you some new sounds. In this section, we give you some basic pronunciation hints that are important both for surfing through this book and for good articulation when you speak Italian. (If you tried to read and pronounce Italian words in the English manner, Italian speakers would have problems understanding you, just as you may sometimes have trouble understanding Italians when they speak English. For example, have you ever heard an Italian pronounce the names of American celebrities?)

First, we'd like to make a deal with you. Next to the Italian words throughout this book you find the pronunciation in parentheses. In the following sections, we give you some helpful hints about how to read these pronunciations — that is, how to pronounce the Italian words. The deal is that we have to agree on which letters refer to which sounds. You have to follow this code all through this book.

In the pronunciations, we separate the syllables with a hyphen, like this: **casa** *(_kah_-sah)* (house). Furthermore, we underline the stressed syllable, which means that you put the stress of the word on the underlined syllable. (See the section "Stressing Words Properly," later in this chapter, for more information about stresses.)

Vowels

We'll start with the tough ones: vowels. Vowels are difficult because you have to cope with new sounds. Well, the sounds are not that new, but the connection between the written letter and the actual pronunciation is not the same as it is in English.

Italian has five written vowels: *a, e, i, o,* and *u.* The following sections tell you how to pronounce each of them.

The vowel "a"

When "we foreigners" try to learn English, we are shocked to discover how many different sounds the English *a* can have. In Italian, the letter *a* has just one pronunciation. Just think of the sound of the *a* in the English word *far*. The Italian *a* sounds just like that.

To prevent you from falling back to the other *a* sounds found in English, we transcribe the Italian *a* as *(ah),* as shown earlier in **casa** *(kah-sah)* (house). Here are some other examples:

- ✔ **albero** *(ahl-beh-roh)* (tree)
- ✔ **marmellata** *(mahr-mehl-lah-tah)* (jam)
- ✔ **sale** *(sah-leh)* (salt)

The vowel "e"

Forget all you know about the English *e*. Try to think of the sound in the French word *gourmet* (you don't pronounce the *t*). This sound comes very close to the Italian *e*. In this book, we transcribe the *e* sound as *(eh)*. For example:

- ✔ **sole** *(soh-leh)* (sun)
- ✔ **peso** *(peh-zoh)* (weight)
- ✔ **bere** *(beh-reh)* (to drink)

The vowel "i"

The Italian *i* is simply pronounced *(ee),* as in the English word *see.* Here are some examples:

- ✔ **cinema** *(chee-neh-mah)* (cinema)
- ✔ **bimbo** *(beem-boh)* (little boy)

    Surprised you, didn't we? In American English, the word *bimbo* has almost the opposite meaning, doesn't it?

- ✔ **vita** *(vee-tah)* (life)

The vowel "o"

The Italian *o* is pronounced as in the English (from the Italian) *piano.* We therefore list the pronunciation as *(oh)*. The *h* is there to remind you not to pronounce *o* in the English way. Try it out on the following words:

- ✔ **domani** *(doh-<u>mah</u>-nee)* (tomorrow)
- ✔ **piccolo** *(<u>peek</u>-koh-loh)* (little; small)
- ✔ **dolce** *(<u>dohl</u>-cheh)* (sweet)

The vowel "u"

The Italian **u** sounds always like the English *(oo),* as in **zoo.** Therefore, we use *(oo)* to transcribe the Italian **u.** Here are some sample words:

- ✔ **tu** *(too)* (you)
- ✔ **luna** *(<u>loo</u>-nah)* (moon)
- ✔ **frutta** *(<u>froot</u>-tah)* (fruit)

That's it, at least as far as the vowels are concerned.

Consonants

Italian has the same consonants that English does. You pronounce most of them the same way in Italian as you pronounce them in English, but others have noteworthy differences. We start with the easy ones and look at those that are pronounced identically:

- ✔ **b:** As in **bene** *(<u>beh</u>-neh)* (well)
- ✔ **d:** As in **dare** *(<u>dah</u>-reh)* (to give)
- ✔ **f:** As in **fare** *(<u>fah</u>-reh)* (to make)
- ✔ **l:** As in **ladro** *(<u>lah</u>-droh)* (thief)
- ✔ **m:** As in **madre** *(mah-dreh)* (mother)
- ✔ **n:** As in **no** *(noh)* (no)
- ✔ **p:** As in **padre** *(<u>pah</u>-reh)* (father)
- ✔ **t:** As in **treno** *(treh-noh)* (train)
- ✔ **v:** As in **vino** *(<u>vee</u>-noh)* (wine)

Finally there are some consonants that do not really exist in Italian except in some foreign words that have entered the language.

- ✔ **j:** Exists mostly in foreign words such as *jogging, junior,* and *jeans.*
- ✔ **k:** The same as *j;* you find it in words like *okay, ketchup,* and *killer.*
- ✔ **w:** As with *j* and *k,* you find it in some foreign words (for the most part English words), like *whisky, windsurf,* and *wafer.*

✔ x: As with *j, k,* and *w, x* doesn't really exist in Italian, with the difference that "*x* words" derive mostly from Greek. Examples include **xenofobia** *(kseh-noh-foh-bee-ah)* (xenophobia) and **xilofono** *(ksee-loh-foh-noh)* (xylophone).

✔ y: The letter *y* normally appears only in foreign words, like *yogurt, hobby,* and *yacht.*

Now we'll go on to the consonants that are pronounced differently than they are in English.

The consonant "c"

The Italian *c* has various sounds, depending on which letter follows it:

✔ When *c* is followed by *a, o, u,* or any consonant, you pronounce it as in the English word *cat.* We transcribe this pronunciation as *(k).* Examples include **casa** *(kah-sah)* (house), **colpa** *(kohl-pah)* (guilt), and **cuore** *(koo-oh-reh)* (heart).

✔ When *c* is followed by *e* or *i,* you pronounce it as you do the first and last sound in the English word *church;* therefore, we give you the pronunciation *(ch).* Examples include **cena** *(cheh-nah)* (dinner), **cibo** *(chee-boh)* (food), and **certo** *(chehr-toh)* (certainly).

✔ To obtain the "ch" sound before *a, o,* or *u,* you have to insert an *i.* This *i,* however, serves only to create the "ch" sound; you do not pronounce it. Examples include **ciao** *(chah-oh)* (hello; goodbye), **cioccolata** *(chok-koh-lah-tah)* (chocolate), and **ciuccio** *(choo-choh)* (baby's pacifier).

✔ To obtain the "k" sound before *e* and *i,* you must put an *h* between the *c* and the *e* or *i.* Examples include **che** *(keh)* (what), **chiesa** *(kee-eh-zah)* (church), and **chiave** *(kee-ah-veh)* (key).

This pronunciation scheme sounds terribly complicated, but in the end, it's not that difficult. Here we present it in another way, which you can take as a little memory support:

casa	**co**lpa	**cu**ore	**che**	**chi**ave	= **k**
cena	**ci**bo	**ce**rto	**cio**ccolata	**cia**o	= **ch**

The consonant "g"

The Italian *g* behaves the same as the *c.* Therefore, we present it the same way:

✔ When *g* is followed by *a, o, u,* or any consonant, you pronounce it as you pronounce the *g* in the English word *good.* We transcribe this pronunciation as *(g).* Examples include **gamba** *(gahm-bah)* (leg), **gomma** *(gohm-mah)* (rubber), and **guerra** *(goo-eh-rah)* (war).

✔ When *g* is followed by *e* or *i,* you pronounce it as you do the first sound in the English word *job;* therefore we write the pronunciation as *(j).* Examples include **gentile** *(jehn-tee-leh)* (kind), **giorno** *(johr-noh)* (day), and **gelosia** *(jeh-loh-zee-ah)* (jealousy).

✔ To obtain the "j" sound before *a, o,* or *u,* you have to insert an *i.* The *i* serves only to indicate the proper sound; you do not pronounce it. Examples include **giacca** *(jahk-kah)* (jacket), **gioco** *(joh-koh)* (game), and **giudice** *(joo-dee-cheh)* (judge).

✔ To obtain the "g" sound before *e* or *i,* you must put an *h* between the letter *g* and the *e* or *i.* Examples include **spaghetti** *(spah-geht-tee)* (spaghetti), **ghiaccio** *(gee-ahch-choh)* (ice), and **ghirlanda** *(geer-lahn-dah)* (wreath).

Here's another little pattern to help you remember these pronunciations:

gamba	**go**mma	**gue**rra	**ghia**ccio	spa**ghe**tti	= **g**
gentile	**gio**rno	**gia**cca	**gio**co	**giu**dice	= **j**

The consonant "h"

The consonant *h* has only one function: namely, to change the sound of *c* and *g* before the vowels *e* and *i,* as described earlier. It also appears in foreign expressions such as *hostess, hit parade,* and *hobby,* and in some forms of the verb **avere** *(ah-veh-reh)* (to have), but there it's always silent.

The consonant "q"

Q exists only in connection with *u* followed by another vowel; that is, you always find *qu.* The *q* is pronounced like *(k),* and *qu* is therefore pronounced *(koo).* Examples include **quattro** *(koo-aht-troh)* (four), **questo** *(koo-ehs-toh)* (this), and **quadro** *(koo-ah-droh)* (picture).

The consonant "r"

The Italian *r* is not pronounced with the tongue in the back, as it is in English, but trilled at the alveolar ridge, which is the front part of your palate, right behind your front teeth. You have to practice it. In the beginning, you may not find this pronunciation manageable, but practice makes perfect!

Here are some words to help you practice:

✔ **radio** *(rah-dee-oh)* (radio)

✔ **per favore** *(pehr fah-voh-reh)* (please)

✔ **prego** *(preh-goh)* (you're welcome)

The consonant "s"

S is sometimes pronounced as the English *s*, as in *so.* In this case, we give you the pronunciation *(s).* In other cases, it's pronounced like the English *z,* as in *zero;* in these cases, we list *(z)* as the pronunciation. Examples include **pasta** *(pahs-tah)* (pasta), **solo** *(soh-loh)* (only), **chiesa** *(kee-eh-zah)* (church), and **gelosia** *(jeh-loh-zee-ah)* (jealousy).

The consonant "z"

A single *z* is pronounced *(dz)* — the sound is very similar to the English *z* in **zero,** with a *d* added at the beginning, as in **zio** *(dzee-oh)* (uncle). Just try it. When the *z* is doubled, you pronounce it more sharply, like *(t-ts),* as in **tazza** *(taht-tsah)* (cup; mug).

Double consonants

When you encounter double consonants in Italian, you have to pronounce each instance of the consonant or lengthen the sound. The difficult part is that there's no pause between the consonants.

Doubling the consonant usually changes the meaning of the word. So, to make sure that your Italian is understandable, emphasize doubled consonants well. To make you pronounce words with double consonants correctly, we write the first consonant at the end of one syllable and the other one at the beginning of the following one, as in these examples:

- **nono** *(noh-noh)* (ninth)
- **nonno** *(nohn-noh)* (grandfather)
- **capello** *(kah-pehl-loh)* (hair)
- **cappello** *(kahp-pehl-loh)* (hat)

But don't worry too much about your pronunciation of double consonants, because in a conversation, the context helps you be understood. Try it once again:

- **bello** *(behl-loh)* (beautiful)
- **caffè** *(kahf-feh)* (coffee)
- **occhio** *(ohk-kee-oh)* (eye)
- **spiaggia** *(spee-ahj-jah)* (beach)

Consonant clusters

Certain consonant clusters have special sounds in Italian. Here they are:

- ✔ **gn** is pronounced as the English "ny." The sound is actually the same as in a Spanish word we're sure you know: **señorita** *(seh-nyoh-ree-tah)* (miss).

- ✔ **sc** is pronounced as in the English *scooter* when it comes before *a, o, u,* or *h* — that is, as in **scala** *(skah-lah)* (scale), **sconto** *(skohn-toh)* (discount), and **scuola** *(scoo-oh-lah)* (school). Before *e* and *i,* it is pronounced like the *sh* in *cash.* Examples of this pronunciation include **scena** *(sheh-nah)* (scene), **scesa** *(sheh-sah)* (descent), and **scimmia** *(sheem-mee-ah)* (monkey).

Stressing Words Properly

Stress is the audible accent that you put on a syllable as you speak it. One syllable always gets more stress than all the others. (A reminder: In this book we underline the syllable to stress.)

Some words give you a hint as to where to stress them: They have an accent (`) or (´) above one of their letters. Here are some examples:

- ✔ **caffè** *(kahf-feh)* (coffee)
- ✔ **città** *(cheet-tah)* (city)
- ✔ **lunedì** *(loo-neh-dee)* (Monday)
- ✔ **perché** *(pehr-keh)* (why)
- ✔ **però** *(peh-roh)* (but)
- ✔ **università** *(oo-nee-vehr-see-tah)* (university)
- ✔ **virtù** *(veer-too)* (virtue)

Only vowels can have accents, in Italian all vowels at the end of a word can have this accent (`), but only the *e* can have both (`) and (´). The difference lies only in the pronunciation. That is, *è* is pronounced very open as in *hell,* whereas *é* is more closed as in *gourmet.*

If there's no accent in the word, you're unfortunately left on your own. A rough tip is that Italian tends to have the stress on the penultimate (the next-to-last) syllable. But there are too many rules and exceptions to list them all here!

Modern Italy

Every country and culture has common stereotypes. You may notice common, national traits during a **vacanza** *(vah-kahn-tsah)* (vacation) or while watching an old film. Just remember that stereotypes don't necessarily reflect the facts.

Everyone knows the stereotypes that circulate about **gli italiani** *(lyee ee-tah-lee-ah-nee)* (the Italians). Yes, it's true that Italians have **buon gusto** *(boo-ohn goos-toh)* (good taste) in **moda** *(moh-dah)* (fashion) and in **cucina** *(koo-chee-nah)* (the kitchen), and they certainly do live in a lovely little spot. But Italy is a **paese moderno** *(pah-eh-zeh moh-dehr-noh)* (modern country). Nowadays, **donne** *(dohn-neh)* (women) don't give birth to countless **bambini** *(bahm-bee-nee)* (kids); on the contrary, Italy has a declining birth rate. Also, the power of the **chiesa** *(kee-eh-zah)* (church) is no longer what it was 50 years ago. Actually, Italy is one of the leading industrial countries in **Europa** *(eh-oo-roh-pah)* (Europe).

Counteracting the stereotypes about Italy and Italians is certainly not an easy job. Thanks to the many movies about Italians and the gastronomic culture Italy exports, everyone has some notion about how Italians act and think. We hope that nobody comes to Italy expecting to meet only beautiful women and charming men who spend all their time singing, drinking **Chianti** *(kee-ahn-tee)* (Chianti wine), and eating mountains of spaghetti. In Italy, not every woman looks like *la Sofia nazionale (lah soh-fee-ah nah-tsee-oh-nah-leh)* (the national treasure Sophia [Loren]), and not every man jumps around and makes jokes like *il nostro Roberto (eel nohs-troh roh-behr-toh)* (our Roberto [Benigni]).

Every country has its own code of behavior. Gestures or behaviors that may be impolite somewhere else are perfectly acceptable in Italy. So don't worry; you're not always in the middle of an argument. Italians just love to communicate, and often in a loud voice. It's not unusual to start a conversation with a neighbor on the bus, to make jokes with people waiting in line, or to stay for a chat with the vegetable seller.

Stereotypes aside, it is true to say that Italians like to enjoy life. Thanks to the good weather Italy enjoys, people like to be outside, to meet friends in cafés, restaurants, or pizzerias, and to have a good time together.

You find a lot of accents in written Italian. They are always on the vowels and can have different functions:

- ✔ The accent tells you where to stress the word.
- ✔ The accent gives you clues about how to pronounce the stressed vowel.
- ✔ The most important function of an accent is to change a word's meaning. Fortunately, only a few words have the same spelling and only an accent to distinguish them. But it can be a very important distinction, as in the following example:

é (eh) (and) and *è (eh)* (he/she/it is) are distinguished only by the accent on the vowel, which means "is" or "to be."

Using Gestures

Italians love to emphasize their words with gestures. Actually, Italians could talk without words and understand each other. For example, there are gestures to express the following feelings: **Ho fame** *(oh fah-meh)* (I'm hungry), **Me ne vado** *(meh neh vah-doh)* (I'm leaving), and **E chi se ne importa?** *(eh kee seh neh eem-pohr-tah)* (Who cares?). Needless to say, a flood of rude gestures exist as well.

Unfortunately, describing the gestures in words is too difficult, because Italian body language is a science and is hard for foreigners to copy. You also have to make the right facial expressions when performing these gestures; if you don't, you're immediately exposed as a non-Italian. Further, these gestures must come very naturally and spontaneously, which is really hard if you don't exercise them beginning in the cradle.

The following saying expresses this sentiment:

> **L'abitudine è una seconda natura.**
> *lah-bee-too-dee-neh eh oo-nah seh-kohn-dah nah-too-rah*
> Habit is second nature.

Still, we won't let you go off without some of the practical, useful gestures that strangers are allowed to make. Greeting and saying goodbye, for example, are accompanied by a common gesture — hugging and kissing. Italians seek direct contact when greeting one another. When you're not very familiar with a person, you shake hands. But when you know a person well or you have an immediate good feeling, you kiss cheek to cheek; that is, you don't really touch with your lips, but only with your cheek. Actually, you get to decide whether to kiss, barely kiss, or only touch cheek to cheek; it is a question of sympathy and confidence. If, however, you have closer contact — say the other person is a family member or is someone you know well — you can give a kiss to the cheek and a loving hug.

Incidentally, Italians kiss twice — once on the left, once on the right. As they say:

> **Paese che vai, usanza che trovi.**
> *pah-eh-zeh keh vah-ee oo-zahn-tsah keh troh-vee*
> Other countries, other habits.

Chapter 2

The Nitty Gritty: Basic Italian Grammar and Numbers

- -

- -

*T*his chapter gives you grammatical hints and rules about how to use Italian. You know that each language has special speaking and writing patterns which make understanding easier. If everyone decided not to follow these rules, you'd have a hard time understanding even someone speaking your native tongue. Don't look at grammar as a burden, but more as a scaffolding that helps you to construct your sentences.

At the end of this chapter, we give you numbers and their various usages because they're pretty basic, too.

Setting Up Simple Sentences

Becoming a fluent speaker of a foreign language takes a lot of work. Simply communicating or making yourself understood in a foreign language is much easier. Even if you only know a few words, you can usually communicate successfully in common situations such as at a restaurant or a hotel.

Forming simple sentences is, well, simple. The basic sentence structure of Italian is *subject-verb-object* — the same as in English. In the following examples, you can see how this structure works:

- **Carla parla inglese.** *(kahr-lah pahr-lah een-gleh-zeh)* (Carla speaks English.)

- **Pietro ha una macchina.** *(pee-eh-troh ah oo-nah mahk-kee-nah)* (Pietro has a car.)

One major difference between English and Italian is that Italian doesn't usually put the subject before the verb when the subject is a personal pronoun, such as *I, you, he, she,* and so on. This may sound odd, but the verb changes according to the its subject. Consequently, if you know the different verb forms, you automatically understand who the subject is. The verb form tells you the unspoken subject, as in this example: **Ho una macchina** *(oh oo-nah mahk-kee-nah)* means "I have a car."

Check out the following table of the verb **avere** *(ah-veh-reh)* (to have) — with pronouns as subjects:

Conjugation	*Pronunciation*
io ho	ee-oh oh
tu hai	too ah-ee
lui/lei ha	loo-ee/lay ah
noi abbiamo	noh-ee ahb-bee-ah-moh
voi avete	voh-ee ah-veh-teh
loro hanno	loh-roh ahn-noh

We included the subject in the preceding example simply to allow you to see which verb form corresponds to which personal pronoun. Using the verb in a sentence, however, a native Italian speaker would say:

- **Ho un cane.** *(oh oon kah-neh)* (I have a dog.)

- **Hai un cane.** *(ah-ee oon kah-neh)* (You have a dog.)

The rest of the pronouns in the list continue in the same manner.

Whenever the subject in a sentence is not very clear — for instance, when speaking about a third person (in the following example, Luca) — or the sentence is confusing, say the subject. Once named, however, the noun or pronoun drops out:

Luca ha fame. Mangia una mela. *(loo-kah ah fah-meh mahn-jah oo-nah meh-lah)* (Luca is hungry. [He] eats an apple.)

Coping with Gendered Words (Articles and Adjectives)

The main grammatical difference between English and Italian is that English has only one article for all kinds of words — *the* — and no gender differences in nouns. Italian differentiates both gender and number. The result is that Italian uses a couple of articles to distinguish between masculine/feminine and singular/plural.

Definite feminine articles

The singular feminine article is **la** *(lah)* (the) — for example, **la casa** *(lah kah-sah)* (the house). Feminine nouns end, in most cases, with **-a.** If a feminine noun begins with a vowel, replace the **a** in **la** and the space between the article and noun with an apostrophe — as in **l'amica** *(lah-mee-kah)* (the friend [f]). The plural feminine article is **le** *(leh)* — for example, **le case** *(leh kah-seh)* (the houses). Never apostrophize the plural article; therefore, it is **le amiche** *(leh ah-mee-keh)* (the friends [f]).

Definite masculine articles

Italian contains more than one masculine article. However, the most prominent one is **il** *(eel)* (the), as in **il gatto** *(eel gaht-toh)* (the cat). Its plural form is **i** *(ee),* as in **i gatti** *(ee gaht-tee)* (the cats).

Furthermore, Italian contains another masculine article, **lo** *(loh).* Use **lo** with nouns that begin with **z,** as in **lo zio** *(loh zee-oh)* (the uncle); with **y,** as in **lo yogurt** *(loh yoh-joort)* (the yogurt); with **gn,** as in **lo gnomo** *(loh nyoh-moh)* (the gnome); and with an **s** followed by a consonant, such as **st, sb, sc, sd,** and so on — for example, **lo studente** *(loh stoo-dehn-teh)* (the student). Also use **lo** for nouns that begin with a vowel, such as **l'amico** *(lah-mee-koh)* (the friend [m]). As you can see, in such a case, you contract **lo.**

As for the plural, we have good news: The plural article for all these cases is **gli** *(lyee)* (the), as in **gli studenti** *(lyee stoo-dehn-tee)* (the students) and **gli amici** *(lyee ah-mee-chee)* (the friends [m]).

Unlike feminine nouns, many masculine nouns end in **-o.** However, many Italian words end in **-e** and can be either feminine or masculine.

Definite articles are certainly useful and, sure enough, indefinite articles also play an important role in Italian.

The indefinite feminine article

The indefinite feminine article is **una** *(oo-nah)* (a) — for example, **una casa** *(oo-nah kah-sah)* (a house). If a feminine noun begins with a vowel, contract the article, as in **un'amica** *(oo-nah-mee-kah)* (a friend [f]).

The indefinite masculine articles

As you can see earlier in this chapter, Italian contains more than one definite masculine article. The same holds true for the indefinite articles. The first indefinite article is **un** *(oon)* (a), as in **un gatto** *(oon gaht-toh)* (a cat). It's plural form is **dei** *(deh-i)*. In contrast to the definite article, you do not contract the indefinite article when the following noun begins with a vowel. Therefore, if a masculine noun begins with a vowel, it's **un amico** *(oon ah-mee-koh)* (a friend [m]). In this case the plural form is **degli,** for instance **degli amici** (some friends).

For the other cases in which you need the definite masculine article **lo** *(loh)* (the), the indefinite counterpart is **uno** *(oo-noh)* (a) — that is **uno studente** *(oo-noh stoo-dehn-teh)* (a student). In this case the plural form is again **degli,** like in **degli studenti** (some students).

To sum up: The masculine articles are **il, lo** (**l'** — before a vowel) (definite singular); **i, gli** (definite plural); and **uno; (un)** (indefinite). The feminine articles are **la (l')** (definite singular); **le** (definite plural); and **una, (un')** (indefinite).

Adjectives

The gender feature of nouns extends to other grammatical categories, including pronouns and adjectives. First, we take a look at the adjectives.

An adjective is a word that describes a noun — whether a person, a thing, or whatever — with a quality or characteristic. Because the adjective and the noun are grammatically connected, they must match in number and gender. The adjective adopts the number and gender of the noun. If, for example, you use the adjective **bello** *(behl-loh)* (beautiful) to refer to a house, which is a feminine noun, the phrase becomes **una bella casa** *(oo-nah behl-lah kah-sah)* (a beautiful house). Incidentally, the infinitive form of a verb — that is the form which can stand on its own and that you find in the dictionary — is always the masculine singular adjective.

Some examples of how adjectives change according to their referents include:

✔ **il ragazzo italiano** *(eel rah-gahts-tsoh ee-ta-lee-ah-noh)* (the Italian boy)

✔ **i ragazzi italiani** *(ee rah-gahts-tsee ee-ta-lee-ah-nee)* (the Italian boys)

✔ **la ragazza italiana** *(lah rah-gahts-tsah ee-ta-lee-ah-nah)* (the Italian girl)

✔ **le ragazze italiane** *(leh rah-gahts-tseh ee-ta-lee-ah-neh)* (the Italian girls)

Several adjectives end in **-e,** such as **grande** *(grahn-deh)* (big). These adjectives are valid for both feminine and masculine nouns. In the plural of both genders, change the **-e** to an **-i** — for example, **grandi** *(grahn-dee)* (big).

✔ **il negozio grande** *(eel neh-goh-tsee-oh grahn-deh)* (the big store)

✔ **i negozi grandi** *(ee neh-goh-tsee grahn-dee)* (the big stores)

✔ **la casa grande** *(lah kah-sah grahn-deh)* (the big house)

✔ **le case grandi** *(leh kah-seh grahn-dee)* (the big houses)

In Italian, the position of the adjective is not as rigid as it is in English. In most cases, the adjective follows the noun. Nevertheless, there are some adjectives which can stand before the noun. The position of the adjective does convey a slight difference in meaning — an adjective after the noun gives the adjective a certain emphasis. Both the phrases below mean "a small house," but in the second example the emphasis is on the small size of the house.

una piccola casa *(oo-nah peek-koh-lah kah-sah)*

una casa piccola *(oo-nah kah-sah peek-koh-lah)*

However, there are also adjectives that change in meaning depending on whether they precede or follow the noun. And in these cases their position is fixed to the meaning. Here some examples:

una cara amica *(oo-nah kah-rah ah-mee-kah)* (a dear friend [f])
un CD caro *(oon cheh-deh kah-roh)* (an expensive CD)

un certo signore *(oon chehr-toh see-nyoh-reh)* (a certain gentleman)
una cosa certa *(oo-nah koh-sah chehr-tah)* (a sure thing)

diverse macchine *(dee-vehr-seh mahk-kee-neh)* (various cars)
penne diverse *(pehn-neh dee-vehr-seh)* (different pencils)

un grand'uomo *(oon grahn-doo-oh-moh)* (a great man)
un uomo grande *(oon oo-oh-moh grahn-deh)* (a big; tall man)

un povero ragazzo *(oon poh-veh-roh rah-gah-tsoh)* (an unfortunate boy)
un ragazzo povero *(oon rah-gah-tsoh poh-veh-roh)* (a poor; not well-off boy)

una semplice domanda *(oo-nah sehm-plee-cheh doh-mahn-dah)* (simply a question)
una domanda semplice *(oo-nah doh-mahn-dah sehm-plee-cheh)* (a simple question)

l'unica occasione *(loo-nee-kah ohk-kah-zee-oh-neh)* (the one-and-only opportunity)
un'occasione unica *(oo-nohk-kah-zee-oh-neh oo-nee-kah)* (a unique opportunity)

Talking about Pronouns

A pronoun replaces, as the word itself says, a noun. When you talk about Jim, for example, you can replace his name with **he.** You often use pronouns to avoid repetition.

Personal pronouns

Several types of personal pronouns exist. Presently, the most important ones for you are the *subject pronouns,* which refer either to the speaker(s) *I* or *we,* the person(s) spoken to, *you,* or the person(s) spoken about *he, she, it,* or *they.* In addition, two other types of personal pronouns exist: the *accusative pronouns* — the so-called direct-object pronouns — and the *dative pronouns* — the so-called indirect-object pronouns. Table 2-1 lists subject pronouns.

Table 2-1	Subject Pronouns	
Pronoun	*Pronunciation*	*Translation*
io	ee-oh	I
tu	too	you
lui	loo-ee	he
lei	lay	she
esso/a	ehs-soh/sah	it [m/f]
noi	noh-ee	we
voi	voh-ee	you
loro	loh-roh	they
essi/e	ehs-see/seh	they [m/f]

Italians often drop subject pronouns because the verb ending shows what the subject is. Use a personal pronoun only for contrast, for emphasis, or when the pronoun stands alone.

- ✔ *Contrast:* **Tu tifi per il Milan, ma io per la Juventus.** *(too tee-fee pehr eel mee-lahn mah ee-oh pehr lah yoo-vehn-toos)* (You're a fan of Milan, but I'm a fan of Juventus.)

- ✔ *Emphasis:* **Vieni anche tu alla festa?** *(vee-eh-nee ahn-keh too ahl-lah fehs-tah)* (Are you coming to the party, too?)

- ✔ *Isolated position:* **Chi è? Sono io.** *(kee eh soh-noh ee-oh)* (Who's there? It's me.)

Pronouns are, however, used to replace an already mentioned thing or person to avoid repetitions. More about direct and indirect object pronouns follows. Let's start with the direct pronoun and give you some examples. You will easily understand what they stand for.

Direct object pronouns

As the name explains, the direct object pronoun is directly connected with the verb and has no need of any preposition. Some examples of direct object pronouns in English are:

- ✔ I saw *her.*
- ✔ She called *him.*
- ✔ Do you like *them?*
- ✔ You don't need *me.*

Now, you're surely curious to know what they are in Italian.

- ✔ *Mi* **hai chiamato?** *(mee ah-ee kee-ah-mah-toh)* (Did you call me?)
- ✔ **No, non** *ti* **ho chiamato.** *(noh nohn tee oh kee-ah-mah-toh)* (No, I didn't call you.)
- ✔ **Vorrei ringraziar***la.* *(vohr-ray reen-grah-tsee-ahr-lah)* (I'd like to thank you [formal, singular].)
- ✔ *Lo* **vedo.** *(loh veh-doh)* (I see him; it.)
- ✔ *La* **vedo.** *(lah veh-doh)* (I see her; it.)
- ✔ *Ci* **hanno invitati.** *(chee ahn-noh een-vee-tah-tee)* (They invited/have invited us.)
- ✔ *Vi* **ringrazio.** *(vee reen-grah-tsee-oh)* (I thank you [formal and informal, plural].)
- ✔ *Li* **ho visti.** (i ragazzi) *(lee oh vees-tee)* (I saw/have seen them [m].)
- ✔ *Le* **ho viste.** (le ragazze) *(leh oh vees-teh)* (I saw/have seen them [f].)

Contract **lo** *(loh)* (him) and **la** *(lah)* (her) before a vowel. Occasionally you contract **mi** *(mee)* (me), **ti** *(tee)* (you), **ci** *(chee)* (us), and **vi** *(vee)* (you), also. But never use an apostrophe to contract the plural forms **li** *(lee)* (they [m]) and **le** *(leh)* (they [f]).

Indirect object pronouns

These pronouns may cause a little difficulty for you, because the indirect object means *for* or *to,* which isn't always evident in English. In general, certain verbs dictate the use of the indirect object pronouns — for example, **dare a** *(dah-reh ah)* (to give to) calls for the dative.

- ✔ **Mi hai scritto una lettera?** *(mee ah-ee skreet-toh oo-nah leht-teh-rah)* (Did you write a letter to me?)

- ✔ **Ti ho portato un regalo.** *(tee oh pohr-tah-toh oon reh-gah-loh)* (I've brought a gift for you.)

- ✔ **Le do il mio indirizzo.** *(leh doh eel mee-oh een-dee-reets-tsoh)* (I give you [formal] my address.)

- ✔ **Gli ho chiesto un favore.** *(lyee oh kee-ehs-toh oon fah-voh-reh)* (I asked/have asked him/them a favor.)

- ✔ **Ci hanno telefonato.** *(chee ahn-noh teh-leh-foh-nah-toh)* (They phoned/have phoned us.)

- ✔ **Vi chiedo scusa.** *(vee kee-eh-doh skoo-zah)* (I beg your [formal and informal, plural] pardon.)

- ✔ **Gli ho dato un lavoro.** *(lyee oh dah-toh oon lah-voh-roh)* (I gave him/them a job.)

- ✔ **Le ho dato un bacio.** *(leh oh dah-toh oon bah-choh)* (I gave her a kiss.)

Notice that all of the preceding pronouns stand for **a me** *(ah meh)* (to me), **a te** *(ah teh)* (to you), **a lei** *(ah lay)* (to you [formal]), **a lui** *(ah loo-ee)* (to him), **a lei** *(ah lay)* (to her), **a noi** *(ah noh-ee)* (to us), **a voi** *(ah voh-ee)* (to you [formal and informal, plural]), and **a loro** *(ah loh-roh)* (to them), respectively. Therefore, you can also write the first couple sentences above as follows:

- ✔ **Hai scritto una lettera a me?** *(ah-ee skreet-toh oo-nah leht-teh-rah ah meh)* (Did you write a letter to me?)

- ✔ **Ho portato un regalo a te.** *(oh pohr-tah-toh oon reh-gah-loh ah teh)* (I've brought a gift for you.)

The first versions are more natural. Use the second version only when you want to emphasize a fact.

Saying "you": Formal and informal

You probably already know that many foreign languages contain both formal and informal ways of addressing people. If you didn't know before, now you do! In Italian, you need to respect this important characteristic. Use the informal pronoun **tu** *(too)* (you) with good friends, young people, children, and your family members. When, however, you talk to a person you don't know well or to a person of higher rank (a superior, teacher, professor, and so on), you should address him or her formally — that is, with **lei** *(lay)* (you). When you become more familiar with someone, you may change from formal to informal. According to custom, the elder person initiates the use of **tu**.

Tu requires the verb form of the second person singular — for example, **tu sei** *(too say)* (you are). **Lei** calls for **lei è** *(lay eh)* (you are [formal singular]). The formal plural form with **Loro** is practically never used.

The following examples show the forms of *you:*

- *Informal singular:* **Ciao, come stai?** *(chah-oh koh-meh stah-ee)* (Hi, how are you?)

- *Formal singular:* **Buongiorno, come sta?** *(boo-ohn-johr-noh koh-meh stah)* (Good morning, how are you?)

- *Informal plural:* **Ciao, come state?** *(chah-oh koh-meh stah-teh)* (Hi, how are you?)

Discovering Interrogative Pronouns

In Italian at least one thing is easier than in English: forming questions. In English, in most cases, you need the auxiliary *do* to form a question. In other cases, you need a form of *to be* or *to have.* You also (mostly) have to invert your sentence construction. For example, "He goes to the movies." becomes "Does he go to the movies?"

In Italian, forming questions is very easy: A question has the same structure as an affirmative statement. You identify a question only by the intonation in spoken language and by the use of a question mark in written language. For example:

Luca va a scuola.	**Luca va a scuola?**
loo-kah vah ah skoo-oh-lah	*loo-kah vah ah skoo-oh-lah*
Luca goes to school.	Luca goes to school? or Does Luca go to school?

Italian also contains interrogative pronouns (**when, where, what,** and so on) with which you can start questions. Use the following pronouns:

- **Chi?** *(kee)* (Who?)
- **Cosa?** *(<u>koh</u>-sah)* (What?)
- **Quando?** *(koo-<u>ahn</u>-doh)* (When?)
- **Dove?** *(<u>doh</u>-veh)* (Where?)
- **Perché?** *(pehr-<u>keh</u>)* (Why?)
- **Come?** *(<u>koh</u>-meh)* (How?)

Some sample questions using these interrogative pronouns include:

- **Chi è?** *(kee eh)* (Who is this?)
- **Cosa stai facendo?** *(<u>koh</u>-sah <u>stah</u>-ee fahch-<u>chehn</u>-doh)* (What are you doing?)
- **Quando arrivi?** *(koo-<u>ahn</u>-doh ahr-<u>ree</u>-vee)* (When do you arrive?)
- **Dov'è la stazione?** *(doh-<u>veh</u> lah stah-tsee-<u>oh</u>-neh)* (Where is the station?)
- **Perché non sei venuto?** *(pehr-<u>keh</u> nohn say veh-<u>noo</u>-toh)* (Why didn't you come?)
- **Come stai?** *(<u>koh</u>-meh <u>stah</u>-ee)* (How are you?)

Introducing Regular and Irregular Verbs

What's the difference between regular and irregular verbs? Regular verbs follow a certain pattern in their conjugation: They behave the same way as other verbs in the same category. Therefore, you can predict a regular verb's form in any part of any tense. On the other hand, you cannot predict irregular verbs in this way — they behave a bit like individualists.

Regular verbs

You can divide Italian verbs into three categories, according to their ending in the infinitive form. They are, **-are,** as in **parlare** *(pahr-<u>lah</u>-reh)* (to speak); **-ere,** as in **vivere** *(<u>vee</u>-veh-reh)* (to live); and **-ire,** as in **partire** *(pahr-<u>tee</u>-reh)* (to leave). Verbs in these categories can be regular as well as irregular.

The following tables show you the conjugation of three regular verbs:

Conjugation	Pronunciation
io parlo	<u>ee</u>-oh <u>pahr</u>-loh
tu parli	too <u>pahr</u>-lee
lui/lei parla	<u>loo</u>-ee/lay <u>pahr</u>-lah
noi parliamo	<u>noh</u>-ee pahr-lee-<u>ah</u>-moh
voi parlate	<u>voh</u>-ee pahr-<u>lah</u>-teh
loro parlano	<u>loh</u>-roh <u>pahr</u>-lah-noh

Conjugation	Pronunciation
io vivo	<u>ee</u>-oh <u>vee</u>-voh
tu vivi	too <u>vee</u>-vee
lui/lei vive	<u>loo</u>-ee/lay <u>vee</u>-veh
noi viviamo	<u>noh</u>-ee vee-vee-<u>ah</u>-moh
voi vivete	<u>voh</u>-ee vee-<u>veh</u>-teh
loro vivono	<u>loh</u>-roh <u>vee</u>-voh-noh

Conjugation	Pronunciation
io parto	<u>ee</u>-oh <u>pahr</u>-toh
tu parti	too <u>pahr</u>-tee
lui/lei parte	<u>loo</u>-ee/lay <u>pahr</u>-teh
noi partiamo	<u>noh</u>-ee pahr-tee-<u>ah</u>-moh
voi partite	<u>voh</u>-ee pahr-<u>tee</u>-teh
loro partono	<u>loh</u>-roh <u>pahr</u>-toh-noh

You can apply these patterns to every regular verb. Some regular verbs behave a bit differently, but this doesn't render them irregular. In some cases — for example, *ire* verbs — you insert the letters *isc* between the root and the ending, as in this example of **capire** *(kah-<u>pee</u>-reh)* (to understand):

Conjugation	Pronunciation
io cap**isc**o	<u>ee</u>-oh kah-<u>pees</u>-koh
tu cap**isc**i	too kah-<u>pee</u>-shee
lui/lei cap**isc**e	<u>loo</u>-ee/lay kah-<u>pee</u>-sheh
noi capiamo	<u>noh</u>-ee kah-pee-<u>ah</u>-moh
voi capite	<u>voh</u>-ee kah-<u>pee</u>-teh
loro cap**isc**ono	<u>loh</u>-roh kah-<u>pees</u>-koh-noh

Irregular verbs

Two important verbs, which you often use as auxiliary verbs, are irregular — **avere** *(ah-veh-reh)* (to have) and **essere** *(ehs-seh-reh)* (to be).

Conjugation	*Pronunciation*
io ho	ee-oh oh
tu hai	too ah-ee
lui/lei ha	loo-ee/lay ah
noi abbiamo	noh-ee ahb-bee-ah-moh
voi avete	voh-ee ah-veh-teh
loro hanno	loh-roh ahn-noh

Conjugation	*Pronunciation*
io sono	ee-oh soh-noh
tu sei	too say
lui/lei è	loo-ee/lay eh
noi siamo	noh-ee see-ah-moh
voi siete	voh-ee see-eh-teh
loro sono	loh-roh soh-noh

Other irregular verbs are **andare** *(ahn-dah-reh)* (to go) and **venire** *(veh-nee-reh)* (to come):

Conjugation	*Pronunciation*
io vado	ee-oh vah-doh
tu vai	too vah-ee
lui/lei va	loo-ee/lay vah
noi andiamo	noh-ee ahn-dee-ah-moh
voi andate	voh-ee ahn-dah-teh
loro vanno	loh-roh vahn-noh

Conjugation	*Pronunciation*
io vengo	<u>ee</u>-oh <u>vehn</u>-goh
tu vieni	too vee-<u>eh</u>-nee
lui/lei viene	<u>loo</u>-ee/lay vee-<u>eh</u>-neh
noi veniamo	<u>noh</u>-ee veh-nee-<u>ah</u>-moh
voi venite	<u>voh</u>-ee veh-<u>nee</u>-the
loro vengono	<u>loh</u>-roh <u>vehn</u>-goh-noh

In addition, the verb ending *-rre,* as in **porre** *(<u>pohr</u>-reh)* (to put) is exclusively irregular.

Conjugation	*Pronunciation*
io pongo	<u>ee</u>-oh <u>pohn</u>-goh
tu poni	too <u>poh</u>-nee
lui/lei pone	<u>loo</u>-ee/lay <u>poh</u>-neh
noi poniamo	<u>noh</u>-ee poh-nee-<u>ah</u>-moh
voi ponete	<u>voh</u>-ee poh-<u>neh</u>-teh
loro pongono	<u>loh</u>-roh <u>pohn</u>-goh-noh

Presenting the Simple Tenses: Past, Present, and Future

Clearly, people don't use just one tense. Sometimes you need to report what you did yesterday or outline what you're going to do tomorrow. These three tenses (past, present, and future) are not high grammar — just basic stuff.

✔ **Ieri ho mangiato un gelato.** *(<u>yeh</u>-ree oh mahn-<u>jah</u>-toh oon jeh-<u>lah</u>-toh)* (Yesterday I ate ice cream.)

✔ **Mangio un gelato.** *(<u>mahn</u>-joh oon jeh-<u>lah</u>-toh)* (I am eating/eat ice cream.)

✔ **Domani mangerò un gelato.** *(doh-<u>mah</u>-nee mahn-jeh-<u>roh</u> oon jeh-<u>lah</u>-toh)* (Tomorrow I will eat ice cream.)

Past tense

As you can see, the only compound form in Italian is the past tense, called **passato prossimo** *(pahs-sah-toh prohs-see-moh)*. Generally, it corresponds to the English present perfect tense (I have done). As in the example above, however, Italian uses the passato prossimo even when English uses the simple past (I ate) — that is, for situations that happened in the past.

In passato prossimo, like the English present perfect, a form of the verb **avere** *(ah-veh-reh)* (to have) comes before the past participle of the verb. A past participle expresses a completed action, as in the English *written, gone,* and *been.* To help you acquire a taste for the passato prossimo, some Italian examples follow:

- ✔ **Ho letto il giornale.** *(oh leht-toh eel johr-nah-leh)* (I read/have read the newspaper.)

- ✔ **Maria ha scritto una lettera.** *(mah-ree-ah ah skreet-toh oo-nah leht-teh-rah)* (Maria wrote/has written a letter.)

- ✔ **Abbiamo vinto la partita.** *(ahb-bee-ah-moh veen-toh lah pahr-tee-tah)* (We won/have won the match.)

Some verbs require **essere** *(ehs-seh-reh)* (to be) rather than **avere** (to have) to form the passato prossimo — for example, most verbs that indicate movement fall into this category. Check out the next example to see how things change in this case:

- ✔ **Anna è andata al cinema.** *(ahn-nah eh ahn-dah-tah ahl chee-neh-mah)* (Anna has gone/went to the movies.)

- ✔ **Anche Marco è venuto.** *(ahn-keh mahr-koh eh veh-noo-toh)* (Marco came/has come also.)

A peculiarity of this form is that one past participle ends in *-a* and one ends in *-o.* The reason for this peculiarity is that in one case the subject (the person who does the action) is feminine — Anna — and in the other case the subject is masculine, Marco. When you compound the **passato prossimo** with the present tense of **essere** (to be), the past participle ends according to the subject: feminine singular *-a* (**andata**), masculine singular *-o* (**andato**), feminine plural *-e* (**andate**), masculine plural *-i* (**andati**).

Check out these examples in complete sentences:

- ✔ **Anna è andata a Milano.** *(ahn-nah eh ahn-dah-tah ah mee-lah-noh)* (Anna went/has gone to Milan.)

- ✔ **Marco è andato a Milano.** *(pah-oh-loh eh ahn-dah-toh ah mee-lah-noh)* (Marco went/has gone to Milan.)

   ✔ **Anna e Carla sono andate a Milano.** *(ahn-nah eh kahr-lah soh-noh ahn-dah-teh ah mee-lah-noh)* (Anna and Carla have gone/went to Milan.)

   ✔ **Marco e Paolo sono andati a Milano.** *(mahr-koh eh pah-oh-loh soh-noh ahn-dah-tee ah mee-lah-noh)* (Marco and Paolo have gone/went to Milan.)

Present tense

The present tense doesn't require much attention here; have a look at the simple sentence construction and the verb forms earlier in this section.

Future tense

The Italian future tense isn't a compound form as it is in English (I will/I'm going to). The verb form — or more precisely the verb ending — includes the time marker (will/going to). For example, examine the verb **parlare** *(pahr-lah-reh)* (to speak), which belongs to the family of verbs ending in **-are**. When you cut off the ending, only the verb stem **parl-** remains, to which you can add endings that indicate the grammatical person and the tense. For example, the ending for the first person singular future tense is **-erò/-irò**. Adding it to the stem, you get **parlerò** *(pahr-leh-roh)* (I will speak). In comparison, the first person singular present tense is **parlo** *(pahr-loh)* (I speak). Here are some more examples:

   ✔ **Domani saprò i risultati.** *(doh-mah-nee sah-proh ee ree-zool-tah-tee)* (Tomorrow I will know the results.)

   ✔ **Lunedì vedrai Marco.** *(loo-neh-dee veh-drah-ee mahr-coh)* (Monday you will see Marco.)

   ✔ **Elena partirà domenica.** *(eh-leh-nah pahr-tee-rah doh-meh-nee-kah)* (Elena is going to leave on Sunday.)

   ✔ **Finiremo il lavoro fra poco.** *(fee-nee-reh-moh eel lah-voh-roh frah poh-koh)* (We're going to finish this work soon.)

   ✔ **Quando uscirete dalla chiesa?** *(koo-ahn-doh oo-shee-reh-teh dahl-lah kee-eh-zah)* (When will you come out of the church?)

   ✔ **Verranno da noi in estate.** *(vehr-rahn-noh dah noh-ee een ehs-tah-teh)* (They will come to see/stay with us in the summer.)

See Appendix A for verb tables.

Counting Numbers

Numbers are a basic part of any language, so we've included numbers in this chapter of basic grammar. You can't get away without knowing numbers, even in small talk. Somebody may ask you how old you are, how many days you're visiting, or whatever. You can see how numbers are used at restaurants in Chapter 5, for dealing with money in Chapter 11, and for finding addresses in Chapter 12, where you can also find the Italian ordinal numbers.

Every language follows a certain scheme to formulate higher numbers. When you know the basics — the numbers from one to ten — you're halfway there.

In the Italian scheme, as in the English one, the higher value precedes the lower one, so that to say "22," you first say **venti** *vehn-tee* "twenty" and then **due** *doo-eh* "two" and simply put them together: **ventidue** *(vehn-tee-doo-eh)* (twenty-two). The same is true for higher numbers — like **trecentoventidue** *(treh-chehn-toh-vehn-tee-doo-eh)* (three hundred and twenty-two) and **duemila-trecentoventidue** *(doo-eh-mee-lah-treh-chehn-toh-vehn-tee-doo-eh)* (two thousand three hundred and twenty-two).

One thing merits some further explanation: When two vowels meet [this happens frequently with **uno** *(oo-noh)* (one) and **otto** *(oht-toh)* (eight)] you eliminate the first vowel as in **vent(i)uno** *(vehn-too-noh)* (twenty-one) and **quarant(a)otto** *(koo-ah-rahn-toht-toh)* (forty-eight). So far so good.

Every rule has exceptions, and there are some irregular numbers, which you simply have to memorize. The numbers from 11 to 19 follow their own rules: **undici** *(oon-dee-chee)* (eleven), **dodici** *(doh-dee-chee)* (twelve), **tredici** *(treh-dee-chee)* (thirteen), **quattordici** *(koo-aht-tohr-dee-chee)* (fourteen), **quindici** *(koo-een-dee-chee)* (fifteen), **sedici** *(seh-dee-chee)* (sixteen), **diciassette** *(dee-chahs-seht-teh)* (seventeen), **diciotto** *(dee-choht-toh)* (eighteen), and **diciannove** *(dee-chahn-noh-veh)* (nineteen).

You can see that up to the number 16 the previous rule is reversed — the minor number precedes the major one. The numbers 17, 18, and 19 follow the larger-number-first rule, but are formed in their own individual ways.

In Italian you cannot express a decade in just one word — you use a phrase. When you want to say "in the sixties," you have to say **negli anni sessanta** *(neh-lyee ahn-nee sehs-sahn-tah)*, which literally means "in the years sixty." You form all the other decades using this method also.

One other thing to keep in mind is that the plural of **mille** *(meel-leh)* (one thousand) is **mila** *(mee-lah)*, as in **duemila** *(doo-eh-mee-lah)* (two thousand).

Table 2-2 gives you enough numbers that we hope that you can form the ones not included on your own.

Table 2-2	Numbers	
Italian	*Pronunciation*	*Number*
From 1 to 30		
zero	<u>dzeh</u>-roh	0
uno	<u>oo</u>-noh	1
due	<u>doo</u>-eh	2
tre	treh	3
quattro	koo-<u>aht</u>-troh	4
cinque	<u>cheen</u>-koo-eh	5
sei	say	6
sette	<u>seht</u>-teh	7
otto	<u>oht</u>-toh	8
nove	<u>noh</u>-veh	9
dieci	dee-<u>eh</u>-chee	10
undici	<u>oon</u>-dee-chee	11
dodici	<u>doh</u>-dee-chee	12
tredici	<u>treh</u>-dee-chee	13
quattordici	koo-<u>aht</u>-tohr-dee-chee	14
quindici	<u>koo</u>-een-dee-chee	15
sedici	<u>seh</u>-dee-chee	16
diciassette	dee-chahs-<u>seht</u>-teh	17
diciotto	dee-<u>choht</u>-toh	18
diciannove	dee-chahn-<u>noh</u>-veh	19
venti	<u>vehn</u>-tee	20
ventuno	vehn-<u>too</u>-noh	21
ventidue	vehn-tee-<u>doo</u>-eh	22
ventitré	vehn-tee-<u>treh</u>	23
ventiquattro	vehn-tee-koo-<u>aht</u>-troh	24
venticinque	vehn-tee-<u>cheen</u>-koo-eh	25

(continued)

Table 2-2 (continued)

Italian	Pronunciation	Number
ventisei	vehn-tee-<u>say</u>	26
ventisette	vehn-tee-<u>seht</u>-teh	27
ventotto	vehnt-<u>oht</u>-toh	28
ventinove	vehn-tee-<u>noh</u>-veh	29
trenta	<u>trehn</u>-tah	30
Decades 40 to 90		
quaranta	koo-ah-<u>rahn</u>-tah	40
cinquanta	cheen-koo-<u>ahn</u>-tah	50
sessanta	sehs-<u>sahn</u>-tah	60
settanta	seht-<u>tahn</u>-tah	70
ottanta	oht-<u>tahn</u>-tah	80
novanta	noh-<u>vahn</u>-tah	90
Centuries from 200 to 900		
cento	<u>chehn</u>-toh	100
duecento	doo-eh-<u>chehn</u>-toh	200
trecento	treh-<u>chehn</u>-toh	300
quattrocento	koo-aht-troh-<u>chehn</u>-toh	400
cinquecento	cheen-koo-eh-<u>chehn</u>-toh	500
seicento	say-<u>chehn</u>-toh	600
settecento	seht-teh-<u>chehn</u>-toh	700
ottocento	oht-toh-<u>chehn</u>-toh	800
novecento	noh-veh-<u>chehn</u>-toh	900
Higher numbers		
mille	<u>meel</u>-leh	1,000
duemila	doo-eh-<u>mee</u>-lah	2,000
un milione	oon mee-lee-<u>oh</u>-neh	1,000,000
due milioni	doo-eh mee-lee-<u>oh</u>-nee	2,000,000
un miliardo	oon mee-lee-<u>ahr</u>-doh	1,000,000,000

Part II
Italian in Action

The 5th Wave   By Rich Tennant

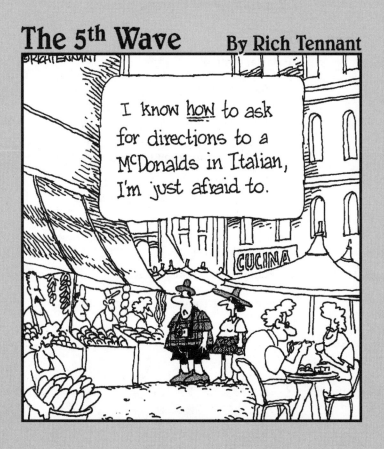

In this part . . .

These chapters help you delve into every-day activities:

- Find out what you need to know to be a good guest: how to introduce yourself and make small talk.

- Dig into the Italian food experience — dining out and going to the market.

- Shop till you drop.

- Explore cultural and recreational activities.

- Talk on the telephone for both business and pleasure.

- Function in an office setting.

So, choose your topic and put some Italian in action!

Chapter 3

Buongiorno! Meeting and Greeting

In This Chapter

▶ Saying hello and good-bye

▶ Responding to a greeting

▶ Asking whether someone speaks English

▶ Describing places and where you come from

▶ Interacting with friends

▶ Looking at the "to be" verbs: **essere** (*ehs*-seh-reh) and **stare** (*stah*-reh)

B*uongiorno!* (*boo-ohn-johr-noh*) (Hello!)

Have you ever counted the number of times you say hello in a single day? You probably say it more often than you realize. When you interact with people, you usually begin the connection with a greeting — and that greeting can have an impact on the first impression you give.

When you have contact with people from other countries or cultures, knowing how they say hello and good-bye is very useful. This chapter explains how to say those things, as well as how to supplement a greeting with some basic small talk.

Looking at Common Greetings and Good-byes

Italians like to have social contact and meet new people. Generally, they're easygoing and anything but stiff. At the same time, they tend to be very respectful and polite.

To give you a good start in greeting people in Italian, we want to familiarize you with the most common greetings and good-byes, followed by examples:

- ✔ **Ciao** *(chah-oh)* (Hello and good-bye: informal)

    Ciao Claudio! *(chah-oh klah-oo-dee-oh)* (Hello, Claudio!)

- ✔ **Salve** *(sahl-veh)* (Hello and good-bye: neutral)

    Salve ragazzi! *(sahl-veh rah-gaht-tsee)* (Hi, folks!)

    Salve is a relic from Latin. In Caesar's time, the Romans used it a lot.

- ✔ **Buongiorno** *(boo-ohn johr-noh)* (Good morning [Literally: Good day] formal)

    Buongiorno signora Bruni! *(boo-ohn johr-noh see-nyoh-rah broo-nee)* (Good morning, Mrs. Bruni!)

    Buongiorno is the most formal greeting. Whenever you're in doubt, use this word. **Buongiorno** also means "good-bye." You frequently hear it when you leave an Italian shop.

- ✔ **Buonasera** *(boo-oh-nah-seh-rah)* (Good afternoon; good evening: formal)

    Buonasera signor Rossi! *(boo-oh-nah-seh-rah see-nyohr rohs-see)* (Good afternoon, Mr. Rossi!)

    You use **buonasera** after 2 p.m. to say both hello and good-bye. Just mind the time of day!

- ✔ **Buonanotte** *(boo-oh-nah-noht-teh)* (Good-night)

    Buonanotte amici! *(boo-oh-nah-noht-teh ah-mee-chee)* (Good-night, friends!)

- ✔ **Buona giornata!** *(boo-oh-nah johr-nah-tah)* (Have a nice day!)

    You often use this phrase when you're leaving somebody or saying good-bye on the phone.

- ✔ **Buona serata!** *(boo-oh-nah seh-rah-tah)* (Have a nice evening!)

    Like **buona giornata,** you use **buona serata** when you're leaving someone or saying good-bye on the phone. The difference is that you use **buona serata,** according to Italian custom, after 2 p.m.

- ✔ **Addìo** *(ahd-dee-oh)* (Good-bye; Farewell)

    Addìo amore mio! *(ahd-dee-oh ah-moh-reh mee-oh)* (Farewell, my love!)

    Addìo is more literary; that is, you see it more frequently in writing. It is used less often in the spoken language.

- ✔ **Arrivederci** *(ahr-ree-veh-dehr-chee)* (Good-bye)

    Arrivederci signora Eva! *(ahr-ree-veh-dehr-chee see-nyoh-rah eh-vah)* (Good-bye, Mrs. Eva!)

Deciding whether to address someone formally or informally

An important feature of Italian culture is that there are two different ways of addressing people. Italian has both a formal and an informal form of address.

✔ You generally use the formal form of address — **lei** *(lay)* (you: formal singular) — with people you don't know: businesspeople, officials, and persons of higher rank, such as supervisors, teachers, professors, and so on. (The exceptions are with children or among young people; in those cases you use the informal.)

✔ When you get to know someone better, depending on your relationship, you may switch to the informal form of address — **tu** *(too)* (you, informal singular). You also use the informal with members of your family and, as already mentioned, with children. Young people speak informally among themselves, too.

Replying to a greeting

When you reply to a greeting in English, you often say "How are you?" as a way of saying "Hello" — you don't expect an answer. In Italian, however, this is not the case; you respond with an answer. Following are common ways to reply to particular greetings.

Formal greeting and reply

Greeting:	**Buongiorno signora, come sta?**
	boo-ohn-johr-noh see-nyoh-rah koh-meh stah
	Hello, ma'am, how are you?
Reply:	**Benissimo, grazie, e lei?**
	beh-nees-see-moh grah-tsee-eh eh lay
	Great, thank you, and you?

Informal greeting and reply

Greeting:	**Ciao, Roberto, come stai?**
	chah-oh roh-behr-toh koh-meh stah-ee
	Hi, Roberto, how are you?
Reply:	**Bene, grazie.**
	beh-neh grah-tsee-eh
	Fine, thanks.

Another typical, rather informal, greeting and reply

Greeting: **Come va?**
koh-me vah
How are things?

Reply: **Non c'è male.**
nohn cheh mah-leh
Not bad.

Using body language

Saying hello or good-bye is generally accompanied by some kind of physical contact, which differs from culture to culture. In Italy, people who are familiar with each other, such as family and friends, commonly hug and kiss. Hugging and kissing are more common between two women or between a man and a woman.

Italians kiss twice: once left, once right. Whether or not you follow this custom is up to you.

Another common physical greeting is the more formal handshake. You shake hands with people you meet for the first time and with those you don't know well.

Specifying your reuniting

Sometimes, you want to say more than just good-bye and specify your next meeting. The following expressions are common and also can be used as good-byes on their own:

- **A presto!** *(ah prehs-toh)* (See you soon!)

- **A dopo!** *(ah doh-poh)* (See you later!)

- **A domani!** *(ah doh-mah-nee)* (See you tomorrow!)

- **Ci vediamo!** *(chee veh dee-ah-moh)* (See you!)

    You can combine **Ci vediamo** with the other phrases. For example:

    - **Ci vediamo presto!** *(chee veh dee-ah-moh prehs-toh)* (See you soon!)

    - **Ci vediamo dopo!** *(chee veh dee-ah-moh doh-poh)* (See you later!)

    - **Ci vediamo domani!** *(chee veh dee-ah-moh doh-mah-nee)* (See you tomorrow!)

To these basic phrases, you can add whatever you want — a weekday, a time, or whatever — to state more precisely your next meeting. For example: **Ci vediamo lunedì alle cinque.** *(chee veh-dee-ah-moh loo-neh-dee ahl-leh cheen-koo-eh)* (See you on Monday at five p.m.)

Chapter 7 talks about times of day and days of the week.

Making Introductions

Every day you approach people you may or may not know. Introducing yourself or asking for a name often begins your contact with those people. In Italian, what you say and how you say it — which form of address you use, and whether you use first names or last names — depends on how well you know the person you're talking to.

You can find information about whether to use the formal or informal form of address earlier in this chapter, in the section "Looking at Common Greetings and Good-byes."

Whether to use first or last names is just as important a consideration. In a job situation, you usually use last names, whereas at private functions, people are more likely to tell you their first names. The fact that someone gives you his or her first name does not necessarily mean that you should use the informal **tu** *(too)* (you), however; using a person's first name with the formal form of address is quite common.

If you're unsure of how to address someone, pay attention to what your Italian acquaintance does and do the same.

Introducing yourself

We want to familiarize you with an important reflexive verb, **chiamarsi** *(kee-ah-mahr-see)* (to call oneself), which you use to introduce yourself and to ask others for their names. Here's how you conjugate this important verb:

Conjugation	Pronunciation
mi chiamo	mee kee-ah-moh
ti chiami	tee kee-ah-mee
si chiama	see kee-ah-mah

Conjugation	*Pronunciation*
ci chiamiamo	chee kee-ah-mee-<u>ah</u>-moh
vi chiamate	vee kee-ah-<u>mah</u>-teh
si chiamano	see kee-<u>ah</u>-mah-noh

So that you can get the ring of the verb **chiamarsi,** practice these easy examples:

- ✔ **Ciao, mi chiamo Eva.** (<u>chah</u>-oh mee kee-<u>ah</u>-moh eh-vah) (Hello, my name is Eva.)

- ✔ **E tu come ti chiami?** (eh too koh-meh tee kee-<u>ah</u>-mee) (And what's your name?)

- ✔ **Lei si chiama?** (lay see kee-<u>ah</u>-mah) (What's your name?)

    You use the same verb form with **lui** (loo-ee) (he) and **lei** (lay) (she) — for example, **lui si chiama** (<u>loo</u>-ee see kee-<u>ah</u>-mah) (his name is).

Incidentally, as in English, you can also introduce yourself simply by saying your name: **Sono Pietro** (<u>soh</u>-noh pee-<u>eh</u>-troh) (I'm Pietro).

Talkin' the Talk

The people in this dialogue are colleagues assigned to work on the same project. They introduce themselves to each other.

Mr. Messa:	**Carlo Messa, piacere!**
	<u>kahr</u>-loh <u>mehs</u>-sah pee-ah-<u>cheh</u>-reh
	Carlo Messa, nice to meet you!

Mr. Rossi:	**Piacere, Marco Rossi.**
	pee-ah-<u>cheh</u>-reh <u>mahr</u>-koh <u>rohs</u>-see
	Nice to meet you, Marco Rossi.

Ms. Pertini:	**Piacere, sono Paola Pertini.**
	pee-ah-<u>cheh</u>-reh <u>soh</u>-noh <u>pah</u>-oh-lah pehr-<u>tee</u>-nee
	Nice to meet you, I'm Paola Pertini.

Ms. Salvi:	**Lieta di conoscerla, Anna Salvi.**
	lee-<u>eh</u>-tah dee koh-<u>noh</u>-shehr-lah <u>ahn</u>-nah <u>sahl</u>-vee
	Pleased to meet you, Anna Salvi.

Mr. Melis:	**Mi chiamo Carlo Melis, piacere.**
	mee kee-ah-moh kahr-loh meh-lees
	My name is Carlo Melis, nice to meet you.
Mr. Foschi:	**Molto lieto, Silvio Foschi.**
	mohl-toh lee-eh-toh seel-vee-oh fohs-kee
	Very pleased to meet you, Silvio Foschi.

Children and young people forgo ceremony and introduce themselves more casually, though still politely — something like this:

Ciao! Sono Giulio.
chah-oh soh-noh joo-lee-oh
Hello! I'm Giulio.

E io sono Giulia, piacere.
eh ee-oh soh-noh joo-lee-ah pee-ah-cheh-reh
And I'm Giulia, nice to meet you.

The following example offers a very informal introduction, used only in a very casual situation, such as on the beach or at a disco:

Come ti chiami?
koh-meh tee-kee-ah-mee
What's your name?

Chiara. E tu?
kee-ah-rah eh too
Chiara, and yours?

Amedeo.
ah-meh-deh-oh
Amedeo.

Talkin' the Talk

 Mr. Versi enters a café, where the only free seats are at tables that are already occupied. He approaches a table with an open chair and asks permission to use it. Because he doesn't know the person he's speaking to, Mr. Versi speaks more formally than he would to a friend. Please note the abbreviation for "signor."

Sig. Versi:	**Posso?**
	pohs-soh
	May I?

Sig. Melis:	**Prego, si accomodi.**
	preh-goh see ahk-koh-moh-dee
	Please, have a seat!

Sig. Versi:	**Grazie mille.**
	grah-tsee-eh meel-leh
	Thanks a lot.

Sig. Versi:	**Permette? Versi.**
	pehr-meht-teh vehr-see
	Permit me to introduce myself. Versi.

Sig. Melis:	**Piacere, Melis.**
	pee-ah-cheh-reh meh-lees
	Nice to meet you, Melis.

Normally, the older person proposes making the switch to the informal form. The older generation tends to be more formal than youngsters and may not switch to the informal as quickly as younger people do. If you're uncertain, it's better to address people formally.

Often, young people start off using the informal form. Take your cue from the people speaking to you.

Talkin' the Talk

Now listen to two young people introducing each other in a less formal setting. One enters the café and comes up to a table occupied by one person.

Mario:	**È libero?**
	eh lee-beh-roh
	Is it free?

Patrizia:	**Sì.**
	see
	Yes.

Mario:	**Grazie. Ti disturbo?**
	grah-tsee-eh tee dees-toor-boh
	Thank you. Am I disturbing you?

Patrizia:	**No, per niente.**
	noh pehr nee-<u>ehn</u>-teh
	Not at all.

Mario:	**Mi chiamo Mario.**
	mee kee-<u>ah</u>-moh mah-<u>ree</u>-oh
	My name is Mario.

Patrizia:	**Ciao, io sono Patrizia.**
	chah-oh <u>ee</u>-oh <u>soh</u>-noh pah-<u>tree</u>-tsee-ah
	Hello, I'm Patrizia.

Mario:	**Aspetti qualcuno?**
	ahs-<u>peht</u>-tee koo-ahl-<u>koo</u>-noh
	Are you waiting for anybody?

Patrizia:	**Sì, due amici.**
	see <u>doo</u>-eh ah-<u>mee</u>-chee
	Yes, two friends.

Amici *(ah-<u>mee</u>-chee)* (friends) is a plural term that you use to refer to more than one friend. Use **amici** to talk about any group that includes at least one male. If the group is composed of only female friends, you say **amiche** *(ah-<u>mee</u>-keh)* (female friends).

Introducing other people

Sometimes you not only have to introduce yourself, but also introduce someone to your friends or to other people.

The following vocabulary may be helpful in making introductions. With it, you can indicate the relationship between you and the person you're introducing:

- ✔ **mio fratello** *(<u>mee</u>-oh frah-<u>tehl</u>-loh)* (my brother)
- ✔ **mia sorella** *(<u>mee</u>-ah soh-<u>rehl</u>-lah)* (my sister)
- ✔ **mia figlia** *(<u>mee</u>-ah <u>fee</u>-lyah)* (my daughter)
- ✔ **mio figlio** *(<u>mee</u>-oh <u>fee</u>-lyoh)* (my son)
- ✔ **mio marito** *(<u>mee</u>-oh mah-<u>ree</u>-toh)* (my husband)

- **mia moglie** (*mee-ah moh-lyee-eh*) (my wife)
- **il mio amico** (*eel mee-oh ah-mee-koh*) (my friend [m])
- **la mia amica** (*lah mee-ah ah-mee-kah*) (my friend [f])
- **il mio collega** (*eel mee-oh kohl-leh-gah*) (my colleague [m])
- **la mia collega** (*lah mee-ah kohl-leh-gah*) (my colleague [f])

You're probably wondering why **la mia amica** has the article *la* and **mia sorella** has none. The reason is that the possessives usually are preceded by an article except when they refer to family members in the singular.

To make life easier we give you here the conjugation of the verb **presentare** (*preh-zehn-tah-reh*) (to present). The pronoun you insert in front of the verb is dependant on the number and relationship of the person to whom you're making the introduction: **ti** (*tee*) (to you: informal singular), **le** (*leh*) (to you: formal singular), **vi** (*vee*) (to you: (informal and formal plural).

Conjugation	*Pronunciation*
io presento	ee-oh preh-zehn-toh
tu presenti	too preh-zehn-tee
lui/lei presenta	loo-ee/lay preh-zehn-tah
noi presentiamo	noh-ee preh-zehn-tee-ah-moh
voi presentate	voh-ee preh-zehn-tah-teh
loro presentano	loh-roh preh-zehn-tah-noh

Talkin' the Talk

The following dialogue, which represents a formal occasion, contains some typical expressions used during introductions. Here, Mrs. Ponti introduces a new colleague. Please note the abbreviation for signora.

Sig.ra Ponti: **Buonasera signora Bruni . . . Signora Bruni, le presento il signor Rossi.**
boo-oh-nah-seh-rah see-nyoh-rah broo-nee see-nyoh-rah broo-nee leh preh-zehn-toh eel see-nyohr rohs-see
Good afternoon, Mr Bruni . . . Mr. Bruni, I'd like to introduce you to Mr. Rossi.

Sig.ra Bruni: **Lieta di conoscerla.**
lee-eh-tah dee koh-noh-shehr-lah
Pleased to meet you.

Sig.ra Rossi: **Il piacere è tutto mio!**
eel pee-ah-cheh-reh eh toot-toh mee-oh
The pleasure is all mine!

Talkin' the Talk

 Of course, friends can be informal with one another, as the next conversation shows. Here Teresa bumps into her old friend Carla. Both are married now and introduce their husbands.

Carla: **Ciao, Teresa, come stai?**
chah-oh teh-reh-zah koh-meh stah-ee
Hello, Teresa. How are you?

Teresa: **Bene, grazie.Carla, ti presento mio marito Franco.**
beh-neh grah-tsee eh kahr-lah tee preh-zehn-toh mee-oh mah-ree-toh frahn-koh
Good, thank you. Carla, I'd like to introduce you to my husband, Franco.

Carla: **Ciao Franco.**
chah-oh frahn-koh
Hello, Franco.

Franco: **Piacere.**
pee-ah-cheh-reh
Nice to meet you.

Carla: **Teresa, questo è Roberto.**
teh-reh-zah koo-ehs-toh eh roh-behr-toh
Teresa, this is Roberto.

Roberto: **Piacere.**
pee-ah-cheh-reh
Nice to meet you.

Words to Know

conoscere	koh-<u>noh</u>-sheh-reh	to meet
marito [m]	mah-<u>ree</u>-toh	husband
moglie [f]	<u>moh</u>-lyee-eh	wife
piacere	pee-ah-<u>cheh</u>-reh	nice to meet you

Getting Acquainted

Introducing yourself is the first step in getting to know someone. If you get a good feeling about the person and want to speak more, a conversation usually follows the introduction. This section tells you about the different topics you might talk about to get to know each other.

Finding out whether someone speaks English

When you meet someone from another country, your first question is probably "Do you speak English?" The English language is used all over the world, so your chances are good that he or she will say yes. But what if the person speaks Italian and not English? In that case, you have an opportunity to try out your newly acquired smattering of Italian.

CULTURAL WISDOM

Two names for married women?

When Italian women marry, they have two names. We're talking about two different names, not a hyphenated name. For example, if Maria Bianchi *(mah-<u>ree</u>-ah bee-<u>ahn</u>-kee)* marries Paolo Verdi *(pah-<u>oh</u>-loh <u>vehr</u>-dee),* she may be called signora Bianchi *(see-<u>nyoh</u>-rah bee-<u>ahn</u>-kee)* or signora Verdi *(see-<u>nyoh</u>-rah vehr-dee)* — usually depending on the occasion. If she works outside the home, her colleagues will probably call her by her maiden name. But in non-work-related situations and with her husband or her children (who take their father's last name), she very likely will be called signora Verdi.

When in Naples . . .

Throughout Italy, in all buses and taxis you usually find the same sign: **Non parlate al conducente!** *(nohn pahr-lah-teh ahl kohn-doo-chehn-teh)* (Don't speak to the driver!). In Naples, however, you find **Non rispondete al conducente!** *(nohn rees-pohn-deh-teh ahl kohn-doo-chehn-teh)* (Don't answer the driver!). Can you guess why?

Neapolitans are famous for talking a lot and with enthusiasm, and for using the sort of language you won't find in this book.

To ask whether someone speaks English, you need to be familiar with the verb **parlare** *(pahr-lah-reh)* (to speak; to talk). This regular verb is from the group that ends in **-are** *(ah-reh)*. Its root is **parl-** *(pahrl)*. (Head to Chapter 2 for an explanation of regular and irregular verbs.) Following are examples of how to use **parlare**:

- ✔ **Parlo molto e volentieri!** *(pahr-loh mohl-toh eh voh-lehn-tee-eh-ree)* (I talk a lot and with enthusiasm!)

- ✔ **Parli con me?** *(pahr-lee kohn meh)* (Are you speaking to me?)

- ✔ **Parla italiano?** *(pahr-lah ee-tah-lee-ah-noh)* (Do you speak Italian?)

- ✔ **Parli inglese?** *(pahr-lee een-gleh-zeh)* (Do you speak English?)

- ✔ **Oggi parliamo di musica americana.** *(ohj-jee pahr-lee-ah-moh dee moo-zee-kah ah-meh-ree-kah-nah)* (Today we talk about American music.)

- ✔ **Parlano sempre di viaggi!** *(pahr-lah-noh sehm-preh dee vee-ahj-jee)* (They always talk about trips!)

Italians have a nice saying: **Parla come mangi!** *(pahr-lah koh-meh mahn-jee)* (Speak the way you eat!) You may want to say this to someone who speaks in a very sophisticated fashion with a touch of arrogance. This phrase reminds people to speak normally — just the way they eat.

Talkin' the Talk

Ilaria and Carmen have recently gotten to know each other. Because Carmen is not Italian, although she lives in Italy, Ilaria is curious to know how many languages she speaks.

Ilaria:	**Quante lingue parli?**
	koo-ahn-teh leen-goo-eh pahr-lee
	How many languages do you speak?

Carmen:	**Tre: italiano, spagnolo e tedesco.**
	treh ee-tah-lee-ah-noh spah-nyoh-loh eh
	teh-dehs-koh
	Three: Italian, Spanish, and German.

Ilaria:	**E qual' è la tua lingua madre?**
	eh koo-ah-leh eh lah too-ah leen-goo-ah mah-dreh
	And which is your mother tongue?

Carmen:	**Lo spagnolo.**
	loh spah-nyoh-loh
	Spanish.

Ilaria:	**Tua madre è spagnola?**
	too-ah mah-dreh eh spah-nyoh-lah
	Is your mother Spanish?

Carmen:	**Sì. E mio padre è austriaco.**
	see eh mee-oh pah-dreh eh ah-oos-tree-ah-koh
	Yes, and my father is Austrian.

Talking about where you come from

You know how interesting meeting people from other countries and nationalities can be. Sometimes hearing of new places makes you curious about what may be different there. But to find out something, you have to ask a questions. Two common questions, phrased here in the formal, are useful to remember:

- **Da dove viene?** *(dah doh-veh vee-eh-neh)* (Where do you come from?)
- **Di dov'è?** *(dee doh-veh-eh)* (Where are you from?)

The answers are, respectively:

- **Vengo da . . .** *(vehn-goh dah)* (I come from . . .)
- **Sono di . . .** *(soh-noh dee)* (I'm from . . .)

Now you can play with these phrases. You can insert the names of continents, countries, cities, or places.

Talkin' the Talk

Il signor Belli is sitting in his favorite café in Milan drinking his coffee and notices somebody at the next table who is examining a city plan. Il signor Belli is a curious person:

Sig. Belli: **Non è di qui, vero?**
nohn eh dee koo-ee veh-roh
You're not from here, are you?

Sig. Verdi: **No, sono di Perugia.**
noh soh-noh dee peh-roo-jee-ah
No, I'm from Perugia.

Sig. Belli: **Una bella città!**
oo-nah behl-lah cheet-tah
A beautiful town!

Sig. Verdi: **Sì, è piccola ma molto bella.**
see eh peek-koh-lah mah mohl-toh behl-lah
Yes, it is small but very beautiful.

Sig. Belli: **È antica?**
eh ahn-tee-kah
Is it old?

Sig. Verdi: **Sì, medievale.**
see meh-dee-eh-vah-leh
Yes, medieval.

Sig. Belli: **È tranquilla?**
eh trahn-koo-eel-lah
Is it quiet?

Sig. Verdi: **Sì, forse troppo.**
see fohr-seh trohp-poh
Yes, perhaps too much.

If you want to talk about nationalities, however, things change a bit. As you say in English, "Are you American?" or "I'm Canadian," you say the same in Italian:

✔ **È americano?** *(eh ah-meh-ree-kah-noh)* (Are you American?)

✔ **No, sono canadese.** *(noh soh-noh kah-nah-deh-zeh)* (No, I'm Canadian.)

After you know the basics for such a situation, you're ready to chitchat.

Talkin' the Talk

Il signor Bennati, meets a Canadian, Mr. Walsh. Because they are strangers, their exchange is in the formal form.

Sig. Bennati: **Di dov'è?**
                dee doh-veh
                Where are you from?

Mr Walsh: **Sono canadese.**
                soh-noh kah-nah-deh-zeh
                I'm Canadian.

Sig. Bennati: **Di dove esattamente?**
                dee doh-veh eh-zaht-tah-mehn-teh
                From where, exactly?

Mr Walsh: **Di Montreal. Lei è italiana?**
                dee mohn-treh-ahl lay eh ee-tah-lee-ah-nah
                From Montreal. Are you Italian?

Sig. Bennati: **Sì, di Firenze.**
                see dee fee-rehn-tseh
                Yes, from Florence.

In English, you must put the pronoun in front of the verb. You may have noticed that this is not the case in Italian. Because the verb form is different for each pronoun, you can easily leave out the pronoun — you understand who is meant from the verb ending and from the context. You use the pronoun only when the subject isn't clear enough or when you want to emphasize a fact — for example, **Loro sono americani, ma io sono italiano** *(loh-roh soh-noh ah-meh-ree-kah-nee mah ee-yoh soh-noh ee-tahl-yah-noh)* (They are Americans, but I am Italian).

Use adjectives ending in *-o* (singular) and *-i* (plural) to refer to males and adjectives ending in *-a* (singular) and *-e* (plural) to refer to females. Adjectives that end in *-e* in the singular refer to both males and females and end in the plural with *-i.*

Some adjectives indicating nationality end with *-e:* This form is both feminine and masculine. Table 3-1 gives some examples.

Table 3-1	Genderless Nationalities and Countries	
Nationality/ Country	**Pronunciation**	**Translation**
canadese Canada	kah-nah-<u>deh</u>-zeh <u>kah</u>-nah-dah	Canadian Canada
cinese Cina	chee-<u>neh</u>-zeh <u>chee</u>-nah	Chinese China
francese Francia	frahn-<u>cheh</u>-zeh <u>frahn</u>-chah	French France
giapponese Giappone	jahp-poh-<u>neh</u>-zeh jahp-<u>poh</u>-neh	Japanese Japan
inglese Inghilterra	een-<u>gleh</u>-zeh een-geel-<u>tehr</u>-rah	English England
irlandese Irlanda	eer-lahn-<u>deh</u>-zeh eer-<u>lahn</u>-dah	Irish Ireland
portoghese Portogallo	pohr-toh-<u>geh</u>-zeh pohr-toh-<u>gahl</u>-loh	Portuguese Portugal
svedese Svezia	sveh-<u>deh</u>-zeh <u>sveh</u>-tsee-ah	Swedish Sweden

In other cases, nationalities have a feminine, masculine, plural feminine, and plural masculine form as Table 3-2 shows.

Table 3-2	Gender-Specific Nationalities and Countries	
Nationality/ Country	**Pronunciation**	**Translation**
americana/o/e/i America	ah-meh-ree-<u>kah</u>-nah/noh/neh/nee ah-<u>meh</u>-ree-kah	American America
brasiliana/o/e/i Brasile	brah-see-lee-<u>ah</u>-nah/noh/neh/nee brah-<u>see</u>-leh	Brazilian Brazil
italiana/o/e/i Italia	ee-tah-lee-<u>ah</u>-nah/noh/neh/nee ee-<u>tah</u>-lee-ah	Italian Italy
marocchina/o/e/i Marocco	mah-rohk-<u>kee</u>-nah/noh/neh/nee mah-<u>rohk</u>-koh	Moroccan Morocco
russa/o/e/i Russia	<u>roos</u>-sah/soh/seh/see <u>roos</u>-see-ah	Russian Russia

(continued)

Table 3-2 (continued)

Nationality/ Country	Pronunciation	Translation
spagnola/o/e/i Spagna	spah-<u>nyoh</u>-lah/loh/leh/lee <u>spah</u>-nyah	Spanish Spain
svizzera/o/e/i Svizzera	<u>sveet</u>-tseh-rah/roh/reh/ree <u>sveet</u>-tseh-rah	Swiss Switzerland
tedesca/o/e/i Germania	teh-<u>dehs</u>-kah/koh/keh/kee jehr-<u>mah</u>-nee-ah	German Germany

Instead of saying **sono americano** (<u>soh</u>-noh ah-meh-ree-<u>kah</u>-noh) (I'm American), you can also say **vengo dall'America** (vehn-goh dahl-lah-<u>meh</u>-ree-kah) (I'm from America). The same is true for all countries.

Following we show you the conjugation of the verb **venire** (veh-<u>nee</u>-reh) (to come), which is helpful to know when you want to tell people where you come from or ask other people where their home is. The right verb/preposition combination in this case is **venire da** (veh-<u>nee</u>-reh dah) (to come from), as in: **Vengo dalla Francia** (<u>vehn</u>-goh <u>dahl</u>-lah <u>frahn</u>-chah) (I come from France).

Conjugation	Pronunciation
io vengo	<u>ee</u>-oh <u>vehn</u>-goh
tu vieni	too vee-<u>eh</u>-nee
lui/lei viene	<u>loo</u>-ee/lay vee-<u>eh</u>-neh
noi veniamo	<u>noh</u>-ee veh-nee-<u>ah</u>-moh
voi venite	<u>voh</u>-ee veh-<u>nee</u>-teh
loro vengono	<u>loh</u>-roh <u>vehn</u>-goh-noh

The following examples give you more practice with this construction.

- **Veniamo dall'Italia.** (veh-nee-<u>ah</u>-moh dahl-lee-<u>tah</u>-lee-ah) (We come from Italy.)

- **Viene dalla Francia.** (vee-<u>eh</u>-neh <u>dahl</u>-lah <u>frahn</u>-chah) (He/she comes from France.)

- **Vengono dalla Spagna.** (<u>vehn</u>-goh-noh <u>dahl</u>-lah <u>spah</u>-nyah) (They come from Spain.)

- **Venite dalla Russia.** (veh-<u>nee</u>-teh <u>dahl</u>-lah <u>roos</u>-see-ah) (You [plural] come from Russia.)

- **Vieni dalla Svizzera.** (vee-<u>eh</u>-nee <u>dahl</u>-lah <u>sveet</u>-tseh-tah) (You come from Switzerland.)

- ✔ **Vengo dal Giappone.** (*vehn-goh dahl jahp-poh-neh*) (I come from Japan.)

- ✔ **Veniamo dal Canada.** (*veh-nee-ah-moh dahl kah-nah-dah*) (We come from Canada.)

- ✔ **Veniamo dagli U. S. A.** (*veh-nee-ah-moh dah-lyee oo-ehs-ah*) (We come from the U. S. A.)

You may have noticed that some countries are feminine (those with a final **-a**), and others are male (those with the endings **-e, -a,** and **-o**). Canada is an exception; it is masculine but ends in **-a.** And the U.S. uses a plural article because there are many states.

The following are some other frequently used, informal questions that you might ask to initiate a conversation:

- ✔ **Sei di qui?** (*say dee koo-ee*) (Are you from here?)

- ✔ **Dove vivi?** (*doh-veh vee-vee*) (Where do you live?)

- ✔ **Dove sei nato?** (*doh-veh say nah-toh*) (Where were you born?)

If you travel to Italy and make new friends, you'll probably be asked these informal questions:

- ✔ **Ti piace l'Italia?** (*tee pee-ah-cheh lee-tah-lee-ah*) (Do you like Italy?)

- ✔ **Sei qui per la prima volta?** (*say koo-ee pehr lah pree-mah vohl-tah*) (Is this your first time here?)

- ✔ **Sei qui in vacanza?** (*say koo-ee een vah-kahn-tsah*) (Are you on vacation?)

- ✔ **Quanto rimani?** (*koo-ahn-toh ree-mah-nee*) (How long are you staying?)

- ✔ **Ti stai divertendo?** (*tee stah-ee dee-vehr-tehn-doh*) (Are you enjoying it?)

Talkin' the Talk

In the following dialogue, you can catch some typical expressions for describing a city.

Tokiko: **Ti piace Venezia?**
tee pee-ah-cheh veh-neh-tsee-ah
Do you like Venice?

Dolores: **Sì, è molto romantica.**
see eh mohl-toh roh-mahn-tee-kah
Yes, it's very romantic.

Tokiko:	**È bellissima!** *eh behl-lees-see-mah* It's very beautiful!
Dolores:	**Com'è Tokio?** *kohm-eh toh-kee-oh* What's Tokyo like?
Tokiko:	**È grandissima, moderna.** *eh grahn-dees-see-mah moh-dehr-nah* It's huge, modern.
Dolores:	**Ma è molto bella, no?** *mah eh mohl-toh behl-lah noh* But it's very beautiful, isn't it?
Tokiko:	**Sì, e molto cara.** *see eh mohl-toh kah-rah* Yes, and very expensive.
Dolores:	**Cara e affollata?** *kah-rah eh ahf-fohl-lah-tah* Expensive and crowded?
Tokiko:	**Sì, come Venezia!** *see koh-meh veh-neh-tsee-ah* Yes, like Venice!

Being you, being there: Using the verbs "essere" and "stare" to describe things

Essere (*eh-sseh-reh*) (to be) is the most important verb in the Italian language. You use this verb the most frequently and it is definitely a necessary verb in meeting, greeting, and talking with people. Following is **essere** conjugated.

Conjugation	*Pronunciation*
io sono	*ee-oh soh-noh*
tu sei	*too say*
lui/lei è	*loo-ee/lay eh*
noi siamo	*noh-ee see-ah-moh*
voi siete	*voh-ee see-eh-teh*
loro sono	*loh-roh soh-noh*

Besides the verb **essere** *(ehs-seh-reh)* (to be), another verb also means roughly "to be": **stare** *(stah-reh)* (to be there; to stay). **Stare** indicates the current state of affairs rather than an unchanging condition. For example, if you say, **"Oggi sto a casa"** *(ohj-jee stoh ah kah-sah)* (Today I stay home), it means that you probably won't go out, whereas saying **"Oggi sono a casa"** *(ohj-jee soh-noh ah kah-sah)* (Today I'm at home) just indicates that you're in your house. **Stare** is also used to express the way you feel: **Stai bene?** *(stah-ee beh-neh)* means "Are you okay?" and **Maria sta male** *(mah-ree-ah stah mah-leh)* means "Maria doesn't feel well."

The following examples show how to use the verb **stare:**

- **Sei americana?** *(say ah-meh-ree-kah-nah)* (Are you American?)

  No, sono australiana. *(noh soh-noh ah-oo-strah-lee-ah-nah)* (No, I'm Australian.)

- **Com'è Paola?** *(koh-meh pah-oh-lah)* (How is Paola?)

  È un po' arrogante. *(eh oon poh ahr-roh-gahn-teh)* (She's a little bit arrogant.)

- **Siete qui in vacanza?** *(see-eh-teh koo-ee een vah-kahn-tsah)* (Are you here on vacation?)

  No, siamo qui per studiare l'italiano. *(noh see-ah-moh koo-ee pehr stoo-dee-ah-reh lee-tah-lee-ah-noh)* (No, we're here to study Italian.)

- **Dove sono Elena e Sara?** *(doh-veh soh-noh eh-leh-nah eh sah-rah)* (Where are Elena and Sara?)

  Sono in biblioteca. *(soh-noh een bee-blee-oh-teh-kah)* (They are in the library.)

Here's how you conjugate the verb **stare:**

Conjugation	Pronunciation
io sto	ee-oh stoh
tu stai	too stah-ee
lui/lei sta	loo-ee/lay stah
noi stiamo	noh-ee stee-ah-moh
voi state	voh-ee stah-teh
loro stanno	loh-roh stahn-noh

The following examples show you how to use the verb **stare:**

- **In che albergo stai?** *(een keh ahl-behr-goh stah-ee)* (What hotel are you in?)

- **Sto al Miramare.** *(stoh ahl mee-rah-mah-reh)* (I'm in the Miramare.)

✔ **State un po' con me?** (*stah-teh oon poh kohn meh*) (Will you stay with me for a while?)

    Perché, non stai bene? (*pehr-keh nohn stah-ee beh-neh*) (Why, don't you feel good?)

✔ **Oggi stiamo a casa!** (*ohj-jee stee-ah-moh ah kah-sah*) (Let's stay home today!)

    Come mai? (*koh-meh mah-ee*) (How come?)

✔ **Daniela sta a dieta!** (*dah-nee-eh-leh stah ah dee-eh-tah*) (Daniela is on a diet!)

    Stanno tutti a dieta! (*stahn-noh toot-tee ah dee-eh-tah*) (They are all on a diet!)

Extending and responding to invitations

Italians are very hospitable. It's not unusual to be invited for a meal in an Italian home, especially if you're traveling in Italy. You may also be asked to join an Italian friend for a meal in a restaurant.

When you want to invite someone to dinner, you can use the following phrases:

✔ **Andiamo a cena insieme?** (*ahn-dee-ah-moh ah cheh-nah een-see-eh-meh*) (Should we have dinner together?)

✔ **Vieni a cena da noi/me?** (*vee-eh-nee ah cheh-nah dah noh-ee meh*) (Are you coming to dinner with us/me?)

✔ **Posso invitarti stasera?** (*pohs-soh een-vee-tahr-tee stah-seh-rah*) (Can I invite you for this evening?)

To accept an invitation, you can use the following expressions:

✔ **Volentieri, grazie!** (*voh-lehn-tee-eh-ree grah-tsee-eh*) (I'd like to, thank you!)

✔ **Con piacere, grazie!** (*kohn pee-ah-cheh-reh grah-tsee-eh*) (With pleasure, thank you!)

Of course, you can't accept every invitation you receive. Following are expressions you can use to decline an invitation:

✔ **Mi dispiace ma non posso.** (*mee dees-pee-ah-cheh mah nohn pohs-soh*) (I'm sorry, but I can't.)

✔ **Magari un'altra volta, grazie.** (*mah-gah-ree oon-ahl-trah vohl-tah grah-tsee-eh*) (Perhaps another time, thank you.)

✔ **Sono occupata stasera, mi dispiace.** *(soh-noh ohk-koo-pah-tah stah-seh-rah mee dees-pee-ah-cheh)* (I'm busy tonight, I'm sorry.)

✔ **Mi dispiace, ho già un altro impegno.** *(mee dees-pee-ah-cheh oh jah oon ahl-troh eem-peh-nyoh)* (I'm sorry, but I'm already engaged.)

Talkin' the Talk

Francesca talks to Giovanni to get the particulars for their date that evening.

Francesca: **A che ora ci vediamo?**
ah keh oh-rah chee veh-dee-ah-moh
At what time are we going to meet?

Giovanni: **Alle nove.**
ahl-leh noh-veh
At nine o' clock.

Francesca: **Dove ci vediamo?**
doh-veh chee veh-dee-ah-moh
Where are we going to meet?

Giovanni: **Al bar Centrale.**
ahl bahr chehn-trah-leh
In the café "Centrale."

Francesca: **Dove vogliamo andare?**
doh-veh voh-lyah-moh ahn-dah-reh
Where are we going?

Giovanni: **Al cinema!**
ahl chee-neh-mah
To the movies!

CULTURAL WISDOM

Bearing gifts

In Italy, it's very common to bring **il dolce** *(eel dohl-cheh)* (sweets) as a small gift when you're invited for dinner. This sweet can be **una torta** *(oo-nah tohr-tah)* (a cake), **gelato** *(jeh-lah-toh)* (ice cream), or something from **una pasticceria** *(oo-nah pahs-teech-cheh-ree-ah)* (a bakery). Equally welcome are **fiori** *(fee-oh-ree)* (flowers) or **una bottiglia di vino** *(oo-nah both-tee-lyah dee vee-noh)* (a bottle of wine). Other gifts are welcome, too — especially among youngsters.

Words to Know

andare	ahn-dah-reh	to go
mi scusi	mee skoo-zee	excuse me
numero [m]	noo-meh-roh	number
ora [f]	oh-rah	hour
ciao	chah-oh	hello
arrivederci	ahr-ree-veh-dehr-chee	good-bye
grazie	grah-tsee-eh	thank you

Fun & Games

A chance meeting leads to a quick introduction in this short dialogue. Fill in the blanks in the Italian, using the phrases below.

le presento, il piacere, e lei, come sta, conoscerla

Gayle: **Buonasera, signora Frederick. _____?**
Good afternoon, Ms. Frederick. How are you?

Ms. Frederick: **Benissimo, grazie, _____?**
Very well, thank you, and you?

Gayle: **Bene, grazie. _____ mio amico, George.**
Fine, thanks. I'd like to introduce my friend, George.

George: **Lieta di _____, signora.**
Pleased to meet you, ma'am.

Ms. Frederick: **_____ è mio.**
The pleasure is mine.

Answers: come sta, e lei, le presento, conoscerla, il piacere

Chapter 4

Getting to Know You: Making Small Talk

* *

In This Chapter

▶ Asking simple questions

▶ Making small talk with strangers

▶ Talking about yourself and your family

▶ Discussing the weather, temperature, and seasons

* *

*E*veryone engages in small talk. It's a starting point for getting to know someone, having a short chat with your neighbor, or beginning a conversation with the person next to you in an airplane. Sometimes casual chit-chat leads to interesting topics. Even if you have only a few minutes and you know you won't see the other person again, there's still something special about small talk.

Small talk is probably most useful when you're in the company of strangers. Not only can you find out about another person, but you may learn something about a different culture, too. After all, international understanding doesn't take place only through political treaties, but also through private exchanges.

In this chapter, we present phrases that you can use to make small talk in Italian.

Italians *like* small talk. They're always open to new ideas and people. In Italy, it's not unusual for strangers to meet and talk on the street. Italians always seem to have time to talk and to listen.

Asking Simple Questions

You usually ask a question to start a conversation. Of course, you don't necessarily have to ask the well-known: "Nice weather today, isn't it?" You have lots of other possibilities for framing a question. A few simple key words for asking questions are:

- **Chi?** *(kee)* (Who?)

- **Che?** *(keh)* (What?)

- **Che cosa?** *(keh koh-zah)* (What?) (This is the preferred use.)

- **Dove?** *(doh-veh)* (Where?)

- **Quando?** *(koo-ahn-doh)* (When?)

- **Perché?** *(pehr-keh)* (Why?)

- **Come?** *(koh-meh)* (How?)

- **Quanto?** *(koo-ahn-toh)* (How much?)

- **Quale?** *(koo-ah-leh)* (Which?)

To be sure, these single words won't help you that much in starting a conversation. You may want to have the following practical examples up your sleeve when a chance for small talk arises:

- **Chi è?** *(kee eh)* (Who's that?)

- **Scusi, che ore sono?** *(skoo-zee kee oh-reh soh-noh)* (Excuse me, what time is it?)

- **Che cosa ha detto?** *(keh koh-zah ah deht-toh)* (What did you say?) (formal)

- **Dov'è la stazione?** *(doh-veh lah sta-tsee-oh-neh)* (Where is the station?)

- **Quando parte l'aereo?** *(koo-ahn-doh pahr-teh lah-eh-reh-oh)* (When is the plane leaving?)

- **Perché va a Milano?** *(pehr-keh vah ah mee-lah-noh)* (Why are you going to Milan?)

- **Com'è il tempo?** *(kohm-eh eel tehm-poh)* (How is the weather?)

- **Quanto dura il volo?** *(koo-ahn-toh doo-rah eel voh-loh)* (How long is the flight?)

- **Qual è l'autobus per il centro?** *(koo-ahl-eh lah-oo-toh-boos pehr eel chehn-troh)* (Which is the bus to downtown?)

Here's a tiny, but practical, grammar hint. You know that little things in life can change the world. Although not as dramatic, a tiny little accent can change the meaning of a word. You may have already noticed the word **è** *(eh)* (he/she/it is) and its accent. This accent distinguishes this word from another little word, **e** *(eh)* (and), which looks the same but has another meaning. Needless to say, both of these words are used very frequently.

è *(eh)* = he/she/it is

e *(eh)* = and

You may wonder how Italians make out the difference between the two sounds. Quite easily! You can see the accent in written communication and when speaking, the difference lies first in hearing the pronunciation — the *è* is slightly more open, as in *hell* — whereas the *e* sounds more like the *e* in *gourmet.* And second, when speaking, you don't need to differentiate between the two words because the context tells you which is which.

Begging Your Pardon?

When you're getting familiar with a new language, you don't always understand everything said to you, and you often find yourself asking to have things repeated. For those instances, the following three sentences are very helpful:

- ✔ **Non ho capito.** *(nohn oh kah-pee-toh)* (I didn't understand.)
- ✔ **Mi dispiace.** *(mee dees-pee-ah-cheh)* (I'm sorry.)
- ✔ **Come scusa?** (informal) *(koh-meh skoo-zah)* or **Come scusi?** (formal) *(koh-meh skoo-zee)* (Pardon?)

If you want to be very polite, you can combine these three expressions: **Scusi! Mi dispiace, non ho capito.** *(skoo-zee mee dees-pee-ah-cheh nohn oh kah-pee-toh)* (Excuse me! I'm sorry, I didn't understand).

Incidentally, **scusa** *(skoo-zah)* and **scusi** *(skoo-zee)* also mean "excuse me" and you use them when you need to beg pardon — for example, when you bump into someone.

Talkin' the Talk

 On Flight Number 223, from Palermo to Milan, Mr. Brancato wants to take his seat, but he has to pass a woman who has the seat beside his. In this dialogue, they speak formally.

Sig. Brancato:	**Permesso?** *pehr-mehs-soh* May I?
Ms. Roe:	**Prego.** *preh-goh* Please.
Sig. Brancato:	**Grazie. Aldo Brancato.** *grah-stee-eh ahl-doh brahn-kah-toh* Thank you. Aldo Brancato.

Ms. Roe:	**Piacere, Kathy Roe . . . Bel decollo!**
	pee-ah-<u>cheh</u>-reh Kathy Roe behl deh-<u>kohl</u>-loh
	Pleasure. Kathy Roe . . . Nice takeoff!
Sig. Brancato:	**Meno male!**
	<u>meh</u>-noh <u>mah</u>-leh
	Thank goodness!
Ms. Roe:	**È il suo primo volo?**
	eh eel <u>soo</u>-oh <u>pree</u>-moh <u>voh</u>-loh
	Is this your first flight?
Sig. Brancato:	**No, ma ho sempre paura.**
	noh mah oh <u>sehm</u>-preh pah-<u>oo</u>-rah
	No, but I'm always scared.
Ms. Roe:	**La capisco perfettamente.**
	lah kah-<u>pees</u>-koh
	I understand you perfectly.

The next dialogue provides you with some vocabulary that you can use when talking about your family.

Talkin' the Talk

 Mr. Brancato and Ms. Roe continue with their small talk on the plane:

Sig. Brancato:	**Ha un accento particolare.**
	ah oon ahch-<u>chehn</u>-toh pahr-tee-koh-<u>lah</u>-reh
	You have a distinctive accent.
Ms. Roe:	**Sono canadese, di Winnipeg.**
	<u>soh</u>-noh kah-nah-<u>deh</u>-zeh dee winnipeg
	I'm Canadian, from Winnipeg.
Sig. Brancato:	**Viene spesso in Italia?**
	vee-<u>eh</u>-neh <u>spehs</u>-soh een ee-<u>tah</u>-lee-ah
	Do you come often to Italy?
Ms. Roe:	**Sì, mia sorella vive a Milano.**
	see <u>mee</u>-ah soh-<u>rehl</u>-lah <u>vee</u>-veh ah mee-<u>lah</u>-noh
	Yes, my sister lives in Milan.
Sig. Brancato:	**Vacanze in famiglia!**
	vah-<u>kahn</u>-tseh een fah-<u>mee</u>-lyee-ah
	A vacation with your family!

Ms. Roe:	**Sì, e lei, di dov'è?** *see eh lay dee doh-<u>veh</u>* And where are you from?
Sig. Brancato:	**Sono di Palermo, ma vivo a Milano.** *<u>soh</u>-noh dee pah-<u>lehr</u>-moh mah <u>vee</u>-voh ah* *mee-<u>lah</u>-noh* I come from Palermo but I live in Milan.
Ms. Roe:	**E la sua famiglia?** *eh lah <u>soo</u>-ah fah-<u>mee</u>-lyee-ah* And your family?
Sig. Brancato:	**I miei genitori sono a Palermo.** *ee mee-<u>ay</u> jeh-nee-<u>toh</u>-ree <u>soh</u>-noh ah* *pah-<u>lehr</u>-moh* My parents are in Palermo.
Ms. Roe:	**Ha sorelle o fratelli?** *ah soh-<u>rehl</u>-leh oh frah-<u>tehl</u>-lee* Do you have sisters or brothers?
Sig. Brancato:	**Una sorella che vive a Roma.** *<u>oo</u>-nah soh-<u>rehl</u>-lah keh <u>vee</u>-veh ah <u>roh</u>-mah* One sister, who lives in Rome.

CULTURAL WISDOM

Many people from the south of Italy actually live in the north because the north offers more job opportunities: Most of the industry in Italy is situated in the north.

Words to Know

vivere	<u>vee</u>-veh-reh	to live
il volo [m]	eel <u>voh</u>-loh	flight
capire	kah-<u>pee</u>-reh	to understand
dove	<u>doh</u>-veh	where
spesso	<u>spehs</u>-soh	often

Talking about Yourself and Your Family

Small talk often focuses on family: an opportunity to tell a bit about yourself and home, and learn something about the other person's family and home too.

Italian families today are not the same as those of 30 to 40 years ago. Multi-generational families, with **nonna** (*nohn-nah*) (grandmother) and **nonno** (*nohn-noh*) (grandfather) living with their children and their **nuore** (*noo-oh-reh*) (daughters-in-law) and **generi** (*jeh-neh-ree*) (sons-in-law) and **nipoti** (*nee-poh-teh*) (grandchildren), are far less common than they once were. Today, **fili** (*fee-lee*) (children) move out of their parents' homes when they find a job (although that may happen at a later age than is common in other countries).

Other topics you may find yourself chatting about are common in many countries:

✔ **il tempo** (*eel tehm-poh*) (the weather)

✔ **il lavoro** (*eel lah-voh-roh*) (work)

✔ **lo sport** (*loh spohrt*) (sports)

Talkin' the Talk

Here's another formal dialogue in the plane. Mr. Melis and Mr. Belli have already introduced themselves and are chatting a bit about their families. Mr. Melis comes from Cagliari and lives in Milano.

Sig. Belli:	**Di dov'è, signor Melis?**
	dee doh-veh see-nyohr meh-lees
	Where are you from, Mr. Melis?
Sig. Melis:	**Sono di Cagliari.**
	soh-noh dee kah-lyah-ree
	I'm from Cagliari.
Sig. Belli:	**Vive solo a Milano?**
	vee-veh soh-loh ah mee-lah-noh
	Do you live on your own in Milan?
Sig. Melis:	**No, con mio fratello.**
	noh kohn mee-oh frah-tehl-loh
	No, with my brother.
Sig. Belli:	**I suoi genitori?**
	ee soo-oh-ee jeh-nee-toh-ree
	Your parents?

Sig. Melis:	**Mia madre vive in Sardegna.**
	mee-ah mah-dreh vee-veh een sahr-deh-nyah
	My mother lives in Sardinia.

Sig. Belli:	**E suo padre?**
	eh soo-oh pah-dreh
	And your father?

Sig. Melis:	**Purtroppo è morto.**
	poor-trohp-poh eh mohr-toh
	Unfortunately, he's dead.

Sig. Belli:	**Mi dispiace.**
	mee dees-pee-ah-cheh
	I'm sorry.

We go on with a dialogue which contains vocabulary material for a chat about marital status.

Talkin' the Talk

Still in the plane, two women, la signora Tosi and la signora Amici, are talking about another colleague.

Sig.ra Tosi:	**Anna è sposata, vero?**
	ahn-nah eh spoh-zah-tah veh-roh
	Anna is married, isn't she?

Sig.ra Muti:	**Credo, perché?**
	kreh-doh pehr-keh
	I think so, why?

Sig.ra Tosi:	**Non è mai con suo marito.**
	nohn eh mah-ee kohn soo-oh mah-ree-toh
	She is never with her husband.

Sig.ra Muti:	**Forse è vedova.**
	fohr-seh eh veh-doh-vah
	Perhaps she's a widow.

Sig.ra Tosi:	**Oppure è divorziata.**
	ohp-poo-reh eh dee-vohr-tsee-ah-tah
	Or she's divorced.

Words to Know

sposata	spoh-_zah_-tah	married
vedova [f]	_veh_-doh-vah	widow
divorziata	dee-vohr-tsee-_ah_-tah	divorced
mi dispiace	mee dees-pee-_ah_-cheh	I'm sorry
mio marito [m]	_mee_-oh mah-_ree_-toh	my husband
mia madre [f]	_mee_-ah _mah_-dreh	my mother
mio padre [m]	_mee_-oh _pah_-dreh	my father

Talkin' the Talk

 Farther back in the plane, two youngsters, Martina and Fabio, are chatting to each other. Of course, they address each other informally.

Martina: **Quanti siete in famiglia?**
koo-_ahn_-tee see-_eh_-teh een fah-_mee_-lyee-ah
How many are in your family?

Fabio: **Siamo cinque.**
see-_ah_-moh _cheen_-koo-eh
There are five of us.

Martina: **Hai fratelli?**
_ah_-ee frah-_tehl_-lee
Do you have brothers?

Fabio: **Una sorella e un fratello.**
_oo_-nah soh-_rehl_-lah eh oon frah-_tehl_-loh
One sister and one brother.

Martina: **Beato te!**
beh-_ah_-toh teh
Lucky you!

Fabio:	**Perché?**
	pehr-keh
	Why?

Martina:	**Io sono figlia unica.**
	ee-oh soh-noh fee-lyah oo-nee-kah
	I'm an only child.

Fabio:	**Beata te!**
	beh-ah-tah teh
	Lucky you!

Sharing special news with an old friend is always satisfying, even if, as with Anna and Marta in the following dialogue, you haven't spoken in a while.

Talkin' the Talk

This phone call is between Anna and Marta who have a long-standing friendship but haven't heard from each other for a long time.

Anna:	**Pronto, Marta, sono Anna.**
	prohn-toh mahr-tah soh-noh ahn-nah
	Hello, Marta, this is Anna.

Marta:	**Anna, che sorpresa!**
	ahn-nah keh sohr-preh-zah
	Anna, what a surprise!

Anna:	**Marta, sai che sono nonna?**
	mahr-tah sah-ee keh soh-noh nohn-nah
	Marta, do you know that I'm a grandmother?

Marta:	**Nonna? Tu?**
	nohn-nah too
	Grandmother? You?

Anna:	**Sì, mia figlia Carla ha una bambina.**
	see mee-ah fee-lyah kahr-lah ah oo-nah bahm-bee-nah
	Yes, my daughter Carla has a little girl.

Marta:	**Tanti auguri! Come si chiama?**
	than-tee ah-oo-*goo*-ree *koh*-meh see kee-*ah*-mah
	Congratulations! What's her name?

Anna:	**Teresa, come la suocera di Carla.**
	teh-reh-zah koh-meh lah soo-oh-cheh-rah dee kahr-lah
	Teresa, like Carla's mother-in-law.

There doesn't really exist a neutral term for brothers and sisters in Italian, like **sibling** in English. You have to say **sorelle e fratelli** (*soh-rehl-leh eh frah-tehl-lee*) (sisters and brothers). But to avoid using this long expression, Italians often reduce it to **fratelli**, which includes both.

Words to Know

mia moglie [f]	mee-ah moh-lyee-eh	my wife
mia figlia [f]	mee-ah fee-lyah	my daughter
mio figlio [m]	mee-oh fee-lyoh	my son
mia sorella [f]	mee-ah soh-rehl-lah	my sister
mia cognata [f]	mee-ah koh-nyah-tah	my sister-in-law
mio cognato [m]	mee-oh koh-nyah-toh	my brother-in-law
mia zia [f]	mee-ah dzee-ah	my aunt
mio zio [m]	mee-oh dzee-oh	my uncle
mia cugina [f]	mee-ah koo-jee-nah	my cousin (female)
mio cugino [m]	mee-oh koo-jee-noh	my cousin (male)

Chatting about the Weather

Whenever you're in conversational trouble and don't know what to say, you can always talk about the weather: "It's very hot today, isn't it?" Or, you can ask, "Is Spring your rainy season?" Talking about the weather can save your conversation in many situations!

CULTURAL WISDOM

Weather wise

Italy is a fortunate country, at least as far as weather is concerned. It has a mild climate, and gets a lot of sun. No wonder it's a popular vacation destination!

The summers are for the most part warm — sometimes *too* hot. The winters can be very cold, but snow is rare, except in some ski areas in the north. The south is a little bit warmer in both summer and winter.

Summer in the cities is generally terribly hot, so most Italians take their vacation in August and flee to cooler places: the sea or the lakes or the mountains. As a matter of fact, in August, it is hard to find actual residents in the big cities. The only people you find there are likely to be tourists and those Italians who have to work.

Because the weather is such an important topic, you must be armed with the necessary vocabulary. In this section, we talk about the **quattro stagioni** *(koo-aht-troh stah-joh-nee)* (four seasons).

The fact that both the famous concertos by Antonio Vivaldi *(ahn-toh-nee-oh vee-vahl-dee)* and an oh-so-good pizza are named *Quattro stagioni* is no accident. Both are subdivided into four parts, and each part refers to one season.

- **primavera** *(pree-mah-veh-rah)* (spring)
- **estate** *(ehs-tah-teh)* (summer)
- **autunno** *(ah-oo-toon-noh)* (autumn; fall)
- **inverno** *(een-vehr-noh)* (winter)

Talkin' the Talk

Our friends Mr. Brancato and Ms. Roe, from the plane, are now talking about the weather.

Ms. Roe:	**Le piace Milano?**
	leh pee-ah-cheh mee-lah-noh
	Do you like Milan?

Sig. Brancato:	**Sì, ma non il clima.**
	see mah nohn eel klee-mah
	Yes, but not its climate.

Ms. Roe:	**Fa molto freddo?** *fah mohl-toh frehd-doh* Is it very cold?
Sig. Brancato:	**In inverno sì.** *een een-vehr-noh see* In winter it is.
Ms. Roe:	**E piove molto, no?** *eh pee-oh-veh mohl-toh noh* And it rains a lot, doesn't it?
Sig. Brancato:	**Sì, e c'è sempre la nebbia.** *see eh cheh sehm-preh lah nehb-bee-ah* Yes, and there is always fog.
Ms. Roe:	**Com' è il clima di Palermo?** *kohm-eh eel klee-mah dee pah-lehr-moh* What's Palermo's climate like?
Sig. Brancato:	**Temperato, mediterraneo.** *tehm-peh-rah-toh meh-dee-tehr-rah-neh-oh* Temperate, Mediterranean.
Ms. Roe:	**Non fa mai freddo?** *nohn fah mah-ee frehd-doh* Is it never cold?
Sig. Brancato:	**Quasi mai.** *koo-ah-zee mah-ee* Almost never.

An expression that shows a difference between cultures is: **Una rondine non fa primavera** *(oo-nah-rohn-dee-neh nohn fah pree-mah-veh-rah)* (One swallow does not make a summer). Note the difference: In English, the expression refers to summer; in Italian it refers to spring. This difference may be due to the fact that the birds come earlier in Italy and later to other countries.

Talkin' the Talk

Il signor Brancato and Ms. Roe, airplane seatmates, are still talking about the weather.

Ms. Roe:	**Piove molto a Milano?** *pee-oh-veh mohl-toh ah mee-lah-noh* Does it rain a lot in Milan?

Sig. Brancato:	**No, un po' in inverno.**
	noh oon poh een een-<u>vehr</u>-noh
	No, a little bit in winter.

Ms. Roe:	**E l'estate com'è?**
	e lehs-<u>tah</u>-teh cohm-<u>eh</u>
	What's the summer like?

Sig. Brancato:	**Molto calda e lunga.**
	<u>mohl</u>-toh <u>kahl</u>-dah eh <u>loon</u>-gah
	Very hot and long.

Ms. Roe:	**E la primavera?**
	eh lah pree-mah-<u>veh</u>-rah
	And the spring?

Sig. Brancato:	**La mia stagione preferita.**
	lah <u>mee</u>-ah stah-<u>joh</u>-neh preh-feh-<u>ree</u>-tah
	My favorite season.

Ms. Roe:	**Davvero?**
	dahv-<u>veh</u>-roh
	Really?

Sig. Brancato:	**Sì, perché è mite.**
	see pehr-<u>keh</u> eh <u>mee</u>-teh
	Yes, because it's mild.

Ms. Roe:	**Come l'autunno in Canada.**
	<u>koh</u>-meh lah-oo-<u>toon</u>-noh een <u>kah</u>-nah-dah
	Like the fall in Canada.

When you're talking about the weather, the following expressions, which are very idiomatic, will make you sound like a native speaker!

- ✔ **Fa un caldo terribile!** *(fah oon <u>kahl</u>-doh tehr-<u>ree</u>-bee-leh)* (It's terribly hot!)

- ✔ **Oggi il sole spacca le pietre!** *(<u>ohj</u>-jee eel <u>soh</u>-leh <u>spahk</u>-kah leh pee-<u>eh</u>-treh)* (The sun today is breaking the stones!)

- ✔ **Fa un freddo cane!** *(fah oon <u>frehd</u>-doh <u>kah</u>-neh)* (It's terribly cold!)

- ✔ **Fa un freddo/un caldo da morire!** *(fah oon <u>frehd</u>-doh/oon <u>kahl</u>-doh dah moh-<u>ree</u>-reh)* (It's deadly cold/warm!)

Da morire *(dah moh-ree-reh)* (deadly) is a typical expression used for emphasis in Italian. You can use it in all kinds of situations: For example, **sono stanco da morire** *(soh-noh stahn-koh dah moh-ree-reh)* (I'm deadly tired) or **ho sete da morire** *(oh seh-teh dah moh-ree-reh)* (I'm deadly thirsty).

Talkin' the Talk

Back in the plane, there is more small talk about the weather as the plane goes in for its landing.

Voice over the loudspeaker:	**Signore e Signori!** *see-nyoh-reh eh see-nyoh-ree* Ladies and gentlemen!
Sig. Brancato:	**Che succede?** *kee soo-cheh-deh* What's up?
Voice:	**Stiamo atterrando a Milano Malpensa.** *stee-ah-moh aht-tehr-rahn-doh ah mee-lah-noh mahl-pehn-sah* We're landing now at Milan Malpensa.
Sig. Brancato:	**Meno male!** *meh-noh mah-leh* Thank goodness!
Voice:	**Il cielo è coperto.** *eel cheh-loh eh koh-pehr-toh* The sky is overcast.
Ms. Roe:	**Come al solito!** *koh-meh ahl soh-lee-toh* As usual!
Voice:	**E la temperatura è di cinque gradi.** *eh lah tehm-peh-rah-too-rah eh dee cheen-koo-eh grah-dee* And the temperature is five degrees.

You probably know that in Europe the Celsius scale is used to measure temperature. So, in the preceding dialogue, "five degrees" converts to 41 degrees Fahrenheit.

Words to Know

come al solito	koh-meh ahl <u>soh</u>-lee-toh	as usual
umido	<u>oo</u>-mee-doh	humid
tempo incerto [m]	<u>tehm</u>-poh een-<u>chehr</u>-toh	uncertain weather
Piove!	pee-oh-veh	It's raining

Piove sul bagnato *(pee-<u>oh</u>-veh sool bah-<u>nyah</u>-toh)* (Literally: it rains on the wet) is an idiomatic expression that Italians use when something positive happens to someone who doesn't really need it. For example, if a millionaire wins the lottery, you may say **piove sul bagnato** to indicate your feeling that you should have won instead.

Talking Shop

Another popular topic for small talk is work. Knowing what another person does is always interesting. Certainly, there are also taboo topics about work, like asking how much someone makes, for example. But otherwise, most everyone is happy to talk about work.

When you talk about your profession in Italian, you don't need to use the article *a*, as in "I'm a doctor." You simply say **sono medico** *(<u>soh</u>-noh <u>meh</u>-dee-koh)*.

Talkin' the Talk

Back on the plane, we hear la signora Basile and her neighbor il signor Corsi speaking formally, which is very typical in a conversation between people who are conversing because of circumstance.

Sig.ra Basile: **Viaggia per lavoro?**
vee-<u>ahj</u>-jah pehr lah-<u>voh</u>-roh
Are you traveling because of your job?

Sig. Corsi: **Sì, per un'intervista.**
see pehr oon een-tehr-vees-tah
Yes, for an interview.

Sig.ra Basile: **È giornalista?**
eh johr-nah-lees-tah
Are you a journalist?

Sig. Corsi: **Sì, giornalista televisivo.**
see johr-nah-lees-tah teh-leh-vee-zee-voh
Yes, a television journalist.

Sig.ra Basile: **Per quale società lavora?**
pehr koo-ah-leh soh-cheh-tah lah-voh-rah
Which company do you work for?

Sig. Corsi: **Sono libero professionista.**
soh-noh lee-beh-roh proh-fehs-see-oh-nees-tah
I'm a freelancer.
E lei che lavoro fa?
eh lay keh lah-voh-roh fah
And what is your job?

Sig.ra Basile: **Sono architetto.**
soh-noh ahr-kee-teht-toh
I'm an architect.

Sig. Corsi: **Anche lei è free lance?**
ahn-keh lay eh free lance
Are you also a freelancer?

Sig.ra Basile: **No, lavoro in uno studio di design.**
nohn lah-voh-rah een oo-noh stoo-dee-oh dee deh-sihn
No, I work in a design studio.

Sig. Corsi: **Grande?**
grahn-deh
A big one?

Sig.ra Basile: **Siamo sei colleghi.**
see-ah-moh say kohl-leh-gee
There are six of us.

CULTURAL WISDOM

Titular titles and abbreviations

In Italy, you often hear **"Buongiorno dottore!"** *(boo-ohn-johr-noh doht-toh-reh)* (Hello, doctor!), and you may wonder how many doctors Italy has. The fact is, any person who has a university education is called **dottore** [m] *(doht-toh-reh)* or **dottoressa** [f] *(doht-toh-rehs-sah)*. Of course, you also address a medical doctor with this term.

You may have noticed abbreviations in the Talkin' the Talk sections: **Sig.ra** for **signora** and **Sig.** for **signor**. These are used only in written language — there is no spoken contraction. Italian is less sexist than English in that it uses the same title for married and unmarried women, and **signor** for all men.

Words to Know

giornalista [f/m]	johr-nah-<u>lees</u>-tah	journalist
regista [f/m]	reh-<u>jees</u>-tah	film director
architetto [f/m]	ahr-kee-<u>teht</u>-toh	architect
avvocato [f/m]	ahv-voh-<u>kah</u>-toh	lawyer
ingegnere [f/m]	een-jeh-<u>nyeh</u>-reh	engineer
medico [f/m]	<u>meh</u>-dee-koh	doctor
insegnante [f/m]	een-seh-<u>nyahn</u>-the	teacher
commessa [f]/ commesso [m]	kohm-<u>mehs</u>-sah kohm-<u>mehs</u>-soh	clerk
meccanico [f/m]	mehk-<u>kah</u>-nee-koh	mechanic

Getting Addresses and Phone Numbers

In nearly all your everyday activities, you use numbers. Perhaps you call a friend and arrange to meet her at the corner of Sixteenth Street and First Avenue. You buy two apples to get the 250 lire in change you need to catch the number 46 bus to meet your friend. Following are the numbers from one to ten to get you started. A more complete listing of numbers is in Chapter 2.

- ✔ **zero** (_dzeh_-roh) (zero)
- ✔ **uno** (_oo_-noh) (one)
- ✔ **due** (_doo_-eh) (two)
- ✔ **tre** (_treh_) (three)
- ✔ **quattro** (koo-_aht_-troh) (four)
- ✔ **cinque** (_cheen_-koo-eh) (five)
- ✔ **sei** (_say_) (six)
- ✔ **sette** (_seht_-teh) (seven)
- ✔ **otto** (_oht_-toh) (eight)
- ✔ **nove** (_noh_-veh) (nine)
- ✔ **dieci** (dee-_eh_-chee) (ten)

Since 1998, Italians have to dial the area code even for local calls. Don't forget to do this if you visit Italy.

Talkin' the Talk

Marina and Luca got to know each other at a party and want to meet again. Marina asks for Luca's address and phone number.

Marina: **Mi dai il tuo indirizzo?**
mee _dah_-ee eel _too_-oh een-dee-_reet_-tsoh
Can you give me your address?

Luca: **Via Alberto Ascari, otto.**
vee-ah ahl-_behr_-toh _ahs_-kah-ree _oht_-toh
Alberto Ascari Street, eight.

Marina: **Codice postale?**
koh-dee-cheh pohs-_tah_-leh
Zip code?

Luca:	**Zero zero uno quattro due, Roma.**
	dzeh-roh dzeh-roh oo-noh koo-aht-troh doo-eh roh-mah
	Zero zero one four two, Rome.
Marina:	**Telefono?**
	teh-leh-foh-noh
	Phone?
Luca:	**Cinque uno nove due sette tre tre.**
	cheen-koo-eh oo-noh noh-veh doo-eh seht-teh treh treh
	Five one nine two seven three three.
Marina:	**Il prefisso?**
	eel preh-fees-soh
	The area code?
Luca:	**Zero sei.**
	dzeh-roh say
	Zero six.

Nowadays many people have another address: e-mail. In Italian, you can say "e-mail" or **posta elettronica** *(pohs-tah eh-leht-troh-nee-kah)* (electronic mail). In English, you use *at* to refer to this symbol: @. Italians have given it a more fanciful name: **chiocciola** *(kee-ohch-choh-lah)* (snail) or even **chiocciolina** *(kee-ohch-choh-lee-nah)* (little snail) — or you can refer to it in the English way *at*. The format for an Italian e-mail address is like an e-mail address anywhere:

```
nome@server.it
```

By the way, **nome** *(noh-meh)* is "name"; @, or *at,* is taken from English; the Italian for "period" is **punto** *(poon-toh)*; and **it** *(eet)* stands for Italy.

Talkin' the Talk

La signora Damiani and il signor Bianchi are thinking about becoming business partners. They want to remain in contact, and so they exchange addresses.

Sig.ra Damiani:	**Ha un biglietto da visita?**
	ah oon bee-lyeht-toh dah vee-see-tah
	Do you have a business card?

Sig. Bianchi:	**Purtroppo no.** *poor-trohp-poh noh* Unfortunately not.
Sig.ra Damiani:	**Il Suo indirizzo?** *eel soo-oh een-dee-reet-tsoh* Your address?
Sig. Bianchi:	**Corso Sempione, cinque.** *kohr-soh sehm-pee-oh-neh cheen-koo-eh* Corso Sempione, five.
Sig.ra Damiani:	**Codice?** *koh-dee-cheh* Zip code?
Sig. Bianchi:	**Non mi ricordo!** *nohn mee ree-kohr-doh* I can't remember!
Sig.ra Damiani:	**Numero di telefono?** *noo-meh-roh dee teh-leh-foh-noh* Phone number?
Sig. Bianchi:	**Zero due cinque nove zero uno uno sei tre.** *dzeh-roh doo-eh cheen-koo-eh noh-veh dzeh-roh oo-noh oo-noh say treh* Zero two five nine zero one one six three.
Sig.ra Damiani:	**Ha un fax?** *ah oon fahks* Do you have a fax?
Sig. Bianchi:	**Sì, è lo stesso numero.** *see eh loh stehs-soh noo-meh-roh* Yes, it's the same number.

Just as in English, Italian streets are called by different names and each name of the street incorporates a word meaning street, avenue, boulevard, and so on. You'll find streets named, for example, **Via Antonio Vivaldi**, **Viale Regina Margherita, corso Mazzini,** or **strada statale 12**.

What's the difference between **via, viale, corso,** and **strada?** In general, if you want to say "it's a big road," you say **è una strada grande** *(eh oo-nah strah-dah grahn-deh)*, although some people say **via** in such a case. A similar concept applies to the words for "avenue": Use **il viale** *(eel vee-ah-leh)* when you mean any wide, tree-lined avenue or boulevard, and **il corso** *(eel kohr-soh)* when you include the avenue's name or mean a street in the shopping district.

Most Italians who live in a city stay in an apartment or flat. Due to the population density, there aren't many detached houses in urban areas. Those who can afford it often have a house up in the mountains or at a lake.

However, people usually refer to their **appartamento** *(ahp-pahr-tah-mehn-toh)* (apartment) as their **casa** *(kah-sah)* (house). Italians care a lot for their homes, they take pride in them, and have, for the most part, very tastefully furnished ones. To give you some terms concerning flats and houses, read this excerpt from an essay by a little girl from primary school.

> **Casa mia è la più bella del mondo.**
> *kah-sah mee-ah eh lah pee-oo behl-lah dehl mohn-doh*
> My home is the most beautiful in the world.
>
> **È grande, con tante finestre e due terrazze.**
> *eh grahn-deh kohn than-teh fee-nehs-treh eh doo-eh tehr-raht-tseh*
> It's big, with many windows and two terraces.
>
> **Il palazzo non è tanto grande, ha quattro piani.**
> *eel pah-laht-tsoh nohn eh than-toh grahn-deh ah koo-aht-troh pee-ah-neh*
> The building is not very big, it has four floors.
>
> **Io abito al secondo.**
> *ee-oh ah-bee-toh ahl she-kohn-doh*
> I live on the second (floor).
>
> **C'è un bel giardino.**
> *cheh oon behl jahr-dee-noh*
> There is a beautiful garden.

In Italian, you have two words that mean "to live":

- **vivere** *(vee-veh-reh)* (to live) is generally used in the sense of being alive, and to say that you have lived in a place for a long period. You wouldn't use this verb to talk about where you stayed on your vacation, but to tell where your home is.

- **abitare** *(ah-bee-tah-reh)* (to live; to stay) is used more to indicate which street you live on.

But in the end, nobody makes a fuss about it; you can use either. The conjugations for both follow:

Conjugation	*Pronunciation*
io vivo	<u>ee</u>-oh <u>vee</u>-voh
tu vivi	too <u>vee</u>-vee
lui/lei vive	<u>loo</u>-ee/lay <u>vee</u>-veh
noi viviamo	<u>noh</u>-ee vee-vee-<u>ah</u>-moh
voi vivete	<u>voh</u>-ee vee-<u>veh</u>-teh
loro vivono	<u>loh</u>-roh <u>vee</u>-voh-noh

Conjugation	*Pronunciation*
io abito	<u>ee</u>-oh <u>ah</u>-bee-toh
tu abiti	too <u>ah</u>-bee-tee
lui/lei abita	<u>loo</u>-ee/lay <u>ah</u>-bee-tah
noi abitiamo	<u>noh</u>-ee ah-bee-tee-<u>ah</u>-moh
voi abitate	<u>voh</u>-ee ah-bee-<u>tah</u>-teh
loro abitano	<u>loh</u>-roh <u>ah</u>-bee-tah-noh

If you are visiting a city and want to tell someone where you're staying, use **abitare**. Actually, in this case you can also say, **sono all'albergo Quattro Stagioni** (*<u>soh</u>-noh ahl-lahl-<u>behr</u>-goh koo-<u>aht</u>-troh stah-<u>joh</u>-nee*) (I am at the hotel Quattro Stagioni). Following are some other examples:

- ✔ **Sono al Quattro Fontane.** (*<u>soh</u>-noh ahl koo-<u>aht</u>-troh fohn-<u>tah</u>-neh*) (I am at the Quattro Fontane.)

- ✔ **Stiamo all'albergo Il giardino** (*stee-<u>ah</u>-moh ahl-lahl-<u>behr</u>-goh eel jahr-<u>dee</u>-noh*) (We are staying at the hotel Il Giardino.)

Fun & Games

Last but not least, we want to give you a little personal questionnaire (asked in formal form). You can probably understand the questions without translations, but if you need them, they are printed upside down at the bottom of this page.

You can answer these questions with a simple *Yes* or *No.* If you feel confident enough, you can, of course, answer them in whole sentences. Answer this first batch formally.

1. **È americano?**

2. **È sposato?**

3. **Piove?**

4. **Ha un fratello?**

5. **Fa freddo?**

6. **Vive a Palermo?**

In this batch, answer informally:

7. **Sei giornalista?**

8. **Hai un fax?**

9. **Hai una sorella?**

Remember: **Conta più la pratica che la grammatica.** *(<u>kohn</u>-tah pee-<u>oo</u> lah <u>prah</u>-tee-kah keh lah grahm-<u>maht</u>-tee-kah)* (Practice makes perfect.)

Answers: 1. Are you American? 2. Are you married? 3. Is it raining? 4. Do you have a brother? 5. Is it cold? 6. Do you live in Palermo? 7. Are you a journalist? 8. Do you have a fax? 9. Do you have a sister?

Chapter 5

Food, Glorious Food — and Don't Forget the Drink

- -

In This Chapter

▶ Eating, Italian style

▶ Reserving your table and paying for your meal

▶ Getting three meals a day (at least)

▶ Shopping for food

- -

*T*his chapter invites you to have a closer look at the world-renowned Italian cuisine — all about our special food and drink. You no doubt are already familiar with a great many Italian foods, like spaghetti and other pastas, pizza, risotto, espresso, and so on. Reading these sections you'll find lots of vocabulary about meals, and you also learn how to say that you're hungry or thirsty. We also tell you how to order your food in a restaurant, as well as how meals are taken in Italy. Have fun and serve yourself!

Eating and Drinking Italian Style

There are several ways to communicate that demanding, hungry feeling in your stomach:

> ✔ **Ho fame.** *(oh fah-meh)* (I'm hungry.)
>
> ✔ **Andiamo a mangiare qualcosa** *(ahn-dee-ah-moh ah mahn-jah-reh koo-qhl-koh-sah)* (Let's get something to eat.)
>
> ✔ **Hai sete?** *(ah-ee seh-teh)* (Are you thirsty?)

Italians have three main meals: **la (prima) colazione** *(lah pree-mah koh-lah-tsee-oh-neh)* (breakfast), **il pranzo** *(eel prahn-tsoh)* (lunch) and **la cena** *(lah cheh-nah)* (dinner). **Uno spuntino** *(oo-noh spoon-tee-noh)* (a snack) is taken when you're hungry between main meals.

"I'm so hungry I could eat a horse!"

Every language has exaggerated ways to express being hungry or thirsty. To be sure, Italians are in no way inferior in coming up with ways to express how hungry or thirsty they are. Here are some common expressions:

✔ **Muoriamo di sete!** *(moo-oh-ree-ah-moh dee seh-teh)* (We're dying of thirst!)

✔ **Ho una fame da lupi!** *(oh oo-nah fah-meh dah loo-pee)* (I'm hungry as wolves are!; What a terrible hunger!)

✔ **Ho una fame che non ci vedo!** *(oh oo-nah fah-meh keh nohn chee veh-doh)* (I cannot see with hunger!)

Drinking, Italian Style

This section talks about almost every sort of drink Italians usually have. Starting, obviously, with their good coffee, but covering also water, tea and many sorts of spirits.

Expressing your love for espresso

You may have to order an espresso at your favorite coffee emporium in the States to get the rich, dark brew you crave, but in Italy, you get the same drink by asking for **caffè** *(kahf-feh)* (coffee). In Italy, you rarely hear the word *espresso,* unless **il cameriere** *(eel kah-meh-ree-eh-reh)* (the waiter) says, **"un espresso per la signora"** *(oon ehs prehs-soh pehr lah see-nyoh-rah)* (one espresso for the lady), as an announcement that this espresso is yours.

Of course, even in Italy, people drink more than just **caffè.** You can enjoy a nice cup of **cioccolata** *(chohk-koh-lah-tah)* (cocoa), various sorts of **te** *(teh)* (tea), **succhi di frutta** *(sook-kee dee froot-tah)* (fruit juices), and a wider selection of water than most North Americans enjoy.

In Italy, even water is not just water. If you travel to Italy and ask only for water, you may be surprised when you are served with a glass of **acqua naturale** *(ahk-koo-ah nah-too-rah-leh)* (natural water), which comes from the faucet. If you like **acqua minerale** *(ahk-koo-ah mee-neh-rah-leh)* (mineral water), which can be **acqua gassata/gasata** *(ahk-koo-ah gas-sah-tah/ gah-zah-tah)* (carbonated water), also called **acqua frizzante** *(ahk-koo-ah freez-zahn-teh),* or **acqua liscia** *(ahk-koo-ah lee-shah)* (noncarbonated water).

In **estate** *(ehs-tah-teh)* (summer), you may want your coffee or tea over **ghiaccio** *(gee-ahch-choh)* (ice). Ask for **caffè freddo/shakerato** *(kahf-feh frehd-doh/sheh-keh-rah-toh)* (iced coffee) or **tè freddo** *(teh frehd-doh)* (iced tea).

CULTURAL WISDOM

Italy's national drink: Espresso

In this sidebar, we initiate you into the various sorts of Italian coffee. There are so many different sorts of this good, strong, brown liquid.

By the way, *espresso* is short for **espressamente preparato per chi lo richiede** *(ehs-prehs-sah-<u>mehn</u>-teh preh-pah-<u>rah</u>-toh pehr kee loh ree-kee-<u>eh</u>-deh)* (expressly prepared for who requests it).

Caffè Hag *(kahf-<u>feh</u> ahg)* is a popular brand of decaffeinated coffee — every Italian knows it.

- **caffè** *(kahf-<u>feh</u>):* When you order **caffè**, you automatically get an espresso. It is also called **caffè normale** *(kahf-<u>feh</u> nohr-<u>mah</u>-leh)* (normal coffee).

- **ristretto** *(<u>ree</u>-streht-toh):* Very strong and concentrated espresso.

- **doppio** *(<u>dohp</u>-pee-oh):* Double espresso.

- **lungo** *(<u>loon</u>-goh):* Espresso with more water to make it less concentrated.

- **corretto** *(kohr-<u>reht</u>-toh):* Espresso with a bit of cognac or other liquor.

- **cappuccino** *(kahp-pooch-<u>chee</u>-noh):* Espresso with frothed milk.

- **caffellatte** *(kahf-fehl-<u>laht</u>-teh):* Espresso with plenty of milk.

- **macchiato** *(mahk-kee-<u>ah</u>-toh):* Espresso with a touch of milk.

- **latte macchiato** *(<u>laht</u>-teh mahk-kee-<u>ah</u>-toh):* Milk with just a touch of espresso.

- **caffè americano** *(kahf-<u>feh</u> ah-meh-ree-<u>kah</u>-noh):* American coffee but stronger — this type of coffee has become a new fashion.

- **decaffeinato** *(deh-kahf-feh-ee-<u>nah</u>-toh):* Decaffeinated coffee.

- **caffè d'orzo** *(kahf-<u>feh</u> <u>dohr</u>-zoh):* Coffee substitute made from germinated, dried, and roasted barley. You can have it strong or light.

When do you pay for your drinks in an Italian coffee bar? It depends. Normally, you have your coffee or whatever first and pay afterward. In little Italian bars, where just one or two people work behind the bar, you simply tell the cashier what you had and pay then. In bigger bars, you get a sales slip and then you go to pay at the cash register.

TIP

When you order a drink in Italy, you need to specify how much you want — a whole bottle, a carafe, or just a glass. You can use the following words:

- **Una bottiglia di. . .** *(<u>oo</u>-nah boht-<u>tee</u>-lyah dee)* (A bottle of. . .)

- **Una caraffa di. . .** *(<u>oo</u>-nah kah-<u>rahf</u>-fah dee)* (A carafe of. . .)

- **Un bicchiere di. . .** *(oon beek-kee-<u>eh</u>-reh dee)* (A glass of. . .)

- **Una tazza di. . .** *(<u>oo</u>-nah <u>taht</u>-tsah dee)* (A cup of. . .)

- **Una tazzina di caffè** *(<u>oo</u>-nah taht-<u>tsee</u>-nah dee kahf-<u>feh</u>)* (A small cup of coffee)

Beverages with even more of a kick

Italy is also famous for its **vini** *(vee-nee)* (wines) and other fermented beverages. Just the sight of a Chianti bottle brings thoughts of candlelight dinners and romance to people worldwide. **Grappa** *(grahp-pah)* (brandy), though not a big export, is a very popular liquor in Italy. Be sure to try it if you get the opportunity.

Talkin' the Talk

Friends eating a casual meal in a pizzeria debate what type of wine to have with their meal.

Laura: **La lista dei vini, per favore?**
lah *lees*-tah day *vee*-nee pehr fah-*voh*-reh
The wine list, please?

Server: **È l'ultima pagina.**
eh *lool*-tee-mah *pah*-jee-nah
It's on the last page.

Laura: **Ah, eccola.**
ah *ehk*-koh-lah
Ah, here it is.

Server: **Che tipo di vino volete?**
keh *tee*-poh dee *vee*-noh voh-*leh*-teh
What type of wine would you like?

Silvio: **Di solito bevo vino bianco, ma oggi preferisco il rosso.**
dee *soh*-lee-to *beh*-voh *vee*-noh bee-*ahn*-koh mah *ohj*-jee preh-feh-*rees*-koh eel *rohs*-soh
Usually I drink white wine, but I prefer red today.

Laura: **Che ne dici di una bottiglia di Chianti?**
keh neh *dee*-chee dee *oo*-nah boht-*tee*-lyah dee kee-*ahn*-tee
How about a bottle of Chianti?

Silvio: **Perfetto!**
pehr-*feht*-toh
Perfect!

Words to Know

il vino [m]	eel <u>vee</u>-noh	wine
bianco [m]	bee-<u>ahn</u>-koh	white
rosso [m]	<u>rohs</u>-soh	red
oggi [m]	<u>ohj</u>-jee	today
perfetto	pehr-<u>feht</u>-toh	perfect

You can't talk in Italian about beverages, drinks, and so on without knowing how to say "to drink." Here's a useful conjugation of the verb **bere** *(<u>beh</u>-reh):*

Conjugation	*Pronunciation*
io bevo	<u>ee</u>-oh <u>beh</u>-voh
tu bevi	too <u>beh</u>-vee
lui/lei beve	<u>loo</u>-ee/lay <u>beh</u>-veh
noi beviamo	<u>noh</u>-ee beh-vee-<u>ah</u>-moh
voi bevete	<u>voh</u>-ee beh-<u>veh</u>-teh
loro bevono	<u>loh</u>-roh <u>beh</u>-voh-noh

Talkin' the Talk

Il signor Di Leo and la signora Fazio are lunching together. They summon their server to order their drinks.

Server: **Desiderano un aperitivo?**
deh-<u>zee</u>-deh-rah-noh oon ah-peh-ree-<u>tee</u>-voh
Would you like an aperitif?

Sig.ra Fazio: **Io prendo un Campari. E tu?**
<u>ee</u>-oh <u>prehn</u>-doh oon kahm-<u>pah</u>-ree eh too
I'll have a Campari. And you?

Sig. Di Leo: **Per me un Martini rosso, grazie.**
pehr meh oon mahr-<u>tee</u>-nee <u>rohs</u>-soh <u>grah</u>-tsee-eh
For me a red Martini, thank you.

Server: **E da bere?**
eh dah beh-reh
And to drink?

Sig.ra Fazio: **Che cosa ci consiglia?**
keh koh-zah chee kohn-see-lyah
What do you recommend?

Server: **Abbiamo un ottimo Chianti.**
ahb-bee-ah-moh oon oht-tee-moh kee-ahn-tee
We have a very good Chianti.

Sig. Di Leo: **Io preferisco vino bianco.**
ee-oh preh-feh-rees-koh vee-noh bee-ahn-koh
I prefer white wine.

Sig.ra Fazio: **Un bianco allora.**
oon bee-ahn-koh ahl-loh-rah
A white one then.

You may be interested in a **aperitivo** *(ah-peh-ree-tee-voh)* (aperatif) before or after your meal, or perhaps a **birra** *(beer-rah)* (beer), either in a **bottiglia** *(boht-tee-lyah)* (bottle) or **alla spina** *(ahl-lah spee-nah)* (draft beer). You can combine Italian specialties, as il signor Di Leo does by adding **grappa** to his **espresso** in the following dialogue.

Talkin' the Talk

To top off an exquisite meal, il signor Di Leo and la signora Fazio order after-dinner drinks.

Server: **La casa offre caffè e amaro.**
lah kah-sah ohf-freh kahf-feh eh ah-mah-roh
We offer coffee and after-dinner drinks.

Sig.ra Fazio: **Per me caffè.**
pehr meh kahf-feh
For me, espresso.

Sig. Di Leo: **Per me caffè corretto, grazie.**
pehr meh kahf-feh kohr-reht-toh grah-tsee-eh
For me, espresso with a bit of liquor, thank you.

Server: **Con grappa?**
kohn grahp-pah
Laced with grappa?

Sig. Di Leo:	**Perfetto!**
	pehr-feht-toh
	Perfect!

The Start and Finish of Dining Out

One of the more enjoyable (if potentially fattening) ways to explore a new culture is to sample the native cuisine. People interested in Italian cuisine are lucky — Italian-style restaurants are plentiful in North America. You can eat in a pizza joint, or enjoy a traditional, multi-course meal in a classy restaurant. And, if you're fortunate enough to actually travel to Italy, your taste buds are in for a real treat!

This section discusses the beginning and endings of meals — making reservations, and paying the tab. **Buon appetito!** *(boo-ohn-ahp-peh-tee-toh)* (Enjoy your meal!)

Making reservations

Unless you're going to a pizzeria, or the **trattoria** *(traht-toh-ree-ah)* (little restaurant) down the street, you often need to reserve a table in a nice Italian restaurant.

The following dialogue demonstrates the phrases you use to make a reservation at a restaurant.

Talkin' the Talk

Mr. Di Leo calls for reservations at his favorite restaurant.

Waiter:	**Pronto. Ristorante Roma.**
	prohn-toh rees-toh-rahn-teh roh-mah
	Hello! Roma Restaurant.

Sig. Di Leo:	**Buonasera. Vorrei prenotare un tavolo.**
	boo-oh-nah-seh-rah vohr-ray preh-noh-tah-reh oon
	tah-voh-loh
	Good afternoon! I would like to reserve a table.

Waiter:	**Per stasera?**
	pehr stah-seh-rah
	For this evening?

Sig. Di Leo:	**No, per domani.**
	noh pehr doh-mah-nee
	No, for tomorrow.

Waiter:	**Per quante persone?**
	pehr koo-ahn-teh pehr-soh-neh
	For how many people?

Sig. Di Leo:	**Per due.**
	pehr doo-eh
	For two.

Waiter:	**A che ora?**
	ah keh oh-rah
	At what time?

Sig. Di Leo:	**Alle nove.**
	ahl-leh noh-veh
	At nine.

Waiter:	**A che nome?**
	ah keh noh-meh
	In whose name?

Sig. Di Leo:	**Di Leo.**
	dee leh-oh
	Di Leo.

Words to Know

tavolo [m]	tah-voh-loh	table
cameriere [m]	kah-meh-ree-eh-reh	waiter
domani [m]	doh-mah-nee	tomorrow
prenotazione [f]	preh-noh-tah-tsee-oh-neh	reservation
stasera [f]	stah-seh-rah	this evening

Paying for your meal

Not in all restaurants do you have to pay cash, there are a lot, mostly higher standard ones, where you can pay with your credit card, too. In these cases it's written at the entrance.

You can certainly leave a tip for the waiter on the plate with the bill. In good restaurants, people usually leave 10 percent of the bill. In pizzerias, young people sometimes "forget" to tip.

When you want the bill, you ask the waiter "to bring" it to you. Here is the Italian conjugation of the verb **portare** *(pohr-_tah_-reh)*:

Conjugation	Pronunciation
io porto	<u>ee</u>-oh <u>pohr</u>-toh
tu porti	too <u>pohr</u>-tee
lui/lei porta	<u>loo</u>-ee/lay <u>pohr</u>-tah
noi portiamo	<u>noh</u>-ee pohr-tee-<u>ah</u>-moh
voi portate	<u>voh</u>-ee pohr-<u>tah</u>-teh
loro portano	<u>loh</u>-roh <u>pohr</u>-tah-noh

Talkin' the Talk

Mr. Di Leo and his wife just had a fabulous dinner. Mr. Di Leo calls the waiter to ask for the check.

Sig. Di Leo: **Ci porta il conto, per favore?**
chee <u>pohr</u>-tah eel <u>kohn</u>-toh pehr fah-<u>voh</u>-reh
Could you bring us the check, please?

Server: **Subito!**
<u>soo</u>-bee-toh
Immediately!

Sig.ra Di Leo: **Scusi, dov'è il bagno?**
<u>skoo</u>-zee doh-<u>veh</u> eel <u>bah</u>-nyoh
Excuse me, where are the restrooms?

Server: **Al piano di sotto a sinistra.**
ahl pee-<u>ah</u>-noh dee <u>soht</u>-toh ah see-<u>nees</u>-trah
Downstairs on the left.

Sig.ra Di Leo: **Grazie.**
grah-tsee-eh
Thank you.

Server: **Prego, signore.**
preh-goh see-_nyoh_-reh
Here's the bill, sir.

Sig. Di Leo: **Accettate carte di credito?**
ahch-cheht-_tah_-teh _kahr_-teh dee _kreh_-dee-toh
Do you accept credit cards?

Server: **Certo!**
chehr-toh
Of course!

Real Italian restaurants

In Italy, before you satisfy your hunger, you have to choose where to do that. However, with the variety of restaurants in Italy, this is not a simple decision. You have many possibilities:

✔ **bar** _(bahr):_ An Italian bar where you can have all sorts of drinks and little snacks.

✔ **paninoteca** _(pah-nee-noh-_teh_-kah):_ Here you can get virtually all kinds of filled and topped rolls and toasts, served hot or cold.

✔ **osteria** _(ohs-teh-_ree_-ah):_ A little inn where you get simple but very flavorful food. The prices are usually rather low.

✔ **trattoria** _(traht-toh-_ree_-ah):_ The **trattoria** is something in between an **osteria** and a restaurant. It is usually medium-priced.

✔ **taverna** _(tah-_vehr_-nah):_ Also serves food and drink whose quality is somewhat below the trattoria level.

✔ **ristorante** _(rees-toh-_rahn_-teh):_ In Italy, you can find very good restaurants, but the prices vary. The best strategy is to check the prices outside first and then decide.

✔ **pizzeria** _(peet-tsah-_ree_-ah):_ Most of them have a wide range of pizzas. Pizza is always good in Italy (do you wonder why?). You can also get pasta and salads there.

✔ **tavola calda** _(_tah_-voh-lah_ kahl_-dah):_ Sort of a fast food restaurant or carry out, where you get warm food, like **pollo arrosto** _(_pohl_-loh ahr-_rohs_-toh)_ (roasted chicken), **patate arrosto** _(pah-_tah_-teh ahr-_rohs_-toh)_ (roasted potatoes), and so on.

Osterie, trattorie, and **taverne** are all sure bets for a good meal — you generally find more Italians than tourists in them.

Save that sales slip

In some Italian bars, especially those located in train or bus stations or other confusing environments, you pay before you get your drink. You go to the register, tell them what you want, and pay there, and *then* you go to the bar to get it.

Be sure to keep **lo scontrino** *(loh skohn-tree-noh)* (the sales slip), at least until you leave an Italian bar or any kind of shop or restaurant. This is important in Italy, because **la Guardia di Finanza** *(lah goo-ahr-dee-ah dee fee-nahn-tsah)* (the customs office) often checks. If you leave without a sales slip and are caught, you have to pay a fine. And that's not so fine!

Having Breakfast

Your first meal of the day is always **la prima colazione** *(lah pree-mah koh-lah-tsee-oh-neh)* (breakfast).

Many Italians begin **la giornata** *(lah johr-nah-tah)* (the day) with **un caffè** *(oon kahf-feh)* (espresso) at home, and stop for another one in **un bar** *(oon bahr)* (an espresso bar) on their way to work. They may also get **un cornetto** *(oon kohr-neht-toh)* (croissant) filled with **la marmellata** *(lah mahr-mehl-lah-tah)* (jam), **crema** *(kreh-mah)* (cream), or **cioccolata** *(chohk-koh-lah-tah)* (chocolate).

In Sicily, you can even get **brioche con il gelato** *(bree-ohsh kohn eel jeh-lah-toh)* (croissant-like pastry with ice cream).

An Italian bar is not the same bar as the one you go to in the United States or Canada to have a beer in the evening. In Italy, you can go **al bar** *(ahl bahr)* (to the bar) any time during the day. These bars offer espresso, cappuccino, wine, **grappa** *(grahp-pah)* (a special type of Italian spirit), as well as light meals. You find these bars on virtually every street corner.

Italians have their breakfast standing up by the counter, so it takes only a few minutes. Twenty years ago, most Italian bars didn't even have tables. Nowadays tables are becoming more and more common because of tourists.

We can't talk about meals and dishes without the basic verb **mangiare** *(mahn-jah-reh)* (to eat).

Conjugation	*Pronunciation*
io mangio	<u>ee</u>-oh <u>mahn</u>-joh
tu mangi	too <u>mahn</u>-jee
lui/lei mangia	<u>loo</u>-ee/lay <u>mahn</u>-jah
noi mangiamo	<u>noh</u>-ee mahn-<u>jah</u>-moh
voi mangiate	<u>voh</u>-ee mahn-<u>jah</u>-teh
loro mangiano	<u>loh</u>-roh <u>mahn</u>-jah-noh

Talkin' the Talk

The man behind the counter in a coffee bar in Italy is called **il barista** *(eel bah-<u>rees</u>-tah)* (the barman).

Barman: **Buongiorno!**
boo-ohn-<u>johr</u>-noh
Good morning!

Sig. Zampieri: **Buongiorno! Un caffè, per favore.**
boo-ohn-<u>johr</u>-noh oon kahf-<u>feh</u> pehr fah-<u>voh</u>-reh
Good morning! One espresso, please.

Barman: **Qualcosa da mangiare?**
koo-ahl-<u>koh</u>-zah dah mahn-<u>jah</u>-reh
Anything to eat?

Sig. Zampieri: **No, grazie.**
noh <u>grah</u>-tsee-eh
No, thanks.

Barman: **Nient'altro?**
nee-ehnt-<u>ahl</u>-troh
Anything else?

Sig. Zampieri: **Una spremuta d'arancia, per favore.**
<u>oo</u>-nah spreh-<u>moo</u>-tah dah-<u>rahn</u>-chah pehr fah-<u>voh</u>-reh
One fresh-squeezed orange juice, please.

Barman: **Prego.**
<u>preh</u>-goh
Here you are.

Words to Know

acqua [f]	ahk-koo-ah	water
certo	chehr-toh	certainly
scusi	skoo-zee	sorry
spremuta d'arancia	spreh-moo-tah dah-rahn-chah	squeezed orange juice
buongiorno	boo-ohn-johr-noh	good morning
tazza [f]	taht-tsah	cup
tazzina [f]	taht-tsee-nah	small cup

Eating Lunch

For working folk in most of the English-speaking world, **il pranzo** *(eel prahn-tsoh)* (lunch) is an opportunity for a quick break from the job; a chance to get out and pick up **qualcosa di caldo** *(koo-ahl-koh-zah dee kahl-doh)* (something warm).

Italians do it differently. They may eat **un panino** *(oon pah-nee-noh)* (a sort of sandwich) from the **alimentari** *(ah-lee-mehn-tah-ree)* (food shop) around the corner, but most working people normally have from one to three hours for their lunch break. Some of the traditional courses are:

- ✔ **antipasti** *(ahn-tee-pahs-tee)* (appetizers): Usually served cold, **antipasti** range from **verdure miste** *(vehr-doo-reh mees-teh)* (mixed vegetables) to **frutti di mare** *(froot-tee dee mah-reh)* seafood.

- ✔ **primo piatto** *(pree-moh pee-aht-toh)* (first course): This is usually the main, filling course of the meal. You may have all kinds of **pasta** *(pahs-tah)* (pasta), **risotto** *(ree-zoht-toh)* (risotto), or **riso** *(ree-zoh)* (rice) dishes or **minestra** *(mee-nehs-trah)* (soup).

A beloved **primo** *(pree-moh)* (main course) is **spaghetti con le vongole** *(spah-geht-tee kohn leh vohn-goh-leh)* (spaghetti with clams), and many times it is called **spaghetti alle veraci** *(spah-geht-tee ahl-leh veh-rah-chee)*. **Verace** *(veh-rah-cheh)* means "genuine, authentic," and in this case it means "with genuine Neapolitan clams." Now you know where this recipe comes from! If you're interested in learning how to cook Italian, pick up *Italian Cooking For Dummies* by Cesare Casella and Jack Bishop, published by IDG Books Worldwide, Inc.

✔ **il secondo** *(eel seh-kohn-doh)* (the second course): This generally consists of **carne** *(kahr-neh)* (meat), **pesce** *(peh-sheh)* (fish), or *piatti vegetariani* *(pee-aht-tee veh-jeh-tah-ree-ah-nee)* (vegetarian dishes). **Contorni** *(kohn-tohr-nee)* (side dishes) may be ordered separately.

✔ **il dolce** *(eel dohl-cheh)* (the dessert): Last, but certainly not least, dessert may be **un dolce** *(oon dohl-cheh)* (a sweet) or **frutta** *(froot-tah)* (fruit).

You may experience a similar variety of foods and courses in finer Italian restaurants in the United States and Canada.

The verb **prendere** *(prehn-deh-reh)* (literally: to take, but here, to have) is very helpful in talking about food and drinks.

Conjugation	Pronunciation
io prendo	ee-oh prehn-doh
tu prendi	too prehn-dee
lui/lei prende	loo-ee/lay prehn-deh
noi prendiamo	noh-ee prehn-dee-ah-moh
voi prendete	voh-ee prehn-deh-teh
loro prendono	loh-roh prehn-doh-noh

When it comes to soups, there are several kinds of preparations and certainly different tastes. You can have **una minestra** *(oo-nah mee-nehs-trah)* (soup) or **una zuppa** *(oo-nah zoop-pah)* (thick soup). **Il minestrone** *(eel mee-nehs-troh-neh)* (thick vegetable soup) is often made with small-sized pasta as well as vegetables. **Il brodo** *(eel broh-doh)* (stock) can be **vegetale** *(veh-jeh-tah-leh)* (vegetable stock), **di pollo** *(dee pohl-loh)* (chicken stock), **di manzo** *(dee mahn-zoh)* (beef stock), or **di pesce** *(dee peh-sheh)* (fish stock).

La zuppa *(lah zoop-pah)* (thick soup) is usually prepared with **legumi** *(leh-goo-mee)* (legumes), **cereali** *(cheh-reh-ah-lee)* (grains), or vegetables. A few of the choices are: **zuppa di piselli** *(zoop-pah dee pee-sehl-lee)* (pea soup), **di ceci** *(dee cheh-chee)* (chickpea soup), **di lenticchie** *(dee lehn-teek-kee-eh)* (lentil soup), **di patate** *(dee pah-tah-teh)* (potato soup), **di pomodori** *(dee poh-moh-doh-ree)* (tomato soup), but also **di pesce** *(dee peh-sheh)* (fish soup). To this group belong also **pasta e fagioli** *(pahs-tah eh fah-joh-lee)* (bean soup), a very popular, nourishing specialty from Tuscany. And don't be surprised if you find **la zuppa inglese** *(zoo-pah een-gleh-zeh)* — literally "English soup" — on the dessert list!

Talkin' the Talk

La signora Fazio and il signor Di Leo are ordering their first course.

Server: **Per primo, signori?**
pehr pree-moh see-nyoh-ree
For your first course?

Sig.ra Fazio: **Che cosa consiglia la casa?**
keh koh-zah kohn-see-lyah lah kah-sah
What are your specials?

Server: **Oggi abbiamo, penne all'arrabbiata, risotto alla milanese e tortelli di zucca.**
ohj-jee ahb-bee-ah-moh pehn-neh
ahl-lahr-rahb-bee-ah-tah ree-zoht-toh
ahl-lah mee-lah-neh-zeh eh tohr-tehl-lee
dee dzook-kah
Today we have penne with red hot tomato sauce, Milan risotto, and pumpkin tortelli.

Sig. Di Leo: **C'è formaggio nei tortelli?**
cheh fohr-mahj-joh nay tohr-tehl-lee
Is there cheese in the tortelli?

Server: **No, soltanto zucca.**
noh sohl-tahn-toh zook-kah
No, just pumpkin.

Sig. Di Leo: **Nelle penne c'è aglio o peperoncino?**
nehl-leh pehn-neh cheh ahl-lyoh oh
peh-peh-rohn-chee-noh
Does the penne have garlic or paprika?

Server: **Sì, tutt'e due.**
see toot-teh doo-eh
Yes, both.

Sig. Di Leo: **Sono molto piccanti?**
soh-noh mohl-toh peek-kahn-tee
Are they very spicy?

Server: **Un po', ma molto saporite.**
oon poh mah mohl-toh sah-poh-ree-teh
A little, but they're very tasty.

Sig. Di Leo: **Allora le prendo.**
ahl-loh-rah leh prehn-doh
Then I'll have them.

CULTURAL WISDOM

The many meanings of "prego"

Prego *(preh-goh)* has several meanings. When you say it in response to **grazie** *(grah-tsee-eh)* (thank you), it means "you're welcome." But clerks and servers also use it to ask you what you would like or if they can help you. You often hear **prego** when you enter a public office or shop. You also use **prego** when you give something to someone. In this case, the word is translated as "here you are." **Prego** is also a very formal answer when you ask for permission. Following are a few examples of how **prego** is used:

↙ **Grazie.** *(grah-tsee-eh)* (Thank you.)

 Prego. *(preh-goh)* (You're welcome.)

↙ **Prego?** *(preh-goh)* (Can I help you?)

 Posso entrare? *(pohs-soh ehn-trah-reh)* (May I come in?)

 Prego. *(preh-goh)* (Please.)

↙ **Prego, signore.** *(preh-goh see-nyoh-reh)* (Here you are, sir.)

 Grazie. *(grah-tsee-eh)* (Thank you.)

Pasta usually means durum wheat made with flour and water. The different types include: **spaghetti** *(spah-geht-tee)* (spaghetti), **bucatini** *(boo-kah-tee-nee)* (thick, tube-like spaghetti), **penne** *(pehn-neh)* (short, cylinder-shaped pasta shaped to a point at each end), **fusilli** *(foo-zeel-lee)* (spiral-shaped pasta), **rigatoni** *(ree-gah-toh-nee)* (short, cylinder-shaped, and grooved pasta), and so on.

On the other hand, **pasta fresca** *(pahs-tah frehs-kah)* (fresh pasta) means **pasta all'uovo** *(pahs-tah ahl-loo-oh-voh)* (egg noodles), also called **pasta fatta in casa** *(pahs-tah faht-tah een kah-sah)* (home made pasta). These are **tagliatelle** *(tah-lyah-tehl-leh)* (flat noodles), **fettuccine** *(feht-tooch-chee-neh)* (narrow, flat noodles), and **tonnarelli** *(tohn-nah-rehl-lee)* (tubular noodles), to mention just a few.

Incidentally, when you have a bite of pasta, you should make sure that it is **al dente** *(ahl dehn-teh)* (Literally: to the tooth. It means that the pasta is a little hard so that you really need to use your teeth!)

The following conjugation shows you the polite form of the verb **volere** *(voh-leh-reh)* (to want). You have another verb for when you're being polite: "to like." Italian, however, uses a conditional to express politeness.

Conjugation	*Pronunciation*
io vorrei	<u>ee</u>-oh vohr-<u>ray</u>
tu vorresti	too vohr-<u>rehs</u>-tee
lui/lei vorrebbe	<u>loo</u>-ee/lay vohr-<u>rehb</u>-beh
noi vorremmo	<u>noh</u>-ee vohr-<u>rehm</u>-moh
voi vorreste	<u>voh</u>-ee vohr-<u>rehs</u>-teh
loro vorrebbero	<u>loh</u>-roh vohr-<u>rehb</u>-beh-roh

Words to Know

soltanto	sohl-<u>tahn</u>-toh	only; just
saporito	sah-poh-<u>ree</u>-toh	tasty
piccante	peek-<u>kahn</u>-teh	spicy
verdura [f]	vehr-<u>doo</u>-rah	vegetables
tutt'e due	<u>toot</u>-teh <u>doo</u>-eh	both

Enjoying Dinner

Italians often have **la cena** *(lah <u>cheh</u>-nah)* (dinner) at home, but they also eat out. More important for you is certainly the situation outside, say in a restaurant. In the evening, you're more likely to go either to a restaurant or to a pizzeria.

In Italy, a restaurant and a pizzeria differ not only in the food they offer, but also in style. Your dealings in a pizzeria are normally more casual, whereas in a restaurant, especially a higher quality one, you speak more formally. In a pizzeria, you are more likely to use the informal plural "you" — **voi** *(<u>voh</u>-ee)* — whereas in a restaurant, you probably hear, and use, **loro** *(<u>loh</u>-roh)* (you: plural, formal) more often.

Talkin' the Talk

 A group of friends gather at a local pizzeria for dinner. Their exchanges are quite informal.

Sandra: **Che cosa prendiamo?**
keh koh-zah prehn-dee-ah-moh
What should we have?

Laura: **Non lo so! Guardiamo il menù.**
nohn loh soh goo-ahr-dee-ah-moh eel meh-noo
I don't know! Let's look at the menu.

Silvio: **Hai fame?**
ah-ee fah-meh
Are you hungry?

Laura: **Ho fame e sete!**
oh fah-meh eh seh-teh
I'm hungry and thirsty!

Sandra: **Anch'io!**
ahn-kee-oh
Me too!

Silvio: **Sandra, che cosa prendi?**
sahn-drah keh koh-zah prehn-dee
Sandra, what are you going to have?

Sandra: **Vorrei qualcosa di leggero.**
vohr-ray koo-ahl-koh-zah dee lehj-jeh-roh
I'd like something light.

Silvio: **Spaghetti al pomodoro?**
spah-geht-tee ahl poh-moh-doh-roh
Spaghetti with tomato sauce?

Sandra: **E un'insalata mista.**
eh onn-een-sah-lah-tah mees-tah
And a mixed salad.

Silvio: **Poco originale . . .**
pohk-koh oh-ree-jee-nah-leh
Kind of boring . . .

Sandra: **. . . ma buona e leggera!**
mah boo-oh-nah eh lehj-jeh-rah
. . . but good and light!

Most Italian pizzerias have a wide range of pizzas. You can also get pasta and salads there, and afterwards a dessert.

Words to Know

leggero [m]	lehj-<u>jeh</u>-roh	light
insalata mista [f]	een-sah-<u>lah</u>-tah <u>mees</u>-tah	mixed salad
buono	boo-<u>oh</u>-noh	good
il menù [m]	eel meh-<u>noo</u>	menu
avere fame	ah-<u>veh</u>-reh <u>fah</u>-meh	being hungry

Savoring Dessert

You have certainly heard of Italian **gelato** *(jeh-<u>lah</u>-toh)* (ice cream). It is very rich and creamy — and delicious! You can choose between **gelati confezionati** *(jeh-<u>lah</u>-tee kohn-feh-tsee-oh-<u>nah</u>-tee)* (packed ice cream) and **gelati artigianali** *(jeh-<u>lah</u>-tee ahr-tee-jah-<u>nah</u>-lee)* (homemade ice cream — made in a shop). If you choose the latter one, you have to decide whether you want it in a **cono** *(<u>koh</u>-noh)* (cone) or a **coppetta** *(kohp-<u>peht</u>-tah)* (cup).

You also have to decide which **gusto** *(<u>goos</u>-toh)* (flavor) you want, how many **palline** *(pahl-<u>lee</u>-neh)* (scoops), and finally whether you want it **con panna** *(kohn <u>pahn</u>-nah)* (with whipped cream) or **senza panna** *(<u>sehn</u>-tsah <u>pahn</u>-nah)* (without whipped cream).

Talkin' the Talk

 Later on, Laura and Silvio stop for some ice cream.

Server: **Prego?**
<u>preh</u>-goh
What would you like?

Laura:	**Due coni, per favore.**
	doo-eh koh-nee pehr fah-voh-reh
	Two ice cream cones, please.

Server:	**Quante palline?**
	koo-ahn-teh pahl-lee-neh
	How many scoops?

Silvio:	**Per me due.**
	pehr meh doo-eh
	For me two.

Laura:	**Per me quattro.**
	pehr meh koo-aht-troh
	For me four.

Server:	**Che gusti?**
	keh goos-tee
	Which flavors?

Silvio:	**Fragola e limone.**
	frah-goh-lah eh lee-moh-neh
	Strawberry and lemon.

Server:	**Prego. E lei?**
	preh-goh eh lay
	Here you are. And you?

Laura:	**Crema, cioccolato, cocco, e noce.**
	kreh-mah chohk-koh-lah-tah kook-koh eh noh-cheh
	Cream, chocolate, coconut, and nut.

Server:	**Panna?**
	pahn-nah
	Whipped cream?

Laura:	**No, grazie. Sono a dieta!**
	noh grah-tsee-eh soh-noh ah dee-eh-tah
	No, thanks. I'm on a diet!

Italians often have fruit after a meal, either as dessert, a sweet, or even both: **un dolce** *(oon dohl-cheh)* (a sweet) and **frutta fresca** *(froot-tah frehs-kah)* (fresh fruit). Certainly there are many ways of preparing fruit, when you don't like it in its natural form: You can have **una macedonia** *(oo-nah* *mah-cheh-doh-nee-ah)* (fruit salad) or also various fruit drinks, like **spremute di agrumi** *(spreh-moo-teh ah-groo-mee)* (fresh-squeezed juice, often from citrus fruits), **succhi naturali** *(sook-kee nah-too-rah-lee)* (natural juice), **frullati** *(frool-lah-tee)* (mixed fruit juice), **frappé** *(frahp-peh)* (frappé, which can be a fruit milk shake or a frozen fruit shake) or **infusi di frutta** *(een-foo-zee dee froot-tah)* (fruit infusions).

Words to Know

cioccolato [m]	chok-koh-lah-toh	chocolate
crema [f]	kreh-mah	cream
cono [m]	koh-noh	cone
gelato [m]	jeh-lah-toh	ice cream
dieta [f]	dee-eh-tah	diet

Shopping for Food

People do their food shopping in a **supermercato** *(soo-pehr-mehr-kah-toh)* (supermarket) even if there are other places to get it. But many Italian cities have markets on the street and additionally, little shops, called **alimentari** *(ah-lee-mehn-tah-ree),* where you can get everything from **latte** *(laht-teh)* (milk) over **biscotti** *(bees-koht-tee)* (cookies) to all sorts of assorted **salumi** *(sah-loo-mee)* (cold meats), **formaggi** *(fohr-mahj-jee)* (cheeses), and **pane** *(pah-neh)* (bread). These corner markets, with their limited selection of goods, are perfect for supplementing provisions between regular shopping trips.

You may choose to pick out your **carne** *(kahr-neh)* (meat) at a **macellaio** *(mah-chehl-lah-yoh)* (butcher shop) and to get your fresh **prodotti** *(proh-doht-tee)* (produce) at a farmers' market, and your **pane** *(pah-neh)* (bread) at a **panetteria** *(pah-neht-teh-ree-ah)* (bakery), but you can find everything in a supermarket. One thing is for sure: You'll probably always find fresh food. Supermarkets offer non-food products, too. Big ones in Italy also have clothes and televisions.

From the butcher shop you might select items like the following:

- **agnello** *(ah-<u>nyehl</u>-loh)* (lamb)
- **anatra** *(<u>ah</u>-nah-trah)* (duck)
- **coniglio** *(koh-<u>nee</u>-lyoh)* (rabbit)
- **fegato** *(<u>feh</u>-gah-toh)* (liver — if not specified, calf liver)
- **maiale** *(mah-<u>yah</u>-leh)* (pork)
- **manzo** *(<u>mahn</u>-zoh)* (beef)
- **oca** *(<u>oh</u>-kah)* (goose)
- **pollo** *(<u>pohl</u>-loh)* (chicken)
- **vitello** *(vee-<u>tehl</u>-loh)* (veal)
- **bistecca** *(bees-<u>tehk</u>-kah)* (steak)
- **cotoletta** *(koh-toh-<u>leht</u>-tah)* (cutlet)
- **filetto** *(fee-<u>leht</u>-toh)* (filet steak)

When you go **al mercato** *(ahl mehr-<u>kah</u>-toh)* (to the market) — and here, we're talking about an open-air farmers' market — to buy food, you primarily find **frutta** *(<u>froot</u>-tah)* (fruits) and **verdura** *(vehr-<u>doo</u>-rah)* (vegetables). Table 5-1 lists fruits that you can get in **estate** *(ehs-<u>tah</u>-teh)* (summer) and in **autunno** *(ah-oo-<u>toon</u>-noh)* (fall), **agrumi** *(ah-<u>groo</u>-mee)* (citrus fruits), and fruits you can get **tutto l'anno** *(<u>toot</u>-toh <u>lahn</u>-noh)* (year-round). We give you the forms in singular and plural.

Of course you know that eating plenty of fruits and vegetables is important because they are so rich in **vitamine** *(vee-tah-<u>mee</u>-neh)* vitamins.

Table 5-1	Fruits and Vegetables	
Italian/Plural	*Pronunciation*	*Translation*
albicocca/albicocche [f]	ahl-bee-<u>kohk</u>-kah/-keh	apricot
ananas [m]	<u>ah</u>-nah-nahs	pineapple
arancia/arance [f]	ah-<u>rahn</u>-chah/-cheh	orange
asparago/i [m]	ah-<u>spah</u>-rah-goh/-jee	asparagus
banana/e [f]	bah-<u>nah</u>-nah/-neh	banana
broccoli [m]	<u>brohk</u>-koh-lee	broccoli
carota/e [f]	kah-<u>roh</u>-tah/-teh	carrot

Italian/Plural	Pronunciation	Translation
cavolo/i [m]	<u>kah</u>-voh-loh/-lee	cabbage
ciliegia/e [f]	chee-lee-<u>eh</u>-jah/-jeh	cherry
cocomero/i [m]	koh-<u>koh</u>-meh-roh/-ree	watermelon
fico/fichi [m]	<u>fee</u>-koh/-kee	fig
fragola/e [f]	<u>frah</u>-goh-lah/-leh	strawberry
fungo/funghi [m]	<u>foon</u>-goh/-gee	mushroom
limone/i [m]	lee-<u>moh</u>-neh/-nee	lemon
mela/e [f]	meh-lah/-leh	apple
melanzana/e [f]	meh-lahn-<u>zah</u>-nah/-neh	eggplant
melone/i [m]	meh-<u>loh</u>-neh/-nee	melon
peperone/i [m]	peh-peh-roh-neh/-nee	pepper
pera/e [f]	peh-rah/-reh	pear
pesca/pesche [f]	<u>pehs</u>-kah/-keh	peach
pomodoro/i [m]	poh-moh-<u>doh</u>-roh/-ree	tomato
pompelmo/i [m]	pohm-<u>pehl</u>-moh/-mee	grapefruit
prugna/e [f]	<u>proo</u>-nyah/-nyeh	plum
spinaci [m]	spee-<u>nah</u>-chee	spinach
uva [f]	<u>oo</u>-vah	grape
zucchine/i [f/m]	dzook-kee-neh/-nee	zucchini

Don't think that all restaurants serve fresh fish. Sometimes the **pesce** (*peh-sheh)* (fish) is frozen; this is particularly true in big cities. Basically you get good fresh fish when you are close to the sea or a lake. To be sure, the better restaurants have good fish, when they offer it. Getting fresh fish certainly depends on the region and the level of the restaurant. If you are in doubt, it's better to ask somebody or to have a look at a restaurant guide. Better safe than sorry! However, when you're close to the sea, you can virtually be sure to get fresh fish. You can always ask:

> **Dove si può mangiare pesce fresco?**
> *<u>doh</u>-veh see poo-<u>oh</u> mahn-<u>jah</u>-reh <u>peh</u>-sheh <u>frehs</u>-koh*
> Where can we eat fresh fish?

If you finally happen on a good fish restaurant, you can order what your palate desires:

- **acciughe fresche** *(ahch-choo-geh frehs-keh)* (fresh anchovies)
- **calamari** *(kah-lah-mah-ree)* (squid)
- **merluzzo** *(mehr-loot-tsoh)* (cod)
- **polpo/polipo** *(pohl-poh poh-lee-poh)* (octopus)
- **pesce spada** *(peh-sheh spah-dah)* (swordfish)
- **sogliola** *(soh-lyoh-lah)* (sole)
- **spigola** *(spee-goh-lah)* (bass)
- **tonno fresco** *(tohn-noh frehs-koh)* (fresh tuna)
- **frutti di mare** *(froot-tee dee mah-reh)* (seafood)
- **cozze** *(koht-tseh)* (mussels)
- **vongole** *(vohn-goh-leh)* (clams)
- **crostacei** *(krohs-tah-cheh-ee)* (shellfish)
- **aragosta** *(ah-rah-gohs-tah)* (lobster)
- **gamberetti** *(gahm-beh-reht-tee)* (shrimp)
- **gamberi** *(gahm-beh-ree)* (prawns)
- **granchi** *(grahn-kee)* (crab)

In a **panetteria** *(pah-neht-teh-ree-ah)* (bakery), you can try all sorts of different kinds of **pane** *(pah-neh)* (bread), ranging from **il pane integrale** (whole wheat bread) to **dolci** *(dohl-chee)* (pastries).

In most Italian bakeries, you can also find **pizza al taglio** *(peet-tsah ahl tah-lyoh)* (slices of pizza), and pay according to weight. You can choose between **pizza bianca** *(peet-tsah bee-ahn-kah)* (white pizza) — that is, pizza topped only with olive oil — and **pizza rossa** *(peet-tsah rohs-sah)* (red pizza), which is topped with tomatoes or tomato sauce. The flavor can vary from bakery to bakery, as it does from region to region.

The past few years in Italy have seen bread emerge as a fashion. Once Italians preferred white bread, but now there are so many different sorts and tastes — and varying from region to region — that it's hard to know all the names.

CULTURAL WISDOM

The typical Italian market

You may know typical Italian markets from a vacation or maybe watching a film. And these markets really are typical! Some of them seem to be made exclusively for tourists, but Italians themselves use them. In the case of a big market you can get food, of course, and also dresses, leather bags, compact disks, and so on and so forth. These markets can be really chaotic with masses of people pushing you through the streets, and woe betide you if you want to go in the other direction!

Smaller markets in the center of the city have a less dramatic atmosphere. Normally you find fresh fruit, vegetables, and sometimes fish. Some of these markets are open one day a week, but some operate every day, depending on the location. In general these markets are bustling with life and exude a typical Italian atmosphere. People talk to each other and the vegetable seller might ask you **"Da dove viene?"** *(dah doh-veh vee-eh-neh)* (Where do you come from?) when she notices that you're foreign.

In most cases, you have to say what you'd like to have, and the seller will pick it out for you. Prices are according to weight, usually by **chilo** *(kee-loh)* (kilo), and the seller weighs the goods, so you have to trust him. Occasionally you find little baskets or paper bags, which indicate that you can choose your own **frutta** *(froot-tah)* (fruit) or **la verdura** *(vehr-doo-rah)* (vegetables).

A recently passed law in Italy prevents consumers from touching food before buying it. On the one hand, you can't really feel your fruit before buying it, but on the other hand, you also know that your apple hadn't been touched by everybody.

You may think that haggling and bargaining are common at Italian markets, but this is not true. The fruit seller may **mandarti a quel paese** *(mahn-dahr-tee ah koo-ehl pah-eh-zeh)* (send you to blazes) if you try to haggle over the price of his apples.

Talkin' the Talk

This dialogue could take place in one of those bakeries. **Il fornaio** *(eel fohr-nah-yoh)* (the baker) is talking to his clients:

Sig.ra Belli: **Mi da un chilo di pane integrale?**
                 mee dah oon kee-loh dee pah-neh een-teh-grah-leh
                 Would you give me one kilo of whole wheat bread?

Baker: **Ecco a lei.**
                 ehk-koh ah lay
                 Here you are.

Sig.ra Belli:	**Quant'è?**
	koo-ahn-teh
	How much is it?

Baker:	**Duemila e tre.**
	doo-eh-mee-lah eh treh
	Two thousand and three (hundred).

(To another customer):	**Desidera?**
	deh-zee-deh-rah
	What would you like?

Paolo:	**Un pezzo di pizza rossa.**
	oon peht-tsoh dee peet-tsah rohs-sah
	A piece of pizza with tomatoes.

Baker:	**Così va bene?**
	koh-zee vah beh-neh
	Is this okay?

Paolo:	**Sì. Quanto pago?**
	see koo-ahn-toh pah-goh
	Yes. How much do I pay?

Baker:	**Mille e cinque.**
	meel-leh eh cheen-koo-eh
	One thousand five (hundred).

You know that when you hear **un etto** (*oon eht-toh*), it means 100 grams. **Mezz'etto** (*meht-tseht-toh*) is 50 grams, because **mezzo** (*meht-tsoh*) means "half." Likewise, a **mezzo chilo** (*meht-tsoh kee-loh*) is half a kilo.

You say **mille** only in the case of *one* thousand. In all the other cases, you say **mila** (*mee-lah*) (thousands). Assume that you owe 1,500 lire for your food. The cashier may say something like **"milleecinque"** (*meel-leh-eh-cheen-koo-eh*) (one thousand five hundred), which sounds like one word. Actually, the correct form is **mille e cinque** (*meel-leh eh cheen-koo-eh*).

Talkin' the Talk

In this dialogue, Guilio buys fruit from a fruit vendor.

Giulio:	**Mi da un chilo di ciliegie?**
	mee dah oon kee-loh dee chee-lee-eh-jeh
	Could you give me one kilo of cherries?

Vendor: **Sono un po' di più.**
soh-noh oon poh dee pee-oo
They are a little bit more.

Giulio: **Va bene.**
vah beh-neh
Okay.

Vendor: **Che altro?**
keh ahl-troh
What else?

Giulio: **Quanto vengono le albicocche?**
koo-ahn-toh vehn-goh-noh leh ahl-bee-kohk-keh
How much do apricots cost?

Vendor: **Quattromila.**
koo-aht-troh-mee-lah
Four thousand.

Giulio: **Sono carissime!**
soh-noh kah-rees-see-meh
They are very expensive!

Vendor: **Perché sono le prime!**
pehr-keh soh-noh leh pree-meh
Because they are the first ones (of the season)!
Ne provi una.
neh proh-vee oo-nah
Try one.

Giulio: **È dolcissima!**
eh dohl-chees-see-mah
It's very sweet!
Ne prendo mezzo chilo.
neh prehn-doh mehd-dzoh kee-loh
I'll take half a kilo of them.

Vendor: **Altro?**
ahl-troh
Anything else?

Giulio: **Basta così. Quant'è?**
bahs-tah koh-zee koo-ahn-teh
That's enough. How much is it?

Vendor:	**Sono cinquemila.**
	soh-noh cheen-koo-eh-mee-lah
	It's five thousand.

In this dialogue, Giulio asks **quanto vengono** (*koo-ahn-toh vehn-goh-noh*) (how much do they come?), when what he wants to know is **quanto costano** (*koo-ahn-toh kohs-tah-noh*) (how much do they cost?). This is really no big deal; we just wanted to draw your attention to the verb.

Giving a discount is a nice gesture of the seller, and you frequently find this happening at smaller markets.

Words to Know

l' alimentari [m]	lah-lee-mehn-tah-ree	food shop
la drogheria [f]	lah droh-geh-ree-ah	grocery store
la frutteria [f]	lah froot-teh-ree-ah	produce store; greengrocer
il mercato [m]	eel mehr-kah-toh	market
la panetteria [f]/ il forno [m]	lah pah-neht-teh-ree-ah/ eel fohr-noh	bakery
la pescheria [f]	lah pehs-keh-ree-ah	fish store
la salumeria [f]	lah sah-loo-meh-ree-ah	delicatessen

Fun & Games

We talk a lot about food in this chapter. To reward ourselves at the end, we allow ourselves a really good fruit shake. Fill in the Italian for various fruits following. Have fun!

1. pineapple: _ _ _ _ _ _
2. cherry: _ _ _ _ _ _ _ _
3. grape: _ _ _
4. pear: _ _ _ _
5. watermelon: _ _ _ _ _ _ _ _
6. strawberry: _ _ _ _ _ _ _

Answers: 1. ananas, 2. ciliegia, 3. uva, 4. pera, 5. cocomero, 6. fragola

Chapter 6

Shopping Made Easy

. . . .

In This Chapter

▶ Shopping at the department store

▶ Getting the right size

▶ Using definite articles

▶ Finding colors, materials, and accessories to suit you

▶ Trying on shoes

. . . .

Italy is famous throughout the world for its taste and fashion sense, as well as for the **stilisti** *(stee-lees-tee)* (designers) — such as **Armani** *(ahr-mah-nee)*, **Ferré** *(fehr-reh)*, and **Valentino** *(vah-lehn-tee-noh)* — who build on that reputation. Italians like to dress well. Looking at them, you will suddenly feel like going shopping and buying some of these beautiful goods so that you can look as good. And what better place to shop for gorgeous apparel than in Italy, which leads Europe in fashion and shoe production?

Incidentally: In Italian, a famous brand is called **la griffe** *(lah greef)* (a French word) or **la firma** *(lah feer-mah)* that means literally "the signature." So to say that a good is "signed" by a famous stylist we say that it is **griffato** *(greef-fah-toh)* or **firmato** *(feer-mah-toh)* "signed."

Clothing Yourself

Shopping can be an informative and fun way to learn about a culture. Discovering different styles of dress and trying products you don't usually see is both interesting and educational. At any rate, shopping in Italy is fantastic. You can explore lots of boutiques and designer shops, as well as numerous department stores.

Departmentalizing your shopping

North Americans have access to huge **centri commerciali** (*chehn-tree kohm-mehr-chee-ah-lee*) (shopping malls), where you really can find everything. In Italy, people shop in **grandi magazzini** (*grahn-dee mah-gaht-tsee-nee*) (department stores), which are tiny compared to American ones. The biggest Italian department stores are **Standa** (*stahn-dah*), **Upim** (*oo-peem*), and **Rinascente** (*ree-nah-shehn-teh*). **Rinascente** is the priciest, but you can find all three in the downtown area of virtually every Italian city and all three carry all kinds of stuff.

Incidentally, what's shopping in Italian? They say **fare la spesa** (*fah-reh la speh-zah*) (Literally: making the shopping) when you buy food, and **fare spese** for everything else. Good news is that you only have to conjugate the verb **fare.** Here we go:

Conjugation	Pronunciation
io faccio	*ee-oh fahch-choh*
tu fai	*too fah-ee*
lui/lei fa	*loo-ee/lay fah*
noi facciamo	*noh-ee fahch-chah-moh*
voi fate	*voh-ee fah-teh*
loro fanno	*loh-roh fahn-noh*

In any department store, some elementary signs — like the one over the door reading **uscita di sicurezza** (*oo-shee-tah dee see-koo-reht-tsah*) (emergency exit) — can be very useful. Some of these are:

- **entrata** (*ehn-trah-tah*) (entrance)
- **uscita** (*oo-shee-tah*) (exit)
- **spingere** (*speen-jeh-reh*) (to push)
- **tirare** (*tee-rah-reh*) (to pull)
- **orario di apertura** (*oh-rah-ree-oh dee ah-pehr-too-rah*) (business hours)
- **aperto** (*ah-pehr-toh*) (open)
- **chiuso** (*kee-oo-zoh*) (closed)
- **la scala mobile** (*lah skah-lah moh-bee-leh*) (escalator)
- **l'ascensore** (*lah-shehn-soh-reh*) (elevator)
- **la cassa** (*lah kahs-sah*) (cash register)

Italian department stores offer you a great variety of products and still maintain an air of typical Italian style. Prices are clearly labeled in both lire and euros and include sales tax. Often, during **saldi** *(sahl-dee)* (sales) the **il prezzo** *(eel preht-tsoh)* (price) on the label is already reduced, but you may find tags reading **saldi alla cassa** *(sahl-dee ahl-lah kahs-sah)* (reduction at the cash register). For the most part, it's possible to pay with your credit card, but in general Italians like to be paid **in contanti** *(een kohn-than-tee)* (cash) — especially in little places.

The signs pointing to the various **reparti** *(reh-pahr-tee)* (departments) may or may not include the word **da** *(dah)* (for), as in **abbigliamento da donna** *(ahb-bee-lyah-mehn-toh dah dohn-nah)* (women's wear) and **abbigliamento da uomo** *(ahb-bee-lyah-mehn-toh dah oo-oh-moh)* (menswear). But even without the *da*, the signs are pretty clear. Some other departments you may be interested in are:

- **intimo donna** *(een-tee-moh dohn-nah)* (ladies' intimate apparel)
- **intimo uomo** *(een-tee-moh oo-oh-moh)* (men's intimate apparel)
- **accessori** *(ahch-chehs-soh-ree)* (accessories)
- **profumeria** *(proh-foo-meh-ree-ah)* (perfumery)
- **articoli da toletta** *(ahr-tee-koh-lee dah toh-leht-tah)* (toiletries)
- **casalinghi** *(kah-sah-leen-gee)* (housewares)
- **biancheria per la casa** *(bee-ahn-keh-ree-ah pehr lah kah-sah)* (household linens and towels)
- **articoli sportivi** *(ahr-tee-koh-lee spohr-tee-vee)* (sports equipment)
- **articoli da regalo** *(ahr-tee-koh-lee dah reh-gah-loh)* (gifts)

Talkin' the Talk

Here, a clerk is kept busy giving directions for various departments.

Sig.ra Verdi: **Sto cercando l'abbigliamento da bambino.**
stoh chehr-kahn-doh lahb-bee-lyah-mehn-toh dah bahm-bee-noh
I'm looking for children's wear.

Clerk: **Al secondo piano, Sulla destra quando esce dall'ascensore.**
ahl seh-kohn-doh pee-ah-noh sool-lah dehs-trah koo-ahn-doh eh-sheh dahl lah-shehn-soh-reh
On the second floor, go right when you get off the elevator.

Sig. Marchi: **Devo cambiare un paio di pantaloni. Dove dezo andare?**
deh-voh kahm-bee-ah-reh oon pah-yoh dee pahn-tah-loh-nee doh-veh deh-zoh ahn-dah-reh
I need to return a pair of trousers. Where should I go?

Clerk: **Deve rivolgersi al commesso del reparto uomo.**
deh-veh ree-vohl-jehr-see ahl kohm-mehs-soh dehl reh-pahr-toh oo-oh-moh
Please see the clerk in the men's department.

Anna: **Vorrei provare questi abiti. Dove sono i camerini, per favore?**
vohr-ray proh-vah-reh koo-ehs-tee ah-bee-tee doh-veh soh-noh ee kah-meh-ree-nee pehr fah-voh-reh
I want to try on these dresses. Where are the fitting rooms, please?

Clerk: **Vede l'uscita di sicurezza? I camerini sono sulla sinistra.**
veh-deh loo-shee-tah dee see-koo-reht-tsah ee kah-meh-ree-nee soh-noh sool-lah see-nees-trah
Do you see the emergency exit there? The fitting rooms are to the left.

Sig.ra Alberti: **C'è un reparto casalinghi?**
cheh oon reh-pahr-toh kah-sah-leen-gee
Do you have a housewares department?

Clerk: **Sì, è su questo piano dopo le scarpe.**
see eh soo koo-ehs-toh pee-ah-noh doh-poh leh skahr-peh
Yes, we do. It's on this floor, past the shoe section.

Sergio: **Dov'è la scala mobile?**
doh-veh lah skah-lah moh-bee-leh
Where is the escalator?

Clerk: **Dietro a questo bancone.**
dee-_eh_-troh ah koo-_ehs_-toh bahn-_koh_-neh
Behind this counter.

Sergio: **Grazie.**
grah-tsee-eh
Thank you.

Words to Know

centro commerciale [m]	_chehn_-troh kohm-mehr-_chah_-leh	shopping mall
grande magazzino [m]	_grahn_-dee mah-gahd-_dzee_-noh	department store
camerini [f]	kah-meh-_ree_-nee	fitting rooms
libreria [f]	lee-breh-_ree_-ah	bookshop

Avere bisogno di _(ah-_veh_-reh bee-_zoh_-nyoh dee)_ (to need) is a frequent expression in Italian. Above all, you use it in any kind of store. The form that you use as a speaker goes like this:

Ho bisogno di . . . _(oh bee-zoh-nyoh dee)_ (I need . . .)

And you conjugate it like so:

Conjugation	*Pronunciation*
io ho bisogno	_ee_-oh oh bee-_zoh_-nyoh
tu hai bisogno	too _ah_-ee bee-_zoh_-nyoh
lui/lei ha bisogno	_loo_-ee/lay ah bee-_zoh_-nyoh
noi abbiamo bisogno	_noh_-ee ahb-bee-_ah_-moh bee-_zoh_-nyoh
voi avete bisogno	_voh_-ee ah-_veh_-teh bee-_zoh_-nyoh
loro hanno bisogno	_loh_-roh _ahn_-noh bee-_zoh_-nyoh

Talkin' the Talk

 Marisa is looking for a dress but needs some advice from the salesperson.

Marisa:	**Scusi?**
	skoo-zee
	Excuse me?
Saleswoman:	**Prego, signora!**
	preh-goh see-nyoh-rah
	Yes, madam!
Marisa:	**Mi può aiutare? Sto cercando un vestito.**
	mee poo-oh ah-yoo-tah-reh stoh chehr-kahn-doh oon vehs-tee-toh
	Can you help me? I'm looking for a dress.
Saleswoman:	**Elegante?**
	eh-leh-gahn-teh
	Elegant?
Marisa:	**No, per tutti i giorni.**
	noh pehr toot-tee ee johr-nee
	No, for everyday.
Saleswoman:	**Vediamo . . .**
	veh-dee-ah-moh
	Let's see . . .

When you're in a store and have a question or need some advice, you turn to **la commessa** [f] _(lah kohm-mehs-sah)_ or **il commesso** [m] _(eel kohm-mehs-soh)_ (the sales clerk) and say, **Mi può aiutare, per favore** _(mee poo-oh ah-yoo-tah-reh pehr fah-voh-reh)_ (Can you help me, please?) Of course, if you're just looking and a salesperson asks, "**Posso essere d'aiuto?**" _(pohs-soh ehs-seh-reh dah-yoo-toh)_ or "**Desidera?**" _(deh-zee-deh-rah)_ (Can I be of help?; Can I help you?), you answer, "**Sto solo dando un'occhiata, grazie.**" _(stoh soh-loh dahn-doh oon-ohk-kee-ah-tah)_ (I'm just looking, thank you.)

Words to Know

vestiti [m]	vehs-_tee_-tee	clothes
abito [m]	_ah_-bee-toh	suit
camicetta [f]	kah-mee-_cheht_-tah	blouse
camicia [f]	kah-_mee_-chah	shirt
cappotto [m]	kahp-_poht_-toh	coat
completo [m]	kohm-_pleht_-toh	skirt or pants and blouse
giacca [f]	_jahk_-kah	jacket; sports jacket
gonna [f]	_gohn_-nah	skirt
impermeabile [m]	eem-pehr-meh-_ah_-bee-leh	raincoat
paio di jeans [m]	_pah_-yoh dee jeans	pair of jeans
maglia [f]	_mah_-lyah	jumper
maglietta [f]; T-shirt [f]	mahl-_yeht_-tah; _tee_-shirt	T-shirt
pantaloni [m]	pahn-tah-_loh_-nee	pants
tailleur [m]	tah-_lyehr_	skirt or pants and jacket
vestito [m]	vehs-_tee_-toh	dress

Sizing up Italian sizes

You know the problem: Whenever you go to another country, and this is particularly true in Europe, the sizes — called **taglie** (_tah_-lyeh) or **misure** (mee-_zoo_-reh) in Italy — change and you never know which one corresponds to yours. Table 6-1 helps you with this problem by giving you the most common sizes. If you don't fit into any of the sizes in the tables, just go on counting up or down using the same system.

Table 6-1	Clothing Sizes	
Italian Size	*American Size*	*Canadian Size*
Women's dress sizes		
40	4	6
42	6	8
44	8	10
46	10	12
48	12	14
50	14	16
Men's suit sizes		
48	38	40
50	40	42
52	42	44
54	44	46
56	46	48
58	48	50

In Italy you won't have any difficulties with sizes like S, M, L, and XL, because they are used the same way: S for small, M for medium, L for large, and XL for extra large.

Talkin' the Talk

 Giovanna has found the skirt she's been looking for. She asks the saleswoman if she can try it on.

Giovanna: **Posso provare questa gonna?**
pohs-soh proh-vah-reh koo-ehs-tah gohn-nah
May I try on this skirt?

Saleswoman: **Certo. Che taglia porta?**
chehr-toh keh tah-lyah pohr-tah
Sure. Which size do you wear?

Giovanna:	**La quarantadue.**
	lah koo-ah-rahn-tah-doo-eh
	Forty-two.

Saleswoman:	**Forse è un po' piccola.**
	fohr-seh eh oon poh peek-koh-lah
	Perhaps it's a little bit too small.

Giovanna:	**Me la provo.**
	meh lah proh-voh
	I'll try it on.

Giovanna returns from the dressing room.

Saleswoman:	**Va bene?**
	vah beh-neh
	Does it fit?

Giovanna:	**E' troppo stretta. Avete una taglia più grande?**
	eh trohp-poh streht-tah ah-veh-teh oo-nah tah-lyah pee-oo grahn-deh
	It's too tight. Do you have it in a larger size?

Saleswoman:	**Nella sua taglia solo blu.**
	nehl-lah soo-ah tah-lyah soh-loh bloo
	In your size, only in blue.

Giovanna:	**No, il blu non mi sta bene.**
	noh eel bloo nohn mee stah beh-neh
	No, blue doesn't suit me.

Talking definitely: Definite articles

When you're shopping for something, even if you're looking for something as specific as a blue skirt, you don't say, "I'm looking for the blue skirt." Instead, you say that you're looking for *a* blue skirt, where the *a* is an ***indefinite article*** showing that you don't have a specific object in mind — you need to look at *a* skirt here and *a* skirt there before you find ***the*** skirt you want.

You use exactly the same construction in Italian: Italian also uses definite articles — il, la, and l' — as well as indefinite articles, corresponding to the English *a* and *an*. In English, whether you use *a* or *an* depends on what sound the following word starts with — *an* animal, *a* car. The same is true in Italian with just one more condition: The article has to match the gender of the word: Feminine words, which usually end with -*a*, use ***una*** and masculine words ending with -*o* use ***un***. So where you use **la** [f] or **il** or **l'**[m] to indicate ***the*** item, you use ***una*** [f] or ***un*** [m] to indicate ***an*** item.

Just one more thing: A few foreign words end with a consonant — **la T-shirt** [f] and **il gilet** [m] *(eel jee-leh)* (the waistcoat) for example — so you can't tell their gender from the ending. There is no rule; you just need to remember them!

Talkin' the Talk

And just another little dialogue. By now, you're an expert in sizes.

Alberto: **Mi posso provare questa giacca?**
             mee pohs-soh proh-vah-reh koo-ehs-tah jahk-kah
             May I try on this jacket?

Salesman: **Certo, è la sua misura?**
             chehr-toh eh lah soo-ah mee-zoo-rah
             Sure, is it your size?

Alberto: **Che taglia è: la M?**
             keh tah-lyah eh lah ehm-meh
             Which size is it: M?

Salesman: **È la L. Ma forse le sta bene.**
             eh lah ehl-leh mah fohr-seh leh stah beh-neh
             No, it's a large. But perhaps it fits.

Alberto: **È troppo lunga!**
             eh trohp-poh loon-gah
             It's too long!

Salesman: **Sì, è vero.**
             see eh veh-roh
             Yes, it's true.

Alberto: **Non c'è più piccola?**
             nohn cheh pee-oo peek-koh-lah
             Isn't there a smaller one?

Salesman: **No, mi dispiace.**
             noh mee dees-pee-ah-cheh
             No, I'm sorry.

Coloring your words

Of course, knowing some **colori** _(koh-loh-ree)_ (colors) is important. Describing a color using only your hands and feet would be difficult. We want to make life a little easier for you, so we put the most common colors in Table 6-2.

Two important words as far as colors are concerned are **scuro/a/i/e** _(skoo-roh/rah/ree/reh)_ (dark) and **chiaro/a/i/e** _(kee-ah-roh/rah/ree/reh)_ (light). Don't worry over all these vowels at the end of these words. You only have to use one of them at a time according to the gender and case of the noun it modifies. Use **-o** with male singular nouns; **-a** stands for female singular, and **-i** and **-e** are for male plural and female plural, respectively. The same is true for the following colors, but to avoid making it too confusing we just give you the male singular form.

Table 6-2	Colors	
Italian	_Pronunciation_	_Translation_
arancione	ah-rahn-choh-neh	orange
azzurro	ahd-dzoor-roh	sky blue
beige	beh-jeh	beige
bianco	bee-ahn-koh	white
blu	bloo	blue
giallo	jahl-loh	yellow
grigio	gree-joh	grey
marrone	mahr-roh-neh	brown
nero	neh-roh	black
rosa	roh-zah	pink
rosso	rohs-soh	red
verde	vehr-deh	green
viola	vee-oh-lah	purple

Talkin' the Talk

 Matteo is looking for a new suit for the summer.

Salesman: **La posso aiutare?**
              lah <u>pohs</u>-soh ah-yoo-<u>tah</u>-reh
              May I help you?

Matteo: **Sì. Cerco un abito sportivo.**
              see <u>chehr</u>-koh oon <u>ah</u>-bee-toh spohr-<u>tee</u>-voh
              Yes. I'm looking for a suit.

Salesman: **Benissimo. Per l'estate?**
              beh-<u>nees</u>-see-moh pehr lehs-<u>tah</u>-teh
              Very well. For the summer?

Matteo: **Sì, leggero.**
              see lehj-<u>jeh</u>-roh
              Yes, lightweight.

Salesman: **Ecco . . . Provi questo.**
              <u>ehk</u>-koh <u>proh</u>-vee koo-<u>ehs</u>-toh
              Here you are . . . Try this.

Matteo returns with a smile on his face.

Salesman: **Va bene?**
              vah <u>beh</u>-neh
              Okay?

Matteo: **Sì, mi va bene. Lo prendo.**
              see mee va <u>beh</u> neh prehn-doh
              Yes, it fits me well. I'll take it.

Materializing fabrics

Of course, what clothing is made of makes a big difference to the price, dura-bility and comfort. For clothing, you can choose between **fibre naturali** *(<u>fee</u>-breh nah-too-<u>rah</u>-lee)* (natural fibers), or **fibre sintetiche** *(<u>fee</u>-breh seen-teh-<u>tee</u>-keh)* (synthetic fibers) such as **la viscosa** *(<u>lah</u> vees-<u>koh</u>-zah)* (rayon) and **l' acrilico** *(lah-<u>kree</u>-lee-koh)* (acrylic). If you want the fabric to be a hun-dred percent cotton, for example, you can ask, **"È puro cotone?** *(eh <u>poo</u>-roh koh-<u>toh</u>-neh)* (Is it pure cotton?) To which you may get an answer like: **"Il vestito è di lino."** *(eel vehs-<u>tee</u>-toh eh dee <u>lee</u>-noh)* (The dress is linen.)

Words to Know

camoscio [m]	kah-<u>moh</u>-shoh	suede
cotone [m]	koh-<u>toh</u>-neh	cotton
flanella [f]	flah-<u>nehl</u>-lah	flannel
fodera [f]	<u>foh</u>-deh-rah	lining
lana [f]	<u>lah</u>-nah	wool
lino [m]	<u>lee</u>-noh	linen
pelle [f]	<u>pehl</u>-leh	leather
seta [f]	<u>seh</u>-tah	silk
velluto [m]	vehl-<u>loo</u>-toh	velvet
viscosa [f]	vees-<u>koh</u>-zah	rayon

Accessorizing

Of course, you want to decorate your outfit with beautiful **accessori** *(ahch-chehs-<u>soh</u>-ree)* (accessories) to give it that final touch. We list some of them to give you an impression of the variety:

- **berretto** *(behr-<u>reht</u>-toh)* (cap)
- **borsa** *(<u>bohr</u>-sah)* (bag)
- **calze** *(<u>kahl</u>-tseh)* (stockings)
- **calzini** *(kahl-<u>tsee</u>-nee)* (socks)
- **cappello** *(kahp-<u>pehl</u>-loh)* (hat)
- **cintura** *(cheen-<u>too</u>-rah)* (belt)
- **collant** *(kohl-<u>lahn</u>)* (tights)
- **cravatta** *(krah-<u>vaht</u>-tah)* (tie)
- **guanti** *(goo-<u>ahn</u>-tee)* (gloves)
- **ombrello** *(ohm-<u>brehl</u>-loh)* (umbrella)
- **sciarpa** *(<u>shahr</u>-pah)* (scarf)

If you want to go shopping and ask for one of these accessories, you could do it like this:

Talkin' the Talk

Giovanni just wants to buy a scarf. He asks the sales clerk for help.

Giovanni: **Vorrei una sciarpa rossa.**
vohr-ray oo-nah shahr-pah rohs-sah
I'd like a red scarf.

Sales clerk: **Ne abbiamo una bellissima, di cachemire.**
neh ahb-bee-ah-moh oo-nah behl-lees-see-mah dee kahsh-meer
We have a very beautiful cashmere one.

Giovanni: **Deve essere carissima.**
deh-veh ehs-seh-reh kah-rees-see-mah
It must be very expensive.

Sales clerk: **Sì, ma è in saldo. Non ha bisogno di guanti?**
see mah eh een sahl-doh nohn ah bee-zoh-nyoh dee goo-ahn-tee
Yes, but it is on sale. Don't you need gloves?

Giovanni: **Veramente no.**
veh-rah-mehn-teh noh
Not really.

Sales clerk: **Gardi questi: un'occasione.**
goo-ahr-dee koo-ehs-tee oo-nohk-kah-zee-oh-neh
Look at these: a bargain.

Giovanni: **Sono veramente belli.**
soh-noh veh-rah-mehn-teh behl-lee
They're really beautiful.

Sales clerk: **Li vuole provare?**
lee voo-oh-leh proh-vah-reh
Would you like to try them on?

Giovanni: **Sì.**
see
Yes.

Stepping out in style

Oh yes, this is important stuff. You know that Italy is the leader in the shoe industry. You won't believe what good taste Italians have in **scarpe** *(skahr-peh)* (shoes). If you travel to Italy, it is well worth your while to have a look into the various shoe shops you can find in Italian cities. You won't be disappointed and you may well find the shoes of your dreams, whether they be a regular **paio di scarpe** *(pah-yoh dee skahr-peh)* (pair of shoes), **pantofole** *(pahn-toh-foh-leh)* (slippers), **sandali** *(sahn-dah-lee)* (sandals), or **stivali** *(stee-vah-lee)* (boots).

When you try on shoes, some words you may need to use are:

- ✔ **stretta/e** *(streht-tah/teh)* (tight)
- ✔ **larga/e** *(lahr-gah/geh)* (loose)
- ✔ **corta/e** *(kohr-tah/teh)* (short)
- ✔ **lunga/e** *(loon-gah/geh)* (long)

Remember: Because **la scarpa** *(lah skahr-pah)* (the shoe) is female in Italian, we provide you with only the female endings for these adjectives, namely **-a** for singular, and **-e** for plural.

You may notice that Italian uses **numero** *(noo-meh-roh)* (number) to talk about shoes, but **taglia** *(tah-lyah)* or **misura** *(mee-soo-rah)* (size) to talk about clothes.

Talkin' the Talk

If you have seen the pair of shoes of your dreams **in vetrina** *(een veh-tree-nah)* (in the shop window) and you'd like to try them on, you can follow Michela's example:

Michela: · **Vorrei provare un paio di scarpe.**
vohr-ray proh-vah-reh oon pah-yoh dee skahr-peh
I'd like to try on a pair of shoes.

Saleswoman: **Quali sono?**
koo-ah-lee soh-noh
Which ones?

Michela: **Quelle blu, a destra.**
koo-ehl-leh bloo ah dehs-trah
Those there, on the right.

Saleswoman:	**Che numero porta?** *keh <u>noo</u>-meh-roh <u>pohr</u>-tah* Which size do you wear?
Michela:	**Trentasette.** *trehn-tah-<u>seht</u>-teh* Thirty-seven.
Saleswoman:	**Ecco qua. Un trentasette . . . È stretta?** *<u>ehk</u>-koh koo-<u>ah</u> oon trehn-tah-<u>seht</u>-teh eh <u>streht</u>-tah* Here we are. A 37 . . . Is it tight?
Michela:	**No. Sono comodissime.** *noh <u>soh</u>-noh koh-moh-<u>dees</u>-see-meh* No. They are very comfortable.
Saleswoman:	**È un'ottima pelle.** *eh oon-<u>oht</u>-tee-mah <u>pehl</u>-leh* They're made from very good leather.
Michela:	**Quanto vengono?** *koo-<u>ahn</u>-toh <u>vehn</u>-goh-noh* How much do they cost?
Saleswoman:	**Novantamila.** *noh-vahn-tah-<u>meel</u>-lah* Ninety thousand.
Michela:	**Hmm . . .**

Apropos **carina e cara** *(kah-<u>ree</u>-nah eh <u>kah</u>-rah)*, there are three words that are very similar and differ only in the endings:

- ✔ **cara** *(kah-rah)* means "expensive," but also in a abstract sense "dear." (beloved)
- ✔ **carina** *(kah-<u>ree</u>-nah)* has the sense of "nice (girl)."
- ✔ **carissima** *(kah-<u>rees</u>-see-mah)* means "dearest" and "very expensive."

Fun & Games

We give you a lot of information and vocabulary about clothes shopping in this chapter. See how many articles of clothing you can identify on the couple below.

1.
2.
3.
4.
5.

8.

7.

6.

Answers: 1. cappello, 2. camicia, 3. cravatta, 4. completo, 5. pantaloni, 6. scarpe, 7. gonna, 8. camicetta

Chapter 7

Having a Good Time Out on the Town

● ●

In This Chapter

▶ Learning the times of the day and the days of the week

▶ Enjoying movies, art, theater, and other forms of entertainment

▶ Giving and receiving invitations

● ●

Doing the town is always fun, whether you're visiting someplace new or playing **il turista** *(eel too-rees-tah)* (the tourist) in your own hometown. In this chapter, we give you all the information you need to take in cultural attractions and socialize.

In general, Italians are sociable people who enjoy having a good time. You see them having espressos together **al bar** *(ahl bahr)* (in the bar) or drinks at night **sulla piazza** *(sool-lah pee-aht-tsah)* (on the public square). Most Italians love to go out in the evening, crowding the streets until late at night. On the weekend, Italians like to go out in groups: They meet their **amici** *(ah-mee-chee)* (friends) and have enjoyable get-togethers.

Italy is a popular vacation destination, and Italian cities have a great variety of cultural offerings, from open-air festivals and classical music events to city-wide celebrations. The variety is endless, and fun is guaranteed.

Times of Day and Days of the Week

Arranging your social life — whether you want to go to a performance or invite someone to a party — requires knowing the days of the week and times of the day. Table 7-1 gives you the days of the week and the abbreviations for them.

You don't capitalize the days of the week in Italian as you do in English.

Table 7-1	Days of the Week	
Italian/Abbreviation	*Pronunciation*	*Translation*
domenica/do.	doh-<u>meh</u>-nee-kah	Sunday
lunedì/lun.	loo-neh-<u>dee</u>	Monday
martedì/mar.	mahr-teh-<u>dee</u>	Tuesday
mercoledì/mer.	mehr-koh-leh-<u>dee</u>	Wednesday
giovedì/gio.	joh-veh-<u>dee</u>	Thursday
venerdì/ven.	veh-nehr-<u>dee</u>	Friday
sabato/sab.	<u>sah</u>-bah-toh	Saturday

Knowing what time an event starts and being able to communicate that to your date is crucial. If you made a date **ieri** *(ee-<u>eh</u>-ree)* (yesterday), and arranged to meet **domani sera** *(doh-<u>mah</u>-nee <u>seh</u>-rah)* (tomorrow evening) **alle sette e mezza** *(<u>ahl</u>-leh <u>seht</u>-teh eh <u>mehd</u>-dzah)* (at seven-thirty), but you find out **oggi** *(<u>ohj</u>-jee)* (today) that the performance starts **alle sette** *(<u>ahl</u>-leh <u>seht</u>-teh)* (at seven o'clock), you need to tell your date that.

You can see here that half past seven is **le sette e mezza** *(leh <u>seht</u>-teh eh <u>mehd</u>-dzah)* (Literally: seven and a half). A quarter past eight is **le otto e un quarto** *(leh <u>oht</u>-toh eh oon koo-<u>ahr</u>-toh)* (Literally: eight and a quarter). **Un quarto alle nove** *(oon koo-<u>ahr</u>-toh <u>ahl</u>-leh <u>noh</u>-veh)* is a quarter to nine.

When you write the time in Italian, you go from 1.00 to 24.00 (or 00.00). But when you speak, you use just one to twelve, and if there's a doubt about a.m. or p.m., you can add **di mattina** *(dee maht-<u>tee</u>-nah)* (in the morning), **di pomeriggio** *(dee poh-meh-<u>reej</u>-joh)* (in the afternoon) or **di sera** *(dee <u>seh</u>-rah)* (in the evening).

You may find the Italian expression for "the day before yesterday" interesting. It is **l'altro ieri** *(<u>lahl</u>-troh ee-<u>eh</u>-ree),* which literally means "the other yesterday." "The day after tomorrow" is quite similar. It is **dopodomani** *(doh-poh-do-<u>mah</u>-nee); dopo (<u>doh</u>-poh)* means "after."

Some of the ways you might use these expressions are:

- ✔ **Il concerto è martedì sera.** *(eel kohn-<u>chehr</u>-toh eh mahr-teh-<u>dee</u> <u>seh</u>-rah)* (The concert is on Tuesday evening.)

- ✔ **Arrivo a Milano dopodomani.** *(ahr-<u>ree</u>-voh ah mee-<u>lah</u>-noh doh-poh-do-<u>mah</u>-nee)* (I arrive in Milan the day after tomorrow.)

✔ **Dov'eri ieri pomeriggio?** *(doh-veh-ree ee-eh-ree poh-meh-reej-joh)* (Where were you yesterday afternoon?)

✔ **Il concerto è stato l'altro ieri. L'hai perso!** *(eel kohn-chehr-toh eh stah-toh lahl-troh ee-eh-ree lah-ee pehr-soh)* (The concert was the day before yesterday. You missed it!)

Talking about dates and sight-seeing, you also need to know some verbs. The following tables conjugate **vedere** *(veh-deh-reh)* (to see) and **visitare** *(vee-zee-tah-reh)* (to visit):

Conjugation	*Pronunciation*
io vedo	ee-oh veh-doh
tu vedi	too veh-dee
lui/lei vede	loo-ee/lay veh-deh
noi vediamo	noh-ee veh-dee-ah-moh
voi vedete	voh-ee veh-deh-teh
loro vedono	loh-roh veh-doh-noh

Conjugation	*Pronunciation*
io visito	ee-oh vee-zee-toh
tu visiti	too vee-zee-tee
lui/lei visita	loo-ee/lay vee-zee-tah
noi visitiamo	noh-ee vee-zee-tee-ah-moh
voi visitate	voh-ee vee-zee-tah-teh
loro visitano	loh-roh vee-zee-tah-noh

Talkin' the Talk

Now you can see these expressions in a dialogue. Paola tries to convince Martino to visit the cathedral.

Paola: **Andiamo a visitare la cattedrale?**
ahn-dee-ah-moh ah vee-zee-tah-reh lah kaht-teh-drah-leh
Shall we visit the cathedral?

Martino: **Ma no, facciamo una passeggiata!**
mah noh fahch-chah-moh oo-nah pahs-sehj-jah-tah
No, let's take a walk!

Paola:	**Per il centro?** *pehr eel <u>chehn</u>-troh* Through the city center?
Martino:	**Sì, perché no?** *see pehr-<u>keh</u> noh* Yes, why not?
Paola:	**Ma la cattedrale è al centro!** *mah lah kaht-teh-<u>drah</u>-leh eh ahl <u>chehn</u>-troh* But the cathedral is in the center!
Martino:	**Allora mentre io passeggio . . .** *ahl-<u>loh</u>-rah <u>mehn</u>-treh <u>ee</u>-oh pahs-<u>sehj</u>-joh* In that case while I walk around . . .
Paola:	**. . . io visito la chiesa!** *<u>ee</u>-oh <u>vee</u>-zee-toh lah kee-<u>eh</u>-zah* . . . I can visit the church!

Acquiring Culture

No matter where you live or where you travel, most major cities have a weekly **pubblicazione** *(poob-blee-kah-tsee-<u>oh</u>-neh)* (publication) listing information about upcoming events. These publications include dates, descriptions, and time schedules for theaters, exhibitions, festivals, films, and so on. They also provide tips for shopping and restaurants. Of course, advertisements also fill the pages, but the difference between an **annuncio** *(ahn-<u>noon</u>-choh)* (announcment) and **pubblicità** *(pob-blee-chee-<u>tah</u>)* (advertising) is usually easy to determine.

In Italy, these conveniently small weekly magazines usually come out on Thursdays. Larger publications containing additional information also exist. Some of them offer English translations. You can even find a special publication for foreigners in kiosks in the center of Rome. In smaller towns without weekly magazines, you may see events announced on posters. You can also find information in the local newspapers.

Of course, newspapers aren't your only source of information about things to do and see. Asking the following questions can get you answers you want.

- ✔ **Cosa c'è da fare di sera?** *(<u>koh</u>-zah cheh dah <u>fah</u>-reh dee <u>seh</u>-rah)* (Are there any events in the evenings?)

- ✔ **Può suggerirmi qualcosa?** *(poo-<u>oh</u> sooj-jeh-<u>reer</u>-mee koo-ahl-<u>koh</u>-zah)* (Can you recommend something to me?)

✔ **C'è un concerto stasera?** *(cheh oon kohn-chehr-toh stah-seh-rah)* (Is there a concert tonight?)

✔ **Ci sono ancora posti?** *(chee soh-noh ahn-koh-rah pohs-tee)* (Are there any seats left?)

✔ **Dove si comprano i biglietti?** *(doh-veh see kohm-prah-noh ee bee-lyeht-tee)* (Where can we get tickets?)

✔ **Quanto vengono i biglietti?** *(koo-ahn-toh vehn-goh-noh ee bee-lyeht-tee)* (How much are the tickets?)

✔ **Non c'è niente di più economico?** *(nohn cheh nee-ehn-teh dee pee-oo eh-koh-noh-mee-koh)* (Isn't there anything cheaper?)

When you're seeing shows, certain verbs are more helpful than others. We give you the conjugation for two of the more helpful verbs: **cominciare** *(koh-meen-chah-reh)* (to start) and **finire** *(fee-nee-reh)* (to end).

Conjugation	*Pronunciation*
io comincio	ee-oh koh-meen-choh
tu cominci	too koh-meen-chee
lui/lei comincia	loo-ee/lay koh-meen-chah
noi cominciamo	noh-ee koh-meen-chah-moh
voi cominciate	voh-ee koh-meen-chah-teh
loro cominciano	loh-roh koh-meen-chah-noh

Conjugation	*Pronunciation*
io finisco	ee-oh fee-nee-skoh
tu finisci	too fee-nee-shee
lui/lei finisce	loo-ee/lay fee-nee-sheh
noi finiamo	noh-ee fee-nee-ah-moh
voi finite	voh-ee fee-nee-teh
loro finiscono	loh-roh fee-nees-koh-noh

Some tourist or ticket agencies have special offers and sell discounted tickets. But there's no guarantee you can get tickets to the show you want. You can always get your ticket at the theater box office.

Talkin' the Talk

Arturo works at a theater. He is bombarded with questions from patrons before the show.

Sig. Paoli: **Quando comincia lo spettacolo?**
koo-ahn-doh koh-meen-chah loh speht-tah-koh-loh
When does the show start?

Arturo: **Alle sette e mezza.**
ahl-leh seht-teh eh mehd-dzah
At half past seven.

Erika: **A che ora finisce lo spettacolo?**
ah keh oh-rah fee-nee-sheh loh speht-tah-koh-loh
What time is the show going to end?

Arturo: **Verso le dieci.**
vehr-soh leh dee-eh-chee
About ten p.m.

Erika: **C'è un intervallo?**
cheh oon een-tehr-vahl-loh
Is there an intermission?

Arturo: **Sì, tra il secondo e il terzo atto.**
see trah eel seh-kohn-doh eh eel tehr-tsoh aht-toh
Yes, between the second and third acts.

Sig.ra Battiato: **Ha un programma, per favore?**
ah oon proh-grahm-mah pehr fah-voh-reh
May I have a program, please?

Arturo: **Certo signora. Eccolo qua.**
chehr-toh see-nyoh-rah ehk-koh-loh koo-ah
Certainly, madam. Here you are.

Words to Know

a che ora?	ah keh oh-rah	what time?
quando?	koo-ahn-doh	when?
dove?	doh-veh	where?
biglietto [m]	bee-lyeht-toh	ticket
spettacolo [m]	speht-tah-koh-loh	show
cominciare	koh-meen-chah-reh	to start
finire	fee-nee-reh	to end

Going to the movies

Going **al cinema** *(ahl chee-neh-mah)* (to the movies) is a popular activity almost everywhere. You can go **da solo** *(dah soh-loh)* (alone), with **un amico** *(oon ah-mee-koh)* (a friend) or in a **gruppo** *(groop-poh)* (group). Often the **film** *(eel film)* (film) you want to see is playing at a **multisala** *(mool-tee-sah-lah)* (multiplex).

CULTURAL WISDOM

Italian films

It's well known that Italy produces a great number of films, and there are many Italian directors who are famous throughout the world: Fellini, Visconti, Bertolucci, De Sica, and Nanni Moretti. Some of their works are considered important chapters of Italian culture, and we recommend some of them to you, in case you'd like to look for Italian movies in your neighborhood video store.

Le notti di Cabiria (Nights of Cabiria) and *La strada* are among Fellini's masterpieces. The dramatic and moving *Bellissima* is one of the most significant movies by Visconti. To complete the image of the Italian cinema between 1948 and 1957, we can't forget De Sica's *Ladri di biciclette* (The Bicycle Thief). Bertolucci belongs to a more recent period and was discovered through *L'ultimo tango a Parigi* (Last Tango in Paris) whereas Moretti's *Caro diario* made a big contribution to disseminating Italian culture abroad in the mid-1990s.

Then we have Roberto Benigni, who not only directed one of the most successful "foreign" films of modern times but won an Academy Award for acting in *La vita è bella* — Life is Beautiful.

In Italy, American films normally are **doppiati** *(dohp-pee-ah-tee)* (dubbed) into Italian, but you can sometimes find an original English version with Italian subtitles. On the other hand, why not go to an original Italian film? Doing so provides you with a good opportunity to polish your Italian.

Some special questions for the movies include:

✔ **Andiamo al cinema?** *(ahn-dee-ah-moh ahl chee-neh-mah)* (Shall we go to the movies?)

✔ **Cosa danno?** *(koh-zah dahn-noh)* (What's playing?)

✔ **Dove lo danno?** *(doh-veh loh dahn-noh)* or **Dove lo fanno?** *(doh-veh loh fahn-noh)* (Where is [the movie] being shown?)

✔ **E' in lingua (versione) originale?** *(eh een leen-goo-ah [vehr-see-ohn-neh] oh-ree-jee-nah-leh)* (Is the film in the original language?)

✔ **Dov'è il cinema Trianon?** *(doh-veh eel chee-neh-mah tree-ah-nohn)* (Where is the Trianon cinema?)

Often saying the name of the movie theater is sufficient, for example, **Dov'è il Trianon?** *(doh-veh eel tree-ah-nohn)* (Where is the Trianon?). Everyone knows that you mean a movie theater.

Talkin' the Talk

Ugo wants to go to the movies and asks his girlfriend Bianca if she feels like going with him.

Ugo: **Andiamo al cinema?**
ahn-dee-ah-moh ahl chee-neh-mah
Shall we go to the movies?

Bianca: **Che film vuoi vedere?**
keh feelm voo-oh-ee veh-deh-reh
Which movie would you like to see?

Ugo: *La dolce vita*, **naturalmente.**
lah dohl-cheh vee-tah nah-too-rahl-mehn-teh
La dolce vita, of course.

Bianca: **Oh, l'ho visto solo cinque volte!**
oh loh <u>vees</u>-toh <u>soh</u>-loh <u>cheen</u>-koo-eh <u>vohl</u>-teh
Oh, I've seen it only five times!
Dove lo fanno?
<u>doh</u>-veh loh <u>fahn</u>-noh
Where is it being shown?

Ugo: **Al Tiziano, qui vicino.**
ahl tee-tsee-<u>ah</u>-noh koo-<u>ee</u> vee-<u>chee</u>-noh
At the Tiziano, close to here.

Bianca: **A che ora comincia?**
ah keh <u>oh</u>-rah koh-<u>meen</u>-chah
What time does it start?

Ugo: **Esattamente fra cinque minuti!**
*eh-zaht-tah-<u>mehn</u>-teh frah <u>cheen</u>-koo-eh
mee-<u>noo</u>-tee*
In exactly five minutes!

Bianca: **Cosa aspettiamo?**
<u>koh</u>-zah ahs-peht-tee-<u>ah</u>-moh
What are we waiting for?

Italian movie theaters used to be rather small, showing only one movie at a time. Now virtually all large Italian cities have big **multisala** *(<u>mool</u>-tee-sah-lah)* (multiplex) cinemas, with many screens.

Because going to the movies is a popular leisure activity in Italy and films change regularly, people often overcrowd the theaters when the most popular films are playing. Therefore, reserving your **biglietto** *(bee-<u>lyeht</u>-toh)* (ticket) for a movie in advance is always wise. You can reserve in person or by phone.

Talkin' the Talk

Films are an interesting topic of conversation. Here is a typical dialogue between two friends, Chiara and Alberto.

Chiara: **Hai visto l'ultimo film di Bellotti?**
ah-ee vees-toh lool-tee-moh feelm dee behl-loht-tee
Have you seen the new Bellotti film?

Alberto: **Ancora no, e tu?**
ahn-koh-rah noh eh too
Not yet, and you?

Chiara: **Sì, ieri sera.**
see ee-eh-ree seh-rah
Yes, last night.

Alberto: **Com'è?**
koh-meh
How is it?

Chiara: **L'attore è bravissimo!**
laht-toh-reh eh brah-vees-see-moh
The actor is really good!

Alberto: **Ma dai! Lo dici perché è bello!**
mah dah-ee loh dee-chee pehr-keh eh behl-loh
Come on! You say that because he's good looking!

Chiara: **E allora? E il film è così divertente!**
eh ahl-loh-rah eh eel feelm eh koh-zee-dee-vehr-tehn-teh
So what? And the movie is so amusing!

Alberto: **L'ultimo film di Bellotti era così serio.**
lool-tee-moh feelm dee behl-loht-tee eh-rah koh-zee seh-ree-oh
Bellotti's last film was so serious.

Chiara: **È questione di gusti.**
eh koo-ehs-tee-oh-neh dee goos-tee
It's a matter of taste.

Alberto: **Lo vado a vedere.**
loh vah-doh ah veh-deh-reh
I'll go see it.

Words to Know

Chi è il regista?	kee eh eel reh-_jees_-tah	Who is the director?
Chi sono gli attori?	kee _soh_-noh glee aht-_toh_-ree	Who's starring?
attore [m]	aht-_toh_-reh	actor
regista [f/m]	reh-_jees_-tah	director
trama [f]	_trah_-mah	plot
scena [f]	_sheh_-nah	scene

Going to the theater

The language of the theater and the cinema is very similar. Of course, when you attend a play, opera, or symphony performance, where you sit is more of a cause for discussion than it is when you go to a movie. In most cases, seats in the **platea** *(plah-teh-ah)* (orchestra) are **poltronissime** *(pohl-troh-nees-see-meh)* (seats in the first and second rows) and **poltrone** *(pohl-troh-neh)* (seats in the following rows). Or you can choose **posti nei palchi** *(pohs-tee nay pahl-kee)* (box seats). Some theaters indicate seats just by the number of the row: **i primi posti** *(ee pree-mee pohs-tee)* (first seats) are in the first five or six rows, **i secondi posti** *(ee seh-kohn-dee pohs-tee)* (second seats) are in the following ones, and so on.

You may want to avoid certain seats. A doctor who may be called away in the middle of a performance probably doesn't want to sit **centrale/i** *(chehn-trah-leh/lee)* (in the middle of the row). Or maybe you don't like feeling hemmed in and want to choose seats **laterale/i** *(lah-teh-rah-leh/lee)* (on the sides).

In large theaters, and especially in opera houses, you can sit in **il loggione** *(eel lohj-joh-neh)* (the gallery), which is also called **la piccionaia** *(lah peech-choh-nah-yah)* (Literally: the pigeonhouse) because it is high up. The exposed location of the **piccionaia** is a very important one, and these seats are much sought after. You find a special ambience there. For example, it's the place for very important persons in the famous **La Scala di Milano** *(lah skah-lah dee mee-lah-noh),* the well-known opera house in Milan.

Talkin' the Talk

In the following dialogue, Eugenio wants to know whether seats are available for a certain performance of a play he wants to see. He's speaking on the phone with the person at the theater box office.

Ticket Agent: **Pronto?**
prohn-toh
Hello?

Eugenio: **Buongiorno. È il Teatro Valle?**
boo-ohn-johr-noh eh eel teh-ah-tro vahl-leh
Good morning. Is this the Valle Theater?

Ticket Agent: **Sì. Mi dica.**
see mee dee-kah
Yes. Can I help you? (Literally: Tell me.)

Eugenio: **Vorrei prenotare dei posti.**
vohr-ray preh-noh-tah-reh day pohs-tee
I'd like to reserve some seats.

Ticket Agent: **Per quale spettacolo?**
pehr koo-ah-leh speht-tah-koh-loh
For which performance?

Eugenio: *Aspettando Godot,* **domani sera.**
ahs-peht-tahn-doh goh-doh doh-mah-nee seh-rah
Waiting for Godot, tomorrow evening.

Ticket Agent: **Mi dispiace: È tutto esaurito.**
mee dees-pee-ah-cheh eh toot-toh eh-zah-oo-ree-toh
I'm sorry: It's sold out.

Eugenio: **Ci sono repliche?**
chee soh-noh reh-plee-keh
Are there other performances?

Ticket Agent: **L'ultima è dopodomani.**
lool-tee-mah eh doh-poh-doh-mah-nee
The last one is the day after tomorrow.

Did you notice that the title of the play, *Waiting for Godot,* has no preposition in Italian? In English, you wait *for* someone, but Italians say "waiting some-body" — **aspettare qualcuno** *(ahs-peht-tah-reh koo-ahl-koo-noh).* You may also hear **ti aspetto** *(tee ahs-peht-toh)* (I'm waiting for you). You probably think that English is a concise language, but look at how concise Italian is!

Talkin' the Talk

Eugenio asks his friends about changing the date they see the play and then calls the box office again.

Voice: **Pronto?**
prohn-toh
Hello?

Eugenio: **Ho telefonato due minuti fa.**
oh teh-leh-foh-nah-toh doo-eh mee-noo-tee fah
I called two minutes ago.

Voice: **Sì, vuole prenotare per dopodomani?**
see voo-oh-leh preh-noh-tah-reh pehr doh-poh-doh-mah-nee
Yes, do you want to reserve for the day after tomorrow?

Eugenio: **Sì, tre posti.**
see treh pohs-tee
Yes, three seats.

Voice: **Che posti desidera?**
keh pohs-tee seh-zee-deh-rah
Which seats would you like?

Eugenio: **Non troppo cari.**
nohn trohp-poh kah-ree
Not too expensive.

Voice: **La platea viene trentadue.**
lah plah-teh-ah vee-eh-neh trehn-tah-doo-eh
The orchestra is thirty-two (thousand).

Eugenio: **Ci sono tre posti centrali?**
chee soh-noh treh pohs-tee chehn-trah-lee
Are there three middle seats?

Voice: **Un momento . . . sì, ma non insieme.**
oon moh-mehn-toh see mah nohn een-see-eh-meh
Just a moment . . . yes, but not together.

Eugenio:	**In tre file diverse?**
	een treh <u>fee</u>-leh dee-<u>vehr</u>-seh
	In three different rows?
Voice:	**Due in ottava e uno in nona fila.**
	<u>doo</u>-eh een oht-<u>tah</u>-vah eh <u>oo</u>-noh een <u>noh</u>-nah
	<u>fee</u>-lah
	Two in the eighth and one in the ninth row.

If you come to Italy, you must catch an opera by Verdi, Puccini, or Rossini. Their music has enchanted the whole world. Enjoying the operas in wonderful theaters such as Milan's **La Scala** *(lah <u>skah</u>-lah),* Naples's **San Carlo** *(sahn <u>kahr</u>-loh),* and the theaters of Florence and Palermo enhances the experience. In the summer months, actors stage open-air operas in Verona, where you can see the big operas in the old Roman **Arena** *(ah-<u>reh</u>-nah).* You'll surely see an interesting performance. Many other Italian cities also offer beautiful theaters and opera houses.

Following are some phrases concerning performances:

- **la danza classica/moderna/contemporanea** *(lah <u>dahn</u>-tsah <u>klahs</u>-see-kah/ moh-<u>dehr</u>-nah/kohn-tehm-poh-<u>rah</u>-neh-ah)* (classical/modern/contemporary dance)

- **lo spettacolo** *(loh speht-<u>tah</u>-koh-loh)* (the show; the performance)

- **la prova generale pubblica** *(lah <u>proh</u>-vah jeh-neh-<u>rah</u>-leh <u>poob</u>-blee-kah)* (public dress rehearsal)

- **la replica** *(lah <u>reh</u>-plee-kah)* (repeat performance)

- **il matinée** *(eel mah-tee-<u>neh</u>)* (matinee)

- **lo spettacolo pomeridiano** *(loh speht-<u>tah</u>-koh-loh poh-meh-ree-dee-<u>ah</u>-noh)* (afternoon performance)

Talkin' the Talk

Two friends, Stefano and Giorgio, want to attend an opening night.

Giorgio:	**Voglio vedere lo spettacolo al Verdi.**
	<u>voh</u>-lyoh veh-<u>deh</u>-reh loh seht-<u>tah</u>-koh-loh ahl
	<u>vehr</u>-dee
	I want to see the performance at the Verdi Theater.

Stefano:	**Ci sono ancora biglietti per la prima?** *chee <u>soh</u>-noh ahn-<u>koh</u>-rah bee-<u>lyeht</u>-tee pehr lah <u>pree</u>-mah* Are there still tickets for opening night?
Giorgio:	**No, è tutto esaurito.** *noh eh <u>toot</u>-toh eh-zah-oo-<u>ree</u>-toh* No, it's sold out.
Stefano:	**Peccato!** *pehk-<u>kah</u>-toh* That's a pity!
Giorgio:	**Andiamo alla prova generale!** *ahn-dee-<u>ah</u>-moh <u>ahl</u>-lah <u>proh</u>-vah geh-neh-<u>rah</u>-leh* Let's go to the dress rehearsal!
Stefano:	**È pubblica?** *eh <u>poob</u>-blee-kah* Is it open to the public?
Giorgio:	**Penso di sì. Ora telefono.** *<u>pehn</u>-soh dee see <u>oh</u>-rah teh-<u>leh</u>-foh-noh* I think so. I'll call right now.

When you reserve tickets in Italy, you usually have to pay a service charge. Some theaters don't accept telephone reservations; you can only "reserve at the box office" — **prenotazione al botteghino** *(preh-noh-tah-tsee-<u>oh</u>-neh ahl boht-teh-<u>gee</u>-noh)*. You can pay for the tickets and either pick them up immediately or half an hour before the performance begins.

Big theaters offer the option of advanced ordering via phone by using a credit card, but you have to pay an additional charge. In some cities, you can also get your tickets from an agency, like those that provide tourist information. You can find their addresses in the event magazines.

Going to a museum

Exploring the treasures in museums can be an adventure in learning. You can expand your knowledge of history, sociology, anthropology, politics, and communications. Of course, the ancient Roman civilization is the root for much of Western history and culture. The precepts handed down by Roman leaders, artists, and philosophers still influence people and cultures to this day. This history certainly demands a visit to one of the many museums in Italy.

And, don't get us started about Italian artists! You can go into any art museum in the world and probably find a piece by an Italian artist: People everywhere recognize Italian art as some of the very best in the world. Just think of Leonardo da Vinci, Michelangelo, and Tiziano. The list of Italian artists is endless, and you've surely heard of most of them. If you go to Italy, be sure to take a look inside at least one of the many art museums — doing so is really worthwhile!

Talkin' the Talk

Take a look at this dialogue between two friends who are about to go **al museo** *(ahl moo-zeh-oh)* (to the museum).

Luisa: **Ciao, Flavia, dove vai?**
chah-oh flah-vee-ah doh-veh vah-ee
Hello, Flavia, where are you going?

Flavia: **Ciao! Alla mostra di Picasso.**
chah-oh ahl-lah mohs-trah dee pee-kahs-soh
Hello! To the Picasso exhibit.

Luisa: **Ma dai: ci vado anch'io!**
mah dah-ee chee vah-doh ahn-kee-oh
Come on: I'm going there too!

Flavia: **Allora andiamo insieme!**
ahl-loh-rah ahn-dee-ah-moh een-see-eh-meh
In that case, let's go together!

Luisa: **Certo! Viene anche Janet.**
chehr-toh vee-eh-neh ahn-keh jah-neht
Sure! Janet is coming also.

Flavia: **La conosco?**
lah koh-nohs-koh
Do I know her?

Luisa: **Sì, la mia amica americana.**
see lah mee-ah ah-mee-kah ah-meh-ree-kah-nah
Yes, my American friend.

Flavia: **Dove avete appuntamento?**
doh-veh ah-veh-teh ahp-poon-tah-mehn-toh
Where are you meeting?

Luisa:	**Davanti al museo.**
	dah-vahn-tee ahl moo-zeh-oh
	In front of the museum.

Going to a concert

Music is the universal language, and some of the most popular forms, such as **l'opera** *(loh-peh-rah)* (opera), have a close association with Italian.

Italy is full of old and beautiful churches and cathedrals where **musicisti** *(moo-zee-chees-tee)* (musicians) often present classical music concerts. You can also hear concerts in other places — sometimes even in the center of a city in a piazza. Such concerts are spectacular events.

Talkin' the Talk

La signora and il signor Tiberi are reading the morning paper. Suddenly, la signora Tiberi cries out:

Sig.ra Tiberi:	**Guarda qui!**
	goo-ahr-dah koo-ee
	Look here!

Sig. Tiberi:	**Che c'è?**
	keh cheh
	What's up?

Sig.ra Tiberi:	**Martedì c'è Pollini a Roma!**
	mahr-teh-dee cheh pohl-lee-nee ah roh-mah
	Pollini is in Rome on Tuesday!

Sig. Tiberi:	**Dà un concerto?**
	dah oon kohn-chehr-toh
	Is he going to give a concert?

Sig.ra Tiberi:	**Sì, al Conservatorio.**
	see ahl kohn-sehr-vah-toh-ree-oh
	Yes, at the Conservatory.

Sig. Tiberi:	**Sarà tutto esaurito?**
	sah-rah toot-toh eh-zah-oo-ree-toh
	Will it already be sold out?

Sig.ra Tiberi: **Forse no!**
fohr-seh noh
Maybe not!

Sig. Tiberi: **Vai al botteghino?**
vah-ee ahl boht-teh-gee-noh
Are you going to the box office?

Sig.ra Tiberi: **Sì, subito!**
see soo-bee-toh
Yes, immediately!

Maurizio Pollini is an internationally famous Italian pianist who very seldom gives concerts. We do hope that signor and signora Tiberi find two tickets for this rare event. **Buona fortuna!** *(boo-oh-nah fohr-too-nah)* (Good luck!)

Words to Know

musica [f]	moo-zee-kah	music
concerto [m]	kohn-chehr-toh	concert
esaurito	eh-zah-oo-ree-toh	sold out
piano(forte) [m]	pee-ah-noh(-fohr-teh)	piano
museo [m]	moo-zeh-oh	museum
insieme	een-see-eh-meh	together

Maybe you know a musician or someone who plays an instrument in his or her leisure time. You are probably curious about some things, such as:

- ✔ **Che strumento suoni?** *(keh stroo-mehn-toh soo-oh-nee)* (Which instrument do you play?)

  Suono il violino. *(soo-oh-noh eel vee-oh-lee-noh)* (I play the violin.)

- ✔ **Dove suonate stasera?** *(doh-veh soo-oh-nah-teh stah-seh-rah)* (Where are you playing tonight?)

  Suoniamo al Blu Notte. *(soo-oh-nyah-moh ahl bloo noht-teh)* (We play at the Blu Notte.)

✔ **Chi suona in famiglia?** *(kee soo-oh-nah een fah-mee-lyah)* (Who in the family plays?)

Suonano tutti. *(soo-oh-nah-noh toot-tee)* (All of them play.)

Talkin' the Talk

La signora Tiberi meets her neighbor la signora Busi at the box office **in coda** *(een koh-dah)* (in line). They both want tickets for the Pollini concert.

Sig.ra Tiberi: **Buongiorno!**
boo-ohn-johr-noh
Good morning!

Sig.ra Busi: **Anche lei per martedì?**
ahn-keh lay pehr mahr-teh-dee
Do you also need tickets for Tuesday?

Sig.ra Tiberi: **Sì, spero di trovare due biglietti.**
see speh-roh dee troh-vah-reh doo-eh bee-lyeht-tee
Yes, I hope to get two tickets.

Sig.ra Busi: **Le piace il piano?**
leh pee-ah-cheh eel pee-ah-noh
Do you like piano?

Sig.ra Tiberi: **Molto, e lui è così bravo!**
mohl-toh eh loo-ee eh koh-zee brah-voh
Yes, and he's so good!

Sig.ra Busi: **Suona divinamente!**
soo-oh-nah dee-vee-nah-mehn-teh
He plays divinely!

Inviting Fun

Getting or giving **un invito** *(oon een-vee-toh)* (an invitation) is always a pleasureable experience whether you casually invite a friend to come to dinner or receive an invitation to what promises to be **la festa** *(lah fehs-tah)* (the party) of the year.

A party is a good opportunity to meet new and interesting people. When you feel like entertaining, you can say you want **dare una festa** *(dah-reh oo-nah fehs-tah)* (to give a party). You can also use the expression **fare una festa** *(fah-reh oo-nah fehs-tah)* (to make a party).

How do you issue an invitation in Italian? Here we give you the first step — the conjugation of the verb **invitare** *(een-vee-tah-reh)* (to invite).

Conjugation	Pronunciation
io invito	*ee-oh een-vee-toh*
tu inviti	*too een-vee-tee*
lui/lei invita	*loo-ee/lay een-vee-tah*
noi invitiamo	*noh-ee een-vee-tee-ah-moh*
voi invitate	*voh-ee een-vee-tah-teh*
loro invitano	*loh-roh een-vee-tah-noh*

You can use the following expressions to suggest an activity:

- ✔ **Che ne pensa di andare a Roma?** (formal) *(keh neh pehn-sah dee ahn-dah-reh ah roh-mah)* (What do you think of going to Rome?)

- ✔ **Che ne dici di uscire stasera?** (informal) *(keh neh dee-chee dee oo-shee-reh stah-seh-rah)* (What do you say about going out tonight?)

- ✔ **Andiamo in piscina!** *(ahn-dee-ah-moh een pee-shee-nah)* (Let's go to the swimming pool!)

- ✔ **Mangiamo una pizza!** *(mahn-jah-moh oo-nah peet-tsah)* (Let's eat a pizza!)

- ✔ **Perché non andiamo a teatro?** *(pehr-keh nohn ahn-dee-ah-moh ah teh-ah-troh)* (Why don't we go to the theater?)

You can see that suggesting an activity in Italian is not so different from the way you do it in English. You can ask **Perché non . . .** *(pehr-keh nohn)* (Why don't we . . .) or **Che ne pensi . . .** *(keh neh pehn-see)* (What do you think about . . .). The use of *let's* however, is a little different. In Italian, how you say something and the tone you use differentiates a normal sentence from a suggestion. You say **Andiamo!** *(ahn-dee-ah-moh)* (Let's go!) with enthusiasm, and punctuate it with an exclamation point, but **Andiamo al ristorante** *(ahn-dee-ah-moh ahl rees-toh-rahn-teh)* (We're going to the restaurant) is a normal sentence. The actual form of the verb doesn't change.

The word **perché** is special. We use it in this chapter to ask the question "why." However, it can also mean "because." A dialogue can go like this:

Perché non mangi? *(pehr-keh nohn mahn-jee)* (Why don't you eat?)

Perché non ho fame. *(pehr-keh nohn oh fah-meh)* (Because I'm not hungry.)

Talkin' the Talk

Guido has a new job. He's very happy and wants to share his happiness with a couple of friends. He decides to **dare una festa** (*dah-reh oo-nah fehs-tah*) (give a party) and tells his friend Caterina about it.

Guido:	**Ho deciso!** *oh deh-chee-zoh* I've decided!
Caterina:	**Cosa? Dimmi!** *koh-zah deem-mee* What? Tell me!
Guido:	**Faccio una festa!** *fahch-choh oo-nah fehs-tah* I'm giving a party!
Caterina:	**Fantastico! Quando?** *fahn-tahs-tee-koh koo-ahn-doh* Great! When?
Guido:	**Sabato sera.** *sah-bah-toh seh-rah* Saturday night.
Caterina:	**Una festa da ballo?** *oo-nah fehs-tah dah bahl-loh* A dance party?
Guido:	**Certo. Mi aiuti?** *chehr-toh mee ah-yoo-tee* Certainly. Will you help me?
Caterina:	**Come no!** *koh-meh noh* Of course!

Nowadays, you can issue and receive invitations any number of ways. You can receive an invitation by phone, by fax, via e-mail, or you may be asked by your **ospite** (*ohs-pee-teh*) (host) face to face. Occasionally you may even receive the classic engraved invitation!

Talkin' the Talk

 Guido will have a party at his house next Saturday. He calls Sara to invite her.

Sara:	**Ciao Guido, come va?** *chah-oh goo-ee-doh koh-meh vah* Hi Guido, how are you?
Guido:	**Sei libera sabato sera?** *say lee-beh-rah sah-bah-toh seh-rah* Are you free Saturday night?
Sara:	**È un invito?** *eh oon een-vee-toh* Is this an invitation?
Guido:	**Sì, alla mia festa.** *see ahl-lah mee-ah fehs-tah* Yes, to my party.
Sara:	**Fantastico! A che ora?** *fahn-tahs-tee-koh ah keh oh-rah* Great! What time?
Guido:	**Verso le nove.** *vehr-soh leh noh-veh* About nine.
Sara:	**Ci sarò, grazie!** *chee sah-roh grah-tsee-eh* I'll be there, thank you!

Figure 7-1 shows the fax Guido sent to friends he couldn't reach by phone.

INVITO
(een-vee-toh)
(Invitation)

C'è una festa e tu sei invitato.
cheh oo-nah fehs-tah eh too say een-vee-tah-toh
There's a party and you're invited.

Quando?
koo-ahn-doh
When?

Sabato 24 luglio.
sah-bah-toh vehn-tee-koo-aht-troh loo-lyoh
Saturday, July 24.

A che ora?
ah keh oh-rah
What time?

Verso le 9.
vehr-soh leh noh-veh
About 9 o'clock.

Dove?
doh-veh
Where?

A casa mia.
ah kah-sah mee-ah
At my place.

Perché?
pehr-keh
Why?

Per festeggiare insieme!
pehr fehs-tehj-jah-reh een-see-eh-meh
To celebrate together!

Ti aspetto.
tee ahs-peht-toh
I'll be waiting for you.

Guido

Figure 7-1:
A casual
invitation,
suitable for
faxing.

Talkin' the Talk

Both Franco and Emma have received Guido's invitation. They are now talking about whether or not they will go to the party.

Franco: **Vieni alla festa di Guido?**
vee-eh-nee ahl-lah fehs-tah dee goo-ee-doh
Are you going to Guido's party?

Emma: **No, mi annoio alle feste.**
noh mee ahn-noh-yoh ahl-lah fehs-teh
No, I get bored at parties.

Franco: **Ti annoi?**
tee ahn-noh-ee
You get bored?

Emma: **Sì, non ballo e non bevo.**
see nohn bahl-loh eh nohn beh-voh
Yes, I don't dance and don't drink.

Franco: **Ma chiacchieri!**
mah kee-ahk-kee-eh-ree
But you do chat!

Emma: **Sì, ma senza musica di sottofondo.**
see mah sehn-tsah moo-zee-kah dee soht-toh-fohn-doh
Yes, but without background music.

Figure 7-2 is an example of a formal invitation to an opening of an exhibition by artist Elisa Catalani.

La Signoria Vostra è invitata all' inaugurazione della mostra:
lah see-nyoh-ree-ah vohs-trah eh een-vee-tah-tah ahl-leen-ah-oo-goo-rah-tsee-oh-neh dehl-lah mohs-trah
You are invited to the opening of the exhibition:

"Ricordi di una vita"
ree-kohr-dee dee oo-nah vee-tah
"Memories of a Life"

Dipinti a olio e sculture di
dee-peen-tee ah oh-lyoh eh skool-too-reh dee
Oil paintings and sculptures by

Elisa Catalani

Venerdì 28 marzo alle 19, 30
veh-nehr-dee vehnt-oht-toh mahr-tsoh ahl-leh dee-chahn-noh-veh eh trehn-tah
Friday, March 28 at 7:30 p.m.

Galleria Arte & Arte
gahl-leh-ree-ah ahr-teh eh ahr-teh
Gallery Arte & Arte

Via Gabriele Sisti 18

Piacenza

L' artista sarà presente.
lahr-tees-tah sah-rah preh-zehn-teh
The artist will be present.

Figure 7-2:
The classic formal, engraved invitation.

Words to Know

invito [m]	een-_vee_-toh	invitation
festa [f]	_fehs_-tah	party
suonare	soo-oh-_nah_-reh	to play (a musical instrument)
perché	pehr-_keh_	why; because
bere	_beh_-reh	to drink
ballare	bahl-_lah_-reh	to dance

Fun & Games

Now it's your turn to invite an Italian friend to your party. Use the following words to fill in the blanks in this invitation:

aspetto, dove, festa, invitato, ora, perché, sabato, verso

C'è una (1) _____ **e tu sei** (2) _____. (There's a party and you're invited.)

Quando? (3) _____ **24 luglio** (When? Saturday, July 24.)

A che (4) _____? (5) _____ **le 9.** (What time? About 9 o'clock.)

(6) _____? **A casa mia.** (Where? At my place.)

(7) _____? **Per festeggiare insieme!** (Why? To celebrate together!)

Ti (8) _____. (I'll be waiting for you.)

Buon divertimento! (Have a nice time!)

Answers: 1. festa, 2. invitato, 3. sabato, 4. ora, 5. verso, 6. dove, 7. perché, 8. aspetto

Chapter 8

Having Fun Italian Style

• •

In This Chapter

▶ Discovering the great outdoors through animals and plants

▶ Enjoying yourself with reflexive verbs

▶ Exploring sports and other hobbies

• •

*I*n this chapter, we talk about the fun stuff — taking trips, playing sports, and generally enjoying yourself. Plus, we throw in a section about reflexive verbs so that you can talk correctly about enjoying yourself.

Everybody likes to get away from the daily grind and check out new environments and activities during their free time. Vacationers flock **al mare** *(ahl mah-reh)* (to the beach), head **in montagna** *(een mohn-tah-nyah)* (to the mountains) or **in campagna** *(kahm-pah-nyah)* (to the countryside) or take a trip to the big city to see the sights.

Maybe you use your **fine settimana** *(fee-neh seht-tee-mah-nah)* (weekends) as a chance to play sports like **calcio** *(kahl-choh)* (soccer), **tennis** *(tennis)* (tennis), or **pallavolo** *(pahl-lah-voh-loh)* (volleyball). Or perhaps you park yourself in front of the TV to watch **pallacanestro** *(pahl-lah-kah-nehs-troh)* (basketball). In any case, being able to talk sports and other recreational activities is a plus in any language.

Italians love to spend their spare time away from the cities. Especially in summertime, they love to go to the sea, a lake, or up into the mountains. In fact, most Italians are enthusiastic walkers. Hiking and bicycling are creative ways for tourists to see the countryside. The Alps and Dolomites offer marvelous terrain for these sports, particularly during the warm months. In winter, you can use the mountains for skiing. And you will find that Italians are just as enthusiastic about skiing as they are about hiking.

Taking a Tour

Whether you're in a city or rural area, you can usually find fun and interesting sights to see in the area. You can take a car trip, or leave the driving to someone else and sign up for an organized bus tour to take you to special places. Bus tours are, for the most part, organized in great detail and the price generally includes the cost of the hotel, lunch, dinner, and the services of a tour guide.

A guided tour may be the most efficient, cost-effective, and informative way to check out the attractions of an unfamiliar city. You can use the following questions to help find out more about **una gita organizzata** (_oo_-nah jee-tah ohr-gah-nee-_dzah_-tah) (an organized tour). Notice that Italian has two, basically interchangeable ways to say "go on a tour": **fare una gita** (_fah_-reh _oo_-nah _jee_-tah) and **fare un'escursione** (_fah_-reh oon ehs-koor-see-_oh_-neh).

- **Ci sono gite organizzate?** (chee _soh_-noh _jee_-teh ohr-gah-need-_dzah_-teh) (Are there any organized tours?)

- **Che cosa c'è da vedere?** (keh _koh_-zah cheh dah veh-_deh_-reh) (What sights are included?)

- **Quanto costa la gita?** (koo-_ahn_-toh _kohs_-tah lah _jee_-tah) (How much does the tour cost?)

- **C'è una guida inglese?** (cheh _oo_-nah goo-_ee_-dah een-_gleh_-zeh) (Is there an English-speaking guide?)

- **Dove si comprano i biglietti?** (_doh_-veh see _kohm_-prah-noh ee bee-_lyeht_-tee) (Where do you buy tickets?)

Talkin' the Talk

Lucia and Renzo are in a tour office, talking to a tour agent and deciding which trip to go on the next day.

Lucia:	**C'è una bella gita sul lago domani.** cheh _oo_-nah _behl_-lah _gee_-tah sool _lah_-goh doh-_mah_-nee We can take a nice trip to the lake tomorrow.
Renzo:	**Vuoi andare, vero?** voo-_oh_-ee ahn-_dah_-reh _veh_-roh You want to go, don't you?
Lucia:	**Sarebbe carino. E tu?** sah-_rehb_-beh kah-_ree_-noh eh too It would be nice. What about you?
Renzo:	**Non amo le gite in autobus.** nohn _ah_-moh leh _gee_-teh een _ah_-oo-toh-boos I don't like bus trips.

Lucia:	**Ma è una gita a piedi!**
	mah eh <u>oo</u>-nah <u>jee</u>-tah ah pee-<u>eh</u>-dee
	But it's a walking tour!

Renzo:	**Mamma mia!**
	<u>mahm</u>-mah <u>mee</u>-ah
	Oh my goodness!
	A che ora inizia la gita?
	ah keh <u>oh</u>-rah ee-<u>nee</u>-tsee-ah lah <u>jee</u>-tah
	What time does the trip start?

Agent:	**Alle sette e trenta.**
	<u>ahl</u>-leh <u>seht</u>-teh eh <u>trehn</u>-tah
	At seven-thirty a.m.

Lucia:	**Dov'è il punto d'incontro?**
	doh-<u>veh</u> eel <u>poon</u>-toh deen-<u>kohn</u>-troh
	Where is the meeting point?

Agent:	**Sul ponte.**
	sool <u>pohn</u>-teh
	On the bridge.

Renzo:	**Quanto dura?**
	koo-<u>ahn</u>-toh <u>doo</u>-rah
	How long is it going to last?

Agent:	**Circa cinque ore.**
	<u>cheer</u>-kah <u>cheen</u>-koo-eh <u>oh</u>-reh
	About five hours.

Notice in the following sentences that the Italians have appropriated a few English words — picnic and jog.

- ✔ **Mi piace camminare nel verde.** *(mee pee-<u>ah</u>-cheh kahm-mee-<u>nah</u>-reh nehl <u>vehr</u>-deh)* (I like to walk in nature.)

- ✔ **Facciamo un picnic sul prato?** *(fahch-chah-moh oon peek-neek sool prah-toh?)* (Should we have a picnic on the lawn?)

- ✔ **Ti piace il osservare gli uccelli?** *(tee pee-ah-cheh eel ohs-sehr-<u>vah</u>-reh lyee ooch-<u>chehl</u>-lee)* (Do you like bird-watching?)

- ✔ **Faccio jogging nel parco.** *(<u>fahch</u>-choh <u>johg</u>-geeng nehl <u>pahr</u>-koh)* (I go jogging in the park.)

Words to Know

campagna [f]	kahm-_pah_-nyah	countryside
escursione [f]	ehs-koor-see-_oh_-neh	tour
gita [f]	_jee_-tah	tour
fiume [m]	fee-_oo_-meh	river
guida [f]	goo-_ee_-dah	guide
lago [m]	_lah_-goh	lake
mare [f]	_mah_-reh	beach
montagna [f]	mohn-_tah_-nyah	mountain

Maybe you like to go up into the mountains to be close to nature. Even when **ti godi** (*tee _goh_-dee*) (you enjoy) Mother Nature on your own, however, you may want to know some vocabulary to express the wonders you see. Here we go!

✔ **albero** (*_lahl_-beh-roh*) (tree)

✔ **bosco** (*eel _bohs_-koh*) (woods)

✔ **fiore** (*eel fee-_oh_-reh*) (flower)

✔ **pianta** (*lah pee-_ahn_-tah*) (plant)

✔ **pino** (*eel _pee_-noh*) (pine)

✔ **prato** (*eel _prah_-toh*) (meadow; lawn)

✔ **quercia** (*lah koo-_ehr_-chah*) (oak)

Talkin' the Talk

Animals are always an interesting topic, and knowing the names of some of them in another language is always good. Here's a dialogue about animals:

Carla: **Ami gli animali?**
                ah-mee lyee ah-nee-mah-lee
                Do you like animals?

Alessandra: **Sì, ho una piccola fattoria.**
                see oh oo-nah peek-koh-lah faht-toh-ree-ah
                Yes, I have a small farm.

Carla: **Davvero?**
                dahv-veh-roh
                Really?

Alessandra: **Ho un cane, due gatti e un maialino.**
                *oh oon kah-neh doo-eh gaht-tee eh oon
                mah-yah-lee-noh*
                I have a dog, two cats, and a small pig.

Carla: **Ti piacciono i cavalli?**
                tee pee-ahch-choh-noh ee kah-vahl-lee
                Do you like horses?

Alessandra: **No, preferisco le mucche.**
                noh preh-feh-rees-koh leh mook-keh
                No, I prefer cows.

Carla: **Ma dai!**
                mah dah-ee
                Come on!

Alessandra: **Sì, sono così tranquille.**
                see soh-noh koh-zee trahn-koo-eel-leh
                Yes, they are so quiet.

Carla: **Ideali per cavalcare . . .**
                ee-deh-ah-lee pehr kah-vahl-kah-reh
                Ideal to ride . . .

Words to Know

cane [m]	kah-neh	dog
cavallo [m]	kah-vahl-loh	horse
gatto [m]	gaht-toh	cat
maiale [m]	mah-yah-leh	pig
mucca [f]	mook-kah	cow
uccello [m]	ooch-chehl-loh	bird
lupo [m]	loo-poh	wolf
pecora [f]	peh-koh-rah	sheep

Speaking Reflexively

When you say "to enjoy yourself," you use a ***reflexive verb.*** That is, you turn the action back to yourself. The same applies in Italian. But not all Italian reflexive verbs are reflexive in English, and vice versa. Some verbs, such as **riposarsi** *(ree-poh-zahr-see)* (to rest oneself) and **svegliarsi** *(sveh-lyahr-see)* (to wake oneself), are not reflexive in English although they are in Italian.

In Italian, you can tell whether a verb is reflexive by looking at the infinitive form. If the last syllable of the infinitive is ***-si*** *(see),* which translates as "one-self," then the verb is reflexive. When you conjugate a reflexive verb, you must change the last syllable from ***-si*** to something else, just as you change ***oneself*** to ***myself, yourself,*** and so on in English. The following conjugation of **divertirsi** *(dee-vehr-teer-see)* (to enjoy oneself) demonstrates that the conjugation of the verb follows the regular pattern. The only difference is that you add the reflexive pronoun, which refers to the person concerned (the subject).

Conjugation	*Pronunciation*
mi diverto	mee dee-vehr-toh
ti diverti	tee dee-vehr-tee
si diverte	see dee-vehr-teh
ci divertiamo	chee dee-vehr-tee-ah-moh
vi divertite	vee dee-vehr-tee-teh
si divertono	see dee-vehr-toh-noh

Here are some more examples:

- ✔ **Mi diverto molto.** *(mee dee-vehr-toh mohl-toh)* (I enjoy myself a lot.)

- ✔ **Vi annoiate in campagna?** *(vee ahn-noh-yah-teh een kahm-pah-nyah)* (Do you get bored in the country?)

- ✔ **A che ora ti svegli?** *(ah keh oh-rah tee sveh-lyee)* (What time do you wake up?)

- ✔ **Si immaginano una bella gita.** *(see eem-mah-jee-nah-noh oo-nah behl-lah jee-tah)* (They are looking forward to a nice trip.)

Talkin' the Talk

Maria Pia and Mauro are discussing what they enjoy doing on their weekends.

Maria Pia:	**Come passi i fine settimana?** *koh-meh pahs-see ee fee-neh seht-tee-mah-nah* How do you spend your weekends?
Mauro:	**Faccio sport, leggo, incontro amici.** *fahch-choh sport lehg-goh een-kohn-troh ah-mee-chee* I play sports, I read, I meet friends. **Ti piace leggere?** *tee pee-ah-cheh lehj-jeh-reh* Do you like to read?
Maria Pia:	**È la mia passione!** *eh lah mee-ah pahs-see-oh-neh* It's my passion! **Che cosa leggi?** *keh koh-zah lehj-jee* What do you read?
Mauro:	**Soprattutto letteratura contemporanea.** *soh-praht-toot-toh leht-teh-rah-too-rah kohn-tehm-poh-rah-neh-ah* Mostly contemporary literature.

Playing Sports

Playing and talking about sports is a favored pastime of people the world over. And whether you travel to Italy, or just want to invite your Italian neighbor to play tennis, knowing sports terms is always helpful.

Some sports you *do* in Italian. Therefore, you pair those words with **fare** (*fah-reh*) (to do; to practice). With other sports, however, you must use **giocare** (*joh-kah-reh*) (to play) or **andare** (*ahn-dah-reh*) (to go). Table 8-1 lists most sports and the verbs you use with them.

Table 8-1	Sports Verbs	
Italian	*Pronunciation*	*Translation*
fare	**fah-reh**	**to do; to practice**
atletica	aht-leh-tee-kah	athletics
ciclismo	chee-klees-moh	cycling
equitazione	eh-koo-ee-tah-tsee-oh-neh	riding
jogging	johg-geeng	jogging
nuoto	noo-oh-toh	swimming
palestra	pah-lehs-trah	going to the gym
scherma	skehr-mah	fencing
sci nautico	shee nah-oo-tee-koh	water skiing
giocare	**joh-kah-reh**	**to play**
calcio	kahl-cho	soccer
pallacanestro	pahl-lah-kah-nehs-troh	basketball
pallavolo	pahl-lah-voh-loh	volleyball
tennis	tehn-nees	tennis
andare	**ahn-dah-reh**	**to go**
a cavallo	ah kah-vahl-loh	to ride
in bicicletta	een bee-chee-kleht-tah	to cycle

The following conjugations are for these three important sports verbs: **fare**, **andare**, and **giocare**.

Conjugation	*Pronunciation*
io faccio	<u>ee</u>-oh <u>fahch</u>-choh
tu fai	too <u>fah</u>-ee
lui/lei fa	<u>loo</u>-ee/lay fah
noi facciamo	<u>noh</u>-ee fahch-<u>chah</u>-moh
voi fate	<u>voh</u>-ee <u>fah</u>-teh
loro fanno	<u>loh</u>-roh <u>fahn</u>-noh

Conjugation	*Pronunciation*
io vado	<u>ee</u>-oh <u>vah</u>-doh
tu vai	too <u>vah</u>-ee
lui/lei va	<u>loo</u>-ee/lay vah
noi andiamo	<u>noh</u>-ee ahn-dee-<u>ah</u>-moh
voi andate	<u>voh</u>-ee ahn-<u>dah</u>-teh
loro vanno	<u>loh</u>-roh <u>vahn</u>-noh

Conjugation	*Pronunciation*
io gioco	<u>ee</u>-oh <u>joh</u>-koh
tu giochi	too <u>joh</u>-kee
lui/lei gioca	<u>loo</u>-ee/lay <u>joh</u>-kah
noi giochiamo	<u>noh</u>-ee joh-kee-<u>ah</u>-moh
voi giocate	<u>voh</u>-ee joh-<u>kah</u>-teh
loro giocano	<u>loh</u>-roh <u>joh</u>-kah-noh

You can follow sports ranging from sports like tennis to **pugilato** *(poo-jee-<u>lah</u>-toh)* (boxing) to **Formula 1** *(<u>fohr</u>-moo-lah <u>oo</u>-noh)* (Formula One car racing). Or, you can be a bit more active, and participate in sports like **ciclismo** *(chee-<u>klees</u>-moh)* (cycling), **camminare** *(kahm-mee-<u>nah</u>-reh)* (hiking), **fare vela** *(<u>fah</u>-reh <u>veh</u>-lah)* (sailing), **nuoto** *(noo-<u>oh</u>-toh)* (swimming), **pescare** *(<u>pehs</u>-kah-reh)* (fishing), **andare a cavallo** *(ahn-<u>dah</u>-reh ah kah-<u>vahl</u>-loh)* (horseback riding), and **golf.** You can work out at a **palestra** *(pah-<u>lehs</u>-trah)* (gym; fitness center). And don't forget the winter sports — one of the most popular in Italy is **sciare** *(shee-<u>ah</u>-reh)* skiing — as well as **pattinare** *(paht-tee-<u>nah</u>-reh)* (ice skating) and all the other things you can do on the slopes, such as **fare lo snowboarding** *(<u>fah</u>-reh loh <u>snoo</u>-bor-ding)* (snowboarding), **andare in slitta** *(ahn-<u>dah</u>-reh een <u>sleet</u>-tah)* (sledding), and **andare in bob** *(ahn-<u>dah</u>-reh een bohb)* (bobsledding).

Fantasy soccer, Italian style

Here's an interesting note about Italian **calcio**-fanaticism. For some years, many Italians have played a sort of simulation or fantasy soccer game that they call **fantacalcio** *(fahn-tah-kahl-choh)*. You can play this game in groups of eight to ten or even alone, because you can get your statistics from sports newspapers.

You play the game as follows: Everyone builds his or her own soccer team. You may hold auctions with your friends where you buy players for your team with fictious money — and, of course, the players' prices rise with demand. If you're playing alone, you can buy your players through the newspaper, which has a special section for **fantacalcio**. Prices are determined according to the players' performances.

The players you "purchase" are the real, current players. With your virtual team, you "play" the whole soccer season — that is; you watch the actual players and keep track of their individual points scored. At the end of the season, the "manager" whose team scored the most points wins. The personal kick is that you're virtually the manager of your own soccer team.

In Italy, a big difference exists between active and passive sports. The latter means that you follow the action as a spectator and participate either through reading the newspaper or watching TV. The truth is that the passive sports are actually more active than the active ones! To be more precise, certain sports — such as **il calcio** *(eel kahl-choh)* (soccer) and **il ciclismo** *(eel chee-klees-moh)* (cycling) — are definitely the most popular ones, but are almost exclusively spectator sports. Just think of the worldwide event known as **Giro d'Italia** *(jee-roh dee-tah-lee-ah)* — the big, Italian bicycling tour. Of course, some people also go in for actually cycling or playing soccer, but most people just follow the sports on TV.

Many **ragazzi** *(rah-gaht-tsee)* (boys) play **calcio**, but middle-aged men play **calcetto** *(kahl-cheht-toh)* or **calcio a cinque** *(kahl-choh ah cheen-koo-eh)*, which is a game that uses the same rules as soccer, but is played in a gym by teams consisting of five adults. On Sunday, however, these same players become passive and follow real soccer matches on TV or radio. Seeing men with portable radios clutched close to their ears, following the current soccer match, is not unusual.

Talkin' the Talk

Giulia and Stefano have just met at the university and found out that they live in the same neighborhood. On the way to the bus stop Stefano strikes up a conversation about his favorite topic, sports.

Stefano: **Che sport pratichi?**
             keh sport prah-tee-kee
             What sports do you play?

Giulia: **Faccio nuoto e vado a cavallo.**
             fahch-choh noo-oh-toh eh vah-doh ah kah-vahl-loh
             I swim and ride.

Stefano: **Equitazione?**
             eh-koo-ee-tah-tsee-oh-neh
             Riding?

Giulia: **È il mio sport preferito!**
             eh eel mee-oh sport preh-feh-ree-toh
             It's my favorite sport!
             Giochi a tennis?
             joh-kee ah tennis
             Do you play tennis?

Stefano: **No, faccio palestra.**
             noh fahch-choh pah-lehs-trah
             No, I go to the gym.

Giulia: **Body building?**
             boh-dee beeld-eeng
             Body building?

Stefano: **Ma no — aerobica e fitness.**
             mah noh ah-eh-roh-bee-kah eh fit-ness
             Oh no — aerobics and fitness.

Talking about Hobbies and Interests

You can certainly do a lot of other things in your leisure time besides wear yourself out playing sports. We try to give you a variety of them in Italian.

Talkin' the Talk

Have a look at what Serena and Nicoletta are talking about. Nicoletta apparently prefers peaceful and calm activities, whereas Serena likes to participate in sports that make her sweat.

Serena:	**Cosa fai questo fine settimana?**
	koh-zah fah-ee koo-ehs-toh fee-neh-seht-tee-mah-nah
	What are you going to do this weekend?
Nicoletta:	**Vado in campagna.**
	vah-doh een kahm-pah-nyah
	I'm going to the countryside.
Serena:	**È un' idea fantastica!**
	eh oo-nee-deh-ah fahn-tahs-tee-kah
	That's a great idea!
Nicoletta:	**Ho una casetta vicino al lago.**
	oh oo-nah kah-seht-tah vee-chee-noh ahl lah-goh
	I have a small house close to the lake.
Serena:	**Ideale per riposarsi.**
	ee-deh-ah-leh pehr ree-poh-zahr-see
	Ideal for relaxing.
Nicoletta:	**Sì, leggo, scrivo, passeggio lungo il lago.**
	see lehg-goh skree-voh pahs-sehj-joh loon-goh eel lah-goh
	Yes, I read, I write, I take walks around the lake.
Serena:	**Non fai sport?**
	nohn fah-ee sport
	Don't you play any sports?
Nicoletta:	**Vado in bicicletta.**
	vah-doh een bee-chee-kleht-tah
	I bicycle.
Serena:	**Non puoi fare jogging?**
	nohn poo-oh-ee fah-reh johg-geeng
	Can't you jog?
Nicoletta:	**Sì, ma non mi diverto!**
	see mah nohn mee dee-vehr-toh
	Yes, but I don't enjoy it!
Serena:	**Sei troppo pigra!**
	say trohp-poh pee-grah
	You're too lazy!

Obviously, sports isn't the only hobby you can have. Some hobbies are more sedentary, like reading, sewing, playing musical instruments. Coming up, we introduce you to a few of these.

Talkin' the Talk

 Ernesto and Tommaso are discovering that not all sports are physical.

Ernesto:	**Non ti annoi mai?**
	nohn tee ahn-noh-ee mah-ee
	Don't you ever get bored?

Tommaso:	**No, ho molti interessi.**
	noh oh mohl-tee een-teh-rehs-see
	No, I have many interests.

Ernesto:	**Per esempio?**
	pehr eh-zehm-pee-oh
	For example?

Tommaso:	**Amo leggere e andare al cinema.**
	ah-moh lehj-jeh-reh eh ahn-dah-reh ahl chee-neh-mah
	I love to to read and go to the movies.

Ernesto:	**Non fai sport?**
	nohn fah-ee sport
	Don't you play any sports?

Tommaso:	**Soltanto quelli pericolosi!**
	sohl-than-toh koo-ehl-lee peh-ree-koh-loh-zee
	Just the dangerous ones!

Ernesto:	**Per esempio?**
	pehr eh-zehm-pee-oh
	For example?

Tommaso:	**La Formula Uno in televisione!**
	lah fohr-moo-lah oo-noh een teh-leh-vee-zee-oh-neh
	Formula One racing on TV!

Fun & Games

Now it's time for *you* to have some fun! In the box below, try to find the names of some plants and animals we introduced in this chapter. We provide the English, but you have to find the Italian.

Find the Italian for these words: horse, flower, bird, cat, wolf, oak, pine, cow, sheep, tree.

Word Seek

A	J	A	R	O	C	E	P	O	S
U	I	V	S	W	S	O	P	A	B
A	H	C	E	M	L	U	Y	O	A
C	I	K	R	L	L	U	V	G	D
C	G	B	A	E	F	O	L	E	D
U	N	V	M	Z	U	I	N	S	D
M	A	R	X	J	C	Q	O	I	Y
C	G	A	T	T	O	E	I	R	P
A	L	B	E	R	O	P	S	T	E
F	R	H	O	L	L	E	C	C	U

Answers: cavallo, fiore, uccello, gatto, lupo, quercia, pino, mucca, pecora, albero.

Chapter 9

Talking on the Phone

· ·

In This Chapter

▶ Having a phone conversation

▶ Making reservations and appointments over the phone

▶ Getting through to the person you want and leaving messages

▶ Using the past tense

· ·

*I*n this chapter you encounter expressions and phrases about telephones and telecommunication — for example, how to behave when someone calls you and how to leave a message. In addition, we tell you how to make reservations and appointments on the phone, and show you some practical samples of common phone dialogues.

Chatting on the Phone

Pronto! *(prohn-toh)* (Hello!) is the first thing you hear when you talk to an Italian on the phone. There's something special about this word: In most languages, you answer the phone with the same word you use for saying hello, but in Italian, you use **pronto** to say hello only on the phone.

Pronto means more than just hello. It frequently means "ready," in which case it functions as an adjective and therefore changes according to the noun it describes. In other words, when the noun it modifies is masculine, the adjective ends in **-o** (**pronto**). If the noun is feminine, it ends in **-a** — **pronta** *(prohn-tah)*. Consider these examples:

▶ **Martino, sei pronto?** *(mahr-tee-noh say prohn-toh)* (Martino, are you ready?)

▶ **La cena è pronta.** *(lah cheh-nah eh prohn-tah)* (Dinner is ready.)

Another use of **pronto** that you should know is **pronto soccorso** *(prohn-toh sohk-kohr-soh)* (first aid; emergency room). In this context, **pronto** means "rapid."

Italians are fanatical as far as cellular phones are concerned. Ever since this little portable phone became available, you see Italians phoning everywhere. It's hard to find an Italian who doesn't own cellular phone, which they call **il cellulare** *(eel chehl-loo-lah-reh).* They love it so much that they have a affectionate nickname — **il telefonino** *(eel teh-leh-foh-nee-noh),* which literally means "little phone." Italians adopted this useful accessory really as a fashion.

Calling from a public phone

We have to tell you something about **il telefono pubblico** *(eel teh-leh-foh-noh poob-blee-koh)* (the public phone). When you don't have a cellular phone and you're on the street and need to call somebody, you probably look for **una cabina telefonica** *(oo-nah kah-bee-nah teh-leh-foh-nee-kah)* (a telephone booth), which you can find on the street (if you are lucky). These telephone booths are either **un telefono a monete** *(oon teh-leh-foh-noh ah moh-neh-teh)* (a coin-operated phone) or **un telefono a scheda** *(oon teh-leh-foh-noh ah skeh-dah)* (a card phone). The difference is evident: Coin-operated ones need to be fed with money, while you need a phone card for the other ones.

Where can you get a phone card? In Italian, a phone card is called either **la carta telefonica** *(lah kahr-tah teh-leh-foh-nee-kah)* or **la scheda telefonica** *(lah skeh-dah teh-leh-foh-nee-kah),* and you can get one at all **tabaccai** *(tah-bahk-kah-ee)* (kiosks selling tobacco, newspapers, and so on) or at the post office.

Some helpful phone phrases :

- **C' è/avete un telefono?** *(cheh ah-veh-teh oon teh-leh-foh-noh)* (Is there/Do you have a [public] telephone?)

- **E' a monete?** *(eh ah moh-neh-teh)* (Is it coin-operated?)

- **Avete schede telefoniche?** *(ah-veh-teh skeh-deh teh-leh-foh-nee-keh)* (Do you sell phone cards?)

- **Il telefono dà libero.** *(eel teh-leh-foh-noh dah lee-beh-roh)* (The line is free.)

- **Il telefono squilla.** *(eel teh-leh-foh-noh skoo-eel-lah)* (The telephone is ringing.)

- **Il telefono dà occupato.** *(eel teh-leh-foh-noh dah ohk-koo-pah-toh)* (The line is busy.)

- **Rispondi!** (rees-pohn-dee) (Answer!; Pick up the phone!)

- **Attacca!** *(aht-tahk-kah)* (Hang up!)

Talkin' the Talk

 Giorgio is back in Napoli again and decides to give an old friend of his a call.

Simona: **Pronto!**
<u>prohn</u>-toh
Hello!

Giorgio: **Pronto, Simona?**
<u>prohn</u>-toh see-<u>moh</u>-neh
Hello, Simona?

Simona: **Sì, chi parla?**
see kee <u>pahr</u>-lah
Yes, who's speaking?

Giorgio: **Sono Giorgio.**
<u>soh</u>-noh <u>johr</u>-joh
It's Giorgio.

Simona: **Che bella sorpresa!**
keh <u>behl</u>-lah sohr-<u>preh</u>-zah
What a nice surprise!

Giorgio: **Come stai?**
<u>koh</u>-meh <u>stah</u>-ee
How are you?

Simona: **Benissimo, e tu?**
beh-<u>nees</u>-see-moh eh too
Very well, and you?

Giorgio: **Bene, grazie.**
<u>beh</u>-neh <u>grah</u>-tsee-eh
Well, thank you.

Simona: **Sei di nuovo a Napoli?**
say dee noo-<u>oh</u>-voh ah <u>nah</u>-poh-lee
Are you in Naples again?

Giorgio: **Sì, sono arrivato stamattina.**
see <u>soh</u>-noh ahr-ree-<u>vah</u>-toh stah-maht-<u>tee</u>-nah
Yes, I arrived this morning.

Simona:	**Ci vediamo stasera?**
	chee veh-dee-ah-moh stah-seh-rah
	Are we going to meet tonight?

Giorgio:	**Ti chiamo per questo!**
	tee kee-ah-moh pehr koo-ehs-toh
	That's why I'm calling!

In Italy, when you don't know a **numero di telefono** *(noo-meh-roh dee teh-leh-foh-noh)* (phone number), you have three alternatives to get it.

- ✔ The first one is to look it up in the **elenco telefonico** *(eh-lehn-koh teh-leh-foh-nee-koh)* (phone book).

- ✔ If it's a business number you can also either look in the **pagine gialle** *(pah-jee-neh jahl-leh)* (yellow pages), or call the information number available through them.

- ✔ The easiest but most expensive way is to call **il servizio informazioni** *(eel sehr-vee-tsee-oh een-fohr-mah-tsee-oh-nee)* (directory information).

Calling for business or pleasure

Whether you want to find out what time a show starts, make a dental appointment, or just chat with a friend, the easiest way to accomplish any of these tasks is usually to pick up the telephone. This section takes you through the nuts and bolts of talking on the telephone, starting with the conjugation of the word **parlare** *(pahr-lah-reh)* (to speak):

Conjugation	*Pronunciation*
io parlo	*ee-oh pahr-loh*
tu parli	*too pahr-lee*
lui/lei parla	*loo-ee/lay pahr-lah*
noi parliamo	*noh-ee pahr-lee-ah-moh*
voi parlate	*voh-ee pahr-lah-teh*
loro parlano	*loh-roh pahr-lah-noh*

Talkin' the Talk

The following is a formal dialogue between two **signori** (*see-nyoh-ree*) (gentlemen) who have met only once.

Sig. Palladino: **Pronto?**
prohn-toh
Hello?

Sig. Nieddu: **Pronto, il signor Palladino?**
prohn-toh eel see-nyohr pahl-lah-dee-noh
Hello, Mr. Palladino?

Sig. Palladino: **Si. Con chì parlo?**
see kohn kee pahr-loh
Yes. Who am I speaking to?

Sig. Nieddu: **Sono Carlo Nieddu.**
soh-noh kahr-loh nee-ehd-doo
This is Carlo Nieddu.

Sig. Palladino: **Mi dica!**
mee dee-kah
Can I help you? (Literally: Tell me)

Sig. Nieddu: **Si ricorda di me?**
see ree-kohr-dah dee meh
Do you remember me?

Sig. Palladino: **No, mi dispiace.**
noh mee dees-pee-ah-cheh
I don't, I'm sorry.

Sig. Nieddu: **Il cugino di Enza.**
eel koo-jee-noh dee ehn-tsah
Enza's cousin.

Sig. Palladino: **Certo, mi scusi tanto!**
chehr-toh mee skoo-zee tahn-toh
Sure, excuse me!

Sometimes you call just to chat on the phone — **fare due chiacchiere al telefono** (*fah-reh doo-eh kee-ahk-kee-eh-reh ahl teh-leh-foh-noh*). This can be a nice pastime. But the person on the other end of the line may not be prepared for it.

Talkin' the Talk

This is a quick, informal dialogue between Monica and her mother, Lucia.

Monica: **Pronto, mamma, sono io!**
            prohn-toh mahm-mah soh-noh ee-oh
            Hello, Mom, it's me!

Lucia: **Tesoro, ti posso richiamare?**
            teh-zoh-roh tee pohs-soh ree-kee-ah-mah-reh
            Honey, can I call you back?

Monica: **Sei occupata?**
            say ohk-koo-pah-tah
            Are you busy?

Lucia: **Sì, ho molto da fare!**
            see oh mohl-toh dah fah-reh
            Yes, I have a lot to do!

When you are really busy and have not even one second to speak to the person who called you, you may need these phrases. The first is informal, and the second is one you might use at work.

Ti posso richiamare più tardi? *(tee pohs-soh ree-kee-ah-mah-reh peè-oo tahr-dee)* (Can I call you back later?)

or

La posso richiamare fra un mezz'ora? *(lah pohs-soh ree-kee-ah-mah-reh frah oon mehd-dzoh-rah)* (Can I call you back in half an hour?)

Talkin' the Talk

On other occasions your call may be quite welcome, as Monica's is this time:

Monica: **Ciao, mamma, ti disturbo?**
            chah-oh mahm-mah tee dees-toor-boh
            Hello, Mom. Am I disturbing you?

Lucia: **No, affatto.**
            noh ahf-faht-toh
            Not at all.

Monica: **Volevo chiacchierare un po'.**
voh-<u>leh</u>-voh kee-ahk-kee-eh-<u>rah</u>-reh oon poh
I wanted to chat a little bit.

Lucia: **Buona idea!**
boo-<u>oh</u>-nah ee-<u>dee</u>-ah
Good idea!

Monica: **Sai, non ho niente da fare!**
<u>sah</u>-ee nohn oh nee-<u>ehn</u>-teh dah <u>fah</u>-reh
You know, I've nothing to do!

Words to Know

cellulare; telefonino [m]	chehl-loo-<u>lah</u>-reh; teh-leh-foh-<u>nee</u>-noh	cellular phone
cabina telefonica [f]	kah-<u>bee</u>-nah teh-leh-<u>foh</u>-nee-kah	telephone booth
telefono pubblico [m]	teh-<u>leh</u>-foh-noh <u>poob</u>-blee-koh	public phone
telefono a monete [m]	teh-<u>leh</u>-foh-noh ah moh-<u>neh</u>-teh	coin-operated phone
carta/scheda telefonica [f]	<u>kahr</u>-tah <u>skeh</u>-dah teh-leh-<u>foh</u>-nee-kah	phone card

Making Arrangements over the Phone

Making an appointment, reserving a table at a restaurant, ordering tickets for a concert — these are all activities you normally do by phone. In your own language, this is no big deal. In a foreign language, however, it's somewhat tougher. In this section, we gently introduce you to the Italian way to handle these matters.

Talkin' the Talk

Mrs. Elmi calls her doctor's office to make an appointment. She speaks to the doctor's nurse.

Sig.ra Elmi: **Buongiorno, sono la signora Elmi. Vorrei prendere un appuntamento.**
boo-ohn-johr-noh soh-noh lah see-nyoh-rah ehl-mee vohr-ray prehn-deh-reh oon ahp-poon-tah-mehn-toh
Good morning, this is Ms. Elmi. I'd like to make an appointment.

Nurse: **È urgente?**
eh oor-jehn-teh
Is it urgent?

Sig.ra Elmi: **Purtroppo sì.**
poor-trohp-poh see
Unfortunately, it is.

Nurse: **Va bene alle quattro e mezza?**
vah beh-neh ahl-leh koo-aht-troh eh mehd-dzah
Today at four-thirty?

Sig.ra Elmi: **Va benissimo, grazie.**
vah beh-nees-see-moh grah-tsee-eh
That's great, thank you.

Nurse: **Prego. Ci vediamo più tardi.**
preh-goh chee veh-dee-ah-moh pee-oo tahr-dee
You're welcome. See you later.

Sig.ra Elmi: **Arrivederci.**
ahr-ree-veh-dehr-chee
Good-bye.

The expression **a domani** *(ah doh-mah-nee)* (see you tomorrow) is a bit different in Italian, in that it doesn't have a verb. In English, the verb *see* indicates that you will see the other person tomorrow. Italian is more concise; you say **a domani** — literally, "until tomorrow." That you're going to meet or see that person is understood.

Asking for People and Getting the Message

This section offers vocabulary and useful expressions and questions about asking to speak to people and leaving messages. You know how often you use the phone to get in touch with someone either for business or pleasure, so knowing how to ask for the person you want is good information to have. You also know how often the person you want isn't available, so you need to be comfortable getting a message across.

You're familiar with the situation: You're waiting for a call, but the telephone doesn't ring. Then, you have to go out. When you get back, you want to know whether anyone called for you. You can ask that question several ways:

- **Ha chiamato qualcuno per me?** *(ah kee-ah-mah-toh koo-ahl-koo-noh pehr meh)* (Has anybody called for me?)

- **Mi ha chiamato qualcuno?** *(mee ah kee-ah-mah-toh koo-ahl-koo-noh)* (Did anybody call me?)

- **Mi ha cercato nessuno?** *(mee ah chehr-kah-toh nehs-soo-noh)* (Has anybody looked for me?)

- **Chi ha telefonato?** *(kee ah teh-leh-foh-nah-toh)* (Who called?)

- **Chiamate per me?** *(kee-ah-mah-teh pehr meh)* (Are there any calls for me?)

Talkin' the Talk

Leo wants to give Camilla a call, but she's not home. Therefore, he leaves a message for her.

Leo:	**Buongiorno, sono Leo.**
	boo-ohn-johr-noh soh-noh leh-oh
	Good morning, this is Leo.

Voice:	**Ciao Leo.**
	chah-oh leh-oh
	Hello, Leo.

Leo:	**C'è Camilla?**
	cheh kah-meel-lah
	Is Camilla in?

Voice:	**No, è appena uscita.**
	noh eh ahp-peh-nah oo-shee-tah
	No, she's just gone out.

Leo:	**Quando la trovo?** *koo-ahn-doh lah troh-voh* When can I reach her?
Voice:	**Verso le nove.** *vehr-soh leh noh-veh* Around nine.
Leo:	**Le posso lasciare un messaggio?** *leh pohs-soh lah-shah-reh oon mehs-sahj-joh* Can I leave her a message?
Voice:	**Come no, dimmi.** *koh-meh noh deem-mee* Of course, tell me.

Chiamare *(kee-ah-mah-reh)* (to call) is certainly a verb you need in the context of telephones. The conjugation follows:

Conjugation	*Pronunciation*
io chiamo	*ee-oh kee-ah-moh*
tu chiami	*too kee-ah-mee*
lui/lei chiama	*loo-ee/lay kee-ah-mah*
noi chiamiamo	*noh-ee kee-ah-mee-ah-moh*
voi chiamate	*voh-ee kee-ah-mah-teh*
loro chiamano	*loh-roh kee-ah-mah-noh*

Talkin' the Talk

Mr. Marchi calls Mr. Trevi's office to talk about an upcoming meeting. Mr. Trevi's secretary picks up the phone.

Secretary:	**Pronto?** *prohn-toh* Hello?
Sig. Marchi:	**Buongiorno, sono Ennio Marchi.** *boo-ohn-johr-noh soh-noh ehn-nee-oh mahr-kee* Good morning, this is Ennio Marchi.
Secretary:	**Buongiorno, dica.** *boo-ohn-johr-noh dee-kah* Good morning, can I help you?

Sig. Marchi: **Potrei parlare con il signor Trevi?**
poh-<u>tray</u> pahr-<u>lah</u>-reh kohn eel see-<u>nyoh</u>-reh <u>treh</u> vee
Can I speak to Mr. Trevi?

Secretary: **Mi dispiace, è in riunione.**
mee dees-pee-<u>ah</u>-cheh eh een ree-oon-<u>yoh</u>-neh
I'm sorry, he's in a meeting.

Sig. Marchi: **Potrei lasciargli un messaggio?**
poh-<u>tray</u> lah-<u>shahr</u>-lyee oon mehs-<u>sahj</u>-joh
Can I leave him a message?

Secretary: **Certo. Prego.**
<u>chehr</u>-toh <u>preh</u>-goh
Of course. Please.

CULTURAL WISDOM

The Italian spelling alphabet

We want to introduce you to the Italian alphabet. When you need to spell your name or other information, using the following list, which is mostly names of cities, can help ensure that you're understood. You can say either **"A come Ancona"** *(ah <u>koh</u>-meh ahn-<u>koh</u>-nah)* (**A** like Ancona) or simply say **"Ancona,"** and so on.

- A = Ancona *(ahn-<u>koh</u>-nah)*
- B = Bologna *(boh-<u>loh</u>-nyah)*
- C = Catania *(kah-<u>tah</u>-nee-ah)*
- D = Domodossola *(doh-moh-<u>dohs</u>-soh-lah)*
- E = Empoli *(<u>ehm</u>-poh-lee)*
- F = Firenze *(fee-<u>rehn</u>-tseh)*
- G = Genova *(<u>jeh</u>-noh-vah)*
- H = Hotel *(hoh-<u>tehl</u>)*
- I = Imola *(<u>ee</u>-moh-lah)*
- J = Jei *(jay)*/i lunga *(ee <u>loon</u>-gah)*
- K = Kappa *(<u>kahp</u>-pah)*

- L = Lucca *(<u>look</u>-kah)*
- M = Milano *(mee-<u>lah</u>-noh)*
- N = Napoli *(<u>nah</u>-poh-lee)*
- O = Otranto *(<u>oh</u>-trahn-toh)*
- P = Palermo *(pah-<u>lehr</u>-moh)*
- Q = Cu *(koo)*
- R = Roma *(<u>roh</u>-mah)*
- S = Salerno *(sah-<u>lehr</u>-noh)*
- T = Torino *(toh-<u>ree</u>-noh)*
- U = Udine *(<u>oo</u>-dee-neh)*
- V = Venezia *(veh-<u>neh</u>-tsee-ah)*
- W = Vu doppia *(voo <u>dohp</u>-pee-ah)*
- X = Ics *(eeks)*
- Y = Ipsilon *(<u>eep</u>-see-lohn)*
- Z = Zebra *(<u>dzeh</u>-brah)*

Sometimes you don't understand the name of the person you're talking to and you have to ask for the spelling. Names are even harder to understand when they're foreign to you, or when you're speaking a foreign language, so don't be surprised when your name isn't immediately clear to an Italian.

If someone needs you to spell your name, you may hear either of the following questions:

- **Come si scrive?** (*koh-meh-see skree-veh*) (How do you write it?)
- **Può fare lo spelling?** (*poo-oh fah-reh loh spelling*) (Can you spell it?)

See the "The Italian spelling alphabet" sidebar, earlier in this chapter, for tips on how to spell in Italian.

Words to Know

pronto	prohn-toh	hello
arrivederci	ahr-ree-veh-dehr-chee	goodbye
chiacchierare	kee-ahk-kee-eh-rah-reh	to chat
Attenda in linea!	aht-tehn-dah een lee-neh-ah	Hold the line!
chiamare	kee-ah-mah-reh	to call
chiamata [f]	kee-ah-mah-tah	call
informazione [f]	een-fohr-mah-tsee-oh-neh	information
sorpresa [f]	sohr-preh-zah	surprise

What Did You Do Last Weekend? — Talking about the Past

When you speak about something that happened in the past — for example, I have spoken — you mostly use the **passato prossimo** (*pahs-sah-toh prohs-see-moh*) in Italian, which corresponds to the English **present perfect**. But you also use the **passato prossimo** in cases where, in English, you use the **simple past** (I spoke).

The passato prossimo is a compound tense: It consists of more than one word, as in *I have heard.* Take a look at how it works in these examples:

- ✔ **Ho ascoltato un CD.** *(oh ahs-kohl-tah-toh oon cheh-deh)* (I have listened/listened a CD.)

- ✔ **Ho parlato con lui.** *(oh pahr-lah-toh kohn loo-ee)* (I have spoken/spoke to him.)

The structure of the passato prossimo is very similar to the present perfect. It is composed of the present tense of the verb **avere** *(ah-veh-reh)* (to have) plus the past participle of the verb that describes what happened. In the preceding examples, **ascoltato** *(ahs-kohl-tah-toh)* (listened) is the past participle of **ascoltare** *(ahs-kohl-tah-reh)* (to listen), and **parlato** *(pahr-lah-toh)* (spoken) is the past participle of **parlare** *(pahr-lah-reh)* (to speak).

The *past participle* is the form of a verb that can also be an adjective. For example, *spoken* is the past participle of the verb *to speak*. You can say, "I have spoken to him." or "He is the man I have spoken to." Table 9-1 gives you the infinitives and past participles of a number of the verbs that take some form of the verb **avere** *(ah-veh-reh)* (to have).

The complete present tense of **avere** *(ah-veh-reh)* (to have) is:

Conjugation	Pronunciation
io ho	ee-oh oh
tu hai	too ah-ee
lei/lui ha	lay loo-ee ah
noi abbiamo	noh-ee ahb-bee-ah-moh
voi avete	voh-ee ah-veh-teh
loro hanno	loh-roh ahn-noh

Lei *(lay)* is the formal way of saying "you." Use **lei** to address someone you don't know well, or to whom you want to be polite.

Table 9-1	Past Participles Using "Avere" — To Have
Infinitive	**Past Participle**
ascoltare *(ahs-kohl-tah-reh)* (to listen)	**ascoltato** *(ahs-kohl-tah-toh)* (listened)
ballare *(bahl-lah-reh)* (to dance)	**ballato** *(bahl-lah-toh)* (danced)
comprare *(kohm-prah-reh)* (to buy)	**comprato** *(kohm-prah-toh)* (bought)

(continued)

Table 9-1 (continued)

Infinitive	Past Participle
conoscere *(koh-noh-sheh-reh)* (to meet, the first time)	**conosciuto** *(koh-noh-shoo-toh)* (met)
dire *(dee-reh)* (to say)	**detto** *(deht-toh)* (said)
fare *(fah-reh)* (to do)	**fatto** *(faht-toh)* (done)
incontrare *(een-kohn-trah-reh)* (to meet)	**incontrato** *(een-kohn-trah-toh)* (met)
leggere *(lehj-jeh-reh)* (to read)	**letto** *(leht-toh)* (read)
pensare *(pehn-sah-reh)* (to think)	**pensato** *(pehn-sah-toh)* (thought)
scrivere *(skree-veh-reh)* (to write)	**scritto** *(skreet-toh)* (written)
telefonare *(teh-leh-foh-nah-reh)* (to phone)	**telefonato** *(teh-leh-foh-nah-toh)* (called)
vedere *(veh-deh-reh)* (to see)	**visto** *(vees-toh)* (seen)

Asking about last weekend is always a reason to call your friend to hear what he or she did. This question is a good peg to hang a chitchat on.

Talkin' the Talk

Rosa calls her best friend Tiziana to catch up on her weekend.

Rosa: **Che cosa hai fatto questo fine settimana?**
keh koh-zah ah-ee faht-toh koo-ehs-toh fee-neh
seht-tee-mah-nah
What did you do last weekend?

Tiziana: **Ho conosciuto un uomo meraviglioso!**
oh koh-noh-shoo-toh oon oo-oh-moh
meh-rah-vee-lyoh-zoh
I met a wonderful man!

Rosa: **Racconta tutto!**
rahk-kohn-tah toot-toh
Tell me everything!

Tiziana: **Sabato sono andata al mare.**
sah-bah-toh soh-noh ahn-dah-tah ahl mah-reh
Saturday I went to the beach.

Rosa:	**Da sola?**
	dah soh-lah
	Alone?

Tiziana:	**Sì, e lì ho incontrato Enrico.**
	see eh lee oh een-kohn-trah-toh ehn-ree-koh
	Yes, and I met Enrico there.

Rosa:	**Per caso?**
	pehr kah-zoh
	By chance?

Tiziana:	**Sì, è stato proprio carino.**
	see eh stah-toh proh-pree-oh kah-ree-noh
	Yes, it was really nice.

We have one more thing to say about the **passato prossimo**. Not all verbs require the supporting verb **avere** (to have). Most verbs that indicate movement need the verb **essere** (ehs-seh-reh) (to be) to build the **passato prossimo**.

Other examples are a bit different from the ones you already saw.

- ✔ **Anna è andata al mare.** *(ahn-nah eh ahn-dah-tah ahl mah-reh)* (Anna has gone/went to the beach.)
- ✔ **Carlo è appena uscito.** *(kahr-loh eh ahp-peh-nah oo-shee-toh)* (Carlo has just gone/went out.)

In comparison to the previous examples, there are two differences: The first verb is a present tense form of **essere** *(ehs-seh-reh)* (to be) instead of **avere** *(ah-veh-reh)* (to have), and one past participle ends with **-a (andata)** and one ends in **-o (uscito)**.

The reason for this difference is that in one case the subject is a woman, Anna, and in the other case the subject is a man, Carlo. When the **passato prossimo** is compounded with the present tense of **essere** (to be), the past participle ends according to the subject: feminine singular **-a**, masculine singular **-o**, feminine plural **-e**, or masculine plural **-i**.

So just as we gave you the conjugation of **avere** to form certain past participles, we also give you the conjugation of the verb **essere** *(ehs-seh-reh)* (to be) to form the past participles of verbs that indicate movement:

Conjugation	Pronunciation
io sono	<u>ee</u>-oh <u>soh</u>-noh
tu sei	too say
lei/lui è	lay <u>loo</u>-ee eh
noi siamo	<u>noh</u>-ee see-<u>ah</u>-moh
voi siete	<u>voh</u>-ee see-<u>eh</u>-teh
loro sono	<u>loh</u>-roh <u>soh</u>-noh

Table 9-2 lists past participles of verbs that indicate movement and use **essere** to build the **passato prossimo**.

Table 9-2	Past Participles Using "Essere" — To Be
Infinitive	*Past Participle*
andare *(ahn-<u>dah</u>-reh)* (to go)	**andata/-o/-e/-i** *(ahn-<u>dah</u>-tah/toh/teh/tee)* (gone)
arrivare *(ahr-ree-<u>vah</u>-reh)* (to arrive)	**arrivata/-o/-e/-i** *(ahr-ree-<u>vah</u>-tah/toh/teh/tee)* (arrived)
entrare *(ehn-<u>trah</u>-reh)* (to enter)	**entrata/-o/-e/-i** *(ehn-<u>trah</u>-tah/toh/teh/tee)* (entered)
partire *(pahr-<u>tee</u>-reh)* (to leave)	**partita/-o/-e/-i** *(pahr-<u>tee</u>-tah/toh/teh/tee)* (left)
tornare *(tohr-<u>nah</u>-reh)* (to return)	**tornata/-o/-e/-i** *(tohr-<u>nah</u>-tah/toh/teh/tee)* (returned)

Here we present an aspect of Italian verb formation that may confuse you. In English, you build the past participle of *to be* by adding the auxiliary *to have* — for example: *I have been.* In Italian, this is different — you form the past participle of the verb **essere** *(<u>ehs</u>-seh-reh)* (to be) by using **essere** itself. So you say: **Sono stata al cinema** *(<u>soh</u>-noh <u>stah</u>-tah ahl <u>chee</u>-neh-mah)* (I have been to the movies).

Essere and **stare** *(<u>stah</u>-reh)* (to be; to stay) are verbs that don't describe movement but nevertheless take **essere** in the **passato prossimo**:

Infinitive	Past Participle
essere *(<u>ehs</u>-seh-reh)* (to be)	**stata/-o/-e/-i** *(<u>stah</u>-tah/toh/teh/tee)* (been)
stare *(<u>stah</u>-reh)* (to be; to stay)	**stata/-o/-e/-i** *(<u>stah</u>-tah/toh/teh/tee)* (been; stayed)

Words to Know

dimmi	deem-mee	tell me
fine settimana [m]	fee-neh seht-tee-mah-nah	weekend
da solo	dah soh-loh	alone; by oneself
dire	dee-reh	to tell
tutto	toot-toh	everything
proprio	proh-pree-oh	really

Fun & Games

You're Mario's guest, but he's gone out for a moment. The telephone rings and you have to answer it. Fill in the gaps in this incomplete phone conversation.

You: (1) _____ ! (Hello!)

Voice: Ciao, sono Chiara. Con chi (2) _____? (Hello, I'm Chiara. Who am I talking to?)

You: Sono un (3) _____ di Mario. (I'm a friend of Mario's.)

Voice: (4) _____ Mario? (Is Mario in?)

You: No, è (5) _____ uscito. (No, he's just gone out.)

Voice: Gli posso (6) _____? (Can I leave him a message?)

You: Certo (7) _____ (Of course. Please.)

Mario returns and asks:

Mario: Ha (8) _____ qualcuno per me?
            (Has anybody called for me?)

Answers: 1. Pronto, 2. parlo, 3. amico, 4. C'è, 5. appena, 6. lasciare un messaggio, 7. prego, 8. chiamato

Chapter 10

At the Office and Around the House

. . . .

In This Chapter

▶ Talking about the business world

▶ Searching for a home or apartment

▶ Using imperative verbs to order people around

. . . .

*I*t's not always fun to talk about business or to search for an apartment, but getting to know how to do this in Italian can be really fun! In this chapter we talk about all the business stuff that can be important to you, and how to you cope in Italian when looking for a new place to live. Join in!

Discussing Your Job

Business contacts with people in other countries continues to increase in importance. Because modern technology supports the quick exchange of information over vast distances, you may have to talk to foreign business partners — or even travel to their countries. If you happen to have business contacts with Italian companies, knowing some basic Italian business vocabulary may be useful. Because English is the language of business, however, Italian has adopted many English computer and software terms.

Italian has at least three words for "company" — **la compagnia** *(lah kohm-pah-nyee-ah)*, **la ditta** *(lah deet-tah)* (which also means "the firm"), and **la società** *(lah soh-cheh-tah)*. These words are virtually interchangeable.

L'ufficio *(loof-fee-choh)* is Italian for "office," but people often use **stanza** *(stahn-tsah)* (room) to refer to their personal office.

The following sentences give you a taste of the phrases you hear in **uffici** *(oof-fee-chee)* (offices) everywhere:

- ✔ **La mia scrivania è troppo piccola.** *(lah mee-ah skree-vah-nee-ah eh trohp-poh peek-koh-lah)* (My desk is too small.)

- ✔ **È una grande società?** *(eh oo-nah grahn-deh soh-cheh-tah)* (Is it a big company?)

- ✔ **Non proprio, diciamo media.** *(nohn proh-pree-oh dee-chah-moh meh-dee-ah)* (Not really, let's say medium-sized.)

- ✔ **Lavora per una piccola agenzia.** *(lah-voh-rah pehr oo-nah peek-koh-lah ah-jehn-tsee-ah)* (He works for a small agency.)

- ✔ **Amo il mio lavoro.** *(ah-moh eel mee-oh lah-voh-roh)* (I like my job.)

To learn a language you have to work, too. Here we give you the conjugation of the verb **lavorare** *(lah-voh-rah-reh)* (to work).

Conjugation	Pronunciation
io lavoro	ee-oh lah-voh-roh
tu lavori	too lah-voh-ree
lui/lei lavora	loo-ee/lay lah-voh-rah
noi lavoriamo	noh-ee lah-voh-ree-ah-moh
voi lavorate	voh-ee lah-voh-rah-teh
loro lavorano	loh-roh lah-voh-rah-noh

S.p.A. is the Italian abbreviation for **Società per Azioni** *(soh-cheh-tah pehr ah-tsee-oh-nee)* (joint-stock company), whereas a **S.A.S., Società in Accomandita Semplice** *(soh-cheh-tah een ahk-koh-mahn-dee-tah sehm-plee-cheh)* is a limited partnership. Another type of company is an **S.r.l. (Società a responsabilità limitata)** *(soh-cheh-tah ah rehs-pohn-sah-bee-lee-tah lee-mee-tah-tah)* (public limited company, also know as a p.l.c.).

The human element

Even if you are **libero professionista** *(lee-beh-roh proh-fehs-see-oh-nees-tah)* (self-employed), chances are that your **lavoro** *(lah-voh-roh)* (job) puts you in contact with other people. All those people have titles and names, as the following short exchanges show:

✔ **Il mio capo è una donna.** *(eel mee-oh kah-poh eh oo-nah dohn-nah)* (My boss is a woman.)

Il mio è un boss! *(eel mee-oh eh oon boss)* (Mine is bossy!)

This sentence literally translates to "Mine is a boss!" However, Italians say "boss" when someone is bossy.

✔ **Hai un'assistente personale?** *(ah-ee oo-nahs-sees-tehn-teh pehr-soh-nah-leh)* (Do you have a personal assistant?)

No, il nostro team ha un segretario. *(noh eel nohs-troh team ah oon seh-greh-tah-ree-oh)* (No, our team has a secretary.)

✔ **Dov'è il direttore?** *(doh-veh eel dee-reht-toh-reh)* (Where is the director?)

Nella sua stanza. *(nehl-lah soo-ah stahn-tsah)* (In her office.)

Talkin' the Talk

Marta and Elisabetta are talking about their colleagues.

Marta:	**Come sono i tuoi colleghi?** *koh-meh soh-noh ee too-oh-ee kohl-leh-gee* What are your new colleagues like?
Elisabetta:	**Abbastanza simpatici.** *ahb-bahs-tahn-tsah seem-pah-tee-chee* Quite nice.
Marta:	**E i superiori?** *eh ee soo-peh-ree-oh-ree* And the supervisors?
Elisabetta:	**Non me ne parlare!** *nohn meh neh pahr-lah-reh* Don't even mention them!

Office equipment

Even the smallest offices today utilize a wide variety of equipment. Many people couldn't even imagine running a modern business without a computer or photocopier. Fortunately, many of these "technology" words are the same

in Italian as they are in English: computer, fax, and e-mail are used and pronounced as they are in English, and the Italian for "photocopy" and "photocopier" are fairly intuitive — **fotocopia** *(foh-toh-koh-pee-ah)* and
fotocopiatrice *(foh-toh-koh-pee-ah-tree-cheh),* respectively.

The following sentences can help you develop your Italian office vocabulary
to a respectable level.

- **Posso usare la stampante, per favore?** *(pohs-soh oo-zah-reh lah stahm-pahn-teh pehr fah-voh-reh)* (May I use the printer, please?)

- **Il lavoro non va bene.** *(eel lah-voh-roh nohn vah beh-neh)* (The work isn't going well.)

- **Il fax è arrivato.** *(eel fahks eh ahr-ree-vah-toh)* (The fax arrived.)

- **Quando ha spedito l'e-mail?** *(koo-ahn-doh ah speh-dee-toh lee-mail)* (When did you send the e-mail?)

- **Avete già ricevuto gli ordini?** *(ah-veh-teh jah ree-cheh-voo-toh lyee ohr-dee-nee)* (Did you already get the instructions?)

Talkin' the Talk

Mr. Miller, an American businessman, has been trying unsuccess-
fully to send his Italian associate, il signor Tosi, some
important information.

Mr. Miller:	**Ha ricevuto il mio messaggio?**
	ah ree-cheh-voo-toh eel-mee-oh mehs-sahj-joh
	Have you received my message?
Sig. Tosi:	**No, oggi non è arrivato niente.**
	noh ohj-jee nohn eh ahr-ree-vah-toh nee-ehn-teh
	No, nothing has arrived yet today.
Mr. Miller:	**Le mando subito un fax.**
	leh mahn-doh soo-bee-toh oon fahks
	I'll send you a fax immediately.
Sig. Tosi:	**Non funziona: è rotto.**
	nohn foon-tsee-oh-nah eh roht-toh
	It's not working: it's out of order.
Mr. Miller:	**Ha un indirizzo e-mail?**
	ah oon een-dee-reet-tsoh e-mail
	Do you have an e-mail address?

Sig. Tosi:	**Sì. E può mandarmi il file con gli indirizzi?**
	see ee poo-<u>oh</u> mahn-<u>dahr</u>-mee eel file kohn lyee
	een-dee-<u>reet</u>-tsee
	Yes. And can you send me the file with the addresses?

Mr. Miller:	**Certo, glielo mando come allegato, ma avrò bisogno di più tempo per prepararlo.**
	<u>chehr</u>-toh <u>lyee</u>-eh-loh <u>mahn</u>-doh <u>koh</u>-meh
	ahl-leh-<u>gah</u>-toh mah ah-<u>vroh</u> bee-<u>zoh</u>-nyoh
	dee pee-<u>oo</u> <u>tehm</u>-poh pehr preh-pah-<u>rahr</u>-loh
	Of course, I'll send it as an attachment, but it will take me longer to get it ready.

Sig. Tosi:	**Va benissimo. Oggi lavoro fino a tardi.**
	vah beh-<u>nees</u>-see-moh <u>ohj</u>-jee lah <u>voh</u>-roh <u>fee</u>-noh
	ah <u>tahr</u>-dee
	That's okay. I'm working late today.

Words to Know

messaggio [m]	mehs-<u>sahj</u>-joh	message
lavoro [m]	lah-<u>voh</u>-roh	work
È rotto.	eh <u>roht</u>-toh	It's out of order.
macchina [f]	<u>mahk</u>-kee-nah	machine
tempo [m]	<u>tehm</u>-poh	time
tardi	<u>tahr</u>-dee	late

A typical job advertisement

When you're looking for a job, you can check the newspaper advertisements like the example in Figure 10-1.

CULTURAL WISDOM

In Italy, often ads request information on an applicant's personality. Also, job advertisements do not usually contain mailing addresses. Instead, ads list fax or e-mail addresses. You send your **domanda d'assunzione** (doh-_mahn_-dah dahs-soon-tsee-_oh_-neh) (job application) and/or your curriculum vitae or resume via fax or e-mail.

Figure 10-1: An example of a job advertisement.

Agenzia pubblicitaria cerca assistente di direzione. Requisiti: esperienza d'ufficio, perfetto inglese, confidenza con il computer, Caratteristiche: flessibilità, autonomia, senso del team, fantasia. Curriculum Vitae: Agenzia Mondo Fax 01 36 45 08 92 71 e-mail: mondo.age@xxxxxx.it	Advertising bureau is looking for an assistant to the director. Requirements: advertising experience, perfect English, confidence with computers. Characteristics: flexibility, autonomy, team spirit, creativity/imagination. Resumé: **Agenzia Mondo Fax 01 36 45 08 92 71 e-mail: mondo.age@xxxxxx.it**

Talkin' the Talk

Giuliana sent her application to a company several days ago and is anxiously awaiting a reply. Finally the company gets in touch with her.

Anna: **Pronto, la signora Dani?**
prohn-toh lah see-_nyoh_-rah _dah_-nee
Hello, Ms. Dani?

Giuliana: **Sì. Chi parla?**
see kee _pahr_-lah
Yes. Who's speaking?

Anna: **Sono Anna, dell' _Agenzia Mondo._**
soh-noh _ahn_-nah dehl-lah-jehn-_tsee_-ah _mohn_-doh
This is Anna from the Agenzia Mondo.

Giuliana: **Buongiorno! Stavo aspettando la sua chiamata.**
boo-ohn-_johr_-noh _stah_-voh ahs-peht-_tahn_-doh lah _soo_-ah kee-ah-_mah_-tah
Good morning! I've been hoping for a call from you.

Anna:	**Abbiamo ricevuto il suo curriculum vitae e vorremmo conoscerla personalmente.** *ahb-bee-ah-moh ree-cheh-voo-toh eel soo-oh koor-ree-koo-loom vee-tah-eh eh vohr-rehm-moh koh-noh-shehr-lah pehr-soh-nahl-mehn-teh* We received your resume and we'd like to meet you in person. **Può venire martedì prossimo alle 10?** *poo-oh veh-nee-reh mahr-teh-dee prohs-see-moh ahl-leh dee-eh-chee* Could you come next Tuesday at 10?
Giuliana:	**Benissimo. Dov'è l'agenzia?** *beh-nees-see-moh doh-veh lah-jehn-tsee-ah* Very well. Where is the agency?
Anna:	**Via delle Rose 10.** *vee-ah dehl-leh roh-zeh dee-eh-chee* Via delle Rose 10.
Giuliana:	**La ringrazio, a martedì. Arrivederci.** *lah reen-grah-tsee-oh ah mahr-teh-dee ahr-ree-veh-dehr-chee* Thank you, see you Tuesday. Goodbye.

Employers look to hire people they hope are **di responsabilità** *(dee reh-spohn-sah-bee-lee-tah)* (responsible) and **affidabili** *(ahf-fee-dah-bee-lee)* (dependable). So, on Tuesday, Giuliana arrives at the *Agenzia Mondo* at five to ten for her interview with Anna — **La prima cosa è la puntualità!** *(lah pree-mah koh-zah eh lah poon-too-ah-lee-tah)* (The first thing is punctuality!)

Talkin' the Talk

Anna poses the usual **colloquio** *(kohl-loh-koo-ee-oh)* (interview) questions to Giuliana.

Anna:	**Perché vorrebbe cambiare lavoro?** *pehr-keh vohr-rehb-beh kahm-bee-ah-reh lah-voh-roh* Why do you want to change jobs?
Giuliana:	**Vorrei fare qualcosa di nuovo.** *vohr-ray fah-reh koo-ahl-koh-zah dee noo-oh-voh* I'd like to do something new.

Anna:	**È già assistente del direttore.**	
	eh jah ahs-sees-<u>tehn</u>-teh dehl dee-reht-<u>toh</u>-reh	
	You are already assistant to the director.	

Giuliana: **Sì, ma in una compagnia finanziaria.**
see mah een <u>oo</u>-nah kohm-pah-<u>nyee</u>-ah
fee-nahn-tsee-<u>ah</u>-ree-ah
Yes, but in a finance company.

Anna: **È molto diverso?**
eh <u>mohl</u>-toh dee-<u>vehr</u>-soh
Is it very different?

Giuliana: **Penso di sì.**
<u>pehn</u>-soh dee see
I think so.

Words to Know

colloquio [m]	kohl-<u>loh</u>-koo-ee-oh	interview
assistente [f/m]	ahs-sees-<u>tehn</u>-teh	assistant
annuncio [m]	ahn-<u>noon</u>-choh	advertisement
di responsabilità	dee reh-spohn-sah-bee-lee-<u>tah</u>	responsible
affidabile	ahf-fee-<u>dah</u>-bee-leh	dependable
chiamata [f]	kee-ah-<u>mah</u>-tah	call

Inhabiting Your Home

Italians usually speak of **la casa** (*lah <u>kah</u>-sah*) (the house; the home), even though they often mean **l'appartamento** (*lahp-pahr-tah-<u>mehn</u>-toh*) (the apartment). That's why you always say **cerco casa** (*<u>chehr</u>-koh <u>kah</u>-sah*) (I'm looking for a house; apartment).

Hunting for an apartment

When you look for an apartment, several avenues to your goal present themselves. You can find an apartment on your own through newspaper **annunci** *(lahn-noon-chee)* (advertisements) or turn to **un'agenzia immobiliare** *(oon ah-jehn-tsee-ah eem-moh-bee-lyah-reh)* (a real estate agency) for help.

When you turn to an agency, you have to specify your wishes concerning the number of rooms and location. These words can help you do just that:

- **il bagno** *(eel bah-nyoh)* (the bathroom)
- **il balcone** *(eel bahl-koh-neh)* (the balcony)
- **la camera da letto** *(lah kah-meh-rah dah leht-toh)* (the bedroom)
- **la cucina** *(lah koo-chee-nah)* (the kitchen)
- **il soggiorno** *(eel sohj-johr-noh)* (the living room)
- **la stanza** *(lah stahn-tsah)* (the room)

Using the verb "to rent" may be somewhat confusing, but Italians manage to cope with it, so it can't be too difficult. The confusion comes from this: As in English, both **i padroni di casa** *(ee pah-droh-nee dee kah-sah)* (landlords) and **linquilini** *(lyee een-koo-ee-lee-nee)* (tenants) use the verb **affittare** *(ahf-feet-tah-reh)* (to rent). To avoid misunderstandings, landlords also say **dare in affitto** *(dah-reh een ahf-feet-toh)* (Literally: to give in rent) and tenants use **prendere in affitto** *(prehn-deh-reh een ahf-feet-toh)* (Literally: to take in rent).

Talkin' the Talk

Flaminia is looking for an apartment, and Pietro helps her read through the newspaper ads. After a few minutes, Pietro thinks that he's found something interesting.

Pietro:	**Affittasi appartamento zona centro.**
	ahf-feet-tah-see ahp-pahr-tah-mehn-toh dzoh-nah chehn-troh
	Apartment to rent, central area.

Flaminia:	**Continua!**
	kohn-tee-noo-ah
	Go on!

Pietro:	**Due stanze, balcone, garage.**
	doo-eh _stahn_-tseh bahl-_koh_-neh gah-_rahj_
	Two rooms, balcony, garage.

Flaminia:	**Perfetto!**
	pehr-_feht_-toh
	Perfect!

Pietro:	**Tranquillo, in Via Treviso.**
	trahn-koo-_eel_-loh een _vee_-ah treh-_vee_-zoh
	Quiet, on Treviso Street.

Flaminia:	**Chiamo subito. Non è molto centrale.**
	kee-_ah_-moh _soo_-bee-toh nohn eh _mohl_-toh chehn-_trah_-leh
	I'll call immediately. It's not very central.

Pietro:	**No, ma costa sicuramente meno.**
	noh mah _kohs_-tah see-koo-rah-_mehn_-teh _meh_-noh
	No, but it's surely cheaper.

Flaminia:	**È vero.**
	eh _veh_-roh
	It's true!

Pietro:	**Chiama!**
	kee-_ah_-mah
	Call!

When you see a newspaper ad that interests you, reacting immediately is always best — **Chi prima arriva macina** _(kee pree-mah ahr-_ree_-vah _mah_-chee-nah)_ (First come first served). You don't want to hear **Mi dispiace, è già affittato** _(mee dees-pee-_ah_-cheh eh jah ahf-feet-_tah_-toh)_ (I'm sorry, it's already rented).

You may want to know the following words when searching for an apartment (and any other time you are considering making a purchase). **Caro** _(kah-roh)_ means "expensive," and **economico** _(eh-koh-_noh_-mee-koh)_ means "cheap" although Italians seldom use **economico**. Rather, most people say **costa poco** _(kohs-tah poh-koh)_ (it costs little) or **non è caro** _(nohn eh _kah_-roh)_ (it's not expensive). When you want to compare costs, you say **costa meno** _(kohs-tah _meh_-noh)_ (it costs less) or **costa di più** _(kohs-tah dee pee-_oo_)_ (it costs more).

Talkin' the Talk

 Flaminia calls the number given in the ad to find out more about an apartment.

Landlord: **Pronto!**
prohn-toh
Hello!

Flaminia: **Buongiorno, chiamo per l' annuncio. Quant'è l'affitto?**
boo-ohn-_johr_-noh kee-_ah_-moh pehr lahn-_noon_-cho koo-_ahn_-teh lah-_fit_-toh
Good morning! I'm calling about the ad. How much is the rent?

Landlord: **Un milione al mese.**
oon mee-lee-_oh_-neh ahl _meh_-zeh
One million [lire] per month.

Flaminia: **Riscaldamento e acqua sono compresi?**
rees-kahl-dah-_mehn_-toh eh _ahk_-koo-ah _soh_-noh kohm-_preh_-zee
Are heat and water included?

Landlord: **No, sono nelle spese di condominio.**
noh _soh_-noh _nehl_-leh _speh_-zeh dee kohn-doh-_mee_-nee-oh
No, they are included in the maintenance.

Flaminia: **Sono alte?**
soh-noh _ahl_-teh
Are they high?

Landlord: **Dipende dal consumo, come l'elettricità.**
dee-_pehn_-deh dahl kohn-_soo_-moh _koh_-meh leh-leht-tree-chee-_tah_
It depends on your consumption, the same as electricity.

Falminia: **Ci sono elettrodomestici nell'arredamento?**
chee soh-noh eh-leht-troh-doh-mehs-tee-chee nehl-lahr-reh-dah-_mehn_-toh
Are appliances included?

Landlord:	**Sì, ci sono il frigo, la cucina a gas, la lavastoviglie e la lavatrice.** *see chee soh-noh eel free-goh lah koo-chee-nah lah lah-vah-stoh-vee-lyeh eh lah lah-vah-tree-cheh* Yes, there is a refrigerator, a gas stove, a dishwasher, as well as a clothes washer.
Flaminia:	**Quando lo posso vedere?** *koo-ahn-doh loh pohs-soh veh-deh-reh* When can I see it?
Landlord:	**Subito, se vuole.** *soo-bee-toh seh voo-oh-leh* Immediately, if you want.

You'll probably have many other questions if you decide to rent an apartment. Table 10-1 lists some of the more common questions, and some possible answers.

Table 10-1   Common House-Hunting Questions and Answers

Questions	*Possible Answers*
È occupato? *eh ohk-koo-pah-toh* Is it occupied?	**No, è libero.** *noh eh lee-beh-roh* No, it's vacant. **Sì, per il momento.** *see pehr eel moh-mehn-toh* Yes, at the moment. **È libero fra sei mesi.** *eh lee-beh-roh frah say meh-zee* It will be vacant in six months.
Bisogna lasciare un deposito? *bee-zoh-nyah lah-shah-reh oon deh-poh-zee-toh* Is it necessary to put down a deposit?	**Sì, un mese d'affitto.** *see oon meh-zeh dahf-feet-toh* Yes, one month's rent. **Sì, la cauzione** *see lah kah-oo-tsee-oh-neh* Yes, we require a security deposit.
Paghi molto per la casa? *pah-gee mohl-toh pehr lah kah-sah* Do you pay a lot for your house?	**No, l'affitto è veramente basso.** *noh lahf-feet-toh eh veh-rah-mehn-teh bahs-soh* No, the rent is really low.

Questions	Possible Answers
La casa è tua?	**No, sono in affitto.**
lah kah-sah eh too-ah	*noh soh-noh een ahf-feet-toh*
Do you own your home?	No, I rent.
	Sì, l'ho comprata l'anno scorso.
	see loh kohm-prah-tah lahn-noh skohr-soh
	Yes, I bought it last year.

Sprucing up your apartment

When you finally find an apartment, you probably want to furnish it beautifully. The following dialogues show you what Italians call their furniture.

Talkin' the Talk

Valerio has found a new, **non ammobiliato** *(nohn ahm-moh-bee-lee-ah-toh)* (unfurnished) apartment. His friend **Eugenia** is asking him what he needs.

Valerio: **Ho trovato un appartamento! Devo comprare dei mobili.**
oh troh-vah-toh oon ahp-pahr-tah-mehn-toh deh-voh kohm-prah-reh day moh-bee-lee
I just found an apartment! I have to buy some furniture.

Eugenia: **Tutto?**
toot-toh
(Do you need) everything?

Valerio: **No, solo Il letto e l'armadio.**
noh soh-loh eel leht-toh eh lahr-mah-dee-oh
No, just a bed and a wardrobe.

Eugenia: **Nient'altro?**
nee-ehnt-ahl-troh
Nothing else?

Valerio: **Ho due comodini e una cassettiera.**
oh doo-eh koh-moh-dee-nee eh oo-nah kahs-seht-tee-eh-rah
I have two bedside tables and a chest of drawers.

Eugenia: **E per il soggiorno?**
eh pehr eel sohj-johr-noh
Do you have furniture for the living room?

Valerio: **Ho una poltrona. Mi mancano ancora il divano e un tavolino.**
oh oo-nah pohl-troh-nah mee mahn-kah-noh ahn-koh-rah eel dee-vah-noh eh oon tah-voh-lee-noh
Only one chair. I need a couch and a coffee table.

La signora Giorgetti wants to buy secondhand furniture. She reads an interesting ad:

> **Vendesi** *(vehn-deh-see)* (For sale): **tavolo e due sedie** *(tah-voh-loh eh doo-eh seh-dee-eh)* (table and two chairs) **stile Liberty** *(stee-leh lee-behr-tee)* (Liberty style)

"Quello che cercavo!" *(koo-ehl-loh keh chehr-kah-voh)* ("Just what I was looking for!"), she exclaims. She immediately calls the number on the ad. Of course, she needs answers to some questions:

> **Sono autentici?** *(soh-noh ah-oo-tehn-tee-chee)* (Are they authentic?)

> **Sì, comprati ad un' asta.** *(see kohm-prah-tee ahd oon-ahs-tah)* (Yes, [they were] bought at an auction.)

> **Sono in buono stato?** *(soh-noh een boo-oh-noh stah-toh)* (Are they in good condition?)

> **Venga a vederli!** *(vehn-gah ah veh-dehr-lee)* (Come and see them!)

Bending Others to Your Will: Imperatives

When your boss says **Venga nel mio ufficio!** *(vehn-gah nehl mee-oh oof-fee-choh)* (Come in my office!) or you say to your children **Mettete in ordine le vostre camere!** *(meht-teh-teh een ohr-dee-neh leh vohs-treh kah-meh-reh)* (Clean up your rooms!), you use an imperative — a request, a demand, or an invitation for someone to do something. Four forms of imperatives exist:

✔ **Singular informal:** You refer informally to a person you know — for example, a friend or a family member.

In Italian, if a verb ends in **-are**, as in **mandare** *(mahn-dah-reh)* (to send), the informal imperative form ends in **-a**, as in **Manda!** *(mahn-dah)* (Send!). If a verb ends in **-ere** or **-ire**, as in **prendere** *(prehn-deh-reh)* (to take) and **finire** *(fee-nee-reh)* (to finish), the informal imperative ends in **-i**, as in **Prendi!** *(prehn-dee)* (Take!) and **Finisci!** (fee-nee-shee) (Finish!).

✔ **Singular formal:** You refer formally to a person you don't know well.

The command form is different when you refer to a person formally. If the verb ends in **-are**, as in **mandare**, the formal imperative form ends in **-i**, as in **Mandi!** *(mahn-dee)* (Send!). If the verb ends in **-ere** or **-ire**, as in **prendere** or **finire**, the formal imperative ends in **-a**, as in **Prenda!** *(prehn-dah)* (Take!) and **Finisca!** *(fee-nees-kah)* (Finish!). As you can see, you simply switch the informal and formal endings.

✔ **Plural:** You refer to more than one person.

You use the plural imperative form for two or more people, even if you would address the separate individuals formally. Verbs that end in **-are**, like **mandare**, have the plural imperative ending **-ate**, as in **Mandate!** *(mahn-dah-teh)* (Send!). Verbs that end in **-ere** change their endings to **-ete**, as in **Prendete!** *(prehn-deh-teh)* (Take!). Verbs that end in **-ire** change their endings to **-ite**, as in **Finite!** (fee-nee-teh) (Finish!)

✔ **Plural, including yourself:** You include yourself by saying, for example, "Let's go!"

Good news! All verbs, including our examples **mandare**, **prendere**, and **finire,** change their endings to the imperative ending **-iamo** — namely, **Mandiamo!** *(mahn-dee-ah-moh)* (Let's send!), **Prendiamo!** *(prehn-dee-ah-moh)* (Let's take!), and **Finiamo!** *(fee-nee-ah-moh)* (Let's finish!).That's pretty easy, isn't it?

In case you're still struggling to grasp this scheme, Table 10-2 gives a quick overview.

Table 10-2	**Imperative Verb Endings**		
Form	*-are Verb Ending*	*-ere Verb Ending*	*-ire Verb Ending*
Informal singular	-a	-i	-i
Formal singular	-i	-a	-a
Plural	-ate	-ete	-ite
We form	-iamo	-iamo	-iamo

We can't let you get away without looking at some common exceptions to the preceding rules. In the following you see a table with some of these so-called exceptions.

Table 10-3	Exceptional Imperatives	
Informal Singular	*Formal Singular*	*Translation*
Abbi pazienza! (*ahb*-bee pah-tsee-*ehn*-tsah)	**Abbia pazienza!** (ahb-*bee*-ah pah-tsee-*ehn*-tsah)	Be patient!
Da'! (*dah*)	**Dìa!** (*dee*-ah)	Give!
Di' qualcosa! (dee koo-ahl-*koh*-zah)	**Dica qualcosa!** (*dee*-kah koo-ahl-*koh*-zah)	Say something!
Fa' qualcosa! (fah koo-ahl-*koh*-zah)	**Faccia qualcosa!** (*fahch*-chah koo-ahl-*koh*-zah)	Do something!
Sii buono! (*see*-ee boo-*oh*-noh)	**Sia buono!** (*see*-ah boo-*oh*-noh)	Be good!
Sta' fermo! (stah *fehr*-moh)	**Stìa fermo!** (*stee*-ah *fehr*-moh)	Stay still!
Va via! (vah *vee*-ah)	**Vada via!** (*vah*-dah *vee*-ah)	Go away!
Vieni qua! (vee-*eh*-nee koo-ah)	**Venga qua!** (*vehn*-gah koo-ah)	Come here!

Fun & Games

This is an easy one! Identify the various rooms and items marked with a solid, numbered line with their Italian names. For extra credit, keep on naming as many items as you can.

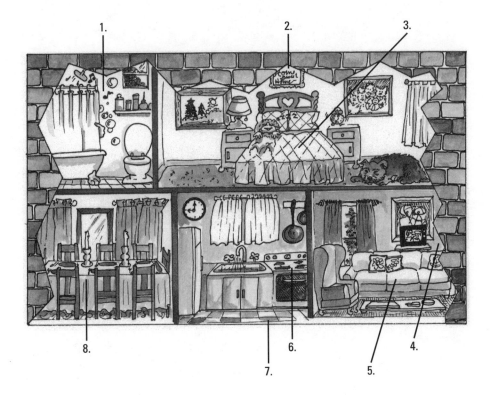

Answers: 1. **il bagno** (the bathroom), 2. **la camera da letto** (the bedroom), 3. **il letto** (the bed), 4. **il soggiorno** (the living room), 5. **il divano** (the couch), 6. **la cucina** (the kitchen), 7. **la stufa** (the stove), 8. **la tavola** (the table).

Part III
Italian on the Go

The 5th Wave   By Rich Tennant

"Don't feel bad-even though asking the gondolier to 'revolve us around a zebra' was a mistake, he did compliment you on how well you rolled your R's."

In this part . . .

The adventure that is traveling! These chapters help you with every aspect of travel — from getting a visa to making hotel reservations and from dealing with foreign currency to asking for directions and getting to your destination. We also include a chapter on handling those unexpected, emergency situations — although we hope you don't need to use it. **Buon viaggio!** (_boo_-ohn vee-_ahj_-joh) (Have a nice trip!)

Chapter 11

Money, Money, Money

• •

• •

*O*n the one hand, you can never have enough of it; on the other hand, money can cause trouble. This is particularly true for situations abroad or when you're dealing with foreign money in general. This chapter doesn't cover only currency — you know how tiresome converting foreign currencies can be — but all the terms you need to know about money.

Going to the Bank

Dealing with banks isn't always fun, but sometimes you can't avoid them. You aren't often in the position of being able to cash a big check; you may have other, more painful, transactions to perform. In this section, we give you some banking terms that can help you manage a dialogue in a bank.

You may need to go to the bank for several reasons. For example, you may want **cambiare dollar** *(kahm-bee-ah-reh dohl-lah-ree)* (to change dollars), **prelevare soldi** *(preh-leh-vah-reh sohl-dee)* (to withdraw money), **versare soldi sul tuo conto** *(vehr-sah-reh sohl-dee sool too-oh kohn-toh)* (to deposit money into your account), or **contrarre un prestito** *(kohn-trahr-reh oon prehs-tee-toh)* (to take out a loan). Other reasons could be **aprire un conto** *(ah-pree-reh oon kohn-toh)* (to open an account), or **riscuotere un assegno** *(rees-koo-oh-teh-reh oon ahs-seh-nyoh)* (to cash a check).

Other phrases you may find helpful include:

✔ **Mi dispiace, il suo conto è scoperto.** *(mee dees-pee-ah-cheh eel soo-oh kohn-toh eh skoh-pehr-toh)* (I'm sorry, your account is overdrawn.)

✔ **Può girare l'assegno per favore?** (poo-_oh_ jee-_rah_-re lahs-_seh_-nyoh pehr fah-_voh_-reh) (Could you endorse the check, please?)

✔ **Avrei bisogno di un credito.** (ah-_vray_ bee-_zoh_-nyoh dee oon _kreh_-dee-toh) (I need a loan.)

✔ **Com'è il tasso d'interesse?** (koh-_meh_ eel _tahs_-soh deen-teh-_rehs_-seh) (What is the interest rate?)

✔ **Vorrei fare un mutuo.** (vohr-_ray_ _fah_-reh oon _moo_-too-oh) (I'd like to apply for a mortgage.)

✔ **Quando può fare il pagamento?** (koo-_ahn_-doh poo-_oh_ _fah_-reh eel pah-gah-_mehn_-toh) (When can you make the payment?)

When you are in the lucky situation of having money left, you may like to invest it. Here is the conjugation for **investire** (een-vehs-_tee_-reh) (to invest):

Conjugation	Pronunciation
io investo	_ee_-oh een-_vehs_-toh
tu investi	too een-_vehs_-tee
lui/lei investe	_loo_-ee/lay een-_vehs_-teh
noi investiamo	_noh_-ee een-vehs-tee-_ah_-moh
voi investite	_voh_-ee een-vehs-_tee_-teh
loro investono	_loh_-roh een-_vehs_-toh-noh

Talkin' the Talk

Il signor Rossi goes to the bank where he wants to open an account. He talks to **un impiegato della banca** (oo-neem-pee-eh-_gah_-toh _dehl_-lah _bahn_-kah) (male bank employee).

Signor Rossi: **Buongiorno!**
boo-ohn-_johr_-noh
Good morning!

Clerk: **Buongiorno. Prego?**
boo-ohn-_johr_-noh _preh_-goh
Good morning. Can I help you?

Signor Rossi: **Vorrei aprire un conto corrente.**
vohr-_ray_ ah-_pree_-reh oon _kohn_-toh kohr-_rehn_-teh
I'd like to open an account.

Clerk:	**Bene: Ho bisogno di alcune informazioni.** *beh-neh oh bee-zoh-nyoh dee ahl-koo-nee* *een-fohr-mah-tsee-oh-nee* Well, I need some information. [a few minutes later]: **Questo è il suo libretto degli assegni.** *koo-ehs-toh eh eel soo-oh lee-breht-toh* *deh-lyee ahs-seh-nyee* Here is your checkbook.
Signor Rossi:	**Quando mi verrà inviata la carta di credito?** *koo-ahn-doh mee vehr-rah een-vee-ah-tah lah* *kahr-tah dee kreh-dee-toh* When will you send my credit card?
Clerk:	**Fra tre settimane circa.** *frah treh seht-tee-mah-neh cheer-kah* In about three weeks.

To make life easier for you and to help you avoid standing in front of closed doors, we give you the hours of Italian banks: Banks are open Monday through Friday, generally from 8:30 a.m. to 1:30 p.m. (sometimes 1:45 p.m.), then they reopen from 2:30 to 4 p.m. These are general guidelines; the hours may be different in different places.

Talkin' the Talk

Il signor Blasio asks for a statement of his account. He talks to **un'impiegata** *(oo-neem-pee-eh-gah-tah)* (a female employee).

Signor Blasio:	**Vorrei riscuotere un assegno.** *vohr-ray rees-koo-oh-teh-reh oon ahs-seh-nyoh* I'd like to cash a check.
Clerk:	**Firmi questa ricevuta, per favore.** *feer-mee koo-ehs-tah ree-cheh-voo-tah pehr* *fah-voh-reh* Please sign this receipt.
Signor Blasio:	**Vorrei anche il mio estratto conto.** *vohr-ray ahn-keh eel mee-oh ehs-traht-toh kohn-toh* I'd like to get my bank statement too.

Clerk: **Il suo numero di conto?**
eel soo-oh noo-meh-roh dee kohn-toh
Your account number?

Signor Blasio: **Sette zero cinque nove.**
seht-teh dzeh-roh cheen-koo-eh noh-veh
Seven zero five nine.

Clerk: **Grazie. Attenda un momento. . .**
grah-tsee-eh aht-tehn-dah oon moh-mehn-toh
Thank you. Wait one moment. . .
Ecco a lei!
ehk-koh ah lay
Here you are!

Signor Blasio: **Grazie mille, arrivederci!**
grah-tsee-eh meel-leh ahr-ree-veh-dehr-chee
Thanks so much, good-bye!

Words to Know

conto [m] corrente	kohn-toh kohr-rehn-teh	checking account
estratto conto [m]	ehs-traht-toh kohn-toh	bank statement
tasso d'interesse	tahs-soh deen-teh-rehs-seh	interest rate
libretto [m] degli assegni	lee-breht-toh deh-lyee ahs-seh-nyee	checkbook
carta di credito	kahr-tah dee kreh-dee-toh	credit card
ricevuta [f]	ree-cheh-voo-tah	receipt
girare	jee-rah-reh	to endorse
riscuotere	rees-koo-oh-teh-reh	to cash

Changing Money

You're more likely to need to change money when you're abroad. Whether you're traveling for business or for pleasure, you always need money. If you're in Italy and want to change some dollars into **lire** *(lee-reh)* (lire), you would go either **in banca** *(een bahn-kah)* (to the bank) or to an **ufficio di cambio** *(oof-fee-choh dee kahm-bee-oh)* (exchange office).

Because Italy is highly frequented by tourists from all over the world, the clerks in exchange offices have experience in dealing with people speaking many different languages — including English. So, you can probably complete a transaction in an exchange office in English. But, we want to show you how to do it in Italian, to make sure that you can manage an exchange in all circumstances.

Talkin' the Talk

Liza Campbell, an American tourist, needs to change some dollars for lira. She goes to a bank and talks to the teller.

Ms. Campbell: **Buongiorno, vorrei cambiare alcuni dollari in lire.**
boo-ohn-johr-noh vohr-ray kahm-bee-ah-reh ahl-koo-nee dohl-lah-ree een lee-reh
Hello, I'd like to change some dollars into lire.

Teller: **Benissimo. Quanti dollari?**
beh-nees-see-moh koo-ahn-tee dohl-lah-ree
Very well. How many dollars?

Ms. Campbell: **Duecento. Quant'è il cambio?**
doo-eh-chehn-toh koo-ahn-teh eel kahm-bee-oh
Two hundred. What's the exchange?

Teller: **Millenovecento lire.**
meel-leh noh-veh-chehn-toh lee-reh
One thousand nine hundred lire.

Ms. Campbell: **E la commissione?**
eh lah kohm-mees-see-oh-neh
And the fee?

Teller: **Trecento lire, signora.**
treh-chehn-toh lee-reh see-nyoh-rah
Three hundred lire, miss.

Ms. Campbell:	**Va bene.**
	vah <u>beh</u>-neh
	Okay.
Teller:	**Ecco. Sono 328000 lire meno la commisione.**
	ehk-koh <u>soh</u>-noh treh-<u>chehn</u>-toh
	vehn-tee-<u>oht</u>-toh <u>meel</u>-leh <u>lee</u>-reh
	<u>meh</u>-noh lah kohm-mees-see-<u>ohn</u>-neh
	Here. It is three hundred twenty-eight thousand
	lire less the commission.
Ms. Campbell:	**Grazie mille!**
	grah-tsee-eh <u>meel</u>-leh
	Thanks a million!

Nowadays, changing money is not the most efficient way to get the local currency. In Italy, as in most Western countries, you can find a **bancomat** *(<u>bahn</u>-koh-maht)* (ATM) almost anywhere. Also, depending on where you shop and eat, you can pay directly with a **carta di credito** *(<u>kahr</u>-tah dee kreh-dee-toh)* (credit card) or with **travelers' cheques** *(<u>treh</u>-vehl-lehr shehks)* (travelers' checks).

Yes, yes, yes, when you want to have something you have to pay for it, even in Italy. Therefore we provide here the conjugation of **pagare** *(pah-<u>gah</u>-reh)* (to pay).

Conjugation	*Pronunciation*
io pago	<u>ee</u>-oh <u>pah</u>-goh
tu paghi	too <u>pah</u>-gee
lui/lei paga	<u>loo</u>-ee/lay <u>pah</u>-gah
noi paghiamo	<u>noh</u>-ee pah-gee-<u>ah</u>-moh
voi pagate	<u>voh</u>-ee pah-<u>gah</u>-teh
loro pagano	<u>loh</u>-roh <u>pah</u>-gah-noh

The following phrases can help you find the cash you need (or at least the cash machine):

- ✔ **Dov'è il prossimo bancomat?** *(doh-<u>veh</u> eel <u>prohs</u>-see-moh <u>bahn</u>-koh-maht)* (Where is the nearest ATM?)

- ✔ **Posso pagare con la carta di credito?** *(<u>pohs</u>-soh pah-<u>gah</u>-reh kohn lah <u>kahr</u>-tah dee <u>kreh</u>-dee-toh)* (Can I pay with my credit card?)

- ✔ **Mi scusi, potrebbe cambiarmi una banconota da 100000 lire?** *(mee <u>skoo</u>-zee poh-<u>trehb</u>-beh kahm-bee-<u>ahr</u>-mee <u>oo</u>-nah bahn-koh-<u>noh</u>-tah da chehn-toh-<u>mee</u>-lah <u>lee</u>-reh)* (Excuse me, do you have change for a 100,000 lire bill?)

✔ **Mi dispiace, non accettiamo carte di credito. Dovrebbe pagare in contanti.** *(mee dees-pee-ah-cheh nohn ahch-cheht-tee-ah-moh kahr-teh dee kreh-dee-toh doh-vrehb-beh pah-gah-reh een kohn-than-tee)* (I'm sorry, we don't accept credit cards. You have to pay cash.)

✔ **Mi dispiace, non ho spiccioli.** *(mee dees-pee-ah-cheh nohn oh speech-choh-lee)* (I'm sorry, I haven't any small change.)

Words to Know

in contanti	een kohn-tahn-tee	in cash
riscuotere	rees-koo-oh-teh-reh	to cash
accettare	ahch-cheht-tah-reh	to accept
bancomat [m]	bahn-koh-maht	ATM
cambiare	kahm-bee-ah-reh	to change
spiccioli [m]	speech-choh-lee	small change

Using Credit Cards

In Canada and the United States you could take care of almost all your financial needs without ever handling cash. You can pay for almost everything with your debit or credit card. You can even use your credit card to get cash at ATMs and in some banks.

In Italy, however, you can't assume that you can pay by credit card or check everywhere. The rule is to ask before you buy something or eat in a restaurant. For the most part, shop and restaurant doors indicate which cards the establishment accepts. There is no definite rule; each shop determines which payment methods they accept, and some establishments welcome neither checks nor credit cards. Cash is still the customary form of payment in some parts of Italy.

Talkin' the Talk

Ms. Johnson wants to withdraw some lira with her credit card but discovers that the ATM is out of order. She enters the bank and asks the cashier what's up.

Ms. Johnson:	**Scusi, il bancomat non funziona.** *skoo-zee eel bahn-koh-maht nohn* *foon-tsee-oh-nah* Excuse me, the ATM isn't working.
Cashier:	**Lo so, signora, mi dispiace!** *loh soh see-nyoh-rah mee dees-pee-ah-cheh* I know, madam, I'm sorry!
Ms. Johnson:	**Ma ho bisogno di contanti.** *mah oh bee-zoh-nyoh dee kohn-tahn-tee* But I need cash.
Cashier:	**Non può prelevarli qui alla cassa?** *nohn poo-oh preh-leh-vahr-lee koo-ee ahl-lah* *kahs-sah* Can't you withdraw it here?
Ms. Johnson:	**Non lo so!** *nohn loh soh* I don't know!
Cashier:	**Vediamo . . .** *veh-dee-ah-moh* Let's see . . .

You can use your credit card in many places in Italy, especially big cities where the major international credit cards are accepted by many merchants. But, when you go to smaller places, be sure to have some cash handy.

You can also use your credit card along with your passport to change money at airports, railway stations, and hotels, but keep in mind that the commission rates in these places are sometimes higher than in banks and exchange offices.

Normally, things go easily and you don't have any problems using credit cards. But you may be asked to show your identification for security purposes. The following phrases can help you be prepared for this situation:

✔ **Potrei vedere la sua carta d'identità, per favore?** *(poh-tray veh-deh-reh lah soo-ah kahr-tah dee-dehn-tee-tah pehr fah-voh-reh)* (Can I please see your identification?)

✔ **Potrebbe darmi il suo passaporto, per favore?** *(poh-trehb-beh dahr-mee eel soo-oh pahs-sah-pohr-toh pehr fah-voh-reh)* (Could you please give me your passport?)

✔ **Il suo indirizzo?** *(eel soo-oh een-dee-reet-tsoh)* (What is your address?)

You may have to wait to exchange money. The following conjugation lets you know how to talk about anybody and everybody waiting — it's of **attendere** *(aht-tehn-deh-reh)* (to wait).

Conjugation	Pronunciation
io attendo	ee-oh aht-tehn-doh
tu attendi	too aht-tehn-dee
lui/lei attende	loo-ee/lay aht-tehn-deh
noi attendiamo	noh-ee aht-tehn-dee-ah-moh
voi attendete	voh-ee aht-tehn-deh-teh
loro attendono	loh-roh aht-tehn-doh-noh

Talkin' the Talk

While Ms. Johnson explores her options with the cashier, another person enters the bank and starts to complain:

Signora Gradi: **Il bancomat ha mangiato la mia carta.**
eel bahn-koh-maht ah mahn-jah-toh lah mee-ah kahr-tah
The cash machine has eaten my card.

Teller: **Ha digitato il numero giusto?**
ah dee-jee-tah-toh eel num-eh-ro joos-toh
Did you enter the right number?

Signora Gradi: **Certo! Che domanda!**
chehr-toh keh doh-mahn-dah
Of course! What a question!

Teller: **Mi scusi, ma può capitare.**
mee skoo-zee mah poo-oh kah-pee-tah-reh
Excuse me, but it can happen.

Signora Gradi: **Cosa posso fare?**
koh-sah pohs-soh fah-reh
What can I do?

Teller:	**Attenda un momento . . .**
	aht-tehn-dah oon moh-mehn-toh
	Wait a moment . . .

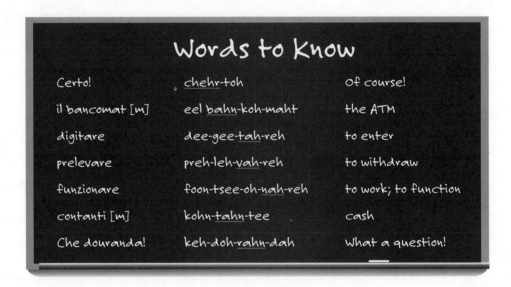

Words to Know

Certo!	chehr-toh	Of course!
il bancomat [m]	eel bahn-koh-maht	the ATM
digitare	dee-gee-tah-reh	to enter
prelevare	preh-leh-vah-reh	to withdraw
funzionare	foon-tsee-oh-nah-reh	to work; to function
contanti [m]	kohn-tahn-tee	cash
Che domanda!	keh-doh-rahn-dah	What a question!

A large part of the Italian population plays the national lottery. In recent years, a real lottery hysteria has broken out. There are even whole TV shows devoted to this phenomenon, where you can see which numbers win and, what's more important, whether you won.

Looking at Various Currencies

The Italian monetary unit is the **lira** (*lee-rah*). The plural form is **lire** (*lee-reh*), and the abbreviation either *L.* or *Lit.* The latter is actually the abbreviation for "Lira italiana," which is the complete name. Several denominations of **monete** (*moh-neh-teh*) (coins) exist, including 50, 100, 200, and 500 lira coins, as well as the recently added 1,000 lire coin. Five, ten, and twenty lire coins used to exist, but are no longer used. The notes exist in the following values: 1,000, 2,000, 5,000, 10,000, 50,000, and 100,000 lire. You can also check out Chapter 2 for Italian numbers.

Lire come in much larger denominations than the dollars you're probably used to, so we're taking this opportunity to list the larger numbers in Table 11-1.

Table 11-1	**Numbers**	
Italian	*Pronunciation*	*Translation*
mille	<u>meel</u>-leh	1,000/one thousand
duemila	doo-eh-<u>mee</u>-lah	2,000/two thousand (**mila** is plural)
cinquemila	cheen-koo-eh-<u>mee</u>-lah	5,000/five thousand
diecimila	dee-eh-chee-<u>mee</u>-lah	10,000/ten thousand
cinquantamila	cheen-koo-ahn-tah-<u>mee</u>-lah	50,000/fifty thousand
centomila	chehn-toh-<u>mee</u>-lah	100,000/one hundred thousand
un milione	oon mee-lee-<u>oh</u>-neh	1 million

Talkin' the Talk

Patrizia is planning her vacation to Spain. She talks to her friend, Milena, about exchanging her money.

Patrizia: **Sai com'è il cambio lire in pesetas?**
<u>sah</u>-ee *koh-<u>meh</u> eel <u>kahm</u>-bee-oh <u>lee</u>-reh een peh-<u>zeh</u>-tahs*
Do you know the exchange rate for lire to pesetas?

Milena: **Non ne ho idea!**
nohn neh oh ee-<u>deh</u>-ah
I have no idea!

Patrizia: **Domani parto per Madrid . . .**
doh-<u>mah</u>-nee <u>pahr</u>-toh pehr mah-<u>dreed</u>
Tomorrow I'm leaving for Madrid . . .

Milena: **. . . e non hai ancora cambiato!**
eh nohn <u>ah</u>-ee ahn-<u>koh</u>-rah kahm-bee-<u>ah</u>-toh
. . . and you haven't changed your money yet!

Patrizia: **Posso farlo all'aeroporto.**
<u>pohs</u>-soh <u>fahr</u>-loh ahl-lah-eh-roh-<u>pohr</u>-toh
I can do it at the airport.

Milena:	**Ma no, è molto più caro!**
	mah noh eh <u>mohl</u>-toh pee-<u>oo</u> <u>kah</u>-roh
	No, that's much more expensive!

Patrizia:	**Mi accompagni in banca?**
	mee ahk-kohm-<u>pah</u>-nyee een <u>bahn</u>-kah
	Will you come with me to the bank?

CULTURAL WISDOM

The **euro** *(eh-<u>oo</u>-roh),* coins and bills, is legal tender in those countries that belong to the European Union (EU). So, if you travel among EU countries after you have euros in your possession, you don't have to change money in every country you visit. In March 2002, the Italian **lira** will disappear, and the euro will be the only valid currency in Italy.

But, until then, Table 11-2 shows the currencies of various countries.

Table 11-2		Currencies	
Italian single/plural	*Pronunciation single/plural*	*English single/plural*	*Where used*
dollaro/dollari	*<u>dohl</u>-lah-roh/ <u>dohl</u>-lah-ree*	dollar/dollars	Canada; United States
franco/franchi	*<u>frahn</u>-koh/<u>frahn</u>-kee*	franc/francs	Belgium; France; Luxembourg; Switzerland
lira/e sterlina/e	*<u>lee</u>-rah/eh stehr-<u>lee</u>-nah/neh*	pound/pounds	Ireland; United Kingdom
marco/marchi	*<u>mahr</u>-koh/<u>mahr</u>-kee*	Mark/Marks	Germany
peseta/pesetas	*peh-<u>zeh</u>-tah/ peh-<u>zeh</u>-tahs*	pesetas/pesetas	Spain

Talkin' the Talk

Patrizia and Milena are at the bank. **Allo sportello** *(<u>ahl</u>-loh spohr-<u>tehl</u>-loh)* (at the counter), they see a sign listing all the exchange rates.

Patrizia:	**Vorrei cambiare cinquecentomila lire in pesetas.**
	vohr-<u>ray</u> kahm-bee-<u>ah</u>-reh <u>cheen</u>-koo-eh- chehn-toh-<u>mee</u>-lah <u>lee</u>-reh een peh-<u>zeh</u>-tahs
	I'd like to change 500,000 lire worth of pesetas.

Teller:	**Per un viaggio?**
	pehr oon vee-<u>ahj</u>-joh
	For a trip?

Patrizia:	**Sì.**
	see
	Yes.

Teller:	**Perché non prende travelers' checks?**
	pehr-<u>keh</u> nohn <u>prehn</u>-deh <u>treh</u>-vehl-lehrs shehks
	Why don't you take travelers' checks?

Patrizia:	**Ha ragione, un po' di contanti . . .**
	ah rah-<u>joh</u>-neh oon poh dee kohn-<u>tahn</u>-tee
	You're right: a bit of cash . . .

Teller:	**. . . e il resto in travelers' checks.**
	eh eel <u>rehs</u>-toh een <u>treh</u>-vehl-ehrs shehks
	. . . and the rest in travelers' checks.

Words to Know

travelers' checks	<u>treh</u>-vehl-lehrs shehks	travelers' checks
prendere	<u>prehn</u>-deh-reh	to take
viaggio [m]	vee-<u>ahj</u>-joh	trip
aeroporto [m]	ah-eh-roh-<u>pohr</u>-toh	airport
cambiare	kahm-bee-<u>ah</u>-reh	to exchange
domani	doh-<u>mah</u>-nee	tomorrow

Fun & Games

Here's a little game for you. Please identify the currency corresponding to the given country in Italian! You have to fill in the plural form. It's not that hard, because we give you one letter for each answer.

1. Canada   _ _ L _ _ _ _

2. Germania   _ _ _ _ H _

3. Francia   _ _ _ N _ _ _

4. Spagna   _ _ _ _ T _ _

5. Inghilterra   _ _ _ _ _ _ _ L _ _ _

Answers: 1. dollari, 2. marchi, 3. franchi, 4. pesetas, 5. lire sterline

Chapter 12

Where Is the Colosseum? Asking Directions

• •

In This Chapter

▶ Asking for directions

▶ Moving verbs

▶ Handling ordinal numbers

• •

*H*ave you ever been lost in a foreign city or country? If so, you realize how helpful it is when you know enough of the native language to be able to ask for directions. Knowing the language also enables you to understand the answer. In this chapter, we give you some helpful conversational tips that make it easier to find your way around.

Finding Your Way: Asking for Specific Places

When asking for directions, it's always polite to start your question with one of the following expressions:

Mi scusi. *(mee skoo-zee)* (Excuse me.)

Scusi. *(skoo-zee)* (Excuse me.)

or

Per favore. *(pehr fah-voh-reh)* (Please.)

Then you can continue with your questions, something like the following:

- ✔ **Dov'è il Colosseo?** *(doh-<u>veh</u> el koh-lohs-<u>seh</u>-oh)* (Where is the Colosseum?)

- ✔ **Questa è via Garibaldi?** *(koo-<u>ehs</u>-tah eh <u>vee</u>-ah gah-ree-<u>bahl</u>-dee)* (Is this via Garibaldi?)

- ✔ **Come si arriva alla stazione?** *(<u>koh</u>-meh see ahr-<u>ree</u>-vah <u>ahl</u>-lah stah-tsee-<u>oh</u>-neh)* (How do I get to the station?)

- ✔ **Può indicarmi la strada per il centro?** *(poo-<u>oh</u> een-dee-<u>kahr</u>-mee lah <u>strah</u>-dah pehr eel <u>chehn</u>-troh)* (Can you show me the way downtown?)

- ✔ **Dove siamo adesso?** *(<u>doh</u>-veh see-<u>ah</u>-moh ah-<u>dehs</u>-soh)* (Where are we now?)

- ✔ **Mi sono perso. Dov'è il duomo?** *(mee <u>soh</u>-noh <u>pehr</u>-soh doh-<u>veh</u> eel doo-<u>oh</u>-moh)* (I've lost my way. Where is the cathedral?)

Some possible answers to the preceding questions are:

- ✔ **Segua la strada principale fino al centro.** *(<u>seh</u>-goo-ah <u>strah</u>-dah preen-chee-<u>pah</u>-leh <u>fee</u>-noh ahl <u>chehn</u>-troh)* (You have to follow the main street to the center of the city.)

- ✔ **Vada sempre dritto.** *(<u>vah</u>-dah <u>sehm</u>-preh <u>dreet</u>-toh)* (Go straight ahead.)

- ✔ **Dopo il semaforo giri a destra.** *(<u>doh</u>-poh eel seh-<u>mah</u>-foh-roh <u>jee</u>-ree ah <u>dehs</u>-trah)* (After the traffic lights, turn right.)

- ✔ **È in fondo a sinistra.** *(eh een <u>fohn</u>-doh ah see-<u>nees</u>-trah)* (It's at the end, on the left side.)

- ✔ **È vicino alla posta.** *(eh vee-<u>chee</u>-noh <u>ahl</u>-lah <u>pohs</u>-tah)* (It's next to the post office.)

- ✔ **Attraversi il ponte, poi c'è una piazza e lì lo vede.** *(aht-trah-<u>vehr</u>-see eel <u>pohn</u>-teh <u>poh</u>-ee cheh <u>oo</u>-nah pee-<u>ahts</u>-tsah eh lee loh <u>veh</u>-deh)* (Cross the bridge, then there's a square and there you see it.)

- ✔ **Ha sbagliato strada.** *(ah sbah-<u>lyah</u>-toh <u>strah</u>-dah)* (You're on the wrong road.)

Mapping the quarters and following directions

Four orientations you already know are the cardinal points of the compass: north, south, east, and west. The four directions are especially helpful to know when you use a map. The following are **i quattro punti cardinali** *(ee koo-<u>aht</u>-troh <u>poon</u>-tee kahr-dee-<u>nah</u>-lee)* (the four cardinal points):

- **nord** *(nohrd)* (north)
- **est** *(ehst)* (east)
- **sud** *(sood)* (south)
- **ovest** *(oh-vehst)* (west)

You may hear the directions used in sentences like the following:

- **Trieste è a nord-est.** *(tree-ehs-teh eh ah nohrd-ehst)* (Trieste is in the northeast.)
- **Napoli è a sud.** *(nah-poh-lee eh ah sood)* (Naples is in the south.)
- **Roma è a ovest.** *(roh-mah eh ah oh-vehst)* (Rome is in the west.)
- **Bari è a sud-est.** *(bah-ree eh ah sood-ehst)* (Bari is in the southeast.)

You need to know how to orient yourself in relation to people and buildings when following or giving directions. Following are useful terms to describe spatial relationships:

- **davanti a** *(dah-vahn-tee ah)* (in front of)
- **dietro a** *(dee-eh-troh ah)* (behind)
- **vicino a** *(vee-chee-noh ah)* (beside; next to)
- **di fronte a** *(dee-frohn-teh ah)* (opposite)
- **dentro** *(dehn-troh)* (inside)
- **fuori** *(foo-oh-ree)* (outside)
- **sotto** *(soht-toh)* (under; below)
- **sopra** *(soh-prah)* (above)

You also need to know relationships between distance and **la direzione** *(lah dee-reh-tsee-oh-neh)* (the direction):

- **dritto** *(dreet-toh)* (straight)
- **sempre dritto** *(sehm-preh dreet-toh)* (straight ahead)
- **fino a** *(fee-noh ah)* (to; up to)
- **prima** *(pree-mah)* (before)
- **dopo** *(doh-poh)* (after)
- **a destra** *(ah dehs-trah)* (on the right)

- ✔ **a sinistra** *(ah see-nees-trah)* (on the left)
- ✔ **dietro l'angolo** *(dee-eh-troh lahn-goh-loh)* (around the corner)
- ✔ **all'angolo** *(ahl-lahn-goh-loh)* (at the corner)
- ✔ **all'incrocio** *(ahl-leen-kroh-choh)* (at the intersection)

More vocabulary you can use for giving and receiving directions:

- ✔ **la calle** *(lah kahl-leh)* (narrow Venetian street)
- ✔ **il largo** *(eel lahr-goh)* (wide square)
- ✔ **il marciapiede** *(eel mahr-chah-pee-eh-deh)* (sidewalk)
- ✔ **la piazza** *(lah pee-ahts-tsah)* (square)
- ✔ **il ponte** *(eel pohn-teh)* (bridge)
- ✔ **il sottopassaggio** *(eel soht-toh-pahs-sahj-joh)* (underpass)
- ✔ **la strada** *(lah strah-dah)* (road; street)
- ✔ **la via** *(lah vee-ah)* (road; street)
- ✔ **la via principale** *(lah vee-ah preen-chee-pah-leh)* (main street)
- ✔ **il viale** *(eel vee-ah-leh)* (parkway; avenue)
- ✔ **il vicolo** *(eel vee-koh-loh)* (alley; lane)

La strada and **la via** are synonymous, but you always use **via** when the name is specified:

- ✔ **E' una strada molto lunga.** *(eh oo-nah strah-dah mohl-toh loon-gah)* (It's a very long road.)
- ✔ **Abito in via Merulana.** *(ah-bee-toh een vee-ah meh-roo-lah-nah)* (I live in Via Merulana.)

We thought you might want to know the translation and pronunciation of a famous Italian proverb you may have heard:

Tutte le strade portano a Roma.
toot-teh leh strah-deh pohr-tah-noh ah roh-mah
All roads lead to Rome.

Talkin' the Talk

 Mary is in Bologna *(boh-loh-nyah)* for the first time. She has visited the city and walked a lot, and now she wants to go back to the train station. Because she can't remember the way, she asks a gentleman.

Mary:	**Scusi?**
	skoo-zee
	Excuse me?
Gentleman:	**Sì?**
	see
	Yes?
Mary:	**Dov'è la stazione centrale?**
	doh-veh lah stah-tsee-oh-neh chehn-trah-leh
	Where is the central station?
Gentleman:	**Prenda la prima a destra.**
	prehn-dah lah pree-mah ah dehs-trah
	Take the first right.
Mary:	**Poi?**
	poh-ee
	Then?
Gentleman:	**Poi la terza a sinistra,**
	poh-ee lah tehr-tsah ah see-nees-trah
	Then the third left,
Mary:	**Sì?**
	see
	Yes?
Gentleman:	**Poi la seconda, no la prima . . .**
	poh-ee lah seh-kohn-dah noh lah pree-mah
	Then the second, no the first . . .
Mary:	**Grazie: Prendo un taxi!**
	grah-tsee-eh prehn-doh oon tah-ksee
	Thank you: I'll take a taxi!

Words to Know

strada principale [f]	strah-dah preen-chee-pah-leh	main street
semaforo [m]	seh-mah-foh-roh	traffic lights
ponte [m]	pohn-teh	bridge
piazza [f]	pee-ahts-tsah	square
centro [m] center	chehn-troh	downtown; city
stazione [f]	stah-tsee-oh-neh	station
duomo [m]	doo-oh-moh	cathedral
posta [f]	pohs-tah	post office

Ordering ordinals

When giving and receiving directions, you need a command of **numeri ordinali** (*noo-meh-ree ohr-dee-nah-lee*) (ordinal numbers). Because ordinal numbers are adjectives, they change according to the noun they describe. For example, you use the feminine forms when referring to **via** (*vee-ah*) or **strada** (*strah-dah*) (street), which are feminine nouns. Table 12-1 includes the ordinal numbers in the masculine form followed by the feminine form.

Table 12-1	Ordinal Numbers	
Italian	*Pronunciation*	*Translation*
il primo/la prima	eel pree-moh/lah pree-mah	the first
il secondo/la seconda	eel seh-kohn-doh/lah seh-kohn-dah	the second
il terzo/la terza	eel tehr-tsoh/lah tehr-tsah	the third
il quarto/la quarta	eel koo-ahr-toh/lah koo-ahr-tah	the fourth
il quinto/la quinta	eel koo-een-toh/lah koo-een-tah	the fifth

Italian	Pronunciation	Translation
il sesto/la sesta	eel <u>sehs</u>-toh/lah <u>sehs</u>-tah	the sixth
il settimo/la settima	eel <u>seht</u>-tee-moh/lah <u>seht</u>-tee-mah	the seventh
l'ottavo/l'ottava	loht-<u>tah</u>-voh/loht-<u>tah</u>-vah	the eighth
il nono/la nona	eel <u>noh</u>-noh/lah <u>noh</u>-nah	the ninth
il decimo/la decima	eel <u>deh</u>-chee-moh/lah <u>deh</u>-chee-mah	the tenth

These examples show you how to use ordinal numbers in sentences:

>**È la terza strada a sinistra.** *(eh lah <u>tehr</u>-tsah <u>strah</u>-dah ah see-<u>nees</u>-trah)* (It's the third street on the left.)

>**È dopo il terzo semaforo a destra.** *(eh <u>doh</u>-poh eel <u>tehr</u>-tsoh seh-<u>mah</u>-foh-roh ah <u>dehs</u>-trah)* (It's after the third traffic light on the right.)

Quant'è lontano?: Asking how far

You may want to know how near or far you are from your destination. Some typical questions and responses are:

- **Quant'è lontano?** *(koo-ahn-<u>teh</u> lohn-<u>tah</u>-noh)* (How far is it?)

- **È molto lontano?** *(eh <u>mohl</u>-toh lohn-<u>tah</u>-noh)* (Is it very far?)

- **Saranno cinque minuti.** *(sah-<u>rahn</u>-noh <u>cheen</u>-koo-eh mee-<u>noo</u>-tee)* (About five minutes.)

- **Circa un chilometro.** *(<u>cheer</u>-kah oon kee-<u>loh</u>-meh-troh)* (About one kilometer.)

- **No, un paio di minuti.** *(noh oon <u>pah</u>-yoh dee mee-<u>noo</u>-tee)* (No, a couple of minutes.)

- **Posso arrivarci a piedi?** *(<u>pohs</u>-soh ahr-ree-<u>vahr</u>-chee ah pee-<u>eh</u>-dee)* (Can I walk there?)

- **Certo, è molto vicino.** *(<u>chehr</u>-toh eh <u>mohl</u>-toh vee-<u>chee</u>-noh)* (Sure, it's very close.)

- **È un po' lontano.** *(eh oon poh lohn-<u>tah</u>-noh)* (It's a bit far away.)

What to say when you don't understand

Occasionally, maybe frequently, you may not understand the directions someone gives you. For those times, you need some useful expressions to ask the other person to repeat their directions.

✔ **Come, scusi?** (*koh-meh skoo-zee*) (I beg your pardon?)

✔ **Mi scusi, non ho capito.** (*mee skoo-zee nohn oh kah-pee-toh*) (I'm sorry, I didn't understand.)

✔ **Può ripetere più lentamente, per favore?** (*poo-oh ree-peh-teh-reh pee-oo lehn-tah-mehn-teh pehr fah-voh-reh*) (Can you please repeat it more slowly?)

When someone does you a favor — explaining the way or giving you directions — you probably want to thank him or her, and that's the easiest task: **Mille grazie!** (*meel-leh grah-stee-eh*) (Thank you very much!)

Other responses to your request for directions might sound something like the following:

✔ **È a circa dieci minuti a piedi.** (*eh ah cheer-kah dee-eh-chee mee-noo-tee ah pee-eh-dee*) (It's about ten minutes on foot.)

✔ **È a cinque minuti in macchina.** (*eh ah cheen-koo-eh mee-noo-tee een mahk-kee-nah*) (It's five minutes by car.)

✔ **Sono tre fermate d'autobus.** (*soh-noh treh fehr-mah-teh dah-oo-toh-boos*) (It's three bus stops.)

✔ **È la seconda fermata.** (*eh lah seh-kohn-dah fehr-mah-tah*) (It's the second stop.)

✔ **È molto lontano da qui.** (*eh mohl-toh lohn-tah-noh dah koo-ee*) (It's very far from here.)

Words to Know

numero [m]	noo-meh-roh	number
minuto [m]	mee-noo-toh	minute
lentamente	lehn-tah-mehn-teh	slowly
autobus [m]	ah-oo-toh-boos	bus
fermata [f]	fehr-mah-tah	bus stop
macchina [f]	mahk-kee-nah	car

Verbs on the Move

You need to know certain verbs when trying to understand directions. Some of the verbs you'll find handy for finding your way are:

- ✔ **andare** *(ahn-dah-reh)* (to go)
- ✔ **girare a destra/a sinistra** *(jee-rah-reh ah dehs-trah/ah see-nees-trah)* (to turn right/left)
- ✔ **prendere** *(prehn-deh-reh)* (to take)
- ✔ **proseguire** *(proh-seh-goo-ee-reh)* (to go on)
- ✔ **seguire** *(seh-goo-ee-reh)* (to follow)
- ✔ **tornare/indietro** *(tohr-nah-reh/een-dee-eh-troh)* (to go back)

Imperatives are useful verb forms to know in a variety of situations, including when you're trying to get around in unfamiliar territory. This list shows the informal verb form followed by the formal verb form. Check out Chapter 3 for help on deciding to use formal or informal forms.

- ✔ **Va/Vada!** *(vah/vah-dah)* (Go!)
- ✔ **Gira/Giri!** *(jee-rah/jee-ree)* (Turn!)
- ✔ **Prendi/Prenda!** *(prehn-dee/prehn-dah)* (Take!)
- ✔ **Prosegui/Prosegua!** *(proh-seh-goo-ee/proh-seh-goo-ah)* (Go on!)
- ✔ **Segui/Segua!** *(seh-goo-ee/seh-goo-ah)* (Follow!)
- ✔ **Torna/Torni!** *(tohr-nah/tohr-nee)* (Go back!)
- ✔ **Attraversa/Attraversi!** *(aht-trah-vehr-sah/aht-trah-vehr-see)* (Cross!)

Notice that the endings of these verbs vary, apparently without any consistent pattern. These aren't typing mistakes — they're determined by the ending of the the infinitive form of the verb *(-are, -ere,* or *-ire).* If you want additional information, please look at Chapter 2. However, you can also simply believe us and memorize the verbs in the preceding list.

No doubt the most frequently used verb in giving and receiving instructions is **andare** *(ahn-dah-reh)* (to go), which we've conjugated for you:

Conjugation	*Pronunciation*
io vado	<u>ee</u>-oh <u>vah</u>-doh
tu vai	too <u>vah</u>-ee
lui/lei va	<u>loo</u>-ee/lay vah
noi andiamo	<u>noh</u>-ee ahn-dee-<u>ah</u>-moh
voi andate	<u>voh</u>-ee ahn-<u>dah</u>-teh
loro vanno	<u>loh</u>-roh <u>vahn</u>-noh

Locations You May Be Looking For

When you're searching for a specific place, these sentences can help you ask the right questions.

- ✔ **Mi sa dire dov'è la stazione?** *(mee sah <u>dee</u>-reh doh-<u>veh</u> lah stah-tsee-<u>oh</u>-neh)* (Can you tell me where the station is?)

- ✔ **Devo andare all'aeroporto.** *(<u>deh</u>-voh ahn-<u>dah</u>-reh ahl-lah-eh-roh-<u>pohr</u>-toh)* (I have to go to the airport.)

- ✔ **Sto cercando il teatro Argentina.** *(stoh chehr-<u>kahn</u>-doh eel teh-<u>ah</u>-troh ahr-jehn-<u>tee</u>-nah)* (I'm looking for the Argentina theatre.)

- ✔ **Dov'è il cinema Astoria, per favore?** *(doh-<u>veh</u> eel <u>chee</u>-neh-mah ahs-<u>toh</u>-ree-ah pehr fah-<u>voh</u>-reh)* (Where is the Astoria cinema, please?)

- ✔ **Come posso arrivare al Museo Romano?** *(<u>koh</u>-meh <u>pohs</u>-soh ahr-ree-<u>vah</u>-reh ahl moo-<u>zeh</u>-oh roh-<u>mah</u>-noh)* (How can I get to the Roman Museum?)

- ✔ **La strada migliore per il centro, per favore?** *(lah <u>strah</u>-dah mee-<u>lyoh</u>-reh pehr eel <u>chehn</u>-troh pehr fah-<u>voh</u>-reh)* (The best way to downtown, please?)

- ✔ **Che chiesa è questa?** *(keh kee-<u>eh</u>-zah eh koo-<u>ehs</u>-tah)* (What church is this?)

- ✔ **Che autobus va all'ospedale?** *(keh <u>ah</u>-oo-toh-boos vah ahl-lohs-peh-<u>dah</u>-leh)* (Which bus goes to the hospital?)

Talkin' the Talk

Peter wants to meet with a friend at a restaurant at the via Torino. After getting off the bus, he asks a girl for directions.

Peter: **Scusa?**
           skoo-zah
           Excuse me?

Girl: **Dimmi.**
           deem-mee
           Yes, please.

Peter: **Sto cercando via Torino.**
           stoh chehr-kahn-doh vee-ah toh-ree-noh
           I'm looking for via Torino.

Girl: **Via Torino!?**
           vee-ah toh-ree-noh
           Via Torino!?

Peter: **È qui vicino, no?**
           eh koo-ee vee-chee-noh noh
           It's close to here, isn't it?

Girl: **No, è lontanissimo.**
           noh eh lohn-tah-nees-see-moh
           No, it's very far away.

Peter: **Oddio, ho sbagliato strada!**
           ohd-dee-oh oh sbah-lyah-toh strah-dah
           Oh, heavens, I went the wrong way!

Girl: **Devi prendere il 20 verso il centro.**
           deh-vee prehn-deh-reh eel vehn-tee vehr-soh eel chehn-troh
           You have to take the [bus number] 20 to the city center.

Words to Know

a destra	ah <u>dehs</u>-trah	to the right
a sinistra	ah see-<u>nees</u>-trah	to the left
stazione [f]	stah-tsee-<u>oh</u>-neh	station
aeroporto [m]	ah-eh-roh-<u>pohr</u>-toh	airport
teatro [m]	teh-<u>ah</u>-troh	theater
cinema [m]	<u>chee</u>-neh-mah	cinema
chiesa [f]	kee-<u>eh</u>-zah	church
ospedale [m]	ohs-peh-<u>dah</u>-leh	hospital

Fun & Games

Please fill in the missing words, which appear at least once in this chapter. We give you a list of words to choose from for each paragraph. These words appear in a random order, so you have to decide the correct order of the words in the sentences.

1. Segui questa _____ (street), all'angolo gira _____ (right). Poi prendi la _____ (third) a sinistra. Attraversa la _____ (square) e vai alla _____ (bus stop).

   Choices: terza, fermata, strada, a destra, piazza

2. Dopo l'incrocio giri _____ (left), sempre _____ (straight ahead) fino al ponte. Attraversi il _____ (the bridge) e il teatro è _____ (opposite) alla posta.

   Choices: di fronte, a sinistra, ponte, dritto

3. Dopo _____ (traffic light) _____ (turn) a destra e poi _____ (at the end) c'è la _____ (church).

   Choices: in fondo, il semaforo, chiesa, gira,

Now try completing these sentences by choosing a word from the list following the sentences.

4. Devo _____ (to go) all'aeroporto.

5. Come posso _____ (to get) al Museo Romano?

6. La strada migliore per _____ (the center)?

7. Che autobus va _____ (to the hospital)?

Choices: il centro, arrivare, andare, all'ospedale

Answers: 1. strada, a destra, terza, piazza, fermata. 2. a sinistra, dritto, ponte, di fronte. 3. il semaforo, gira, in fondo, chiesa. 4. andare, 5. arrivare, 6. il centro, 7. all'ospedale.

Chapter 13

Checking into a Hotel

· ·

· ·

To really get to know Italians and the Italian language and to enjoy the Italian lifestyle, you really should travel to Italy. If you're not lucky enough to have Italian friends who can offer you a place to stay, you have to find a hotel. This chapter shows you how to make yourself understood when you ask for a room or check into a hotel. Plus, we give you a crash course on possessive pronouns and Italian articles.

Reserving a Room

When you reserve a room in a hotel, you use many of the same terms as you do to book a table in a restaurant, just substituting either of the synonyms **la camera** *(lah kah-meh-rah)* or **la stanza** *(lah stahn-tsah),* which both mean "the room," for **il tavolo** *(eel tah-voh-loh)* (the table). Check out Chapter 5 for those specifics.

Italian hotel terms are different than those you're used to and those little differences can cause big trouble if using the wrong ones means you don't get what you want. So we want to spend some time telling you how to ask for what you want in Italian.

La camera singola *(lah kah-meh-rah seen-goh-lah)* is a room with one bed. **La camera doppia** *(lah kah-meh-rah dohp-pee-ah)* is a room with two twin beds, whereas **la camera matrimoniale** *(lah kah-meh-rah mah-tree-moh-nee-ah-leh)* has one big bed for two persons.

Of course, you not only have to choose your room, but also what meals you want provided. You can choose between **la mezza pensione** *(lah mehd-dzah pehn-see-oh-neh),* which includes breakfast and one warm meal, or **la pensione completa** *(lah pehn-see-oh-neh kohm-pleh-tah),* which provides breakfast, lunch, and dinner.

In Italy, people commonly refer to rooms simply as **una doppia, una matrimoniale,** and **una singola.** Everyone understands that you're talking about hotel rooms.

We're sure we don't have to tell you that making reservations in advance is important. This is particularly true for the **alta stagione** *(ahl-tah stah-joh-neh)* (peak season) — in Italy it's the summer months and the weeks around Easter. Italy is a popular country for vacations: Tourists come from all over the world to visit its beautiful sights and to enjoy its history. Be sure to reserve your hotel room in time!

If you run into a situation where you haven't reserved a room and have to request one when you arrive at the hotel, be prepared to not get exactly what you want; you may have to compromise.

When you're making reservations or staying at a hotel, you may have a few questions about the room and the amenities. You'll probably encounter and use some of these common Italian sentences and phrases.

- **La stanza è con bagno?** *(lah stahn-stah eh kohn bah-nyoh)* (Does the room have a bathroom?)

- **Posso avere una stanza con doccia?** *(pohs-soh ah-veh-reh oo-nah stahn-tsah kohn dohch-chah)* (Can I have a room with a shower?)

- **Non avete stanze con la vasca?** *(nohn ah-veh-teh stahn-tseh kohn lah vahs-kah)* (Don't you have rooms with bathtubs?)

- **Avete una doppia al primo piano?** *(ah-veh-teh oo-nah dohp-pee-ah ahl pree-moh pee-ah-noh)* (Do you have a double room on the first floor?)

- **È una stanza tranquillissima e dà sul giardino.** *(eh oo-nah stahn-tsah trahn-koo-eel-lees-see-mah eh dah sool jahr-dee-noh)* (The room is very quiet and looks out onto the garden.)

- **La doppia viene duecentomila a notte.** *(lah dohp-pee-ah vee-eh-neh doo-eh-chehn-toh-mee-lah ah noht-teh)* (A double room costs 200,000 lire per night.)

- **La colazione è compresa?** *(lah koh-lah-tsee-oh-neh eh kohm-preh-zah)* (Is breakfast included?)

- **Può darmi una camera con aria condizionata e televisione?** *(poo-oh dahr-mee oo-nah kah-meh-rah kohn ah-ree-ah kohn-dee-tsee-oh-nah-tah eh teh-leh-vee-zee-oh-neh)* (Can you give me a room with air conditioning and a television?)

✔ **Dove sono i suoi bagagli?** (*doh-veh soh-noh ee soo-oh-ee bah-gah-lyee*) (Where is your baggage?)

✔ **Può far portare le mie borse in camera, per favore?** (*poo-oh fahr pohr-tah-reh leh mee-eh bohr-seh een kah-meh-rah pehr fah-voh-reh*) (Can I have my bags brought to my room, please?)

Talkin' the Talk

Donatella is making reservations for **il soggiorno** *(eel sohj-johr-noh)* (the stay) for five people. The receptionist says that only two double rooms are left, so Donatella has to figure out how to fit all five people.

Donatella:	**Buonasera.**
	boo-oh-nah-seh-rah
	Good evening.
Receptionist:	**Buonasera, prego.**
	boo-oh-nah-seh-rah preh-goh
	Good evening, can I help you?
Donatella:	**Avete stanze libere?**
	ah-veh-teh stahn-tseh lee-beh-reh
	Do you have any vacant rooms?
Receptionist:	**Non ha la prenotazione?**
	nohn ah lah preh-noh-tah-tsee-oh-neh
	You don't have a reservation?
Donatella:	**Eh, no...**
	eh noh
	No...
Receptionist:	**Abbiamo soltanto due doppie.**
	ahb-bee-ah-moh sohl-tahn-toh doo-eh dohp-pee-eh
	We have just two double rooms.
Donatella:	**Non c'è una stanza con tre letti?**
	nohn cheh oo-nah stahn-tsah kohn treh leht-tee
	Isn't there a room with three beds?

Receptionist:	**Possiamo aggiungere un letto.**
	pohs-see-ah-moh ahj-joon-jeh-reh oon leht-toh
	We can add a bed.
Donatella:	**Benissimo, grazie.**
	beh-nees-see-moh grah-tsee-eh
	Very well, thank you.

Following are conjugations for a couple of verbs that can come in handy during a hotel stay — **portare** *(pohr-tah-reh)* (to bring) and **dare** *(dah-reh)* (to give).

Conjugation	*Pronunciation*
io porto	ee-oh pohr-toh
tu porti	too pohr-tee
lui/lei porta	loo-ee/lay pohr-tah
noi portiamo	noh-ee pohr-tee-ah-moh
voi portate	voh-ee pohr-tah-teh
loro portano	loh-roh pohr-tah-noh

Conjugation	*Pronunciation*
io do	ee-oh doh
tu dai	too dah-ee
lui/lei dà	loo-ee/lay dah
noi diamo	noh-ee dee-ah-moh
voi date	voh-ee dah-teh
loro danno	loh-roh dahn-noh

Words to Know

aria condizionata [f]	ah-ree-ah kohn-dee-tsee-oh-<u>nah</u>-tah	air conditioning
camera [f] stanza [f]	kah-meh-rah <u>stahn</u>-tsah	room
camera singola [f]	kah-meh-rah <u>seen</u>-goh-lah	single room
camera doppia [f]	kah-meh-rah <u>dohp</u>-pee-ah	room with two twin beds
camera matrimoniale [f]	kah-meh-rah mah-tree-moh-nee-<u>ah</u>-leh	room with a double bed
colazione [f]	koh-lah-tsee-oh-neh	breakfast
letto supplementare [m]	<u>leht</u>-toh soop-pleh-mehn-<u>tah</u>-reh	extra bed
servizio in camera [m]	sehr-<u>vee</u>-tsee-oh een <u>kah</u>-meh-rah	room service
servizio sveglia [m]	sehr-<u>vee</u>-tsee-oh <u>sveh</u>-lyah	wake-up call

Checking In

Registering at an Italian hotel isn't as difficult as you might imagine. Registration forms list the required information in both Italian and English.

After you're in your room, you may find that you forgot to bring something you need, or discover that you need something in addition to all you brought. Or, you may want special amenities, like **una cassaforte** (*oo-nah kahs-sah-<u>fohr</u>-teh*) (a safe) for your valuables, or **un frigorifero** (*oon free-goh-<u>ree</u>-feh-roh*) (a refrigerator). In these instances, you probably ask the receptionist, the doorman, or the maid for what you need. The following phrases can help you ask for the things you need.

> ✔ **Non trovo l'asciugacapelli.** *(nohn troh-voh lah-shoo-gah-kah-pehl-lee)* (I can't [Literally: don't] find the hair dryer.)
>
> ✔ **Gli asciugamani devono essere cambiati e manca la carta igenica.** *(lyee ah-shoo-gah-mah-nee deh-voh-noh ehs-seh-reh kahm-bee-ah-tee eh mahn-kah lah kahr-tah ee-jeh-nee-kah)* (The towels must be changed and there is no toilet paper.)
>
> ✔ **Potrei avere un'altra saponetta?** *(poh-tray ah-veh-reh oon-ahl-trah sah-poh-neht-tah)* (Could I have a new soap?)
>
> ✔ **Ho finito lo shampoo.** *(oh fee-nee-toh loh shampoo)* (I ran out of shampoo.)
>
> ✔ **È ancora aperto il bar?** *(eh ahn-koh-rah ah-pehr-toh eel bahr)* (Is the bar still open?)
>
> ✔ **Vorrei un'altra coperta e due cuscini, per favore.** *(vohr-ray oon-ahl-trah koh-pehr-tah eh doo-eh koo-shee-nee)* (I'd like one more blanket and two pillows, please.)
>
> ✔ **Dov'è la farmacia più vicina?** *(doh-veh lah fahr-mah-chee-ah pee-oo vee-chee-nah)* (Where is the closest pharmacy?)
>
> ✔ **Vorrei la sveglia domattina.** *(vohr-ray lah sveh-lyah doh-maht-tee-nah)* (I'd like to get an early wake-up call tomorrow.)
>
> ✔ **C'è il telefono nella mia stanza?** *(cheh eel teh-leh-foh-noh nehl-lah mee-ah stahn-tsah)* (Is there a telephone in my room?)

If you want *another* something, notice that you write the feminine form **un'altra** *(oon-ahl-trah)* differently than the masculine **un altro** *(oon ahl-troh)*. Feminine words require an apostrophe; masculine words don't. This is also valid for all other words that begin with a vowel.

The following list contains more words you may find useful during a hotel stay:

> ✔ **fazzolettino di carta** *(faht-tsoh-leht-tee-noh dee kahr-tah)* (tissue)
>
> ✔ **lettino** *(leht-tee-noh)* (cot)
>
> ✔ **negozio di regali** *(neh-goh-tsee-oh dee reh-gah-lee)* (gift shop)
>
> ✔ **parrucchiere** *(pahr-rook-kee-eh-reh)* (hairdresser)
>
> ✔ **portacenere** *(pohr-tah-cheh-neh-reh)* (ashtray)
>
> ✔ **piscina** *(pee-shee-nah)* (swimming pool)

Talkin' the Talk

Mr. Baricco arrives at the hotel where he made reservations two weeks ago. He walks up to the receptionist.

Sig. Baricco: **Buonasera, ho una stanza prenotata.**
*boo-oh-nah-seh-rah oh oo-nah stahn-tsah
preh-noh-tah-tah*
Good evening, I have a reservation.

Receptionist: **Il suo nome, prego?**
eel soo-oh noh-meh preh-goh
Your name, please?

Sig. Baricco: **Baricco.**
bah-reek-koh
Barrico.

Receptionist: **Sì, una singola per due notti.**
see oo-nah seen-goh-lah pehr doo-eh noht-tee
Yes, a single room for two nights.
Può riempire la scheda, per favore?
*poo-oh ree-ehm-pee-reh lah skeh-dah pehr
fah-voh-reh*
Could you fill out the form, please?

Sig. Baricco: **Certo. Vuole un documento?**
chehr-toh voo-oh-leh oon doh-koo-mehn-toh
Sure. Do you want identification?

Receptionist: **Sì, grazie. . . .Bene la sua chiave la stanza numero
quarantadue, signore.**
*see grah-tsee-eh beh-neh lah soo-ah kee-ah-veh lah
stahn-tsah noo-meh-roh koo-ah-rahn-tah-doo-eh
see-nyoh-reh*
Yes, thanks. . . .Here is your key to room number
forty-two, sir.

Sig. Baricco: **Grazie. A che ora è la colazione?**
*grah-tsee-eh ah keh oh-rah eh lah
koh-lah-tsee-oh-neh*
Thank you. What time is breakfast?

Receptionist: **Dalle sette alle nove.**
dahl-leh seht-teh ahl-leh noh-veh
From seven till nine.

Sig. Baricco: **Grazie. Buonanotte.**
grah-tsee-eh boo-oh-nah-noht-teh
Thank you. Good-night.

Receptionist: **Buonanotte.**
boo-oh-nah-noht-teh
Good-night.

Words to Know

avete	ah-<u>veh</u>-the	do you (plural) have
dov'è	doh-<u>veh</u>	where is
dove sono	<u>doh</u>-veh <u>soh</u>-noh	where are
Può ripetere per favore?	poo-<u>oh</u> ree-<u>peh</u>-teh-reh pehr fah-<u>voh</u>-reh	Could you repeat that please?
saldare il conto	sahl-dah-reh eel <u>kohn</u>-toh	to check out
indirizzo [m]	een-dee-<u>reet</u>-tsoh	address

Using Plurals and Pronouns

At times, digging a little bit deeper into grammar helps you understand things better. In this section, we hope to improve your knowledge of plurals and pronouns. You are perfectly aware of how to use them in English, now we show you how they work in Italian.

Making more in Italian

You may have noticed that the plural form in Italian is not as simple as it is in English. In English, you usually add an *s* to the end of a word to make it plural. In Italian, how you make a noun plural depends on both the gender of the word and, as far as the article is concerned, on the first letters in the word. (Check out Chapter 2 for more on the gender of nouns.)

Italian nouns have two genders: masculine or feminine. You use different articles with each gender:

- ✔ The masculine article **il** *(eel)* accompanies masculine nouns, most of which end in *o.*
- ✔ The feminine article **la** *(lah)* accompanies the feminine nouns, most of which end in *a.*

In addition, masculine nouns that begin with a vowel, like **l'amico** *(lah-mee-koh)* (the friend) or with **z**, like **lo zio** *(loh dzee-oh)* (uncle), **gn**, like **lo gnomo** *(loh nyoh-moh)* (the gnome) or **y**, like **lo yogurt** *(loh yoh-goort)*, or **s** followed by another consonant (**sb, sc, sd** and so on), as **lo studente** *(loh stoo-dehn-teh)* (the student), take the masculine article **lo** *(loh)*. When the word begins with a vowel, **lo** is abbreviated as **l'** as in **l'amico**. The same is true for feminine nouns beginning with a vowel; the feminine **la** is reduced to **l'**. The feminine article has no equivalent to the masculine **lo**. In the plural, **lo** and **l'** (for masculine nouns) become **gli** (lyee).

Of course, exceptions exist — some nouns end with **e**, for example, which indicates that the noun can be feminine or masculine. You can identify its gender by the article.

Once you understand these rules, forming the plural is actually quite easy.

- When you have a feminine noun, such as **la cameriera** *(lah kah-meh-ree-eh-rah)* (chambermaid) or **l'entrata** *(lehn-trah-tah)* (hall), change the final **a** (in the article as well as in the word) to an **e**, so that **la cameriera** becomes **le cameriere** and **l'entrata** becomes **le entrate**.

- In the case of masculine nouns, such as **il bagno** *(eel bah-nyoh)* (bathroom), the plural article becomes **i** *(ee)* and so does the final **o** of the word. So, **il bagno** becomes **i bagni** *(ee bah-nyee)*.

- With some exceptions, to make nouns ending with **e** plural, for example **la chiave** *(lah kee-ah-veh)* (the key) and **il cameriere** *(eel kah-meh-ree-eh-reh)* (the waiter), you change the **e** to **i**, and the article changes according to the gender — for example, **le chiavi** *(leh kee-ah-vee)* (keys) and **i camerieri** *(ee kah-meh-ree-eh-ree)* (waiters). The masculine articles **lo** and **l'** change to **gli** *(lyee)*, and the feminine **l'** becomes **le** *(leh)*.

Table 13-1 shows the plural form of several hotel-related words with their proper articles.

Table 13-1	Making Plurals	
Singular Plural	*Pronunciation*	*Translation*
la cameriera	lah kah-meh-ree-eh-rah	chambermaid
le cameriere	leh kah-meh-ree-eh-reh	chambermaids
il bagno	eel bah-nyoh	bathroom
i bagni	ee bah-nyee	bathrooms
la chiave	lah kee-ah-veh	key
le chiavi	leh kee-ah-vee	keys

(continued)

Table 13-1 *(continued)*

Singular Plural	Pronunciation	Translation
il cameriere	eel kah-meh-ree-<u>eh</u>-reh	waiter
i camerieri	ee kah-meh-ree-<u>eh</u>-ree	waiters
lo specchio	loh <u>spehk</u>-kee-oh	mirror
gli specchi	lyee <u>spehk</u>-kee	mirrors
l'albergo	lahl-<u>behr</u>-goh	hotel
gli alberghi	lyee ahl-<u>behr</u>-gee	hotels
la stanza	lah <u>stahn</u>-tsah	room
le stanze	leh <u>stahn</u>-tseh	rooms
la camera	lah <u>kah</u>-meh-rah	room
le camere	leh <u>kah</u>-meh-reh	rooms
la persona	lah pehr-<u>soh</u>-nah	person
le persone	leh pehr-<u>soh</u>-neh	persons
il letto	eel <u>leht</u>-toh	bed
i letti	ee <u>leht</u>-tee	beds
la notte	lah <u>noht</u>-teh	night
le notti	leh <u>noht</u>-tee	nights
l'entrata	lehn-<u>trah</u>-tah	hall
le entrate	leh ehn-<u>trah</u>-teh	halls

Personalizing pronouns

As you know, a pronoun is a word you use in a place of a noun: When you say "I go," you substitute your name with *I*. *I* is the *personal pronoun*. Sometimes you use a pronoun that not only takes the place of a noun but also indicates to whom it belongs. For example, when you say "My bag is red and yours is black," the possessive pronoun *yours* represents *bag* and indicates to whom the bag belongs.

This or these: Demonstrative pronouns

In English, you use the pronouns *this* and *these* (called *demonstrative pronouns*) to indicate or specify what you're talking about. *This* is singular, and *these* is plural. In English you can use *this* or *these* with any noun — as long as you get the number right: this book, these girls, and so on. In Italian, however, which word you use depends on both number *and* gender because there are masculine and feminine articles. Consider these examples:

> ✔ **Questa è la sua valigia?** *(koo-ehs-tah eh lah soo-ah vah-lee-jah)* (Is this your suitcase?)

> ✔ **No, le mie sono queste.** *(noh leh mee-eh soh-noh koo-ehs-teh)* (No, these are mine.)

In the preceding, you see the feminine version of singular and plural (**questa** and **queste**, respectively). The following shows the masculine version of singular and plural (**questo** and **questi**):

> ✔ **Signore, questo messaggio è per lei.** *(see-nyoh-reh koo-ehs-toh mehs-sahj-joh eh pehr lay)* (Sir, this message is for you.)

> ✔ **Questi prezzi sono eccessivi!** *(koo-ehs-tee preht-tsee soh-noh ehch-chehs-see-vee)* (These prices are excessive!)

Yours, mine, and ours: Possessive pronouns

Possessive pronouns (such as *my, your, his*) indicate possession of something (the noun). In Italian, these words vary according to the gender of the item they refer to. The possessive pronoun must agree in number and gender with the possessed thing or person. Unlike in English, in Italian you almost always put the article in front of the possessive determiner. The following table shows the singular and plural articles for each gender:

Gender	Number	Article
Feminine	Singular	la/l'
Feminine	Plural	le
Masculine	Singular	il/l'/lo
Masculine	Plural	i/gli

When you want to show that something belongs to you and that something is a feminine noun, the possessive **mia** ends in *a* — such as **la mia valigia** *(lah mee-ah vah-lee-jah)* (my suitcase). When you refer to a masculine word, the possessive ends in *o,* as in **il mio letto** *(eel mee-oh leht-toh)* (my bed).

So, these pronouns get their form from the possessor — **il mio** *(eel mee-oh)* (mine), **il tuo** *(eel too-oh)* (yours), and so on — and their number and gender from the thing possessed. For example, in **è la mia chiave** *(eh lah mee-ah kee-ah-veh)* (it's my key), **la chiave** is singular and feminine and is, therefore, replaced by the possessive pronoun **mia.** Table 13-2 lists possessive pronouns and their articles.

Table 13-2	Possessive Pronouns			
Possessive Pronoun	*Singular Masculine*	*Singular Feminine*	*Plural Masculine*	*Plural Feminine*
my/mine	il mio	la mia	i miei	le mie
your/yours	il tuo	la tua	i tuoi	le tue
yours (formal)	il suo	la sua	i suoi	le sue
his/her/hers	il suo	la sua	i suoi	le sue
our/ours	il nostro	la nostra	i nostri	le nostre
your/yours (formal and informal)	il vostro	la vostra	i vostri	le vostre
their/theirs	il loro	la loro	i loro	le loro

Following are some practical examples using possessive pronouns:

- ✔ **È grande la vostra stanza?** *(eh grahn-deh lah vohs-trah stahn-tsah)* (Is your room big?) (plural)

- ✔ **Dov'è il tuo albergo?** *(doh-veh eel too-oh ahl-behr-goh)* (Where is your hotel?)

- ✔ **Ecco i vostri documenti.** *(ehk-koh ee vohs-tree doh-koo-mehn-tee)* (Here are your documents.) (plural)

- ✔ **Questa è la sua chiave.** *(koo-ehs-tah eh lah soo-ah kee-ah-veh)* (This is your [formal] key.) and also (This is his/her key.)

- ✔ **La mia camera è molto tranquilla.** *(lah mee-ah kah-meh-rah eh mohl-toh trahn-koo-eel-lah)* (My room is very quiet.)

- ✔ **Anche la nostra. E la tua?** *(ahn-keh lah nohs-trah eh lah too-ah)* (Ours too. And yours [singular]?)

Following are two conjugations tables for **appartenere** *(ahp-pahr-teh-neh-reh)* (to belong) and **possedere** *(pohs-seh-deh-reh)* (to own).

Conjugation	*Pronunciation*
io appartengo	ee-oh ahp-pahr-tehn-goh
tu appartieni	too ahp-pahr-tee-eh-nee
lui/lei appartiene	loo-ee/lay ahp-pahr-tee-eh-neh
noi apparteniamo	noh-ee ahp-pahr-teh-nee-ah-moh
voi appartenete	voh-ee ahp-pahr-teh-neh-teh
loro appartengono	loh-roh ahp-pahr-tehn-goh-noh

Conjugation	*Pronunciation*
io possiedo	<u>ee</u>-oh pohs-see-<u>eh</u>-doh
tu possiedi	too pohs-see-<u>eh</u>-dee
lui/lei possiede	<u>loo</u>-ee/lay pohs-see-<u>eh</u>-deh
noi possediamo	<u>noh</u>-ee pohs-seh-dee-<u>ah</u>-moh
voi possedete	<u>voh</u>-ee pohs-seh-<u>deh</u>-teh
loro possiedono	<u>loh</u>-roh pohs-see-<u>eh</u>-doh-noh

Talkin' the Talk

You frequently use possessive pronouns, so you need to know how to use them. The following dialogue takes between members of a family who are trying to sort out who has whose luggage.

Mamma: **Dove sono le vostre borse?**
<u>doh</u>-veh <u>soh</u>-noh leh <u>vohs</u>-treh <u>bohr</u>-seh
Where are your [plural] bags?

Michela: **La mia è questa.**
lah <u>mee</u>-ah eh koo-<u>ehs</u>-tah
Mine is this one.

Mamma: **E la tua, Carla?**
eh lah <u>too</u>-ah <u>kahr</u>-lah
And yours, Carla?

Carla: **La porta Giulio.**
lah <u>pohr</u>-tah <u>joo</u>-lee-oh
Giulio is carrying it.

Mamma: **No, Giulio porta la sua.**
noh <u>joo</u>-lee-oh <u>pohr</u>-tah lah <u>soo</u>-ah
No, Giulio is carrying his.

Carla: **Giulio, hai la mia borsa?**
<u>joo</u>-lee-oh <u>ah</u>-ee lah <u>mee</u>-ah <u>bohr</u>-sah
Giulio, do you have my bag?

Giulio: **No, sono le mie!**
noh <u>soh</u>-noh le <u>mee</u>-eh
No, they're mine!

Carla: **Sei sicuro?**
say see-koo-roh
Are you sure?

Giulio: **Com'è la tua?**
koh-meh lah too-ah
What does yours look like?

Carla: **È rossa.**
eh rohs-sah
It's red.

Words to Know

bagaglio [m]	bah-gah-lyoh	baggage
borsa [f]	bohr-sah	bag
cameriera [f]	kah-meh-ree-eh-rah	chambermaid
garage [m]	gah-rahj	car park, garage
messaggio [m]	mehs-sahj-joh	message
portiere [m]	pohr-tee-eh-reh	doorman
valigia [f]	vah-lee-jah	suitcase

Fun & Games

· ·

This exercise focuses on words you're likely to hear in a hotel. First, write the correct answer, in Italian, in each blank. Taking the letter indicated in parenthesis from each correct answer, in order, gives you one of the two Italian words for **_room_**. Only one of these words is the solution to the puzzle.

   1. **You call her when you need something in your room.** _____ **(1st)**

   2. **You carry all your stuff in it.** _____ **(2nd)**

   3. **You may even find one in a bottle.** _____ **(1st)**

   4. **It's simply the best place to rest.** _____ **(2nd)**

   5. **You pay there for a bed.** _____ **(5th)**

   6. **Perfect for taking you up and down.** _____ **(1st)**

Answers: 1. Cameriera, **2.** Valigia, **3.** Messaggio, **4.** Letto, **5.** Albergo, **6.** Ascensore

· ·

Chapter 14

Getting Around: Planes, Trains, Taxis, and Buses

● ●

In This Chapter
▶ Traveling by airplane
▶ Declaring your goods to customs
▶ Renting a car
▶ Using public transportation
▶ Understanding maps and schedules
▶ Arriving early, late, or on time

● ●

*W*hether you're visiting Italy or you just need to explain to an Italian-speaking friend how to get across town, transportation vocabulary really comes in handy. This chapter helps you make your way through the airport and also helps you secure transportation to get where you're going once you're on the ground, either by taxi, bus, car, or train. Further, we show you how to declare and to behave at customs as well as how to rent a car. Let's go!

Getting through the Airport

You're lucky, because it's very likely that you can get by with English when you're at an Italian airport. Normally, both Italian and English are spoken there. But, you may be in a situation where the person next to you in an airport only knows Italian. Just in case, though, we want to provide you with some useful linguistic material. Besides, you'll probably want a chance to practice the language in which you will be immersed once you step outside the airport.

Checking in

The moment you finally get rid of your luggage is called check-in — in Italian **accettazione** (*ahch-cheht-tah-tsee-oh-neh*). Actually, people often use "check-in" in Italian, too. You also pick up your boarding pass at the check-in counter, so speaking is usually inevitable. The following dialogue contains some of the sentences people commonly exchange.

Talkin' the Talk

Ms. Adami is checking in. She shows her ticket and passport to the agent and leaves her suitcases at the counter.

Agent: **Il suo biglietto, per favore.**
eel soo-oh bee-lyeht-toh pehr fah-voh-reh
Your ticket, please.

Sig.ra Adami: **Ecco.**
ehk-koh
Here it is.

Agent: **Passaporto?**
pahs-sah-pohr-toh
Passport?

Sig.ra Adami: **Prego.**
preh-goh
Here you are.

Agent: **Quanti bagagli ha?**
koo-ahn-tee bah-gah-lyee ah
How many suitcases do you have?

Sig.ra Adami: **Due valigie e una borsa a mano.**
doo-eh vah-lee-jeh eh oo-nah bohr-sah ah mah-noh
Two suitcases and one piece of carry-on luggage.

Agent: **Fumatori o non fumatori?**
foo-mah-toh-ree oh nohn foo-mah-toh-ree
Smoking or non-smoking?

Sig.ra Adami: **Non fumatori.**
nohn foo-mah-toh-ree
Non-smoking.

Agent: **Preferisce un posto vicino al finestrino o al corridoio?**
preh-feh-<u>ree</u>-sheh oon <u>pohs</u>-toh vee-<u>chee</u>-noh ahl fee-nehs-<u>tree</u>-noh oh ahl kohr-ree-<u>doh</u>-ee-oh
Do you prefer a window or an aisle seat?

Sig.ra Adami: **Preferisco il finestrino, grazie.**
preh-feh-<u>rees</u>-koh eel fee-nehs-<u>tree</u>-noh <u>grah</u>-tsee-eh
I prefer the window, thanks.

Agent: **Ecco la sua carta d'imbarco.**
<u>ehk</u>-koh lah <u>soo</u>-ah <u>kahr</u>-tah deem-<u>bahr</u>-koh
Here is your boarding pass.
L'imbarco è alle nove e quindici, uscita tre.
leem-<u>bahr</u>-koh eh <u>ahl</u>-leh <u>noh</u>-veh eh koo-<u>een</u>-dee-chee oo-<u>shee</u>-tah treh
Boarding is at 9:15, gate 3.

Words to Know

imbarco [m]	eem-<u>bahr</u>-koh	boarding
valigia [f]	vah-<u>lee</u>-jah	suitcase
fumatori	foo-mah-<u>toh</u>-ree	smoking
uscita [f]	oo-<u>shee</u>-tah	gate
borsa [f] a mano	<u>bohr</u>-sah ah <u>mah</u>-noh	carry-on luggage
passaporto [m]	pahs-sah-<u>pohr</u>-toh	passport
bagaglio [m]	bah-<u>gah</u>-lyoh	baggage

Dealing with excess baggage

Sometimes you take so many things with you, and your suitcases are so heavy, that the airline charges an extra fee to transport your luggage. The following weightless sentences, which you can carry in your head, prepare you for just such an event. The truth is that you really can't say much; you simply have to pay.

✔ **Ha un eccesso di bagaglio.** *(ah oon ehch-ches-soh dee bah-gah-lyoh)* (You have excess luggage.)

✔ **Deve pagare un supplemento.** *(deh-veh pah-gah-reh oon soop-pleh-mehn-toh)* (You have to pay a surcharge.)

✔ **Per ogni chilo in più sono ____ lire.** *(pehr oh-nyee kee-loh een pee-oo soh-noh lee-reh)* (For each kilogram of excess luggage, it's ____ lire.)

✔ **Questa borsa a mano è troppo ingombrante.** *(koo-ehs-tah bohr-sah ah mah-noh eh trohp-poh een-gohm-brahn-teh)* (This carry-on luggage is too large.)

Waiting to board the plane

Before boarding, you may encounter unforeseen situations, such as delays. If you do, you'll probably want to ask some questions. Read the following dialogue for an example of what you can say when you're dealing with a delay.

Talkin' the Talk

Mr. Campo is in the boarding area. He asks the agent if his flight is on time.

Sig. Campo: **Il volo è in orario?**
              eel voh-loh eh een oh-rah-ree-oh
              Is the flight on time?

Agent: **No, è in ritardo.**
              noh eh een ree-tahr-doh
              No, there has been a delay.

Sig. Campo: **Di quanto?**
              dee koo-ahn-toh
              How much?

Agent: **Circa quindici minuti.**
              cheer-kah koo-een-dee-chee mee-noo-tee
              About fifteen minutes.

While you're waiting to board, two other questions may come in handy:

- ✔ **Dov'è il bar?** *(doh-veh eel bahr)* (Where is the bar?)
- ✔ **Dove sono i servizi?** *(doh-veh soh-noh ee sehr-vee-tsee)* (Where are the bathrooms?)

Words to Know

supplemento [m]	soop-pleh-mehn-toh	supplement
ingombrante	een-gohm-brahn-teh	large
circa	cheer-kah	about
servizi [m]	sehr-vee-tsee	the bathrooms
in ritardo	een ree-tahr-doh	late; delayed
volo [m]	voh-loh	flight
in orario	een oh-rah-ree-oh	on time

Coping after landing

After you exit a plane in Italy, you are immediately hit by voices speaking a foreign language. You don't have time to decide on your first impressions about the language, however, you have to take care of necessities, such as finding a bathroom, changing money, looking for the baggage claim area, and securing a luggage cart and a taxi. The following dialogues give you an idea of how these situations may play out.

Talkin' the Talk

Mrs. Johnson just arrived at the airport in Milan. First, she wants to change money to pay for a taxi. She asks the first passerby she sees where she can do so.

Mrs. Johnson:	**Mi scusi?** *mee _skoo_-zee* Excuse me?
Passerby:	**Prego!** *_preh_-goh* Yes, please!
Mrs. Johnson:	**Dov'è un bancomat?** *doh-_veh_ oon _bahn_-koh-maht* Where is an ATM?
Passerby:	**All'uscita, signora.** *ahl-loo-_shee_-tah see-_nyoh_-rah* At the exit, madam.
Mrs. Johnson:	**C'è anche una banca?** *cheh _ahn_-keh _oo_-nah _bahn_-kah* Is there also a bank?
Passerby:	**No, c'è soltanto uno sportello di cambio.** *noh cheh sohl-_tahn_-toh _oo_-noh spohr-_tehl_-loh dee _kahm_-bee-oh* No, there is only a change counter.
Mrs. Johnson:	**Benissimo. Dove?** *beh-_nees_-see-moh _doh_-veh* Very well. Where [is it]?
Passerby:	**In fondo alla hall.** *een _fohn_-doh _ahl_-lah hall* At the end of the hall.
Mrs. Johnson:	**Grazie mille.** *_grah_-tsee-eh _meel_-leh* Thank you very much.

Mrs. Johnson changes some money and then needs to pick up her luggage. She asks a woman passing by where she can find a luggage cart.

Mrs. Johnson:	**Dove sono i carrelli?** *_doh_-veh _soh_-noh ee kahr-_rehl_-lee* Where are the luggage carts?
Woman:	**Al ritiro bagagli.** *ahl ree-_tee_-roh bah-_gah_-lyee* At baggage claim.

Mrs. Johnson:	**Servono monete?** *sehr-voh-noh moh-neh-teh* Do I need coins?
Woman:	**Sì, da cinquecento o da mille lire.** *see dah cheen-koo-eh-chehn-toh oh dah meel-leh lee-reh* Yes, 500 or 1,000 lire.

Visitors from countries in the European Union need only **la carta d'identità** *(lah kahr-tah dee-dehn-tee-tah)* (the identity card) to enter Italy. Nationals of all other countries need a valid **passaporto** *(pahs-sah-pohr-toh)* (passport), and sometimes also a visa. Normally, at **controllo passaporti** *(kohn-trohl-loh pahs-sah-pohr-tee)* (passport control), you don't exchange many words, and the ones you do exchange are usually routine. The following section gives you a typical dialogue at passport control.

Talkin' the Talk

Mrs. Smith and her young daughter are passing through passport control. The officer wants to see their passports.

Officer:	**Buongiorno. Passaporti, per favore.** *boo-ohn-johr-noh pahs-sah pohr-tee pehr fah-voh-reh* Good morning. Passports, please.
Mrs. Smith:	**Ecco! Mia figlia è sul mio.** *ehk-koh mee-ah fee-lyah eh sool mee-oh* Here you are! My daughter is on my passport.
Officer:	**Viene in Italia per lavoro?** *vee-eh-neh een ee-tah-lee-ah pehr lah-voh-roh* Are you coming to Italy on business?
Mrs. Smith:	**No, siamo qui in vacanza.** *noh see-ah-moh koo-ee een vah-kahn-tsah* No, we're here on vacation.

Words to Know

arrivo [m]	ahr-<u>ree</u>-voh	arrival
partenza [f]	pahr-<u>tehn</u>-tsah	departure
vacanza [f]	vah-kahn-tsah	vacation
riconsegna bagagli [f]	ree-kohn-<u>seh</u>-nyah bah-gah-lyee	baggage claim
cambio [m]	<u>kahm</u>-bee-oh	money exchange
destinazione [f]	dehs-tee-nah-zee-<u>oh</u>-neh	destination
entrata [f]	ehn-<u>trah</u>-tah	entrance

Going through Customs

You can't get into a foreign country without going through customs. When you have something to declare, you do so **alla dogana** (ahl-lah doh-<u>gah</u>-nah) (at customs). These examples should relieve you of any possible linguistic worries:

✔ **Niente da dichiarare?** (nee-<u>ehn</u>-teh dah dee-kee-ah-<u>rah</u>-reh) (Anything to declare?)

No, niente. (noh nee-<u>ehn</u>-teh) (No, nothing.)

✔ **Per favore, apra questa valigia.** (pehr fah-<u>voh</u>-reh <u>ah</u>-prah koo-<u>ehs</u>-tah vah-<u>lee</u>-jah) (Please, open this suitcase.)

✔ **È nuovo?** (eh noo-<u>oh</u>-voh) (Is it new?)

Sì, ma è per uso personale. (see mah eh pehr <u>oo</u>-zoh pehr-soh-<u>nah</u>-leh) (Yes, but it's for personal use.)

✔ **Per questo deve pagare il dazio.** (pehr koo-<u>ehs</u>-toh <u>deh</u>-veh pah-<u>gah</u>-reh eel <u>dah</u>-tsee-oh) (You have to pay duty on this.)

When you pass through customs, you must honestly declare any goods that you purchased.

Ho questo/queste cose da dichiarare. (oh koo-<u>ehs</u>-toh/koo-<u>ehs</u>-teh <u>koh</u>-zeh dah dee-kee-ah-<u>rah</u>-reh) (I have to declare this/these things.)

Words to Know

dogana [f]	doh-<u>gah</u>-nah	customs
dichiarare	dee-kee-ah-<u>rah</u>-reh	to declare
niente	nee-<u>ehn</u>-teh	nothing
pagare	pah-<u>gah</u>-reh	to pay
uso personale	<u>oo</u>-zoh pehr-soh-<u>nah</u>-leh	personal use

Renting a Car

Italy is a beautiful country, and if you visit, you may want to consider taking driving tours of the cities and the countryside. If you don't have a car, renting one to visit various places is a good idea, but don't forget that Italian traffic is not very relaxed, and finding a place to park can tax your patience — especially in town centers. We don't want to scare you, though; just enjoy the adventure!

To drive a car or motorcycle in Italy, you must be at least 18 years old. Furthermore, you need an international driving permit or a valid national **patente** *(pah-tehn-teh)* (driver's license) with a certified translation. If you decide to rent a car, you should know that small, local companies generally offer cars cheaper than international or large, well-known companies. On the other hand, finding the big companies is easier because they're usually at or near the airport.

Whether you rent a car by phone or directly from a rental service, the process is the same: Just tell the rental company what kind of car you want and under what conditions you want to rent it. The following dialogue represents a typical conversation on this topic.

Talkin' the Talk

Mr. Brown is staying in Italy for two weeks and wants to rent a car to visit different cities. He enters a rental service and talks to **l'impiegato** *(leem-pee-eh-<u>gah</u>-toh)* (the employee).

Mr. Brown: **Vorrei noleggiare una macchina.**
vohr-<u>ray</u> noh-lehj-<u>jah</u>-reh <u>oo</u>-nah <u>mahk</u>-kee-nah
I would like to rent a car.

Agent: **Che tipo?**
keh tee-poh
What kind?

Mr. Brown: **Di media cilindrata col cambio automatico.**
dee meh-dee-ah chee-leen-drah-tah kohl kahm-bee-oh ah-oo-toh-mah-tee-koh
A mid-size with an automatic transmission.

Agent: **Per quanto tempo?**
pehr koo-ahn-toh tehm-poh
For how long?

Mr. Brown: **Una settimana.**
oo-nah seht-tee-mah-nah
One week.
Quanto costa a settimana?
koo-ahn-toh kohs-tah ah seht-tee-mah-nah
What does it cost for a week?

Agent: **C'è una tariffa speciale.**
cheh oo-nah tah-reef-fah speh-chah-leh
There is a special rate.

Mr. Brown: **L'assicurazione è inclusa?**
lahs-see-koo-rah-tsee-oh-neh eh een-kloo-zah
Is insurance included?

Agent: **Sì, con la polizza casco.**
see kohn lah poh-leets-tsah kahs-koh
Yes, a comprehensive policy.

Mr. Brown: **Il chilometraggio è limitato?**
eel kee-loh-meh-trahj-joh eh lee-mee-tah-toh
Is the mileage limited?

Agent: **No.**
noh
No.

Mr. Brown: **E posso consegnare la macchina all'areoporto?**
eh pohs-soh kohn-seh-nyah-reh lah mahk-kee-nah ahl-lah-reh-oh-pohr-toh
Can I return the car at the airport?

Agent: **Certo.**
chehr-toh
Certainly.

Mr. Brown:	**L'ultima domanda: che benzina ci vuole?**
	lool-tee-mah doh-mahn-dah keh behn-dzee-nah
	chee-voo-oh-leh
	Last question: What kind of fuel does the car need?
Agent:	**Normale senza piombo.**
	nohr-mah-leh sehn-tsah pee-ohm-boh
	Normal unleaded.

Other vocabulary words that you may need when renting a car or getting fuel at a gas station include the following:

- **l'aria condizionata** (*lah-ree-ah kohn-dee-tsee-oh-nah-tah*) (air conditioning)

- **il cabriolet** (*eel kah-bree-oh-leh*) (convertible)

- **fare benzina** (*fah-reh behn-dzee-nah*) (to put in gas)

- **faccia il pieno** (*fahch-chah eel pee-eh-noh*) (fill it up)

- **la benzina senza piombo** (*lah behn-dzee-nah sehn-tsah pee-ohm-boh*) (unleaded fuel)

- **la benzina super** (*lah behn-dzee-nah soo-pehr*) (premium fuel)

- **controlli l'olio** (*kohn-trohl-lee loh-lee-oh*) (check the oil)

Navigating Public Transportation

If you'd rather not drive yourself, you can get around quite comfortably using public transportation, such as taxis, trains, and buses. The following sections tell you how to do so in Italian.

Calling a taxi

The process of hailing a taxi is the same in Italy as it is in the United States — you even use the same word: **Taxi** (*tah-ksee*) has entered the Italian language. The only challenge for you is that you have to communicate in Italian. Here are some phrases to help you on your way:

- **Può chiamarmi un taxi?** (*poo-oh kee-ah-mahr-mee oon tah-ksee*) (Can you call me a taxi?)

- **Vorrei un taxi, per favore.** (*vohr-ray oon tah-ksee pehr fah-voh-reh*) (I'd like a taxi, please.)

In case you are asked **quando?** *(koo-ahn-doh)* (when?), you need to be prepared with an answer. Following are some common ones:

- **subito** *(soo-bee-toh)* (right now)

- **fra un'ora** *(frah oon-oh-rah)* (in one hour)

- **alle due del pomeriggio** *(ahl-leh doo-eh dehl poh-meh-reej-joh)* (at 2:00 p.m.)

- **domani mattina** *(doh-mah-nee math-tee-nah)* (tomorrow morning)

After you seat yourself in a taxi, the driver will ask where to take you. Here are some potential destinations:

- **Alla stazione, per favore.** *(ahl-lah stah-tsee-oh-neh pehr fah-voh-reh)* (To the station, please.)

- **All'areoporto.** *(ahl-lah-reh-oh-pohr-toh)* (To the airport.)

- **In via Veneto.** *(een vee-ah veh-neh-toh)* (To via Veneto.)

- **A questo indirizzo: via Leopardi, numero 3.** *(ah koo-ehs-toh een-dee-ree-tsoh vee-ah leh-oh-pahr-dee noo-meh-roh treh)* (To this address: via Leopardi, number 3.)

Finally, you have to pay. Simply ask the driver **Quant'è?** *(koo-ahn-teh)* (How much is it?) For more information about money, see Chapter 11.

In Italy, as in the United States, you usually tip the taxi driver. The general rule is to tip 10 to 15 percent.

Moving by train

You can buy a train ticket **alla stazione** *(ahl-lah stah-tsee-oh-neh)* (at the station) or at **un'agenzia di viaggi** *(oo-nah-jehn-tsee-ah dee vee-ahj-jee)* (a travel agency). If you want to take a **treno rapido** *(treh-noh rah-pee-doh)* (express train) that stops only in the main stations, you pay a **supplemento** *(soop-pleh-mehn-toh)* (surcharge). These faster trains in Italy are called Inter City (IC) — or Euro City (EC) if their final destination is outside Italy. The Euro Star is an even faster option.

Keep in mind that in Italy you have to validate your ticket before entering **il binario** *(eel bee-nah-ree-oh)* (the platform; the track). Therefore, the train station positions validation boxes in front of the platforms.

Talkin' the Talk

 Bianca is at the train station in Roma. She goes to the **informazioni** *(een-fohr-mah-tsee-<u>oh</u>-nee)* (information counter) to ask about a connection to Perugia.

Bianca: **Ci sono treni diretti per Perugia?**
chee <u>soh</u>-noh <u>treh</u>-nee dee-<u>reht</u>-tee pehr peh-<u>roo</u>-jah
Are there direct trains to Perugia?

Agent: **No, deve prendere un treno per Terni.**
noh <u>deh</u>-veh <u>prehn</u>-deh-reh oon <u>treh</u>-noh pehr <u>tehr</u>-nee
No, you have to take a train to Terni.

Bianca: **E poi devo cambiare?**
eh <u>poo</u>-ee <u>deh</u>-voh kahm-bee-<u>ah</u>-reh
And then do I have to change [trains]?

Agent: **Sì, prende un locale per Perugia.**
see <u>prehn</u>-deh oon loh-<u>kah</u>-leh pehr peh-<u>roo</u>-jah
Yes, you take a slow train to Perugia.

Bianca: **A che ora parte il prossimo treno?**
ah keh <u>oh</u>-rah <u>pahr</u>-teh eel <u>prohs</u>-see-moh <u>treh</u>-noh
At what time is the next train?

Agent: **Alle diciotto e arriva a Terni alle diciannove.**
<u>ahl</u>-leh dee-<u>choht</u>-toh eh ahr-<u>ree</u>-vah ah <u>tehr</u>-nee
<u>ahl</u>-leh dee-chahn-<u>noh</u>-veh
At 6 p.m. It arrives in Terni at 7 p.m.

Bianca: **E per Perugia?**
eh pehr peh-<u>roo</u>-jah
And to Perugia?

Agent: **C'è subito la coincidenza.**
cheh <u>soo</u>-bee-toh lah koh-een-chee-<u>dehn</u>-tsah
There is an immediate connection.

After exploring your options, you have to make a decision and buy a ticket. In the following dialogue, Bianca does just that.

Talkin' the Talk

 Bianca goes to the ticket counter and buys her ticket.

Bianca: **Un biglietto per Perugia, per favore.**
oon bee-lyeht-toh pehr peh-roo-jah pehr fah-voh-reh
One ticket to Perugia, please.

Agent: **Andata e ritorno?**
ahn-dah-tah eh ree-tohr-noh
Round trip?

Bianca: **Solo andata. Quanto viene?**
soh-loh ahn-dah-tah koo-ahn-toh vee-eh-neh
One-way. How much does it cost?

Agent: **In prima classe quarantamila lire.**
*een pree-mah klahs-seh koo-ah-rahn-tah-meelah
lee-reh*
First class [costs] 40,000 lire.

Bianca: **E in seconda?**
eh een seh-kohn-dah
And second [class]?

Agent: **Ventitré.**
vehn-tee-treh
23,000.

Bianca: **Seconda classe, per favore. Da che binario parte?**
*seh-kohn-dah klahs-seh pehr fah-voh-reh dah keh
bee-nah-ree-oh pahr-teh*
Second class, please. From which track does it leave?

Agent: **Dal tre.**
dahl treh
From [track number] 3.

Notice that the employee replies only **ventitré** instead of **ventitremilalire**
(*vehn-tee-treh-mee-lah-lee-reh*). When the context is clear and the meaning is
implicit, this is a common way of giving a price.

Words to Know

binario [m]	bee-<u>nah</u>-ree-oh	platform; track
biglietto [m]	bee-<u>lyeht</u>-toh	ticket
andata [f]	ahn-<u>dah</u>-tah	one way
ritorno [m]	ree-<u>tohr</u>-noh	return trip
supplemento [m]	soop-pleh-<u>mehn</u>-toh	surcharge

Going by bus or tram

You're not always in the lucky situation of having a car, or maybe you have one, but want to avoid driving in the city traffic. To get from point A to point B without a car, you most likely take the bus or tram. We provide the appropriate Italian vocabulary for such situations in this section.

Some Italian cities have streetcars, or trams, and most have buses. Incidentally, in Italian they spell it **il tram** and pronounce it *eel trahm.* The Italian word for bus is **l'autobus** *(<u>lah</u>-oo-toh-boos)* — and the little buses are called **il pullmino** *(eel pool-<u>mee</u>-noh).* Big buses that take you from one city to another are called **il pullman** *(eel <u>pool</u>-mahn)* or **la corriera** *(lah kohr-ree-<u>eh</u>-rah).*

You can buy bus or tram tickets in Italian bars, **dal giornalaio** *(dahl johr-nah-<u>lah</u>-ee-oh)* (at newspaper stands), or a **dal tabaccaio** *(dahl tah-bahk-<u>kah</u>-ee-oh)* (tobacco shop). The latter are little shops where you can purchase cigarettes, stamps, newspapers, and so on. You can find them on virtually every street corner in Italy; they're recognizable by either a black-and-white sign or a blue-and-white sign with a big T on it.

Talkin' the Talk

Gherardo wants to get to the train station. He's standing at a bus stop but is a little unsure about which bus to take. He asks **un signore** *(oon see-<u>nyoh</u>-reh)* (a gentleman) waiting there.

Gherardo: **Mi scusi, signore.**
              mee <u>skoo</u>-zee see-<u>nyoh</u>-reh
              Excuse me, sir.

Gentleman:	**Prego?**
	preh-goh
	Yes?

Gherardo:	**Quest'autobus va alla stazione?**
	koo-ehs-tah-oo-toh-boos vah ahl-lah stah-tsee-oh-neh
	Does this bus go to the station?

Gentleman:	**Sì.**
	see
	Yes.

Gherardo:	**Dove si comprano i biglietti?**
	doh-veh see kohm-prah-noh ee bee-lyeht-teh
	Where can I buy tickets?

Gentleman:	**In questo bar.**
	een koo-ehs-toh bahr
	In this bar.

You probably aim to take the most convenient and fastest means of transport. To know which one this is, you have to know what's what and your way about. If you don't, hopfully you can find a nice person to help you.

Talkin' the Talk

 Tom, a Canadian tourist, wants to visit the cathedral downtown. He asks about the bus, but a woman advises him to take the subway because it takes less time.

Tom:	**Scusi, che autobus va al Duomo?**
	skoo-zee keh ah-oo-toh-boos vah ahl doo-oh-moh
	Excuse me, which bus goes to the Cathedral?

Woman:	**Perché non prende la metropolitana?**
	pehr-keh nohn prehn-deh lah
	meh-troh-poh-lee-tah-nah
	Why don't you take the subway?

Tom:	**È meglio?**
	eh meh-lyoh
	Is it better?

Woman:	**Sì, ci mette cinque minuti!**
	see chee meht-teh cheen-koo-eh mee-noo-tee
	Yes, it takes five minutes!

Tom:	**Dov'è la fermata della metropolitana?**
	doh-veh lah fehr-mah-tah dehl-lah
	meh-troh-poh-lee-tah-nah
	Where is the subway station?

Woman:	**Dietro l'angolo.**
	dee-eh-troh lahn-goh-loh
	Around the corner.

Tom:	**Per il Duomo?**
	pehr eel doo-oh-moh
	[How far] To the Cathedral?

Woman:	**La prossima fermata.**
	lah pros-see-mah fehr-mah-tah
	The next stop.

Tom:	**Grazie!**
	grah-tsee-eh
	Thanks!

Woman:	**Prego.**
	preh-goh
	You're welcome.

Reading maps and schedules

You don't need to know much about reading maps except for the little bit of vocabulary written on them. At the least, you must know the four directions: **nord** *(nohrd)* (north), **est** *(ehst)* (east), **sud** *(sood)* (south), and **ovest** *(oh-vehst)* (west). If you're traveling in Italy and you don't want to risk relying on your Italian, you can find city maps in English in most **edicole** *(eh-dee-koh-leh)* (newstands).

Reading a schedule can be more difficult for travelers because the schedules are usually written only in Italian. You frequently find the following words on schedules:

- **l'orario** *(loh-rah-ree-oh)* (the timetable)

- **partenze** *(pahr-tehn-tseh)* (departures)

- **arrivi** *(ahr-ree-vee)* (arrivals)

- **giorni feriali** *(johr-nee feh-ree-ah-lee)* (weekdays)

- **giorni festivi** *(johr-nee fehs-tee-vee)* (Sundays and holidays)

- **il binario** *(eel bee-nah-ree-oh)* (the track; the platform)

Keep in mind that Europeans don't write a.m. or p.m.; they count the hours from 0.00 to 24.00. Therefore, 1.00 is the hour after midnight, whereas 1:00 p.m. is 13.00.

Being Early or Late

You don't always arrive on time, and you may have to communicate that you'll be late or early, or apologize to someone for being delayed. The following list contains important terms that you can use to do so:

- ✔ **essere in anticipo** *(ehs-seh-reh een ahn-tee-cee-poh)* (to be early)

- ✔ **essere puntuale** *(ehs-seh-reh poon-too-ah-leh)* (to be on time)

- ✔ **essere in ritardo** *(ehs-seh-reh een ree-tahr-doh)* (to be late)

- ✔ **arrivare/venire troppo presto** *(ahr-ree-vah-reh veh-nee-reh trohp-poh prehs-toh)* (to arrive; to come too early)

These examples use the preceding phrases in sentences:

- ✔ **Mi scusi, sono arrivata in ritardo.** *(mee skoo-zee soh-noh ahr-ree-vah-tah een ree-tahr-doh)* (I'm sorry, I arrived late.)

- ✔ **Sono venuti troppo presto.** *(soh-noh veh-noo-tee trohp-poh prehs-toh)* (They came too early.)

- ✔ **Meno male che sei puntuale.** *(meh-noh mah-leh keh say poon-too-ah-leh)* (Fortunately you're on time.)

When talking about someone's lateness, you probably can't avoid the verb **aspettare** *(ahs-peht-tah-reh)* (to wait). Following are a few examples of this verb:

- ✔ **Aspetto da un'ora.** *(ahs-peht-toh dah oo-noh-rah)* (I've been waiting for an hour.)

- ✔ **Aspetta anche lei il ventitré?** *(ahs-peht-tah ahn-keh lay eel vehn-tee-treh)* (Are you also waiting for the number 23 bus?)

- ✔ **Aspettate un momento!** *(ahs-peht-tah-teh oon moh-mehn-toh)* (Wait a moment!)

- ✔ **Aspettiamo Anna?** *(ahs-peht-tee-ah-moh ahn-nah)* (Should we wait for Anna?)

- ✔ **Chi aspetti?** *(kee ahs-peht-tee)* (For whom are you waiting?)

Please note that the verb **aspettare** takes no preposition, as the English **to wait for** does.

Fun & Games

What a mess! This schedule is really jumbled. The Italian words for **train**, **bus stop**, **train station**, **track**, **ticket**, **one way**, **return trip**, and **surcharge** are hidden in the following puzzle. If you want to get to your train on time, you have to solve it. Hurry up!

Word Seek

B	S	M	T	A	T	A	M	R	E	F	O
I	T	U	D	H	G	L	T	X	L	N	C
N	S	Y	P	V	X	L	A	B	E	D	G
A	P	J	Y	P	B	E	I	R	S	H	D
R	K	D	A	J	L	G	T	X	F	X	V
I	V	D	U	Y	L	E	M	R	C	D	Q
O	I	D	Y	I	K	A	M	G	G	D	R
R	Z	J	E	L	X	S	T	E	E	L	K
B	C	T	C	P	M	D	Q	A	N	C	I
B	T	H	P	R	S	P	U	F	D	T	K
O	R	I	T	O	R	N	O	S	O	N	O
S	T	A	Z	I	O	N	E	Z	A	G	A

Answers: treno, fermata, stazione, binario, biglietto, andata, ritorno, supplemento

Chapter 15

Planning a Trip

● ●

In This Chapter

▶ Making travel plans

▶ Coming and going: **Arrivare** and **partire**

▶ Obtaining passports and visas

▶ Looking forward to your trip: The simple future

● ●

*W*henever you plan a trip, especially to a foreign country, you always have a long list of things to do. Be sure to first decide which cities you want to visit. Then you can book your flight, make your hotel accommodations, and check to see that your passport is valid. Above all, **Buon viaggio!** *(boo-ohn-vee-ahj-joh)* (Have a nice trip!) or **Buone vacanze!** *(boo-oh-neh vah-kahn-tseh)* (Have a nice vacation!)

Deciding When and Where to Go

Deciding when to take a trip can be just as important as choosing your destination. You probably don't want to visit India during the monsoon season, or Washington, D.C. in August when the weather can be unbearably hot and humid. Italy also has cities that it's better to avoid in the heat of the summer. In fact, many Italians living in those cities escape in the hottest months to cooler places. On the other hand, summer months are **l'alta stagione** *(lahl-tah stah-joh-neh)* (high season) for tourists and the cities are bustling with life. Table 15-1 lists the months, which you need to plan a vacation.

Table 15-1	Months	
Italian	*Pronunciation*	*Translation*
gennaio	gehn-nah-ee-oh	January
febbraio	fehb-brah-ee-oh	February
marzo	mahr-tsoh	March

(continued)

Table 15-1 (continued)

Italian	Pronunciation	Translation
aprile	ah-<u>pree</u>-leh	April
maggio	<u>mahj</u>-joh	May
giugno	<u>joo</u>-nyoh	June
luglio	<u>loo</u>-lyoh	July
agosto	ah-<u>gohs</u>-toh	August
settembre	seht-<u>tehm</u>-breh	September
ottobre	oht-<u>toh</u>-breh	October
novembre	noh-<u>vehm</u>-breh	November
dicembre	dee-<u>chehm</u>-breh	December

Talkin' the Talk

Enzo is telling Cristina about their vacation for the summer. He has it all figured out already, but Cristina is skeptical.

Enzo: **Quest'anno andiamo in montagna!**
koo-ehs-<u>than</u>-noh ahn-dee-<u>ah</u>-moh een mohn-<u>tah</u>-nyah
This year we're going to the mountains!

Cristina: **Stai scherzando?**
<u>stah</u>-ee skehr-<u>tsahn</u>-doh
Are you kidding?

Enzo: **È rilassante: boschi, aria fresca . . .**
eh ree-lahs-<u>sahn</u>-teh <u>bohs</u>-kee <u>ah</u>-ree-ah <u>frehs</u>-kah
It's relaxing: woods, fresh air. . . .

Cristina: **È noioso! E non si può nuotare!**
eh noh-<u>yoh</u>-zoh eh nohn see poo-<u>oh</u> noo-oh-<u>tah</u>-reh
It's boring. And you can't swim!

Enzo: **Ci sono le piscine!**
chee <u>soh</u>-noh leh pee-<u>shee</u>-neh
There are swimming pools!

Cristina:	**Ma dai, pensa al mare, al sole. . . .**
	mah dah-ee pehn-sah ahl mah-reh ahl soh-leh
	Come on, think of the sea, the sun. . . .

Enzo:	**E la campagna?**
	eh lah kahm-pah-nyah
	What about the country?

Cristina:	**Oh no. Rimango a casa!**
	oh noh ree-mahn-goh ah kah-sah
	Oh no. I'll stay home!

Booking a Trip

When you're ready to book your flight or hotel, you may want to consider using **un'agenzia viaggi** (*oo-nah-jehn-tsee-ah vee-ahj-jee*) (a travel agency). This approach is a convenient way to get plane tickets, hotel reservations, or complete tour packages all in one place.

For information about booking hotel rooms, see Chapter 13.

Talkin' the Talk

If you want to travel from Italy to another country, you may have a conversation like this in a travel agency. Alessandro, who wants to fly to India, is talking to Giorgio, **l'impiegato** (*leem-pee-eh-gah-toh*) (the employee).

Giorgio:	**Buongiorno, mi dica.**
	boo-ohn-johr-noh mee dee-kah
	Good morning, can I help you? (Literally: Tell me.)

Alessandro:	**Vorrei fare un viaggio in India.**
	vohr-ray fah-reh oon vee-ahj-joh een een-dee-ah
	I'd like to travel to India.

Giorgio:	**Dove, esattamente?**
	doh-veh eh-zaht-tah-mehn-teh
	Where exactly?

Alessandro:	**Da Bombay al sud.**
	dah bohm-bay ahl sood
	From Bombay to the south.

Giorgio:	**Un viaggio organizzato?**
	oon vee-ahj-joh ohr-gah-nee-zah-toh
	An organized trip?

Alessandro:	**No, vorrei soltanto prenotare i voli.**
	noh vohr-ray sohl-tahn-toh preh-noh-tah-reh
	ee voh-lee
	No, I'd like to book just the flights.

Giorgio:	**Anche interni?**
	ahn-keh een-tehr-nee
	Also within the country?

Alessandro:	**No, in India vorrei viaggiare in treno.**
	noh een een-dee-ah vohr-ray vee-ahj-jah-reh een
	treh-noh
	No, in India I'd like to travel by train.

Giorgio:	**Quando vuole partire?**
	koo-ahn-doh voo-oh-leh pahr-tee-reh
	When do you want to leave?

Alessandro:	**La prima settimana di Febbraio.**
	lah pree-mah seht-tee-mah-nah dee fehb-brah-ee-oh
	The first week of February.

Giorgio:	**E il ritorno?**
	eh eel ree-tohr-noh
	And return?

Alessandro:	**Fine Marzo.**
	fee-neh mahr-tsoh
	The end of March.

If you fly to Italy, the main airports are **Malpensa** *(mahl-pehn-sah)* in Milan, and **Linate** *(lee-nah-teh)* and **Leonardo da Vinci** *(leh-oh-nahr-doh dah veen-chee)* in Rome.

Several years ago, a new vacation concept became popular in Italy in a very short time: **l'agriturismo** *(lah-gree-too-rees-moh)* (the farm holiday). During these types of vacations, people travel to the country or the mountains where they stay in farmhouses or old castles. The prices for this type of lodging are lower than hotel rates, you eat the traditional food of the region, and you're miles away from formal, impersonal hotels. Farm holidays are extremely popular with both Italians and foreigners.

Another popular type of lodging is the bed and breakfast, which you can find throughout the countryside as well in big cities like Rome and Milan.

Words to Know

campagna [f]	kahm-<u>pah</u>-nyah	country
esattamente	eh-zaht-tah-<u>mehn</u>-teh	exactly
mare [m]	<u>mah</u>-reh	sea
montagna [f]	mohn-<u>tah</u>-nyah	mountain
è noioso	eh noh-<u>yoh</u>-zoh	it's boring
prenotare	preh-noh-<u>tah</u>-reh	to reserve
rimanere	ree-mah-<u>neh</u>-reh	to stay
scherzare	skehr-<u>zah</u>-reh	to kid; to joke
in treno	een <u>t</u>reh-noh	by train
viaggiare	vee-ahj-<u>jah</u>-reh	to travel
viaggio organizzato [m]	vee-<u>ahj</u>-joh ohr-gah-nee-<u>dzah</u>-toh	organized trip
volo [m]	<u>voh</u>-loh	flight

Talkin' the Talk

Alessandro sits together with his friend Carolina and tells her that he plans a trip to India. Carolina seems quite surprised.

Carolina: **Perché in India?**
pehr-<u>keh</u> een <u>een</u>-dee-ah
Why to India?

Alessandro: **È un paese bellissimo.**
eh oon pah-<u>eh</u>-zeh behl-<u>lees</u>-see-moh
It's a very beautiful country.

Carolina: **Ma non l'ideale per rilassarsi.**
mah nohn lee-deh-<u>ah</u>-leh pehr ree-lahs-<u>sahr</u>-see
But not the ideal place to relax.

Alessandro: **Perché no?**
pehr-<u>keh</u> noh
Why not?

Carolina: **Ti muoverai molto.**
tee moo-oh-veh-<u>rah</u>-ee <u>mohl</u>-toh
You'll travel around a lot.

Alessandro: **Viaggerò e farò delle pause al mare.**
vee-ahj-jeh-<u>roh</u> eh fah-<u>roh</u> <u>dehl</u>-leh <u>pah</u>-oo-zeh ahl <u>mah</u>-reh
I'll take trips and have some breaks at the sea.

Carolina: **Ci sono belle spiagge?**
chee <u>soh</u>-noh <u>behl</u>-leh spee-<u>ahj</u>-jeh
Are there nice beaches?

Alessandro: **Sì, e la campagna . . .**
see eh lah kahm-<u>pah</u>-nyah
Yes, and the countryside . . .

Carolina: **Ho visto fotografie incredibili.**
oh <u>vees</u>-toh foh-toh-grah-<u>fee</u>-eh een-kreh-<u>dee</u>-bee-lee
I've seen incredible photographs.

Arriving and Leaving: The Verbs "Arrivare" and "Partire"

To help you understand the verbs **arrivare** *(ahr-ree-<u>vah</u>-reh)* (to arrive) and **partire** *(pahr-<u>tee</u>-reh)* (to leave), we use them in some simple sentences in the list following. As you can see, when you use these verbs in connection with a specific place **arrivare** is always followed by the preposition **a** *(ah)* (at) and **partire** is always followed by the preposition **da** *(dah)* (from).

The following examples demonstrate how to use the verbs **partire** and **arrivare** when referring to the time before departure or arrival.

✔ **Luca parte da Torino alle cinque.** *(<u>loo</u>-kah <u>pahr</u>-teh dah toh-<u>ree</u>-noh <u>ahl</u>-leh <u>cheen</u>-koo-eh)* (Luca leaves from Turin at 5 o'clock.)

✔ **Arrivo a casa nel pomeriggio.** *(ahr-<u>ree</u>-voh ah <u>kah</u>-sah nehl poh-meh-<u>reej</u>-joh)* (I arrive home in the afternoon.)

✔ **A che ora parte l'aereo da Madrid?** *(ah keh <u>oh</u>-rah <u>pahr</u>-teh lah-<u>eh</u>-reh-oh dah <u>mah</u>-dreed)* (What time does the flight leave from Madrid?)

Sometimes the verbs are separated from their preposition by other words. Here's an example:

Parto stasera da Milano. *(<u>pahr</u>-toh stah-<u>seh</u>-rah dah mee-<u>lah</u>-noh)* (I leave this evening from Milan.)

The verb forms change, however, when you refer to the moment of your arrival or departure or the time afterwards. In these cases, **essere** *(<u>ehs</u>-seh-reh)* (to be) is added to the verb and, as usual, changes according to the number and gender of the person concerned. When you refer to a female, the verb ends in *a* when it's singular and in *e* when it's plural. When you refer to a male, the verb ends in *o* when it's singular and in *i* when it's plural.

The following examples demonstrate this construction:

✔ **Sono partita stamattina.** *(<u>soh</u>-noh pahr-<u>tee</u>-tah stah-maht-<u>tee</u>-nah)* (I left this morning.)

✔ **Sono appena arrivato alla stazione.** *(<u>soh</u>-noh ahp-<u>peh</u>-nah ahr-ree-<u>vah</u>-toh <u>ahl</u>-lah stah-tsee-<u>oh</u>-neh)* (I've just arrived at the station.)

✔ **Sono arrivate in ritardo alla lezione.** *(<u>soh</u>-noh ahr-ree-<u>vah</u>-teh een ree-<u>tahr</u>-doh <u>ahl</u>-lah leh-tsee-<u>oh</u>-neh)* (They arrived at the lesson late.)

✔ **Siamo partiti da lì dopo pranzo.** *(see-<u>ah</u>-moh pahr-<u>tee</u>-tee dah lee <u>doh</u>-poh <u>prahn</u>-tsoh)* (We left from there after lunch.)

And here we go with the whole conjunction of **partire** *(pahr-<u>tee</u>-reh)* (to leave) and **arrivare** *(ahr-ree-<u>vah</u>-reh)* (to arrive).

Conjugation	Pronunciation
io parto	<u>ee</u>-oh <u>pahr</u>-toh
tu parti	too <u>pahr</u>-tee
lui/lei parte	<u>loo</u>-ee/lay <u>pahr</u>-teh
noi partiamo	<u>noh</u>-ee pahr-tee-<u>ah</u>-moh
voi partite	<u>voh</u>-ee pahr-<u>tee</u>-teh
loro partono	<u>loh</u>-roh <u>pahr</u>-toh-noh

Conjugation	Pronunciation
io arrivo	<u>ee</u>-oh ahr-<u>ree</u>-voh
tu arrivi	too ahr-<u>ree</u>-vee
lui/lei arriva	<u>loo</u>-ee/lay ahr-<u>ree</u>-vah
noi arriviamo	<u>noh</u>-ee ahr-ree-vee-<u>ah</u>-moh
voi arrivate	<u>voh</u>-ee ahr-ree-<u>vah</u>-teh
loro arrivano	<u>loh</u>-roh ahr-<u>ree</u>-vah-noh

Talkin' the Talk

Filippo and Marzia are spending some time together before Filippo has to catch a plane. While Filippo seems rather relaxed, Marzia is quite worried about him making it to the airport in time.

Marzia: **A che ora parte l'aereo?**
ah keh <u>oh</u>-rah <u>pahr</u>-teh lah-<u>eh</u>-reh-oh
What time does the plane leave?

Filippo: **Alle nove.**
<u>ahl</u>-leh <u>noh</u>-veh
At nine.

Marzia: **Alle sette devi essere all'aeroporto!**
<u>ahl</u>-leh <u>seht</u>-teh <u>deh</u>-vee <u>ehs</u>-seh-reh
ahl-lah-eh-roh-<u>pohr</u>-toh
You have to be at the airport at seven.

Filippo: **Ma no, un'ora prima basta.**
mah noh oon <u>oh</u>-rah <u>pree</u>-mah <u>bahs</u>-tah
No, one hour before is enough.

Marzia: **Hai fatto la valigia?**
<u>ah</u>-ee <u>faht</u>-toh lah vah-<u>lee</u>-jah
Have you packed your suitcase?

Filippo: **Ancora no, c'è tempo.**
ahn-<u>koh</u>-rah noh cheh <u>tehm</u>-poh
Not yet, there is time.

Marzia: **Sei pazzo! Sono già le sei!**
say <u>paht</u>-tsoh <u>soh</u>-noh jah leh say
You're crazy! It's already six!

Filippo:	**E allora? Mi porto solo poche cose.**
	eh ahl-loh-rah mee pohr-toh soh-loh poh-keh koh-zeh
	So what? I'm taking just a few things.
Marzia:	**Certo, poi sono sempre tre valigie e due borse!**
	chehr-toh poh-ee soh-noh sehm-preh treh vah-lee-jeh eh doo-eh bohr-seh
	Sure, but you always end up with three suitcases and two bags!

Words to Know

aereo [m]	ah-eh-reh-oh	plane
aeroporto [m]	ah-eh-roh-pohr-toh	airport
arrivare a	ahr-ree-vah-reh ah	to arrive at
borsa [f]	bohr-sah	bag
partire da	pahr-tee-reh dah	to leave from
in ritardo	een ree-tahr-doh	late
tempo [m]	tehm-poh	time
valido	vah-lee-doh	valid
viaggio [m]	vee-ahj-joh	journey
visto [m]	vees-toh	visa

Traveling to Foreign Lands

If you're traveling to Italy from the United States, Canada, the European Union, Australia, New Zealand, or Ireland, you normally don't need a visa. Visitors from these countries need only a valid passport. But Italians visiting the United States always need a visa.

Talkin' the Talk

Ms. Alessi needs a visa, so she calls the consulate of the country she wants to visit. She speaks to the secretary.

Sig.ra Alessi:	**Ho bisogno di un visto.** *oh bee-<u>zoh</u>-nyoh dee oon <u>vees</u>-toh* I need a visa.
Secretary:	**È un viaggio di lavoro?** *eh oon vee-<u>ahj</u>-joh dee lah-<u>voh</u>-roh* Is it a business trip?
Sig.ra Alessi:	**No, una vacanza.** *noh <u>oo</u>-nah vah-<u>kahn</u>-tsah* No, a vacation.
Secretary:	**Abbiamo bisogno del suo passaporto valido.** *ahb-bee-<u>ah</u>-moh bee-<u>zoh</u>-nyoh dehl <u>soo</u>-oh pahs-sah-<u>pohr</u>-toh <u>vah</u>-lee-doh* We need your valid passport.
Sig.ra Alessi:	**Nient'altro?** *nee-ehn-<u>tahl</u>-troh* Nothing else?
Secretary:	**Sì, deve pagare una tassa di quarantamila lire.** *see <u>deh</u>-veh pah-<u>gah</u>-reh <u>oo</u>-nah <u>tahs</u>-sah dee koo-ah-rahn-tah-<u>meel</u>-lah <u>lee</u>-reh* Yes, you have to pay forty thousand lire.
Sig.ra Alessi:	**Ci vuole molto tempo?** *chee voo-<u>oh</u>-leh <u>mohl</u>-toh <u>tehm</u>-poh* Does it take a long time?
Secretary:	**Due o tre giorni.** *<u>doo</u>-eh oh treh <u>johr</u>-nee* Two or three days.

Using the Simple Future Tense

Sometimes you need a verb form that indicates that something will happen in the near future. In Italian, this tense is called **futuro semplice** *(foo-<u>too</u>-roh <u>sehm</u>-plee-cheh)* (simple future). To be sure, it's not the only tense to use in such a situation — you can also use the present tense when referring to a point in the future. The following sentences use the simple future tense:

- ✔ **Andrò in Italia.** *(ahn-droh een ee-tah-lee-ah)* (I will go to Italy.)

- ✔ **Quando arriverai a Palermo?** *(koo-ahn-doh ahr-ree-veh-rah-ee ah pah-lehr-moh)* (When will you arrive at Palermo?)

- ✔ **Anche Anna verrà alla festa di sabato sera.** *(ahn-keh ahn-nah vehr-rah ahl-lah fehs-tah dee sah-bah-toh seh-rah)* (Anna will come to the party on Saturday night, too.)

- ✔ **Non torneremo troppo tardi.** *(nohn tohr-neh-reh-moh trohp-poh tahr-dee)* (We won't be back too late.)

- ✔ **Sarete lì anche voi?** *(sah-reh-teh lee ahn-keh voh-ee)* (Will you be there, too?)

- ✔ **Arriveranno un po' in ritardo.** *(ahr-ree-veh-rahn-noh oon poh een ree-tahr-doh)* (They will arrive a bit late.)

In addition to the description of a point in the future, the simple future has several other functions. It also expresses, for instance, a definite conviction or plan:

> **Domani sarò a Roma e farò un giro turistico della città.**
> *doh-mah-nee sah-roh ah roh-mah eh fah-roh oon jee-roh too-rees-tee-koh dehl-lah cheet-tah*
> Tomorrow I will be in Rome, and I will take a sightseeing tour around the city.

You also can use the simple future in *if* sentences, where you would use the present tense in English:

> **Se domani pioverà, andrò al museo.** *(seh doh-mah-nee pee-oh-veh-rah ahn-droh ahl moo-zeh-oh)* (If it rains tomorrow, I will go to the museum.)

In Italian, you can also use the present tense to express the same thing:

> **Se domani piove, andrò al museo.** *(seh doh-mah-nee pee-oh-veh ahn-droh ahl moo-zeh-oh)* (If it rains tomorrow, I will go to the museum.)

or even

> **Se domani piove, vado al museo.** *(seh doh-mah-nee pee-oh-veh vah-doh ahl moo-zeh-oh)* (If it rains tomorrow, I'll go to the museum.)

Check Appendix A for more verb conjugations.

Fun & Games

Fill in the missing words with one of three possible answers under each sentence. Have fun!

1. **Quest'anno andiamo in _____.** (This year we're going to the mountains.)

   a. albergo

   b. montagna

   c. aereo

2. **Il volo parte _____ Palermo alle tre.** (The flight leaves from Palermo at three o'clock.)

   a. da

   b. su

   c. a

3. **Passo le vacanze in _____.** (I spend my vacation in the country.)

   a. mar

   b. campagna

   c. montagna

4. **Dov'è la mia _____?** (Where is my suitcase?)

   a. stanza

   b. piscina

   c. valigia

5. **È un _____ organizzato.** (It's an organized trip.)

   a. viaggio

   b. treno

   c. volo

Answers: 1. b, 2. a, 3. b, 4. c, 5. a

Chapter 16

Handling Emergencies

• •

In This Chapter

▶ Asking for help

▶ Dealing with car troubles

▶ Describing what ails you

▶ Alerting the police to an emergency

▶ Protecting your legal rights

• •

Asking for help is never fun, because you only need help when you're in a jam. For the purposes of this chapter, think about what unfortunate things could happen to you and in what difficulties you may find yourself. Some of these situations are minor, and others are much more serious. We give you the language tools you need to communicate your woes to the people who can help.

Here is a general sampling of asking-for-help sentences:

> ✔ **Aiuto!** *(ah-yoo-toh)* (Help!)
>
> ✔ **Mi aiuti, per favore.** *(mee ah-yoo-tee pehr fah-voh-reh)* (Help me, please.)
>
> ✔ **Chiamate la polizia!** *(kee-ah-mah-teh lah poh-lee-tsee-ah)* (Call the police!)
>
> ✔ **Ho bisogno di un medico.** *(oh bee-zoh-nyoh dee oon meh-dee-koh)* (I need a doctor.)
>
> ✔ **Chiamate un'ambulanza!** *(kee-ah-mah-teh oo-nahm-boo-lahn-tsah)* (Call an ambulance!)

As you may have noticed, you conjugate sentences directed at a group of people in the plural form. In an emergency situation, you address anyone who may be listening to you.

In some situations, you must ask for a competent authority who speaks English. Do so by saying:

- ✔ **Mi scusi, parla inglese?** *(mee skoo-zee pahr-lah een-gleh-zeh)* (Excuse me, do you speak English?)

- ✔ **C'è un medico che parli inglese?** *(cheh oon meh-dee-koh keh pahr-lee een-gleh-zeh)* (Is there a doctor who speaks English?)

- ✔ **Dove posso trovare un avvocato che parli inglese?** *(doh-veh pohs-soh troh-vah-reh oon ahv-voh-kah-toh keh pahr-lee een-gleh-zeh)* (Where can I find a lawyer who speaks English?)

If you can't find a professional who speaks English, you may be able to find **un interprete** *(oon een-tehr-preh-teh)* (an interpreter) to help you.

Dealing with Car Trouble

You don't have to be involved in a car crash to experience car trouble. Perhaps some sort of mechanical problem makes your car break down. In such cases you need to call an auto mechanic who can help you out of this situation.

Talkin' the Talk

 Raffaella's car broke down. She calls **il soccorso stradale** *(eel sohk-kohr-soh strah-dah-leh)* (roadside assistance) from her cell phone.

Mechanic: **Pronto.**
prohn-toh oh
Hello.

Raffaella: **Pronto, ho bisogno d'aiuto!**
prohn-toh oh bee-zoh-nyoh dah-yoo-toh
Hello, I need help!

Mechanic: **Che succede?**
keh sooch-cheh-deh
What's wrong?

Raffaella: **Mi si è fermata la macchina.**
mee see eh fehr-mah-tah lah mahk-kee-nah
My car broke down.

Mechanic:	**Dove si trova?**
	doh-veh see troh-vah
	Where are you?
Raffaella:	**Sull'autostrada A 1 prima dell'uscita Firenze Nord.**
	sool au-to-strah-dah ah oo-noh pree-mah
	dehl-loo-shee-tah fee-rehn-tseh nohrd
	On the highway A 1 before the Florence North exit.
Mechanic:	**Bene. Mando un carro attrezzi.**
	beh-neh mahn-doh oon cahr-roh aht-treht-tzee
	Okay. I'll send a tow truck.
Raffaella:	**Ci vorrà molto?**
	chee vohr-rah mohl-toh
	Will it take a long time?
Mechanic:	**Dipende dal traffico.**
	dee-pehn-deh dahl trahf-fee-koh
	It depends on the traffic.
Raffaella:	**Venite il più presto possibile!**
	veh-nee-teh eel pee-oo prehs-toh pohs-see-bee-leh
	Come as soon as possible!

Words to Know

aiuto [m]	ah-yoo-toh	help
fermare	fehr-mah-reh	to stop
macchina [f]	mahk-kee-nah	car
il più presto possibile	eel pee-oo prehs-toh pohs-see-bee-leh	as soon as possible
soccorso stradale [m]	sohk-kohr-soh strah-dah-leh	roadside assistance
traffico [m]	trahf-fee-koh	traffic
meccanico [m]	mehk-kah-nee-koh	mechanic
carro attrezzi [m]	kahr-roh aht-treht-tsee	tow truck

Talking to Doctors

When you're in **l'ospedale** *(lohs-peh-dah-leh)* (the hospital) or at **il medico** *(eel meh-dee-koh)* (the doctor), you must explain where you hurt or what the problem is. This task isn't always easy, because pointing to a spot may not be sufficient. But don't worry, we won't leave you in the lurch. This section shows you, among other things, how to refer to your body parts in Italian (in Table 16-1) and what to say in a medical emergency.

Table 16-1	Basic Body Parts	
Italian	*Pronunciation*	*Translation*
il braccio	eel brahch-choh	the arm
il collo	eel kohl-loh	the neck
la gamba	lah gahm-bah	the leg
la mano	lah mah-noh	the hand
la pancia	lah pahn-chah	the belly
il petto	eel peht-toh	the breast
il piede	eel pee-eh-deh	the foot
lo stomaco	loh stoh-mah-koh	the stomach
la testa	lah tehs-tah	the head

These phrases help you put the body parts in context:

- ✔ **Mi sono rotto una gamba.** *(mee soh-noh roht-toh oo-nah gahm-bah)* (I broke my leg.)

- ✔ **Ho la gola arrossata.** *(oh lah goh-lah ahr-rohs-sah-tah)* (I have a sore throat.)

- ✔ **Ho la pelle irritata.** *(oh lah pehl-leh eer-ee-tah-tah)* (My skin is irritated.)

- ✔ **Mi sono storto il piede.** *(mee soh-noh stohr-toh eel pee-eh-deh)* (I sprained my foot.)

- ✔ **Ho mal di schiena.** *(oh mahl dee skee-eh-nah)* (I have a backache.)

- ✔ **Ho disturbi al cuore.** *(oh dees-toor-bee ahl koo-oh-reh)* (I have heart problems.)

✔ **Il dentista mi ha tolto un dente.** *(eel dehn-tees-tah mee ah tohl-toh oon dehn-teh)* (The dentist pulled out my tooth.)

✔ **Mi fa male lo stomaco.** *(mee fah mah-leh loh stoh-mah-koh)* (My stomach hurts.)

✔ **Mi bruciano gli occhi.** *(mee broo-chah-noh lyee ohk-kee)* (My eyes burn.)

✔ **Mi sono slogata la spalla.** *(mee soh-noh sloh-gah-tah lah spahl-lah)* (I've dislocated my shoulder.)

✔ **Ho mal di testa.** *(oh mahl dee tehs-tah)* (I have a headache.)

✔ **Mi fa male tutto il corpo.** *(mee fah mah-leh toot-toh eel kohr-poh)* (My whole body aches.)

When you want to indicate the left or right body part, you must know that body part's gender. For a masculine part, you say **destro** *(dehs-troh)* (right) and **sinistro** *(see-nees-troh)* (left), whereas for a feminine part you change the ending: **destra** *(dehs-trah)* and **sinistra** *(see-nees-trah)*.

Another little hurdle is the plural form. Where body parts are concerned, a lot of irregular plurals exist. We show you some of the most frequent irregular plural forms in Table 16-2.

Table 16-2	Body Parts Plurals	
Singular (Pronunciation)	*Plural (Pronunciation)*	*Translation*
il braccio (eel brahch-choh)	le braccia (leh brahch-chah)	arm(s)
il dito (eel dee-toh)	le dita (leh dee-tah)	finger(s)
il ginocchio (eel jee-nohk-kee-oh)	le ginocchia (leh jee-nohk-kee-ah)	knee(s)
la mano (lah mah-noh)	le mani (leh mah-nee)	hand(s)
l'orecchio (loh-rehk-kee-oh)	le orecchie (leh oh-rehk-kee-eh)	ear(s)
l'osso (lohs-soh)	le ossa (leh ohs-sah)	bone(s)

Describing what ails you

Generally speaking, if you need to tell someone that you're not feeling well, you can always say **mi sento male** *(mee sehn-toh mah-leh)* (I feel sick), which derives from the verb **sentirsi male** *(sehn-teer-see mah-leh)* (to feel sick). Following we give you the whole conjugation:

Conjugation	Pronunciation
mi sento male	mee sehn-toh mah-leh
ti senti male	tee sehn-tee mah-leh
si sente male	see sehn-teh mah-leh
ci sentiamo male	cee sehn-tee-ah-moh mah-leh
vi sentite male	vee sehn-tee-teh mah-leh
si sentono male	see sehn-toh-noh mah-leh

Sometimes "I feel sick" doesn't describe what's bothering you. When you're at the doctor or in a hospital, you have to be more precise.

You can choose from two ways to describe what ails you: You can use either the expression **fare male** *(fah-reh mah-leh)* (to hurt) or **avere mal di** *(ah-veh-reh mahl dee)* (to hurt). The latter is the easier way to express your ailments, because you only have to know the form **ho** *(oh)* (I have) of the verb **avere** *(ah-veh-reh)* (to have). You simply add the body part hurting you, like **ho mal di testa** *(oh mahl dee tehs-tah)* (I have a headache).

The first verb, **fare male**, is a little bit trickier because the subject is the aching part or parts. If your head hurts, you can say **mi fa male la testa** *(mee fah mah-leh lah tehs-tah)* (my head hurts). If more than one part aches, you must use the plural verb form — for example, **mi fanno male il collo e le spalle** *(mee fahn-noh mah-leh eel kohl-loh eh leh spahl-leh)* (my neck and shoulders hurt).

You may have noticed that **fa male** is preceded by **mi** *(mee)* (me). This word changes according to the speaker and the person who feels the pain. A doctor may ask you **Cosa Le fa male?** *(koh-zah leh fah mah-leh)* (What hurts you?). **Le** is the indirect object pronoun for the formal "you."

Talkin' the Talk

 Gloria goes to the doctor because her leg is swollen. Without further examination, however, the doctor can't determine the problem.

Gloria: **Mi fa molto male questa gamba.**
mee fah <u>mohl</u>-toh <u>mah</u>-leh koo-<u>ehs</u>-tah <u>gahm</u>-bah
This leg hurts very much.

Doctor: **La sinistra, vero?**
lah see-<u>nees</u>-trah <u>veh</u>-roh
The left one, correct?

Gloria: **Sì, è gonfia.**
see eh <u>gohn</u>-fee-ah
Yes, it's swollen.

Doctor: **Vediamo . . .**
veh-dee-<u>ah</u>-moh
Let's see . . .

Gloria: **Devo andare all'ospedale?**
<u>deh</u>-voh ahn-<u>dah</u>-reh ahl-lohs-peh-<u>dah</u>-leh
Do I have to go to the hospital?

Doctor: **Sì, almeno per i raggi.**
see ahl-<u>meh</u>-noh pehr ee <u>rahj</u>-jee
Yes, at least for X-rays.

Words to Know

fare male	<u>fah</u>-reh <u>mah</u>-leh	to hurt
ospedale [m]	ohs-peh-<u>dah</u>-leh	hospital
raggi [m]	<u>rahj</u>-jee	X-rays
sinistra/o [f/m]	see-<u>nees</u>-trah/troh	left
gonfia/o [f/m]	gohn-fee-ah/oh	swollen

Understanding professional medical vocabulary

Various professional people — not all of them doctors — can offer you medical help. They include:

- ✔ **il medico** *(eel meh-dee-koh)* (doctor, both female and male)

- ✔ **il dottore** *(eel doht-toh-reh)* (doctor, both female and male)

  The female form of this noun, **la dottoressa** *(lah doht-toh-rehs-sah),* is less common.

You can use either of these words for "doctor."

- ✔ **la/lo specialista [f/m]** *(lah/loh speh-chah-lees-tah)* (specialist)

- ✔ **la/il dentista [f/m]** *(lah/eel dehn-tees-tah)* (dentist)

- ✔ **l'infermiera** *(leen-fehr-mee-eh-rah)* (female nurse)

- ✔ **l'infermiere** *(leen-fehr-mee-eh-reh)* (male nurse)

Here are questions that you may need to ask in a doctor's office, with typical replies:

- ✔ **Devo prendere qualcosa?** *(deh-voh prehn-deh-reh koo-ahl-koh-sah)* (Do I have to take anything?)

  No, si riposi e beva molte bevande calde. *(noh see ree-poh-zee eh beh-vah mohl-teh beh-vahn-deh kahl-deh)* (No, rest and drink a lot of hot fluids.)

  Ecco la ricetta. *(ehk-koh lah ree-cheht-tah)* (Here is your prescription.)

- ✔ **Devo tornare per un'altra visita?** *(deh-voh tohr-nah-reh pehr oon-ahl-trah vee-zee-tah)* (Do I have to return for another examination?)

  No, è tutto a posto. *(noh eh toot-toh ah pohs-toh)* (No, it's all right.)

  Sì, ripassi la settimana prossima. *(see ree-pahs-see lah seht-tee-mah-nah prohs-see-mah)* (Yes, come see me again next week.)

If you need **una medicina** *(oo-nah meh-dee-chee-nah)* (a medicine) you will probably look for the next **farmacia** *(fahr-mah-chee-ah)* (pharmacy). Normal pharmacy hours are from 8:30 a.m. to 8:00 p.m., generally with a lunch break from 1:00 to 4:00 p.m. You can find the address of the open pharmacy written on all pharmacy doors and in the local newspaper, where you can also find a phone number to call for information.

Talkin' the Talk

Elena has just witnessed an accident. She calls the police.

Officer:	**Polizia.** *poh-lee-tsee-ah* Police.
Elena:	**C'è un' incidente.** *cheh oon een-chee-dehn-teh* There's been an accident!
Officer:	**Dove?** *doh-veh* Where?
Elena:	**Piazza Mattei.** *pee-aht-tsah maht-tay* Piazza Mattei.
Officer:	**Che succede?** *keh sooch-cheh-deh* What happened?
Elena:	**C'è un ferito.** *cheh oon fehr-ee-toh* Someone is injured.
Officer:	**C'è bisogno di un'ambulanza?** *cheh bee-zoh-nyoh dee oo-nahm-boo-lahn-tsah* Is an ambulance needed?
Elena:	**Penso di sì. Fate presto, è urgente!** *pehn-soh dee see fah-teh prehs-toh eh oor-jehn-teh* I think so. Hurry, it's urgent!

If you are in Italy and you have an emergency, call 113, the Italian national police, who will send you also an ambulance if you need one. This number is valid for all of Italy.

Words to Know

ambulanza [f]	ahm-boo-lahn-tsah	ambulance
Che succede?	keh sooch-cheh-deh	What happened?
emergenza (f)	eh-mehr-jehn-tsah	emergency
è urgente	eh oor-jehn-the	it's urgent

I've Been Robbed! Knowing What to Do and Say When the Police Arrive

We hope you are never the target of a robbery. If you are, however, we want you to be prepared with the important phrases you will need when the police arrive.

✔ **Sono stata/o derubata/o.** (*soh-noh stah-tah/toh deh-roo-bah-tah/toh*) (I've been robbed.) [f/m]

✔ **C'è stato un furto nel mio appartamento.** (*cheh stah-toh oon foor-toh nehl mee-oh ahp-pahr-tah-mehn-toh*) (There was a burglary in my apartment.)

✔ **Sono entrati dei ladri in casa nostra.** (*soh-noh ehn-trah-tee day lah-dree een kah-sah nohs-trah*) (Thieves broke into our house.)

✔ **Mi hanno rubato la macchina.** (*mee ahn-noh roo-bah-toh lah mahk-kee-nah*) (My car has been stolen.)

✔ **Mi hanno scippata.** (*mee ahn-noh sheep-pah-tah*) (My handbag was snatched.)

Talkin' the Talk

A motorcyclist stole Anna's **borsa** (*bohr*-sah) (handbag). Distraught, she calls 113 for the police **denunciare** *(deh-noon-chah-reh)* (to report) **il furto** *(eel foor-toh)* (the theft).

Officer:	**Polizia.**
	poh-lee-tsee-ah
	Police.
Anna:	**Mi hanno appena scippata!**
	mee ahn-noh ahp-peh-nah sheep-pah-tah
	They just snatched my handbag!
Officer:	**Si calmi e venga in questura.**
	see kahl-mee eh vehn-gah een koo-ehs-too-rah
	Calm down and come to police headquarters.
Anna:	**È stato un uomo sul motorino.**
	eh stah-toh oon oo-oh-moh sool moh-toh-ree-noh
	It was a man on a moped.
Officer:	**Ho capito, ma deve venire.**
	oh kah-pee-toh mah deh-veh veh-nee-reh
	I got it, but you have to come here.
Anna:	**Dov'è la questura?**
	doh-veh lah koo-ehs-too-rah
	Where is police headquarters?
Officer:	**Dietro la posta centrale.**
	dee-eh-troh lah pohs-tah chehn-trah-leh
	Behind the main post office.
Anna:	**Vengo subito.**
	vehn-goh soo-bee-toh
	I'm coming at once.

Words to Know

borsa [f]	<u>bohr</u>-sah	handbag
furto [m]	<u>foor</u>-toh	theft
denunciare	deh-noon-<u>chah</u>-reh	to report
motorino [m]	moh-toh-<u>ree</u>-noh	moped
questura [f]	koo-ehs-<u>too</u>-rah	police headquarters
scippare	sheep-<u>pah</u>-reh	to snatch a handbag
scippo [m]	<u>sheep</u>-poh	theft of a handbag

When you have to report someone and describe the thief, you must know some essential words, such as hair color, height, and so on. You can form descriptive sentences like this:

La persona era . . . *(lah pehr-<u>soh</u>-nah <u>eh</u>-rah)* (The person was . . .):

- **alta** *(<u>ahl</u>-tah)* (tall)
- **bassa** *(<u>bahs</u>-sah)* (short)
- **di media statura** *(dee <u>meh</u>-dee-ah stah-<u>too</u>-rah)* (of medium build)
- **grassa** *(<u>grahs</u>-sah)* (fat)
- **magra** *(<u>mah</u>-grah)* (thin)

Note: The preceding adjectives end in **-a** because they refer to the noun **la persona**, which is feminine.)

I capelli erano . . . *(ee kah-<u>pehl</u>-lee <u>eh</u>-rah-noh)* (The hair was . . .)

- **castani** *(kahs-<u>tah</u>-nee)* (brown)
- **biondi** *(<u>byohn</u>-dee)* (blond)
- **neri** *(<u>neh</u>-ree)* (black)
- **rossi** *(<u>rohs</u>-see)* (red)
- **scuri** *(<u>skoo</u>-ree)* (dark)
- **chiari** *(kee-<u>ah</u>-ree)* (fair)

> ✔ **lisci** *(<u>lee</u>-shee)* (straight)
>
> ✔ **ondulati** *(ohn-doo-<u>lah</u>-tee)* (wavy)
>
> ✔ **ricci** *(<u>reech</u>-chee)* (curly)
>
> ✔ **corti** *(<u>kohr</u>-tee)* (short)
>
> ✔ **lunghi** *(<u>loon</u>-gee)* (long)

Aveva gli occhi . . . *(ah-<u>veh</u>-vah lyee <u>ohk</u>-kee)* (His/Her eyes were . . .)

> ✔ **azzurri** *(ahdz-<u>zoo</u>-ree)* (blue)
>
> ✔ **grigi** *(<u>gree</u>-jee)* (gray)
>
> ✔ **marroni** *(mah-<u>roh</u>-nee)* (brown)
>
> ✔ **neri** *(<u>neh</u>-ree)* (black; dark)
>
> ✔ **verdi** *(<u>vehr</u>-dee)* (green)

Era . . . *(<u>eh</u>-rah)* (He was . . .)

> ✔ **calvo** *(<u>kahl</u>-voh)* (bald)
>
> ✔ **rasato** *(rah-<u>zah</u>-toh)* (clean-shaven)

Aveva . . . *(ah-<u>veh</u>-vah)* (He/She had . . .)

> ✔ **la barba** *(lah <u>bahr</u>-bah)* (a beard)
>
> ✔ **i baffi** *(ee <u>bahf</u>-fee)* (a moustache)
>
> ✔ **la bocca larga** *(lah <u>bohk</u>-kah <u>lahr</u>-gah)* (a wide mouth)
>
> ✔ **la bocca stretta** *(lah <u>bohk</u>-kah <u>streht</u>-tah)* (thin lips)
>
> ✔ **la bocca carnosa** *(lah <u>bohk</u>-kah kahr-<u>noh</u>-zah)* (a plump mouth)
>
> ✔ **il naso lungo** *(eel <u>nah</u>-zoh <u>loon</u>-go)* (a long nose)
>
> ✔ **il naso corto** *(eel <u>nah</u>-zoh <u>kohr</u>-toh)* (a short nose)

When You Need a Lawyer: Protecting Your Rights

Many unpleasant moments in life require that you seek the help of an authorized person. Often, this person is a lawyer who can help you in complicated situations. Therefore, knowing how to contact a lawyer is rather important. You can use the following general questions and sentences to request legal help in Italian.

✔ **Mi serve l'aiuto di un avvocato.** *(mee se<u>hr</u>-veh lah-<u>yoo</u>-toh dee oon ahv-voh-<u>kah</u>-toh)* (I need the help of a lawyer.)

✔ **Ho bisogno di assistenza legale.** *(oh bee-<u>zoh</u>-nyoh dee ahs-sees-<u>tehn</u>-tsah leh-<u>gah</u>-leh)* (I need legal assistance.)

✔ **Vorrei consultare il mio avvocato.** *(vohr-<u>ray</u> kohn-sool-<u>tah</u>-reh eel <u>mee</u>-oh ahv-voh-<u>kah</u>-toh)* (I'd like to consult my lawyer.)

✔ **Chiamate il mio avvocato, per favore.** *(kee-ah-<u>mah</u>-teh eel <u>mee</u>-oh ahv-voh-<u>kah</u>-toh pehr fah-<u>voh</u>-reh)* (Call my lawyer, please.)

After you find a lawyer, you can speak to him or her about your situation. Here are some examples of what you may need to say:

✔ **Sono stato truffato.** *(<u>soh</u>-noh <u>stah</u>-toh troof-<u>fah</u>-toh)* (I was cheated.)

✔ **Voglio denunciare un furto.** *(<u>Voh</u>-lyoh deh-noon-<u>chah</u>-reh oon <u>foor</u>-toh)* (I want to report a theft.)

✔ **Devo stipulare un contratto.** *(<u>deh</u>-voh stee-poo-<u>lah</u>-reh oon kohn-<u>traht</u>-toh)* (I have to draw up a contract.)

✔ **Ho avuto un incidente stradale.** *(oh ah-<u>voo</u>-toh oon een-chee-<u>dehn</u>-teh strah-<u>dah</u>-leh)* (I've had a traffic accident.)

✔ **Voglio che mi vengano risarciti i danni.** *(<u>voh</u>-lyoh keh mee <u>vehn</u>-gah-noh ree-sahr-<u>chee</u>-tee ee <u>dahn</u>-nee)* (I want to be compensated for the damages.)

✔ **Sono stato arrestato.** *(<u>soh</u>-noh <u>stah</u>-toh ahr-rehs-<u>tah</u>-toh)* (I've been arrested.)

Talkin' the Talk

Il signor Bruni had un **incidente stradale** *(oon een-chee-<u>dehn</u>-teh strah-<u>dah</u>-leh)* (a road accident) and goes to his lawyer.

Sig. Bruni:	**Ho avuto un incidente stradale.** *oh ah-<u>voo</u>-toh oon een-chee-<u>dehn</u>-teh strah-<u>dah</u>-leh* I had a car accident.
Lawyer:	**Com'è successo?** *koh-<u>meh</u> sooch-<u>chehs</u>-soh* How did it happen?
Sig. Bruni:	**Una macchina ha tamponato la mia.** *<u>oo</u>-nah <u>mahk</u>-kee-nah ah tahm-poh-<u>nah</u>-toh lah <u>mee</u>-ah* A car ran into the back of mine.

Lawyer:	**Ha il numero di targa dell'altra auto?**
	ah eel <u>noo</u>-meh-roh dee <u>tahr</u>-gah dehl-<u>lahl</u>-trah <u>ah</u>-oo-toh
	Do you have the number of the other's car license plate?

Sig. Bruni:	**Sì, ho tutto.**
	see oh <u>toot</u>-toh
	Yes, I have all the information.

Lawyer:	**Si è fatto qualcosa?**
	see eh <u>faht</u>-toh koo-ahl-<u>koh</u>-sah
	Were you injured?

Sig. Bruni:	**Ho una ferita sulla fronte.**
	oh <u>oo</u>-nah feh-<u>ree</u>-tah <u>sool</u>-lah <u>frohn</u>-teh
	I have a wound on my forehead.

Lawyer:	**Scriverò all'assicurazione.**
	skree-veh-<u>roh</u> ahl-lahs-see-koo-rah-tsee-<u>oh</u>-neh
	I'll write to the insurance company.

Words to Know

danno [m]	<u>dahn</u>-noh	damage
denunciare	deh-noon-<u>chah</u>-reh	to report
denuncia [f]	deh-<u>noon</u>-chah	report
incidente stradale [m]	een-cee-<u>dehn</u>-teh strah-<u>dah</u>-leh	traffic accident
macchina [f]	mahk-kee-nah	car
targa [f]	tahr-gah	license plate
ferita [f]	feh-ree-tah	injury
assicurazione [f]	ahs-see-koo-rah-tsee-<u>oh</u>-neh	insurance

Fun & Games

Anna is at the police station to report that someone has snatched her handbag. She gives a detailed personal description of the thief. Fill in the gaps in her description:

Sono stata (1)_____ (bag snatched). **Mi ha** (2)_____ (robbed) **un uomo.**

Era (3)_____ (tall) **é** (4)_____ (thin) **é aveva i capelli** (5)_____ (black) **é** (6)_____ (curly). **Poi aveva** (7)_____ (a moustache) **é gli occhi** (8)_____ (green).

Answers: 1. scippata, 2. derubato, 3. alto, 4. magro, 5. neri, 6. ricci, 7. i baffi, 8. verdi.

Part IV
The Part of Tens

The 5th Wave   By Rich Tennant

"I'm not sure if I'm stressing the right syllable in the wrong word, or stressing the wrong syllable in the right word, but it's starting to stress me out."

In this part . . .

These brief chapters can help you add polish to the basics the rest of the book provides. We give you hints on accelerating your Italian learning curve. We clue you in to Italian holidays. We offer some idiomatic expressions that will make you sound like a native, and we warn you about certain expressions you should never use. Jump right in, these chapters are short and fun!

Chapter 17

Ten Ways to Pick Up Italian Quickly

· ·

In This Chapter

▶ Enjoying Italian food

▶ Listening to Italian

▶ Going to Italian films

▶ Sharing Italian with other people

▶ Surfing the Web

▶ Remembering to enjoy

· ·

*O*f course, you've already chosen one of the quickest ways to learn Italian — you picked up this book! For smaller bites of Italian, nibble on one or all of the suggestions in this chapter.

Read Italian Food Labels

Nowadays, finding Italian food is easy in most countries. If you buy Italian food, read the original label a couple of times before you throw the package away. Usually, you can find an English translation alongside the Italian. In a few weeks, you won't need to read the English part anymore!

Ask for Food in Italian

If you go to an Italian restaurant or pizzeria, don't be shy! Order your favorite dishes by using their original names and Italian pronunciations. Restaurants do not usually translate most of the Italian names, but your pronunciation makes a difference. Think of your exchange with the waiter as a kind of play. Prepare before leaving for the restaurant by looking up the correct pronunciation of a couple of dishes you enjoy. (You can write down the pronunciation phonetically and take it with you!) At the restaurant, ask for the dishes the same way that an Italian would.

Listen to Italian Songs

Everyone knows that the favorite theme of Italian songs is **l'amore** (lah-_moh_-reh) (love). Hopefully, love interests you, too, at least in the way Italians speak (and sing) about it. Reading and singing from a songbook with the original Italian lyrics — alongside their translation — is a perfect way to learn words and expressions. In case you don't have a music book, you can still pick up some words by listening to Italian music and singing along with **la canzone** (lah kahn-_tsoh_-neh) (the song).

Read Italian Publications

Trying to read a newspaper in a foreign language can be very frustrating! Don't worry: Experts say that journalistic language is the most difficult to understand, even in your own country. We suggest that you read the ads and the article titles: You will understand a few words and surely recognize some names of international celebrities. Moreover, don't forget that 60 percent of English words have a Latin origin, and Italian also derives from Latin. (You'll find many *cognates,* or words that look similar in both languages.) The number of words you understand will surprise you. By the way, Italians call the newspaper **il giornale** (eel johr-_nah_-leh).

Watch Italian Movies

We hope you like movies! Watching a movie in the original language is a pleasant way to pick up words, expressions, and names, and you can even discover something about the country where the story takes place. You can find several Italian movies with English subtitles, from classic

neorealismo *(neh-oh-reh-ah-leez-moh)* (neorealism) to the most recent releases. If you know other people who are interested in watching Italian movies, invite them to watch movies together and you'll discover the fun of the **cinema italiano** *(chee-neh-mah ee-tah-lee-ah-noh)* (Italian cinema).

Tune in to Italian Radio and TV Programs

In the past, many Italians had to go abroad to find jobs. Huge groups of people emigrated from Italy to several industrialized countries and never returned. Consequently, many countries deliver radio programs (especially the news) in Italian. Find some Italian programs and listen as often as you can. You can at least understand the basics of what the newscaster says because the speakers usually articulate very clearly and slowly, and most of the news is the same as you'd hear in your own national programs. Again, you can pick up words without much effort.

If you have good Internet access, you can also listen to stations directly from Italy. For example, you can go to windowsmedia.microsoft.com/radio/ Radio5.asp and choose from more than ten Italian stations.

Listen to Italian Language Tapes

You can listen to Italian language tapes — or the audio CD that comes with this book — almost any time: when you jog, clean your apartment or house, cook, or whenever you like. And please, don't forget to *repeat aloud* what you hear. Even though you may not always know what you're saying, practice helps. Every language has special sounds and intonations, and the best way to learn these things is through imitation — the same way children do when they learn to speak. Just be prepared to give an answer in case somebody asks what you're talking about!

Share Your Interest

We consider this a valid tip when learning *any* language: Learning a language with other people is much more pleasant (and easier!) than doing it by yourself. Having company while you broaden your knowledge of Italian is helpful not only because language is primarily a means of communicating with others, but also because fun is a vital element in every learning process. An official Italian institution can surely help you find an Italian conversation group to join. If not, write an ad and put it in the local library or bookshop. Just try!

Surf the Net

Nothing is easier than looking for information on the Internet. To find information about Italy, type **Italia** *(ee-tah-lee-ah)* (Italy) or the name of a famous city or monument in Italian, such as **Venezia** *(veh-neh-tsee-ah)* (Venice) or **Colosseo** *(koh-lohs-seh-oh)* (the Coliseum), to mention just two. First try to browse in Italian; you can surely pick up a couple of words that you understand. Otherwise, view the page in English: Learning about the culture of the country whose language you're studying is a good way to come closer to the language.

You can also make use of online dictionaries, such as the one at www.fac-staff.bucknell.edu/rbeard/diction.HTML, and use online translation services such as Babel Fish at babelfish.altavista.com — although you need to be prepared for some slightly odd translations. Some Web sites (www.travlang.com is one) even offer to help you learn a new language, and this site has more than 70 languages to choose from! Another good Web site is www.rai.it — Radio Televisione Italiana.

Don't Take It Too Seriously

Think of learning a language as play and have fun! This is not a "technique" but an approach. Avoid everything you don't like and attempt whatever you do like in Italian: sing, recite a poem, repeat something that sounds good. Moreover, don't forget a very important verb: **ridere** *(ree-deh-reh)* (to laugh).

Chapter 18

Ten Things Never to Say in Italian

*W*e hope the title to this chapter isn't too dramatic! Remember that you should always approach the learning process as fun. If you don't speak Italian perfectly, you may say something wrong — which might be funny or even embarrassing. Don't worry; messing up is not a tragedy! On the contrary, most people are pleased that foreigners make any attempt to learn their language and allow for mistakes, in both speech and behavior. Nevertheless, we want to give you a little advice to help you avoid such situations.

Ciao-ing Down

Ciao (*chah-oh*) is a common way to say "hello" and "goodbye" that even people who don't speak Italian know. However, please remember that Italians use it only with persons they address with the informal **tu** (*too*) (you) — see Chapter 2 for a discussion of the use of **tu.** Many foreigners use the formal **lei** and still say **ciao**; again, this misstep is not a tragedy, but when you're addressing someone in the formal manner, it's more Italian to say **buongiorno** (*boo-ohn-johr-noh*) (Good morning) or **arrivederci** (*ahr-ree-veh-dehr-chee*) (Goodbye).

Don't Be Literal

A literal translation from English to Italian doesn't work in many cases. Here's a typical example: You may want to ask your Italian friend, "How do you like Los Angeles?" Because you've probably learned a lot, you might translate your question into **"Come ti piace Los Angeles?"** (*koh-meh tee pee-ah-cheh Los Angeles*), knowing that **come** is the translation of "how" and **ti piace** means "do you like." Both are absolutely correct translations, but the whole question doesn't sound Italian. We would ask **"Ti piace Los Angeles?"** (*tee pee-ah-cheh Los Angeles*) (Do you like Los Angeles?). Quite easy, isn't it?

Four Fickle "False Friends"

We consider some words "false friends." These words, called *cognates,* sound and look quite similar in two different languages but, unfortunately, don't have the same meaning. One example is the word *sympathy.* In Italian, **simpatia** (*seem-pah-tee-ah*) is the feeling you have for someone you find nice, funny, and pleasant; it doesn't mean that you feel what the other person feels. **Simpatia**'s translation can be "liking." So to say that you find somebody **simpatico** (*seem-pah-tee-koh*) means that you like him or her — the person is nice. Interestingly, English kept the original Greek meaning of the word *sympathy,* which is "to suffer together."

Another false friend is the word **educazione** (*eh-doo-kah-tsee-oh-neh*). In Italian, it does not mean the level of your schooling, but the way you have grown up — your upbringing. **Educato** (*eh-doo-kah-toh*) [**educata** (*eh-doo-kah-tah*) for a female] translates as "well-brought-up" or "polite." A good Italian word for "education" is **istruzione** (*ees-troo-tsee-oh-neh*).

The surprises aren't over. Guess what the Italian word **sensibile** (*sehn-see-bee-leh*) means? The subject of this section tells you already that it doesn't mean "sensible." Instead, it means "sensitive." You can translate the English "sensible" with the adjective **ragionevole** (*rah-joh-neh-voh-leh*).

The adjective **vecchio** (m) (*vehk-kee-oh*) / **vecchia** (f) (*vehk-kee-ah*) translates as "old," but avoid using it to refer to people. You can use **vecchio** for objects (a car, a book, or whatever), but when referring to a person, say **anziano** (m) (*ahn-tsee-ah-noh*) or **anziana** (f) (*ahn-tsee-ah-nah*). **Anziano** means that the person is not young anymore — but it doesn't sound negative.

How Many Years Do You Have?

Another important point about age: In English, you say "I'm X years old," whereas in Italian, you *have* years. We say **ho 25 anni** *(oh vehn-tee-cheen-koo-eh ahn-nee)* (Literally: I have 25 years). The translation of the English expression would sound quite funny. If you were use the literal translation of "I'm 25 years old," which is **sono vecchio 25 anni**, Italian-speakers would hasten to assure you: "Not at all, you're very young!" Using the word for "age" implies that you are aged.

The Problem with "Play"

We'd like to dedicate the last two points of this chapter to the problematic translations of the verb "to play." In English, this verb has different meanings, all of them describing nice activities. The most usual meaning (and the first given in all dictionaries) corresponds to the Italian **giocare** *(joh-kah-reh)*: "to have fun" or "to do things to pass the time pleasantly, as children do." But *don't* use this verb in the following cases:

We don't use **giocare** for playing the piano, for example. When you want to use "to play" to mean performing on an instrument, the accurate translation is **suonare** *(soo-oh-nah-reh)*. Therefore, the correct sentence is **suono il piano** *(soo-oh-noh eel pee-ah-noh)*.

Another English definition of "to play" is "to act, or to perform onstage." In Italian, we say **l'attrice** *(aht-tree-cheh)* (the actress) **recita un dramma** *(reh-chee-tah oon drahm-mah)* "plays a drama." **Recitare** is a cognate of "to recite." Saying **l'attrice gioca** isn't wrong, but this phrase means that she's amusing herself. Unfortunately, an actress's job is not always about having fun — at least for her!

Being Careful of "False Friends"

The pitfalls surrounding cognates — those "false friends" that look or sound like words you know but have different meanings — can transfer to idiomatic expressions that can be very funny for a foreigner. Just think of the English expression "It's raining cats and dogs," which is the best example of a funny expression for non-native English speakers. You now must know that you wouldn't say **Sta piovendo gatti e cani** *(stah pee-oh-vehn-doh gaht-tee eh kah-nee)*. To express the same sentiment, you say instead **Piove a catinelle** *(pee-oh-veh ah kah-tee-nehl-leh)*.

The same is true for the expression "I'm hungry." In Italian, you "have" hunger; therefore you say **Ho fame** *(oh fah-meh)*. You could also say **Sono affamato** *(soh-noh ahf-fah-mah-toh),* but this sounds more like "I'm starving," which is much stronger.

Chapter 19
Ten Favorite Italian Expressions

● ●

In This Chapter
▶ Expressions you hear all the time
▶ Phrases you can say to sound Italian

● ●

Counting how many times a day Italians use some of the following expressions would be an interesting experiment! They are all very typical, and you hear them often in colloquial Italian. So if you remember some of them and use them on the right occasion, you will seem very Italian. Of course, there are, as in any language, always expressions that sound strange coming from the mouth of a foreigner, but the following can be used without hesitation. Exceptions may be **mamma mia** and **uffa**, because they are very spontaneous. But using any or all of the others can make you really sound Italian.

Mamma mia!

Mamma mia! (*mahm-mah mee-ah*) Please don't think that all Italians are like children just because you notice how often they call for their mommies! In fact, the literal translation is something like "Oh Mama!" and Italians use the exclamation to express surprise, impatience, happiness, sorrow, and so on — in general, a strong emotion. The figurative translation is something like "My goodness!"

Che bello!

Che bello! *(keh behl-loh)* (How lovely! — Literally: How beautiful!) Using this phrase shows that you're enthusiastic about something.

Uffa!

Uffa! (<u>oof</u>-fah) is a very clear way to show that you're annoyed, bored, angry, or simply fed up with a situation. In English, you'd probably express the same by saying, "Aargh!"

Che ne so!

When Italians want to say that they have no idea about something, they shrug their shoulders and say **Che ne so!** (keh neh soh) (How should I know?). We don't need to tell you that it's a quite common expression.

Magari!

Magari! (mah-<u>gah</u>-ree): Just one word, but it expresses so much! It indicates a strong wish or hope. It's a good answer, for instance, if somebody asks you if you'd like to win the lottery. A good translation of this word is "If only!" or "I'd love it!"

Ti sta bene!

Ti sta bene! (tee stah <u>beh</u>-neh): This is the Italian way to say "Serves you right!"

Non te la prendere!

If you see that somebody is sad, worried, or upset, you can try to console him or her by saying **Non te la prendere!** (nohn teh lah <u>prehn</u>-deh-reh) (Don't get so upset!). Sometimes it works.

Che macello!

Figuring out the derivation of this phrase is not difficult. The literal translation of **Che macello!** (keh mah-<u>chehl</u>-loh) is "What a slaughterhouse!" Italians usually say this in situations in which an English speaker would say "What a mess!"

Non mi va!

Non mi va! *(nohn mee vah)* is one of the first phrases Italian children learn. It means that you don't want to do something. The best translation is "I don't feel like it!"

Mi raccomando!

With **Mi raccomando!** *(mee rahk-koh-mahn-doh)*, you express a special emphasis in asking for something — like saying "Please, I beg you!" An example is **Telefonami, mi raccomando!** "Don't forget to call me, please!"

Chapter 20

Ten Important Holidays in Italian-Speaking Countries

*W*e all know and love the red-marked days on the calendar because they're holidays. But, honestly, how often do you know the origins of those days, let alone the stories behind other countries' celebrations? To give you an idea of Italian holidays, we introduce you to some of them.

L' Epifania (La Befana)

Italians observe **l'Epifania** *(leh-pee-fah-nee-ah)* (Epiphany) on January 6 as the last day of the Christmas holidays. This day used to be a public holiday and is still a beloved children's day. The tradition says that **la Befana** *(lah beh-fah-nah),* a kindly old witch who flies on a broom, visits all the children and brings them gifts, according to the children's behavior. Good children receive toys and sweets; the "bad ones" get coal! In every pastry shop, you find a special sugar coal, prepared and sold just on this day. **La Befana** enters the houses through the chimneys and puts her presents in old socks.

Children are extremely excited when they leave their socks in the kitchen the night before — many can't or don't want to sleep because they hope to see her. The word **befana** is a popular derivation of the word **Epifania,** or "Epiphany," the religious name of this day, which celebrates the visit of the Three Kings to the infant Jesus.

Martedì Grasso

Martedì Grasso (mahr-<u>teh</u>-dee <u>grahs</u>-soh) (Literally: fat Tuesday) is the last and most important day of Carnival. Derived from the Latin **carne vale** (<u>kahr</u>-neh <u>vah</u>-leh) (Meat, farewell!), Carnival originated as a feast to say goodbye to meat during the time of fasting between November and February. On **martedì grasso,** children dress up and organize parties, even at school. In many places, people organize huge parades including elaborate caricatures and allegorical floats. Most big cities have lost this tradition, but it is still very strong in small places (especially in the South, Sicily, and Sardinia). People even come from foreign countries to see the artistic Venice Carnival.

La festa della donna

La festa della donna (lah <u>fehs</u>-tah <u>dehl</u>-lah <u>dohn</u>-nah) (Women's Day) is a celebration on March 8, filled with political and cultural events dedicated to women. Italian women typically receive small, beautiful mimosa bunches from male friends, boyfriends, husbands, sons — sometimes even from their bosses!

Pasquetta

Pasquetta (pahs-koo-<u>eht</u>-tah) (Literally: little Easter) is Easter Monday — a day that many people use to leave the city and have a nice picnic. It's a way to celebrate the beginning of the warm season — the first "official" day to spend outdoors.

La Festa del Lavoro

May 1 is **La festa del lavoro** (lah <u>fehs</u>-tah dehl lah-<u>voh</u>-roh) (Labor Day), an official holiday with a strong political meaning. Nearly every political party and labor union organizes demonstrations on this day. In the evening, popular singers usually give free concerts.

Ferragosto

On August 15, the Catholic church celebrates the day of the Assumption. For most people, however, **Ferragosto** *(fehr-rah-gohs-toh)* (Mid-August Holiday) is simply the height of the summer holidays. In many cities and villages (especially on the coasts), people organize big festivals with music, traditional food, and often spectacular fireworks.

Ognissanti

People consider **Ognissanti** *(oh-nyee-sahn-tee)* (All Saints Day) on November 1 to be a very solemn holiday. In the past, November 2 — All Souls Day — was also a public holiday, and people used to honor their dead on that day. As it is no longer a public holiday, people now pay their respects to their dead on **Ognissanti.** In many villages, the tradition of preparing special food for this occasion still exists — probably because families used to spend these days together as an opportunity to meet at least once a year. Nowadays, as communication and transportation have made keeping in touch easier, this holiday is no longer such a special event. However, many people still return to their place of origin to visit the cemetery on this day.

L' Immacolata

Italy is a Catholic country with a special veneration for the Virgin Mary. Although many religious festivities are no longer public holidays, **L'Immacolata** *(leem-mah-koh-lah-tah)* ("the Immaculate Conception") on December 8 is one of the holdovers. When Catholics declared the dogma of the Immaculate Conception some centuries ago, Roman firemen put a statue of the Virgin on the top of an old obelisk in the middle of the city. Every December 8, a special ceremony takes place in Rome to celebrate and renew that moment: A fireman climbs to the top of the obelisk to offer a garland of red roses to the Virgin. Romans love this event very much.

La Festa del Patrono

Every city and village in Italy celebrates its **La festa del patrono** *(lah fehs-tah dehl pah-troh-noh)* (Patron Saint's Day). Many different ways to celebrate this day exist, depending on local tradition. Especially beautiful are the celebrations in small villages — and good food is never missing!

La sagra del paese

La sagra del paese *(lah sah-grah dehl pah-eh-zeh)* is a very popular village fair, with a market, traditional food, and a variety of different events, depending on the place. Every village has its **sagra** *(sah-grah)* (village fair) during the period of the agricultural year that is especially important in the region. For example, in areas of wine production, villages hold **la sagra dell'uva** *(lah sah-grah dehl-loo-vah)* (the grape harvest festival), when you can taste the new wine. Visiting these fairs is a pleasant way to experience the culinary specialties of the region.

Chapter 21

Ten Phrases to Say So That People Think You're Italian

• •

In This Chapter

▶ Wishing someone good luck

▶ Shutting your mouth

▶ Being blessed

▶ Contradicting someone emphatically

▶ Telling someone to dream on!

▶ Being unsympathetic

▶ Saying "Stop it!"

▶ Slowing down

▶ Something's going on

▶ Not knowing what to do

• •

In Chapter 19, we give you ten typical expressions Italians love and use a lot. Using them can help you sound very Italian. In this chapter, we offer more sophisticated expressions to make you sound even more Italian — these are truly idiomatic expressions. Using these expressions may make an Italian gape in astonishment. Have fun!

In bocca al lupo!

Perhaps you have an Italian friend facing a difficult situation and you want to wish her good luck. The literal translation of **buona fortuna!** *(boo-oh-nah fohr-too-nah)* would work, but we think that this phrase makes you sound really Italian: **in bocca al lupo!** *(een bohk-kah ahl loo-poh)*. Literally, this means "in the wolf's mouth!" The upcoming difficulty looks like a big wolf, waiting with mouth open wide. Your friend will probably answer **Crepi il lupo!** *(kreh-pee eel loo-poh)*, which means "Hopefully the wolf will die!"

Acqua in bocca!

When you want to share a secret with somebody — but want to make sure that he or she won't tell anybody else — say **acqua in bocca!** *(ahk-koo-ah een bohk-kah).* This expression means "water in mouth." If your mouth is full of water, you can't speak. Similar idioms in English are "Don't say a word about it!" and "Mum's the word!"

Salute!

This expression sounds like a contradiction: Someone sneezes and you say **salute!** *(sah-loo-teh),* which means "health." In fact, it's a way to wish the person to be healthy very soon. "Bless you!" is the English equivalent.

Macché!

Italians love to talk, no doubt about it. Nevertheless, situations exist in which they prefer to say just one word. One good example is **macché!** *(mahk-keh).* It's a strong and determined way to say "Of course not" or "Certainly not!"

Neanche per sogno!

Similar to the preceding idiom, **neanche per sogno** *(neh-ahn-keh pehr soh-nyoh)* means literally "not even in a dream." It is another way to say "No way!" and is close to the English expression "In your dreams."

Peggio per te!

You don't show much sympathy when saying this phrase, but if you're looking for the Italian equivalent of "Too bad for you!" **peggio per te** *(pehj-joh pehr teh)* is what you need.

Piantala!

This is an informal way to say "Stop it!" The literal translation of **piantala** *(pee-ahn-tah-lah)* is "Plant it!"

Vacci piano!

"Slow down!" is the translation of the Italian expression **Vacci piano!** *(vahch-chee pee-ah-noh)*. Use it when you feel that somebody is going too fast or being too enthusiastic about something.

Gatta ci cova!

La gatta is the female cat, and **covare** *(koh-vah-reh)* means "to brood." When Italians say **gatta ci cova** *(gaht-tah chee koh-vah)* (a female cat is brooding here), we mean "There's something fishy going on here." Fish and cat: There must be a connection between the two expressions!

Sono nel pallone

Please don't ask us where this idiom comes from — we have no idea! In Italy, people say **sono nel pallone** *(soh-noh nehl pahl-loh-neh)* to indicate that somebody doesn't know what to do or how to behave in a difficult situation. An English equivalent would be something like "to be flustered." **Sono** is the translation of "to be," and **pallone** means "ball," but also "balloon": Perhaps it means that the person feels up in the air?

Part V

Appendixes

The 5th Wave   By Rich Tennant

Magnifico!

Molto bello!

"I insisted they learn some Italian.
I couldn't stand the idea of standing
in front of the Trevi Fountain and
hearing, 'gosh,' 'wow,' and 'far out.'"

In this part . . .

We put the real nuts and bolts in this part: Included are verb conjugation tables, a fairly extensive mini-dictionary — with both English to Italian and Italian to English — and instructions on how to use the audio CD that comes with this book.

Appendix A

Verb Tables

• •

Italian Verbs

Regular Verbs Ending with -*are*
For example: parlare (to speak);
Past participle: parlato (spoken)

	Present	Past	Future
io (I)	parlo	ho parlato	parlerò
tu (you, inf.)	parli	hai parlato	parlerai
lui/lei (he/she/you form.)	parla	ha parlato	parlerà
noi (we)	parliamo	abbiamo parlato	parleremo
voi (you)	parlate	avete parlato	parlerete
loro (they/you form. pl.)	parlano	hanno parlato	parleranno

Regular Verbs Ending with -*ere*
For example: vendere (to sell);
Past participle: venduto (sold)

	Present	Past	Future
io (I)	vendo	ho venduto	venderò
tu (you, inf.)	vendi	hai venduto	venderai
lui/lei (he/she/you form.)	vende	ha venduto	venderà
noi (we)	vendiamo	abbiamo venduto	venderemo
voi (you)	vendete	avete venduto	venderete
loro (they/you form. pl.)	vendono	hanno venduto	venderanno

Regular Verbs Ending with *-ire*
For example: partire (to leave);
Past participle: partito (left)

	Present	Past	Future
io (I)	parto	sono partito/a	partirò
tu (you, inf.)	parti	sei partito/a	partirai
lui/lei (he/she/you form.)	parte	è partito/a	partirà
noi (we)	partiamo	siamo partiti/e	partiremo
voi (you)	partite	siete partiti/e	partirete
loro (they/you form. pl.)	partono	sono partiti/e	partiranno

Verb *avere* (to have)
Past Participle: avuto (had)

	Present	Past	Future
io (I)	ho	ho avuto	avrò
tu (you, inf.)	hai	hai avuto	avrai
lui/lei (he/she/you form.)	ha	ha avuto	avrà
noi (we)	abbiamo	abbiamo avuto	avremo
voi (you)	avete	avete avuto	avrete
loro (they/you form. pl.)	hanno	hanno avuto	avranno

Verb *essere* (to be)
Past Participle: stato (been)

	Present	Past	Future
io (I)	sono	sono stato/a	sarò
tu (you, inf.)	sei	sei stato/a	sarai
lui/lei (he/she/you form.)	è	è stato/a	sarà
noi (we)	siamo	siamo stati/e	saremo
voi (you)	siete	siete stati/e	sarete
loro (they/you form. pl.)	sono	sono stati/e	saranno

Reflexive Verbs
For example: lavarsi (to wash oneself)
Past Participle: lavato (washed)

	Present	Past	Future
io (I)	mi lavo	mi sono lavato/a	mi laverò
tu (you, inf.)	ti lavi	ti sei lavato/a	ti laverai
lui/lei (he/she/you form.)	si lava	si è lavato/a	si laverà
noi (we)	ci laviamo	ci siamo lavati/e	ci laveremo
voi (you)	vi lavate	vi siete lavati/e	vi laverete
loro (they/you form. pl.)	si lavano	si sono lavati/e	si laveranno

Irregular Italian Verbs

		Present	Future	Past Participle
	io	vado	andrò	
	tu	vai	andrai	
andare	lui/lei	va	andrà	andato/a/i/e
to go	noi	andiamo	andremo	(w/essere)
	voi	andate	andrete	
	loro	vanno	andranno	

		Present	Future	Past Participle
	io	do	darò	
	tu	dai	darai	
dare	lui/lei	dà	darà	dato
to give	noi	diamo	daremo	(w/avere)
	voi	date	darete	
	loro	danno	daranno	

		Present	Future	Past Participle
dire	*io*	dico	dirò	
to say	*tu*	dici	dirai	
	lui/lei	dice	dirà	detto
	noi	diciamo	diremo	(w/avere)
	voi	dite	direte	
	loro	dicono	diranno	

		Present	Future	Past Participle
dovere	*io*	devo	dovrò	
to have to	*tu*	devi	dovrai	
	lui/lei	deve	dovrà	dovuto/a/i/e
	noi	dobbiamo	dovremo	(w/avere)
	voi	dovete	dovrete	
	loro	devono	dovranno	

		Present	Future	Past Participle
fare	*io*	faccio	farò	
to do;	*tu*	fai	farai	
to make	*lui/lei*	fa	farà	fatto
	noi	facciamo	faremo	(w/avere)
	voi	fate	farete	
	loro	fanno	faranno	

		Present	Future	Past Participle
morire	*io*	muoio	morirò	
to die	*tu*	muori	morirai	
	lui/lei	muore	morirà	morto/a/i/e
	noi	moriamo	moriremo	(w/essere)
	voi	morite	morirete	
	loro	muoiono	moriranno	

		Present	Future	Past Participle
piacere to like	*io*	piaccio	piacerò	
	tu	piaci	piacerai	
	lui/lei	piace	piacerà	piaciuto/a/i/e
	noi	piacciamo	piaceremo	(w/essere)
	voi	piacete	piacerete	
	loro	piacciono	piaceranno	

		Present	Future	Past Participle
porre to put	*io*	pongo	porrò	
	tu	poni	porrai	
	lui/lei	pone	porrà	posto
	noi	poniamo	porremo	(w/avere)
	voi	ponete	porrete	
	loro	pongono	porranno	

		Present	Future	Past Participle
potere can	*io*	posso	potrò	
	tu	puoi	potrai	
	lui/lei	può	potrà	potuto/a/i/e
	noi	possiamo	potremo	(w/avere)
	voi	potete	potrete	
	loro	possono	potranno	

		Present	Future	Past Participle
rimanere to stay; to remain	*io*	rimango	rimarrò	
	tu	rimani	rimarrai	
	lui/lei	rimane	rimarrà	rimasto/a/i/e
	noi	rimaniamo	rimarremo	(w/essere)
	voi	rimanete	rimarrete	
	loro	rimangono	rimarranno	

	Present	Future	Past Participle
io	salgo	salirò	
tu	sali	salirai	
lui/lei	sale	salirà	salito/a/i/e
noi	saliamo	saliremo	(w/avere/essere)
voi	salite	salirete	
loro	salgono	saliranno	

salire
to go up

	Present	Future	Past Participle
io	so	saprò	
tu	sai	saprai	
lui/lei	sa	saprà	saputo
noi	sappiamo	sapremo	(w/avere)
voi	sapete	saprete	
loro	sanno	sapranno	

sapere
to know

	Present	Future	Past Participle
io	scelgo	sceglierò	
tu	scegli	sceglierai	
lui/lei	sceglie	sceglierà	scelto
noi	scegliamo	sceglieremo	(w/avere)
voi	scegliete	sceglierete	
loro	scelgono	sceglieranno	

scegliere
to choose

	Present	Future	Past Participle
io	spengo	spegnerò	
tu	spegni	spegnerai	
lui/lei	spegne	spegnerà	spento
noi	spegniamo	spegneremo	(w/avere)
voi	spegnete	spegnerete	
loro	spengono	spegneranno	

spegnere
to switch off;
to put out

	Present	Future	Past Participle
io	sto	starò	
tu	stai	starai	
lui/lei	sta	starà	stato/a/i/e
noi	stiamo	staremo	(w/essere)
voi	state	starete	
loro	stanno	staranno	

stare — to stay

	Present	Future	Past Participle
io	taccio	tacerò	
tu	taci	tacerai	
lui/lei	tace	tacerà	taciuto
noi	taciamo	taceremo	(w/avere)
voi	tacete	tacerete	
loro	tacciono	taceranno	

tacere — to be silent

	Present	Future	Past Participle
io	tengo	terrò	
tu	tieni	terrai	
lui/lei	tiene	terrà	tenuto
noi	teniamo	terremo	(w/avere)
voi	tenete	terrete	
loro	tengono	terranno	

tenere — to hold

	Present	Future	Past Participle
io	tolgo	toglierò	
tu	togli	toglierai	
lui/lei	toglie	toglierà	tolto
noi	togliamo	toglieremo	(w/avere)
voi	togliete	toglierete	
loro	tolgono	toglieranno	

togliere — to take away

		Present	Future	Past Participle
uscire to go out	*io*	esco	uscirò	
	tu	esci	uscirai	
	lui/lei	esce	uscirà	uscito/a/i/e
	noi	usciamo	usciremo	(w/essere)
	voi	uscite	uscirete	
	loro	escono	usciranno	

		Present	Future	Past Participle
venire to come	*io*	vengo	verrò	
	tu	vieni	verrai	
	lui/lei	viene	verrà	venuto/a/i/e
	noi	veniamo	verremo	(w/essere)
	voi	venite	verrete	
	loro	vengono	verranno	

		Present	Future	Past Participle
volere to want	*io*	voglio	vorrò	
	tu	vuoi	vorrai	
	lui/lei	vuole	vorrà	voluto
	noi	vogliamo	vorremo	(w/avere)
	voi	volete	vorrete	
	loro	vogliono	vorranno	

Italian Verbs with a Special Pattern (-isc-)

		Present	Future	Past Participle
	io	capisco	capirò	
capire	*tu*	capisci	capirai	
to understand	*lui/lei*	capisce	capirà	capito
	noi	capiamo	capiremo	(w/avere)
	voi	capite	capirete	
	loro	capiscono	capiranno	

		Present	Future	Past Participle
	io	finisco	finirò	
finire	*tu*	finisci	finirai	
to finish	*lui/lei*	finisce	finirà	finito
	noi	finiamo	finiremo	(w/avere)
	voi	finite	finirete	
	loro	finiscono	finiranno	

		Present	Future	Past Participle
	io	preferisco	preferirò	
preferire	*tu*	preferisci	preferirai	
to prefer	*lui/lei*	preferisce	preferirà	preferito
	noi	preferiamo	preferiremo	(w/avere)
	voi	preferite	preferirete	
	loro	preferiscono	preferiranno	

Italian-English Mini Dictionary

A

a destra/*ah* <u>*dehs*</u>-*trah*/(on the) right

a domani/*ah doh-*<u>*mah*</u>-*nee*/see you tomorrow

a dopo/*ah* <u>*doh*</u>-*poh*/see you later

a sinistra/*ah see-*<u>*nees*</u>-*trah*/(on the) left

abitare/*ah-bee-*<u>*tah*</u>-*reh*/to live

abito/m/<u>*ah*</u>-*bee-toh*/suit

acqua/f/<u>*ahk*</u>-*koo-ah*/water

aereo/m/*ah-*<u>*eh*</u>-*reh-oh*/airplane

aeroporto/m/*ah-eh-roh-*<u>*pohr*</u>-*toh*/airport

affittare/*ahf-feet-*<u>*tah*</u>-*reh*/to rent

agosto/*ah-*<u>*gohs*</u>-*toh*/August

albergo/m/*ahl-*<u>*behr*</u>-*goh*/hotel

amare/*ah-*<u>*mah*</u>-*reh*/to love

americana/f/**americano**/m/ *ah-meh-ree-*<u>*kah*</u>-*nah*/ *ah-meh-ree-*<u>*kah*</u>-*noh*/American

amica/f/**amico**/m/*ah-*<u>*mee*</u>-*kah*/ *ah-*<u>*mee*</u>-*koh*/friend

amore/m/*ah-*<u>*moh*</u>-*reh*/love

anche/<u>*ahn*</u>-*keh*/also

andare/*ahn-*<u>*dah*</u>-*reh*/to go

andata/f/*ahn-*<u>*dah*</u>-*tah*/one-way (ticket)

andata/f/ **e ritorno**/m/*ahn-*<u>*dah*</u>-*tah eh ree-*<u>*tohr*</u>-*noh*/round trip

anno/m/<u>*ahn*</u>-*noh*/year

antipasti/m/*ahn-tee-*<u>*pahs*</u>-*tee*/appetizers

anziana/f/**anziano**/m/*ahn-tsee-*<u>*ah*</u>-*nah*/ *ahn-tsee-*<u>*ah*</u>-*noh*/old (for persons)

appartamento/m/*ahp-pahr-tah-*<u>*mehn*</u>-*toh*/ apartment

aprile/*ah-*<u>*pree*</u>-*leh*/April

architetto/m/*ahr-kee-*<u>*teht*</u>-*toh*/architect

arrivare/*ahr-ree-*<u>*vah*</u>-*reh*/to arrive

arrivederci/*ahr-ree-veh-*<u>*dehr*</u>-*chee*/see you; good-bye

assegno/m/*ahs-*<u>*seh*</u>-*nyoh*/check

autobus/m/<u>*ah*</u>-*oo-toh-boos*/bus

automobile/f/*ah-oo-toh-*<u>*moh*</u>-*bee-leh*/car

avere/*ah-*<u>*veh*</u>-*reh*/to have

avvocato/m/*ahv-voh-*<u>*kah*</u>-*toh*/lawyer

B

bambina/f/**bambino**/m/*bahm-bee-nah*/ *bahm-*<u>*bee*</u>-*noh*/child

banca/f/<u>*bahn*</u>-*kah*/bank

bella/f/**bello**/m/<u>*behl*</u>-*lah*/<u>*behl*</u>-*loh*/beautiful

bene/<u>*beh*</u>-*neh*/well, good (adverb)

bere/<u>*beh*</u>-*reh*/to drink

bianca/f/**bianco**/m/*bee-*<u>*ahn*</u>-*kah*/ *bee-*<u>*ahn*</u>-*koh*/white

bicchiere/m/*beek-kee-*<u>*eh*</u>-*reh*/glass

bicicletta/f/*bee-chee-*<u>*kleht*</u>-*tah*/bicycle

biglietto/m/*bee-*<u>*lyeht*</u>-*toh*/ticket

birra/f/<u>*beer*</u>-*rah*/beer

blu/f/m/*bloo*/blue

borsa/f/<u>*bohr*</u>-*sah*/bag

bottiglia/f/*both-*<u>*tee*</u>-*lyah*/bottle

braccio/m/<u>*brahch*</u>-*choh*/arm

buona/f/**buono**/m/*boo-oh-nah/ boo-oh-noh*/good

buonanotte/*boo-oh-nah-noht-teh/* good-night

buonasera/*boo-oh-nah-seh-rah*/good evening

buongiorno/*boo-ohn-johr-noh*/good morning; good day

C

c'è/*cheh*/there is

caffè/m/*kahf-feh*/coffee

calcio/m/*kahl-choh*/soccer

calda/f/**caldo**/m/*kahl-dah/kahl-doh*/warm; hot

cambiare/*kahm-bee-ah-reh*/to change

cameriera/f/**cameriere**/m/*kah-meh-ree-eh-rah/kah-meh-ree-eh-reh/* waitress/waiter

camicia/f/*kah-mee-chah*/shirt

campagna/f/*kahm-pah-nyah*/country

canadese/f/m/*kah-nah-deh-zeh*/Canadian

cane/m/*kah-neh*/dog

capelli/m.pl./*kah-pehl-lee*/hair

cappello/m/*kahp-pehl-loh*/hat

cappotto/m/*kahp-poht-toh*/coat

cara/f/**caro**/m/*kah-rah/kah-roh*/dear; expensive

carina/f/**carino**/m/*kah-ree-nah/ kah-ree-noh*/nice

carta di credito/f/*kahr-tah dee kreh-dee-toh*/credit card

casa/f/*kah-sah*/house; home

cassa/f/*kahs-sah*/cash register

cavallo/m/*kah-vahl-loh*/horse

cena/f/*cheh-nah*/dinner

cento/*chehn-toh*/hundred

chi/*kee*/who

chiara/f/**chiaro**/m/*kee-ah-rah/ kee-ah-roh*/light-colored

ci sono/*chee soh-noh*/there are

ciao/*chah-oh*/hello; good-bye

cinema/m/*chee-neh-mah*/cinema

cinquanta/*cheen-koo-ahn-tah*/fifty

cinque/*cheen-koo-eh*/five

cioccolata/f/*choh-koh-lah-tah*/chocolate

città/f/*cheet-tah*/city, town

codice postale/m/*koh-dee-cheh pohs-tah-leh*/zip code

colazione/f/*koh-lah-tsee-oh-neh*/breakfast

collo/m/*kohl-loh*/neck

colore/m/*koh-loh-reh*/color

come/*koh-meh*/how

commessa/f/**commesso**/m/*kohm-mehs-sah/ kohm-mehs-soh*/sales clerk

comprare/*kohm-prah-reh*/to buy

costume da bagno/m/*kohs-too-meh dah bah-nyoh*/bathing suit

cravatta/f/*krah-vaht-tah*/tie

crema/f/*kreh-mah*/cream

D

d'accordo/*dahk-kohr-doh*/all right; okay

dai!/*dah-ee*/come on!

dare/*dah-reh*/to give

dentista/f/m/*dehn-tees-tah*/dentist

dicembre/*dee-chehm-breh*/December

diciannove/*dee-chahn-noh-veh*/nineteen

diciassette/*dee-chahs-seht-teh*/seventeen

diciotto/*dee-choht-toh*/eighteen

dieci/*dee-eh-chee*/ten

dire/*dee-reh*/to say

dito/m/*dee-toh*/finger

dodici/*doh-dee-chee*/twelve

dolce/f/m/*dohl-cheh*/sweet

domani/*doh-mah-nee*/tomorrow

donna/f/_dohn_-nah/woman
dormire/_dohr-mee_-reh/to sleep
dottore/m/_doht-toh_-reh/doctor
dove/_doh_-veh/where
dovere/_doh-veh_-reh/to have to
due/_doo_-eh/two

E

emergenza/f/_eh-mehr-jehn_-tsah/emergency
entrata/f/_ehn-trah_-tah/entrance
entrare/_ehn-trah_-reh/to enter
essere/_ehs_-seh-reh/to be
est/m/_ehst_/east

F

faccia/f/_fahch_-chah/face
facile/f/m/_fah_-chee-leh/easy
fame/f/_fah_-meh/hunger
fare/_fah_-reh/to do
febbraio/_fehb-brah_-yoh/February
festa/f/_fehs_-tah/party, holiday
figlia/f/_fee_-lyah/daughter
figlio/m/_fee_-lyoh/son
fine/f/_fee_-neh/end
finestra/f/_fee-nehs_-trah/window
finire/_fee-nee_-reh/to finish
fiore/m/_fee-oh_-reh/flower
formaggio/m/_fohr-mahj_-joh/cheese
fragola/f/_frah_-goh-lah/strawberry
fratello/m/_frah-tehl_-loh/brother
fredda/f/**freddo**/m/_frehd_-dah/ _frehd_-doh/cold
frutta/f/_froot_-tah/fruit

G

gatto/m/_gaht_-toh/cat
gelato/m/_jeh-lah_-toh/ice cream
gennaio/_jehn-nah_-yoh/January
gente/f/_jehn_-teh/people
ghiaccio/m/_gee-ahch_-choh/ice
giacca/f/_jahk_-kah/jacket; blazer
gialla/f/**giallo**/m/_jahl_-lah/_jahl_-loh/yellow
giardino/m/_jahr-dee_-noh/garden
ginocchio/m/_jee-nohk_-kee-oh/knee
giocare/_joh-kah_-reh/to play
gioco/m/_joh_-koh/game
giornale/m/_johr-nah_-leh/newspaper
giorno/m/_johr_-noh/day
giovane/f/m/_joh_-vah-neh/young
giugno/_joo_-nyoh/June
gonna/f/_gohn_-nah/skirt
grande/f/m/_grahn_-deh/big; tall; large
grande magazzino/m/_grahn_-deh mah-gaht-_tsee_-noh/department store
grazie/_grah_-tsee-eh/thank you
grigia/f/**grigio**/m/_gree_-jah/_gree_-joh/gray

I

ieri/_ee-eh_-ree/yesterday
impermeabile/m/_eem-pehr-meh-ah_-bee-leh/ raincoat
impiegata/f/**impiegato**/m/ _eem-pee-eh-gah_-tah/_eem-pee-eh-gah_-toh/ employee
in ritardo/_een ree-tahr_-doh/late
indirizzo/m/_een-dee-reet_-tsoh/address
infermiera/f/_een-fehr-mee-eh_-rah/nurse
ingegnere/m/_een-jeh-nyeh_-reh/engineer

insalata/f/*een-sah-lah-tah*/salad
invito/m/*een-vee-toh*/invitation
io/*ee-oh*/I
italiana/f/**italiano**/m/*ee-tah-lee-ah-nah/ ee-tah-lee-ah-noh*/Italian

J

jeans/m/*jeans*/jeans

L

lago/m/*lah-goh*/lake
lana/f/*lah-nah*/wool
larga/f/**largo**/m/*lahr-gah/lahr-goh*/large
latte/m/*laht-teh*/milk
lavoro/m/*lah-voh-roh*/work
lei/*lay*/she; formal you
libro/m/*lee-broh*/book
loro/*loh-roh*/they
luglio/*loo-lyoh*/July
lui/*loo-ee*/he

M

ma/*mah*/but
macchina/f/*mahk-kee-nah*/car
madre/f/*mah-dreh*/mother
maggio/*mahj-joh*/May
mai/*mah-ee*/never
malata/f/**malato**/m/*mah-lah-tah/ mah-lah-toh*/ill
mamma/f/*mahm-mah*/mom
mangiare/*mahn-jah-reh*/to eat
mano/f/*mah-noh*/hand
mare/m/*mah-reh*/sea
marito/m/*mah-ree-toh*/husband
marrone/f/m/*mahr-roh-neh*/brown
marzo/*mahr-tsoh*/March

me/*meh*/me
medicina/f/*meh-dee-chee-nah*/medicine
medico/m/*meh-dee-koh*/physician
mercato/m/*mehr-kah-toh*/market
mese/m/*meh-zeh*/month
metropolitana/f/*meh-troh-poh-lee-tah-nah/* subway
mettersi/*meht-tehr-see*/to wear
mia/f/**mio**/m/*mee-ah/mee-oh*/my
mille/*meel-leh*/thousand
moglie/f/*moh-lyeh*/wife
montagna/f/*mohn-tah-nyah*/mountain

N

naso/m/*nah-zoh*/nose
nebbia/f/*nehb-bee-ah*/fog
negozio/m/*neh-goh-tsee-oh*/shop
nera/f/ **nero**/m/*neh-rah/neh-roh*/black
neve/f/*neh-veh*/snow
noi/*noh-ee*/we
noiosa/f/**noioso**/m/*noh-yoh-zah/ noh-yoh-zoh*/boring
nome/m/*noh-meh*/name
nord/m/*nohrd*/north
nove/*noh-veh*/nine
novembre/*noh-vehm-breh*/November
numero/m/*noo-meh-roh*/number
nuoto/m/*noo-oh-toh*/swimming

O

occhio/m/*ohk-kee-oh*/eye
orecchio/m/*oh-rehk-kee-oh*/ear
ospedale/m/*ohs-peh-dah-leh*/hospital
otto/*oht-toh*/eight
ottobre/*oht-toh-breh*/October
ovest/m/*oh-vehst*/west

P

padre/m/*pah-dreh*/father
pagare/*pah-gah-reh*/to pay
pane/m/*pah-neh*/bread
pantaloni/m.pl./*pahn-tah-loh-nee*/pants
parlare/*pahr-lah-reh*/to talk
partire/*pahr-tee-reh*/to leave
passaporto/m/*pahs-sah-pohr-toh*/passport
pasticceria/f/*pahs-teech-cheh-ree-ah*/ pastry shop
per favore/*pehr fah-voh-reh*/please
perché/*pehr-keh*/why; because
pesce/m/*peh-cheh*/fish
piacere/*pee-ah-cheh-reh*/nice to meet you
piazza/f/*pee-aht-tsah*/square
piccola/f/**piccolo**/m/ *peek-koh-lah-peek-koh-loh*/small; short
pioggia/f/*pee-ohj-jah*/rain
piove/*pee-oh-veh*/it's raining
polizia/f/*poh-lee-tsee-ah*/police
potere/*poh-teh-reh*/can; may
pranzo/m/*prahn-tsoh*/lunch
preferire/*preh-feh-ree-reh*/to prefer
prego/*preh-goh*/you're welcome
prendere/*prehn-deh-reh*/to take; to order
presentare/*preh-zehn-tah-reh*/to introduce

Q

qualcosa/*koo-ahl-koh-zah*/something
quale/*koo-ah-leh*/which
quando/*koo-ahn-doh*/when
quanti/*koo-ahn-tee*/how many
quanto/m/*koo-ahn-toh*/how much
quattro/m/*koo-aht-troh*/four
quattordici/m/*koo-aht-tohr-dee-chee*/ fourteen

qui/*koo-ee*/here
quindici/*koo-een-dee-chee*/fifteen

R

ragazza/f/*rah-gaht-tsah*/girl
ragazzo/m/*rah-gaht-tsoh*/boy
ridere/*ree-deh-reh*/to laugh
riso/m/*ree-zoh*/rice
rossa/f/**rosso**/m/*rohs-sah/rohs-soh*/red

S

saldi/m.pl./*sahl-dee*/sales
sale/m/*sah-leh*/salt
scarpa/f/*skahr-pah*/shoe
scura/f/**scuro**/m/*skoo-rah/skoo-roh*/dark
sedici/*seh-dee-chee*/sixteen
segretaria/f/**segretario**/m/*seh-greh-tah-ree-ah/seh-greh-tah-ree-oh*/secretary
sei/*say*/six
sempre/*sehm-preh*/always
sete/f/*seh-teh*/thirst
sette/*seht-teh*/seven
settembre/*seht-tehm-breh*/September
settimana/f/*seht-tee-mah-nah*/week
signora/f/*see-nyoh-rah*/Mrs.; Ms.; a woman
signore/m/*see-nyoh-reh*/Mr.; a gentleman
soldi/m.pl./*sohl-dee*/money
sole/m/*soh-leh*/sun
solo/*soh-loh*/only, just
sorella/f/*soh-rehl-lah*/sister
spalla/f/*spahl-lah*/shoulder
stanca/f/**stanco**/m/*stahn-kah/stahn-koh*/tired
stazione/f/*stah-tsee-oh-neh*/station
strada/f/*strah-dah*/street; road

stretta/f/**stretto**/m/_streht_-tah/
  streht-toh/tight; narrow

sud/_sood_/south

supermercato/m/_soo-pehr-mehr-_kah_-toh_/
  supermarket

T

tazza/f/_taht_-tsah/cup

teatro/m/_teh-_ah_-troh_/theater

telefono/m/_teh-_leh_-foh-noh_/phone

tempo/m/_tehm_-poh/time; weather

tre/_treh_/three

tredici/_treh_-dee-chee/thirteen

treno/m/_treh_-noh/train

troppo/_trohp_-poh/too much

tu/_too_/you

tutti/_toot_-tee/everybody

tutto/_toot_-toh/everything

U

ufficio/m/_oof-_fee_-choh_/office

uno/_oo_-noh/one

uscita/f/_oo-_shee_-tah_/exit

V

vacanza/f/_vah-_kahn_-tsah_/vacation

valigia/f/_vah-_lee_-jah_/suitcase

vedere/_veh-_deh_-reh_/to see

vendere/_vehn_-deh-reh/to sell

venire/_veh-_nee_-reh_/to come

venti/_vehn_-tee/twenty

verde/f/m/_vehr_-deh/green

verdura/f/_vehr-_doo_-rah_/vegetables

vestito/m/_vehs-_tee_-toh_/dress

via/f/_vee_-ah/street

viaggiare/_vee-ahj-_jah_-reh_/to travel

viaggio/m/_vee-_ahj_-joh_/travel

viale/m/_vee-_ah_-leh_/avenue

vino/m/_vee_-noh/wine

voi/_voh_-ee/you

volere/_voh-_leh_-reh_/to want

Z

zero/_dzeh_-roh/zero

zia/f/_dzee_-ah/ant

zio/m/_dzee_-oh/uncle

zucchero/m/_dzook_-keh-roh/sugar

English-Italian Mini Dictionary

A

address/**indirizzo**/m/*een-dee-reet-tsoh*

airplane/**aereo**/m/*ah-eh-reh-oh*

airport/**aeroporto**/m/*ah-eh-roh-pohr-toh*

all right; okay/**d'accordo**/*dahk-kohr-doh*

also/**anche**/*ahn-keh*

always/**sempre**/*sehm-preh*

American/**americana**/f/**americano**/m/
ah-meh-ree-kah-nah/ah-meh-ree-kah-noh

ant/**zia**/f/*dzee-ah*

apartment/**appartamento**/m/
ahp-pahr-tah-mehn-toh

appetizers/**antipasti**/m/*ahn-tee-pahs-tee*

April/**aprile**/*ah-pree-leh*

architect/**architetto**/m/*ahr-kee-teht-toh*

arm/**braccio**/m/*brahch-choh*

arrive/**arrivare**/*ahr-ree-vah-reh*

August/**agosto**/*ah-gohs-toh*

avenue/**viale**/m/*vee-ah-leh*

B

bad/**cattivo**/*kaht-tee-voh*

bag/**borsa**/f/*bohr-sah*

bakery/**pasticceria**/f/
pahs-teech-cheh-ree-ah

bank/**banca**/f/*bahn-kah*

bathing suit/**costume da bagno**/m/
kohs-too-meh dah bah-nyoh

be/**essere**/*ehs-seh-reh*

beach/**spiagga**/f/*spee-ahj-gah*

beautiful/**bella**/f/**bello**/m/*behl-lah/
behl-loh*

because/**perché**/*pehr-keh*

beer/**birra**/f/*beer-rah*

bicycle/**bicicletta**/f/*bee-chee-kleht-tah*

big; tall; large/**grande**/f/m/*grahn-deh*

black/**nera**/f/**nero**/m/*neh-rah/neh-roh*

blue/**blu**/f/m/*bloo*

book/**libro**/m/*lee-broh*

boring/**noiosa**/f/**noioso**/m/
noh-yoh-zah/noh-yoh-zoh

bottle/**bottiglia**/f/*boht-tee-lyah*

boy/**ragazzo**/m/*rah-gaht-tsoh*

bread/**pane**/m/*pah-neh*

breakfast/**colazione**/f/*koh-lah-tsee-oh-neh*

brother/**fratello**/m/*frah-tehl-loh*

brown/**marrone**/f/m/*mahr-roh-neh*

bus/**autobus**/m/*ah-oo-toh-boos*

but/**ma**/*mah*

buy/**comprare**/*kohm-prah-reh*

C

can; may/**potere**/*poh-teh-reh*

Canadian/**canadese**/f/m/*kah-nah-deh-zeh*

car/**automobile**/f/*ah-oo-toh-moh-bee-leh*

car/**macchina**/*mahk-kee-nah*

cash register/f/**cassa**/*kahs-sah*

cat/**gatto**/m/_gaht_-toh

change (v.)/**cambiare**/kahm-bee-_ah_-reh

check/**assegno**/m/ahs-_seh_-nyoh

cheese/**formaggio**/m/fohr-_mahj_-joh

child (female)/**bambina**/f/bahm-_bee_-nah

child (male)/**bambino**/m/bahm-_bee_-noh

chocolate/**cioccolata**/f/choh-koh-_lah_-tah

cinema/**cinema**/m/_chee_-neh-mah

city; town/**città**/f/cheet-_tah_

coat/**cappotto**/m/kahp-_poht_-toh

coffee/**caffè**/m/kahf-_feh_

cold/**fredda**/f/**freddo**/m/_frehd_-dah/
frehd-doh

color/**colore**/m/koh-_loh_-reh

come on/**dai**/_dah_-ee

come/**venire**/veh-_nee_-reh

country/**campagna**/f/kahm-_pah_-nyah

cream/**crema**/f/_kreh_-mah

credit card/**carta di credito**/f/_kahr_-tah
dee _kreh_-dee-toh

cup/**tazza**/f/_taht_-tsah

D

dark/**scura**/f/**scuro**/m/_skoo_-rah/_skoo_-roh

daughter/**figlia**/f/_fee_-lyah

day/**giorno**/m/_johr_-noh

dear/**cara**/f/**caro**/m/_kah_-rah/_kah_-roh

December/**dicembre**/dee-_chehm_-breh

dentist/**dentista**/f/m/dehn-_tees_-tah

department store/**grande magazzino**/m/
grahn-deh mah-gaht-_tsee_-noh

dessert (sweet)/**dolce**/m/ _dohl_-cheh

dinner/**cena**/f/_cheh_-nah

doctor/**dottore**/m/doht-_toh_-reh

dog/**cane**/m/_kah_-neh

dress/**vestito**/m/vehs-_tee_-toh

drink (v.)/**bere**/_beh_-reh

E

ear/**orecchio**/m/oh-_rehk_-kee-oh

east/**est**/m/ehst

easy/**facile**/f/m/_fah_-chee-leh

eat/**mangiare**/mahn-_jah_-reh

eight/**otto**/_oht_-toh

eighteen/**diciotto**/dee-_choht_-toh

eleven/**undici**/_oon_-dee-chee

emergency/**emergenza**/f/
eh-mehr-_jehn_-tsah

employee/**impiegata**/f/**impiegato**/m/
eem-pee-eh-_gah_-tah/eem-pee-eh-_gah_-toh

end/**fine**/f/_fee_-neh

engineer/**ingegnere**/m/een-jeh-_nyeh_-reh

enter/**entrare**/ehn-_trah_-reh

entrance/**entrata**/f/ehn-_trah_-tah

everybody/**tutti**/_toot_-tee

everything/**tutto**/_toot_-toh

exit/**uscita**/f/oo-_shee_-tah

expensive/**cara**/f/**caro**/m/_kah_-rah/_kah_-roh

eye/**occhio**/m/_ohk_-kee-oh

F

face/**faccia**/f/_fahch_-chah

father/**padre**/m/_pah_-dreh

February/**febbraio**/fehb-_brah_-yoh

fifteen/**quindici**/koo-_een_-dee-chee

fifty/**cinquanta**/cheen-koo-_ahn_-tah

finger/**dito**/m/_dee_-toh

finish (v.)/**finire**/fee-_nee_-reh

fish/**pesce**/m/_peh_-cheh

five/**cinque**/_cheen_-koo-eh

flower/**fiore**/f/fee-_oh_-reh

fog/**nebbia**/f/_nehb_-bee-ah

four/**quattro**/koo-_aht_-troh

fourteen/**quattordici**/
koo-aht-tohr-dee-chee

friend/**amica**/f/**amico**/m/*ah-mee-kah/
ah-mee-koh*

fruit/**frutta**/f/*froot-tah*

G

garden/**giardino**/m/*jahr-dee-noh*

girl/**ragazza**/f/*rah-gaht-tsah*

give/**dare**/*dah-reh*

glass/**bicchiere**/m/*beek-kee-eh-reh*

go/**andare**/*ahn-dah-reh*

good/**buona**/f/**buono**/m/*boo-oh-nah/
boo-oh-noh*

good-bye/**ciao**/*chah-oh*

good evening/**buonasera**/
boo-oh-nah-seh-rah

good morning; good day/**buongiorno**/
boo-ohn-johr-noh

good-night/**buonanotte**/
boo-oh-nah-noht-teh

green/**verde**/f/m/*vehr-deh*

gray/**grigia**/f/**grigio**/m/*gree-jah/gree-joh*

H

hair/**capelli**/m/*kah-pehl-lee*

hand/**mano**/f/*mah-noh*

hat/**cappello**/m/*kahp-pehl-loh*

have/**avere**/*ah-veh-reh*

have to/**dovere**/*doh-veh-reh*

he/**lui**/*loo-ee*

hello/**ciao**/*chah-oh*

help/**aiuto**/*ah-yoo-toh*

here/**qui**/*koo-ee*

horse/**cavallo**/m/*kah-vahl-loh*

hospital/**ospedale**/m/*ohs-peh-dah-leh*

hot/**calda**/f/**caldo**/m/*kahl-dah/kahl-doh*

hotel/**albergo**/m/*ahl-behr-goh*

house; home/**casa**/f/*kah-sah*

how/**come**/*koh-meh*

how many/**quanti**/*koo-ahn-tee*

how much/**quanto**/*koo-ahn-toh*

hundred/**cento**/*chehn-toh*

hunger/**fame**/f/*fah-meh*

husband/**marito**/m/*mah-ree-toh*

I

I/**io**/*ee-oh*

ice/**ghiaccio**/m/*gee-ahch-choh*

ice cream/**gelato**/m/*jeh-lah-toh*

ill/**malata**/f/**malato**/m/*mah-lah-tah/
mah-lah-toh*

introduce/**presentare**/*preh-zehn-tah-reh*

invitation/**invito**/m/*een-vee-toh*

Italian/**italiana**/f/**italiano**/m/
ee-tah-lee-ah-nah/ee-tah-lee-ah-noh

J

jacket; blazer/f/**giacca**/*jahk-kah*

January/**gennaio**/*jehn-nah-yoh*

jeans/**jeans**/m/*jeans*

July/**luglio**/*loo-lyoh*

June/**giugno**/*joo-nyoh*

K

knee/**ginocchio**/m/*jee-nohk-kee-oh*

knife/**coltello**/m/*kohl-tehl-loh*

L

lake/**lago**/m/*lah-goh*

large/**larga**/f/**largo**/m/*lahr-gah/lahr-goh*

late/**in ritardo**/*een ree-tahr-doh*

laugh/**ridere**/_ree_-deh-reh
lawyer/**avvocato**/m/_ahv-voh-_kah_-toh_
leave/**partire**/_pahr-_tee_-reh_
(on the) left/**a sinistra**/_ah see-_nees_-trah_
light-colored/**chiara**/f/**chiaro**/m/
    _kee-_ah_-rah/kee-_ah_-roh_
live/**abitare**/_ah-bee-_tah_-reh_
love (v.)/**amare**/_ah-_mah_-reh_
love (n.)/**amore**/m/_ah-_moh_-reh_
lunch/**pranzo**/m/_prahn_-tsoh_

M

March/**marzo**/_mahr_-tsoh_
market/**mercato**/m/_mehr-_kah_-toh_
May/**maggio**/_mahj_-joh_
me/**me**/_meh_
meat/**carne**/f/_kahr_-neh_
medicine/**medicina**/f/_meh-dee-_chee_-nah_
milk/**latte**/m/_laht_-teh_
mom/**mamma**/f/_mahm_-mah_
money/**soldi**/m/_sohl_-dee_
month/**mese**/m/_meh_-zeh_
mother/**madre**/f/_mah_-dreh_
mountain/**montagna**/f/_mohn-_tah_-nyah_
Mr./**signore**/m/_see-_nyoh_-reh_
Mrs./**signora**/f/_see-_nyoh_-rah_
my/**mia**/f/**mio**/m/_mee_-ah/_mee_-oh_

N

name/**nome**/m/_noh_-meh_
neck/**collo**/m/_kohl_-loh_
never/**mai**/_mah_-ee_
newspaper/**giornale**/m/_johr-_nah_-leh_
nice/**carina**/f/**carino**/m/_kah-_ree_-nah/
    _kah-_ree_-noh_
nice to meet you/**piacere**/_pee-ah-_cheh_-reh_
nine/**nove**/_noh_-veh_

nineteen/**diciannove**/_dee-chahn-_noh_-veh_
north/**nord**/m/_nohrd_
nose/**naso**/m/_nah_-zoh_
November/**novembre**/_noh-_vehm_-breh_
now/**ora**/_oh_-rah_
number/**numero**/m/_noo_-meh-roh_
nurse/**infermiera**/f/_een-fehr-mee-_eh_-rah_

O

October/**ottobre**/_oht-_toh_-breh_
office/**ufficio**/m/_oof-_fee_-choh_
old (for persons)/**anziana**/f/**anziano**/m/
    _ahn-tsee-_ah_-nah/ahn-tsee-_ah_-noh_
one/**uno**/_oo_-noh_
one-way (ticket)/**andata**/f/_ahn-_dah_-tah_
only; just/**solo**/_soh_-loh_
order/**prendere**/_prehn_-deh-reh_

P

party; holiday/**festa**/f/_fehs_-tah_
passport/**passaporto**/m/_pahs-sah-_pohr_-toh_
pay/**pagare**/_pah-_gah_-reh_
people/**gente**/f/_jehn_-teh_
phone/**telefono**/m/_teh-_leh_-foh-noh_
physician/**medico**/m/_meh_-dee-koh_
plate/**piatto**/m/_pee_-aht-toh_
play (v.)/**giocare**/_joh-_kah_-reh_
play (n.)/**gioco**/m/_joh_-koh_
please/**per favore**/_pehr fah-_voh_-reh_
police/**polizia**/f/_poh-lee-_tsee_-ah_
prefer/**preferire**/_preh-feh-_ree_-reh_

R

rain/**pioggia**/f/_pee-_ohj_-jah_
raincoat/**impermeabile**/m/
    _eem-pehr-meh-_ah_-bee-leh_

red/**rossa**/f/**rosso**/m/*rohs-sah/rohs-soh*

rent/**affittare**/*ahf-feet-tah-reh*

(on the) right/**a destra**/*ah dehs-trah*

rice/**riso**/m/*ree-zoh*

round trip/**andata**/f/**e ritorno**/m/
   ahn-dah-tah eh ree-tohr-noh

S

salad/**insalata**/f/*een-sah-lah-tah*

sales/**saldi**/m.pl./*sahl-dee*

sales clerk/**commessa**/f/**commesso**/m/
   kohm-mehs-sah/kohm-mehs-soh

salt/**sale**/m/*sah-leh*

say (v.)/**dire**/*dee-reh*

sea/**mare**/m/*mah-reh*

secretary/**segretaria**/f/**segretario**/m/
   seh-greh-tah-ree-ah/seh-greh-tah-ree-oh

see/**vedere**/*veh-deh-reh*

see you; good-bye/**arrivederci**/
   ahr-ree-veh-dehr-chee

see you later/**a dopo**/*ah doh-poh*

see you tomorrow/**a domani**/
   ah doh-mah-nee

sell/**vendere**/*vehn-deh-reh*

September/**settembre**/*seht-tehm-breh*

seven/**sette**/*seht-teh*

seventeen/**diciassette**/*dee-chahs-seht-teh*

she/**lei**/*lay*

shirt/**camicia**/f/*kah-mee-chah*

shoe/**scarpa**/f/*skahr-pah*

shop/**negozio**/m/*neh-goh-tsee-oh*

shoulder/**spalla**/f/*spahl-lah*

sister/**sorella**/f/*soh-rehl-lah*

six/**sei**/*say*

sixteen/**sedici**/*seh-dee-chee*

skirt/**gonna**/f/*gohn-nah*

sleep/**dormire**/*dohr-mee-reh*

small; short/**piccola**/f/**piccolo**/m/
   peek-koh-lah/peek-koh-loh

snow/**neve**/f/*neh-veh*

soccer/**calcio**/m/*kahl-choh*

something/**qualcosa**/*koo-ahl-koh-zah*

son/**figlio**/m/*fee-lyoh*

south/**sud**/m/*sood*

square/**piazza**/f/*pee-aht-tsah*

station/**stazione**/f/*stah-tsee-oh-neh*

strawberry/**fragola**/f/*frah-goh-lah*

street; road/**strada**/f/*strah-dah* or
   via/f/*vee-ah*

subway/**metropolitana**/f/
   meh-troh-poh-lee-tah-nah

sugar/**zucchero**/m/*dzook-keh-roh*

suit/**abito**/m/*ah-bee-toh*

suitcase/**valigia**/f/*vah-lee-jah*

sun/**sole**/m/*soh-leh*

supermarket/**supermercato**/m/
   soo-pehr-mehr-kah-toh

sweet/**dolce**/f/m/*dohl-cheh*

swimming/**nuoto**/m/*noo-oh-toh*

T

take/**prendere**/*prehn-deh-reh*

talk/**parlare**/*pahr-lah-reh*

tax/**dazio**/m/*dah-tsee-oh*

telephone/**telefono**/m/*teh-leh-foh-noh*

ten/**dieci**/*dee-eh-chee*

thank you/**grazie**/*grah-tsee-eh*

theater/**teatro**/m/*teh-ah-troh*

there are/**ci sono**/*chee soh-noh*

there is/**c'è**/*cheh*

they/**loro**/*loh-roh*

thirst/**sete**/f/*seh-teh*

thirteen/**tredici**/*treh-dee-chee*

thousand/**mille**/*meel-leh*

three/**tre**/*treh*

ticket/**biglietto**/m/*bee-lyeht-toh*

tie/**cravatta**/f/*krah-vaht-tah*

tight; narrow/**stretta**/f/**stretto**/m/
streht-tah/streht-toh

time; weather/**tempo**/m/*tehm-poh*

tired/**stanca**/f/**stanco**/m/*stahn-kah/
stahn-koh*

today/**oggi**/*ohj-jee*

tomorrow/**domani**/*doh-mah-nee*

too much/**troppo**/*trohp-poh*

train/**treno**/m/*treh-noh*

travel (v.)/**viaggiare**/*vee-ahj-jah-reh*

travel (n.)/**viaggio**/m/*vee-ahj-joh*

trousers/**pantaloni**/m/*pahn-tah-loh-nee*

twelve/**dodici**/*doh-dee-chee*

twenty/**venti**/*vehn-tee*

two/**due**/*doo-eh*

U

uncle/**zio**/m/*dzee-oh*

V

vacation/**vacanza**/f/*vah-kahn-tsah*

vegetables/**verdura**/f/*vehr-doo-rah*

W

waitress/waiter/**cameriera**/f/**cameriere**/
m/*kah-meh-ree-eh-rah/
kah-meh-ree-eh-reh*

wallet/**borsa**/f/*bohr-sah*

want/**volere**/*voh-leh-reh*

warm/**calda**/f/**caldo**/m/*kahl-dah/kahl-doh*

water/**acqua**/f/*ahk-koo-ah*

we/**noi**/*noh-ee*

wear/**mettersi**/*meht-tehr-see*

week/**settimana**/f/*seht-tee-mah-nah*

well; good (adverb)/**bene**/*beh-neh*

west/**ovest**/m/*oh-vehst*

what/**cosa**/*koh-sah*

when/**quando**/*koo-ahn-doh*

where/**dove**/*doh-veh*

which/**quale**/f/m/*koo-ah-leh*

white/**bianca**/f/**bianco**/m/
bee-ahn-kah/bee-ahn-koh

who/**chi**/*kee*

why/**perché**/*pehr-keh*

wife/**moglie**/f/*moh-lyeh*

window/**finestra**/f/*fee-nehs-trah*

wine/**vino**/m/*vee-noh*

woman/**donna**/f/*dohn-nah*

wool/**lana**/f/*lah-nah*

work/**lavoro**/m/*lah-voh-roh*

Y

year/**anno**/m/*ahn-noh*

yellow/**gialla**/f/**giallo**/m/*jahl-lah/jahl-loh*

yesterday/**ieri**/*ee-eh-ree*

you (formal)/**Lei**/*lay*

you (plural, informal/formal)/**voi**/*voh-ee*

you (singular, informal)/**tu**/*too*

you're welcome/**prego**/*preh-goh*

young/**giovane**/f/m/*joh-vah-neh*

Z

zero/**zero**/*dzeh-roh*

zip code/**codice postale**/m/*koh-dee-cheh
pohs-tah-leh*

Appendix C

About the CD

● ●

*F*ollowing is a list of the tracks that appear on this book's audio CD, which you can find inside the back cover. Note that this is an audio-only CD — just pop it into your stereo (or whatever you use to listen to regular music CDs).

Track 1: Introduction and Pronunciation Guide

Track 2: Chapter 3: Buongiorno! Meeting and Greeting — greeting formally

Track 3: Chapter 3: Buongiorno! Meeting and Greeting — greeting informally

Track 4: Chapter 3: Buongiorno! Meeting and Greeting — making a formal introduction

Track 5: Chapter 3: Buongiorno! Meeting and Greeting — making an informal introduction

Track 6: Chapter 4: Getting to Know You: Making Small Talk — making formal small talk

Track 7: Chapter 4: Getting to Know You: Making Small Talk — talking about where you're from

Track 8: Chapter 4: Getting to Know You: Making Small Talk — chatting — informal small talk between youngsters

Track 9: Chapter 4: Getting to Know You: Making Small Talk — talking about the weather

Track 10: Chapter 5: Food, Glorious Food — and Don't Forget the Drink — calling for reservations

Track 11: Chapter 5: Food, Glorious Food — and Don't Forget the Drink — asking for the check

Track 12: Chapter 5: Food, Glorious Food — and Don't Forget the Drink — paying the bill

Index

• J •

• K •

• L •

• M •

● N ●

● O ●

● P ●

• W •

• X •

• Y •

• Z •

Notes

Notes

Notes

Notes

Notes

Notes

Notes

Notes

 **The world's most trusted name in foreign language learning.**

Get one

Free

lesson

Redeemable at any
Berlitz Language Center in
The United States and Canada

Take a language lesson on us!

Millions of people have learned to speak a new language with Berlitz. Why not you?

No matter where you're going or where you're from, odds are Berlitz is already there. We are the global leader in language services with over 70 locations in the United States and Canada. And right now, you can get a free trial language lesson at any one of them and in any language! Experience the unique Berlitz Method® and start speaking a new language confidently from your very first class. Berlitz has over 120 years of proven success, so no matter what your language needs, you can be sure you're getting the best value for your money.

To schedule your free lesson, call Berlitz toll free at 1-800-457-7958 (outside the U.S. call 609-514-9650) for the Language Center nearest you. Or check your telephone book or visit our Web site at www.berlitz.com.

To confirm availability of a teacher for the language of your choice, you must call 24 hours in advance. No purchase is necessary.

* cut out and bring coupon to your nearest Berlitz Language Center in the U.S. and Canada

This coupon cannot be combined with any other offer or used for adjustments to prior purchases. This offer is not available to Berlitz employees or members of their immediate families.

Learn Italian the Berlitz® Way!

There's no better way to understand more about other cultures and people than by trying to speak their language. Whether you want to speak a few essential phrases during your next business trip or vacation or you want to achieve real fluency, Berlitz can help you reach your goals. Here are some time-honored Berlitz tips to help get you on your way:

- Immerse yourself in the language. Read Italian on the Internet, in newspapers, and in fashion magazines — you'll be surprised at how much you can understand already. Watch Italian news programs on cable TV, rent Italian language films, or consider hosting a Italian-speaking exchange student for the summer. And check out your nearest Berlitz language center for information about special courses and cultural nights.
- Take home a self-study language course and set aside time to work with the material a couple of times a week. Berlitz courses are available in book, cassette, audio CD, and CD-ROM formats.
- Set your own pace, but try to put aside a regular block of time at least twice a week to work with your new language. It's more important to set a steady pace than an intensive one. Several 30-minute sessions during the week are better than one longer session a couple of times per month.
- Speak out loud. Don't just read to yourself or listen to a self-study program. Learning a language is as much a physical workout as it is an intellectual one. You have to train your vocal chords to do things they aren't used to doing. Remember: You only learn to speak by speaking!
- Talk to Italian people! And don't be afraid to make mistakes. You'll notice that most people appreciate an attempt to speak their language.
- Try speaking English with a Italian accent. Then, when you start speaking Italian, your brain will already be in the mood.
- Keep an open mind. Don't expect your new language to work the same as your own, and don't look for a neat set of rules. Accept the differences.
- Enjoy yourself! Learning a foreign language can help you see the world and yourself from an entirely different perspective.

About Berlitz®

The name "Berlitz" has meant excellence in language services for over 120 years. Today, at over 400 locations and in 50 countries worldwide, Berlitz offers a full range of language and language-related services, including instruction, cross-cultural training, document translation, software localization, and interpretation services. Berlitz also offers a wide array of publishing products such as self-study language courses, phrase books, travel guides, and dictionaries.

Berlitz has programs to meet everyone's needs: The world-famous **Berlitz Method®** is the core of all Berlitz language instruction. From the time of its introduction in 1878, millions have used this method to learn a new language. Join any one of the classes available throughout the world, and immerse yourself in a new language and culture with the help of a Berlitz trained native instructor.

For those who may not have time for live instruction, **self-study language courses** may be the answer. In addition to several outstanding courses, Berlitz publishes **Bilingual Dictionaries**, **Workbooks**, and **Handbooks**.

Put the world in your pocket . . . with **Berlitz Pocket Guides** and **Phrase Books**, the renowned series that together are the ideal travel companions that will make the most of every trip. These portable full-color pocket guides are packed with information on history, language, must-see sights, shopping, and restaurant information; the Phrase Books help you communicate with ease and confidence.

Berlitz Kids™ has a complete range of fun products such as the **Kids Language Packs**, **1,000 Words**, and **Picture Dictionaries**. Parents and teachers will find **Help Your Child with a Foreign Language** especially informative and enlightening.

Berlitz Cross-Cultural™ programs are designed to bridge cultural gaps for international travelers and business transferees and their families. From vital information about daily life to social and business do's and don'ts, these programs can prepare you for life in any part of the world.

For more information, please consult your local telephone directory for the Language Center nearest you. Or visit the Berlitz Web site at www.berlitz.com, where you can enroll or shop directly online.

FOR DUMMIES®

The easy way to get more done and have more fun

PERSONAL FINANCE

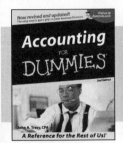

0-7645-5231-7

0-7645-2431-3

0-7645-5331-3

Also available:

Estate Planning For Dummies
(0-7645-5501-4)
401(k)s For Dummies
(0-7645-5468-9)
Frugal Living For Dummies
(0-7645-5403-4)
Microsoft Money "X" For Dummies
(0-7645-1689-2)
Mutual Funds For Dummies
(0-7645-5329-1)

Personal Bankruptcy For Dummies
(0-7645-5498-0)
Quicken "X" For Dummies
(0-7645-1666-3)
Stock Investing For Dummies
(0-7645-5411-5)
Taxes For Dummies 2003
(0-7645-5475-1)

BUSINESS & CAREERS

0-7645-5314-3

0-7645-5307-0

0-7645-5471-9

Also available:

Business Plans Kit For Dummies
(0-7645-5365-8)
Consulting For Dummies
(0-7645-5034-9)
Cool Careers For Dummies
(0-7645-5345-3)
Human Resources Kit For Dummies
(0-7645-5131-0)
Managing For Dummies
(1-5688-4858-7)

QuickBooks All-in-One Desk Reference For Dummies
(0-7645-1963-8)
Selling For Dummies
(0-7645-5363-1)
Small Business Kit For Dummies
(0-7645-5093-4)
Starting an eBay Business For Dummies
(0-7645-1547-0)

HEALTH, SPORTS & FITNESS

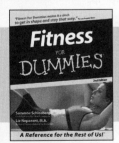

0-7645-5167-1

0-7645-5146-9

0-7645-5154-X

Also available:

Controlling Cholesterol For Dummies
(0-7645-5440-9)
Dieting For Dummies
(0-7645-5126-4)
High Blood Pressure For Dummies
(0-7645-5424-7)
Martial Arts For Dummies
(0-7645-5358-5)
Menopause For Dummies
(0-7645-5458-1)

Nutrition For Dummies
(0-7645-5180-9)
Power Yoga For Dummies
(0-7645-5342-9)
Thyroid For Dummies
(0-7645-5385-2)
Weight Training For Dummies
(0-7645-5168-X)
Yoga For Dummies
(0-7645-5117-5)

FOR DUMMIES®

A world of resources to help you grow

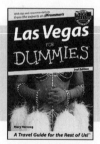

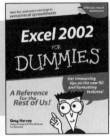

FOR DUMMIES®

Helping you expand your horizons and realize your potential

INTERNET

The Internet FOR DUMMIES

0-7645-0894-6

The Internet ALL-IN-ONE DESK REFERENCE FOR DUMMIES

0-7645-1659-0

eBay FOR DUMMIES

0-7645-1642-6

Also available:

America Online 7.0 For Dummies
(0-7645-1624-8)

Genealogy Online For Dummies
(0-7645-0807-5)

The Internet All-in-One Desk Reference For Dummies
(0-7645-1659-0)

Internet Explorer 6 For Dummies
(0-7645-1344-3)

The Internet For Dummies Quick Reference
(0-7645-1645-0)

Internet Privacy For Dummies
(0-7645-0846-6)

Researching Online For Dummies
(0-7645-0546-7)

Starting an Online Business For Dummies
(0-7645-1655-8)

DIGITAL MEDIA

Digital Photography FOR DUMMIES

0-7645-1664-7

Photoshop Elements 2 FOR DUMMIES

0-7645-1675-2

Digital Video FOR DUMMIES

0-7645-0806-7

Also available:

CD and DVD Recording For Dummies
(0-7645-1627-2)

Digital Photography All-in-One Desk Reference For Dummies
(0-7645-1800-3)

Digital Photography For Dummies Quick Reference
(0-7645-0750-8)

Home Recording for Musicians For Dummies
(0-7645-1634-5)

MP3 For Dummies
(0-7645-0858-X)

Paint Shop Pro "X" For Dummies
(0-7645-2440-2)

Photo Retouching & Restoration For Dummies
(0-7645-1662-0)

Scanners For Dummies
(0-7645-0783-4)

GRAPHICS

PowerPoint 2002 FOR DUMMIES

0-7645-0817-2

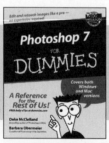

Photoshop 7 FOR DUMMIES

0-7645-1651-5

Macromedia Flash MX FOR DUMMIES

0-7645-0895-4

Also available:

Adobe Acrobat 5 PDF For Dummies
(0-7645-1652-3)

Fireworks 4 For Dummies
(0-7645-0804-0)

Illustrator 10 For Dummies
(0-7645-3636-2)

QuarkXPress 5 For Dummies
(0-7645-0643-9)

Visio 2000 For Dummies
(0-7645-0635-8)

Available wherever books are sold. Go to www.dummies.com or call 1-877-762-2974 to order direct.